Here's what people are saying about Laura Lemay's *Teach Yourself Web Publishing with HTML*

"There are some good HTML primers on the Web itself, but if you're like me, you'll find it easier to learn by cracking a book. The best I've found is Laura Lemay's *Teach Yourself Web Publishing with HTML*." —Marc Frons, *Business Week*

"Laura Lemay delivers on her title's promise. By following her clear sequence of explanations, examples, and exercises, even the absolute Web novice can create serviceable documents within a few days. Better, she moves quickly beyond mechanics to techniques and tools for designing maximally effective and attractive presentations in spite of the medium's limitations." —Michael K. Stone, *Whole Earth Review*

"Of all the HTML books out right now, I think Lemay's is the best, and I recommend it." —Nancy McGough, Infinite Ink

"If you are looking for an easy-to-read introduction to HTML, this book is for you. Lemay has a clear understanding of what works and what doesn't, and she conveys her thoughts in a concise, orderly fashion." —Robert Stewart, *The Virtual Mirror*

"If you want to create a Web page, or even if you already have created one, and you want a *great* book to help you understand it all, check out Laura Lemay's *Teach Yourself Web Publishing with HTML*. I've used mine so much I practically know it by heart!" —Camille Tillman, Book Stacks Unlimited

"All in all, this is a quality 'do-it-yourself' book for beginners of HTML publishing. The ABCs of HTML are explained clearly, and the exercises are instructive and easy to follow." —Jim Duber, *Chorus*

"This is a very thorough book on HTML, and quite accurate. Laura Lemay is a good technical writer who explains things well. This is the book I wish I'd had when I started to learn HTML." —Bob Cunningham, University of Hawaii

"My best recommendation goes to this book by Laura Lemay, entitled *Teach Yourself Web Publishing with HTML*. There is simply no better book available, and many that are much worse than this one. If you study it, you will know more than enough to create stunning Web pages of your own." —Bob Bickford

"If you want a good book that will help you understand how everything is really working, take a look at Sams Publishing's *Teach Yourself Web Publishing with HTML*. It is a very well-written book, and it includes all the information in an easy to understand format." —Ron Loewy, HyperAct, Inc.

"There's a superb new book about HTML called *Teach Yourself Web Publishing with HTML*…. It is very thorough and well-laid out." —Michael MacDonald

"I think Lemay's first book can take some degree of credit for the growth of the Web itself. I wonder how many of the tens of thousands of home pages created in the past six months have been done by folks with dog-eared copies of *Teach Yourself Web Publishing* within arm's reach." —Dave Elliott, The Web Academy

teach
yourself
WEB
PUBLISHING
WITH HTML 3.2
in a week

teach yourself
WEB PUBLISHING
WITH HTML 3.2
in a week

Laura Lemay

201 West 103rd Street
Indianapolis, Indiana 46290

President, Sams Publishing Richard K. Swadley
Publishing Manager Mark Taber
Managing Editor Cindy Morrow
Marketing Manager John Pierce
Assistant Marketing Managers Kristina Perry, Rachel Wolfe

Acquisitions and Development Editor
Fran Hatton

Production Editor
Kristi Hart

Technical Reviewer
Angela Allen

Editorial Coordinator
Bill Whitmer

Technical Edit Coordinator
Lorraine Schaffer

Editorial Assistants
Carol Ackerman, Andi Richter, Rhonda Tinch-Mize

Cover Designer
Tim Amrhein

Book Designer
Gary Adair

Copy Writer
Peter Fuller

Production Supervisor
Brad Chinn

Production
Carol Bowers, Michael Brumitt, Charlotte Clapp Jeanne Clark, Michael Dietsch, Jason Hand, Mike Henry, Louisa Klucznik, Ayanna Lacey, Clint Lahnen, Paula Lowell, Steph Mineart, Ryan Oldfather, Dana Rhodes, Bobbi Satterfield, Ian Smith, Laura A. Smith, Mark Walchle, Jeff Yesh

Indexer
Andrew McDaniel

Overview

Contents

Acknowledgments

To Sams and Sams.net publishing for letting me write the kind of HTML book I wanted to see.

To the Coca-Cola Company, for creating Diet Coke and selling so much of it to me.

To all the folks on the `comp.infosystems.www` newsgroups, the `www-talk` mailing list, and the Web conference on the WELL, for answering questions and putting up with my late-night rants.

To innumerable people who helped me with the writing of this book, including Lance Norskog, Ken Tidwell, Steve Krause, Tony Barreca, CJ Silverio, Peter Harrison, Bill Whedon, Jim Graham, Jim Race, Mark Meadows, and many others I'm sure I've forgotten.

And finally, to Eric Murray, the other half of `lne.com`, for moral support when I was convinced I couldn't possibly finish writing any of this book on time, for setting up all my UNIX and networking equipment and keeping it running, and for writing a whole lot of Perl code on very short notice. (I need a form that calculates the exact weight of the person who submits it based on the phase of the moon, the current gross national debt, and what that person ate for dinner. You can do that in Perl, can't you?) Most of the programs in this book are his work, and as such he deserves a good portion of the credit. Thank you, thank you, thank you, thank you, thank you.

About the Author

Laura Lemay

Laura Lemay is a technical writer and confirmed Web addict. Between spending 12 hours a day in front of a computer and consuming enormous amounts of Diet Coke, she sometimes manages to write a book. She is the author of *Teach Yourself Web Publishing in 14 Days, Professional Reference Edition,* and *Teach Yourself Java in a Week,* and specializes in just about anything related to Web page writing, design, programming, and Web-related publications systems. Her goal for the remainder of the year is to try to get one of her motorcycles to actually run.

You can visit her home page at `http://www.1ne.com/lemay/`.

Introduction

So you've browsed the Web for a while, and you've seen the sort of stuff that people are putting up on the Net. And you're noticing that more and more stuff is going up all the time, and that more and more people are becoming interested in it. "I want to do that," you think. "How can I do that?" If you have the time and you know where to look, you could find out everything you need to know from the information out on the Web. It's all there, it's all available, and it's all free. Or, you could read this book instead. Here, in one volume that you can keep by your desk to read, reference, and squish spiders with, is nearly all the information you need to create your own Web pages—everything from how to write them, to how to link them together, to how to set up your own Web server and use it to manage forms, and to create special programs to process them.

But wait, there's more. This book goes beyond the scope of other books on how to create Web pages, which just teach you the basic technical details such as how to produce a boldface word. In this book, you'll learn why you should be producing a particular effect and when you should use it, as well as how. In addition, this book provides hints, suggestions, and examples of how to structure your overall presentation, not just the words within each page. This book won't just teach you how to create a Web presentation—it'll teach you how to create a good Web presentation.

Also, unlike many other books on this subject, this book doesn't focus on any one computer system. Regardless of whether you're using a PC running Windows, a Macintosh, or some dialect of UNIX (or any other computer system), many of the concepts in this book will be valuable to you, and you'll be able to apply them to your Web pages regardless of your platform of choice.

Sound good? Glad you think so. I thought it was a good idea when I wrote it, and I hope you get as much out of this book reading it as I did writing it.

Who Should Read This Book

Is this book for you? That depends:

- [ ] If you've seen what's out on the Web, and you want to contribute your own content, this book is for you.
- [ ] If you represent a company that wants to create an Internet "presence" and you're not sure where to start, this book is for you.
- [ ] If you're an information developer, such as a technical writer, and you want to learn how the Web can help you present your information online, this book is for you.

☐ If you're doing research or polling and you're interested in creating a system that allows people to "register" comments or vote for particular suggestions or items, this book is for you.

☐ If you're just curious about how the Web works, some parts of this book are for you, although you might be able to find what you need on the Web itself.

☐ If you've never seen the Web before but you've heard that it's really nifty and want to get set up using it, this book isn't for you. You'll need a more general book about getting set up and browsing the Web before moving on to actually producing Web documents yourself.

☐ You've done Web presentations before with text and images and links. Maybe you've played with a table or two and set up a few simple forms. In this case, you may be able to skim the first half of the book, but the second half should still offer you a lot of helpful information.

What This Book Contains

This book is intended to be read and absorbed over the course of two weeks (although it may take you more or less time depending on how much you can absorb in a day). On each day you'll read two chapters, which describe one or two concepts related to Web presentation design.

Day 1 Getting Started: The World Wide Web and You
You get a general overview of the World Wide Web and what you can do with it, and then come up with a plan for your Web presentation.

Day 2 Creating Simple Web Pages
You learn about the HTML language and how to write simple documents and link them together using hypertext links.

Day 3 Doing More with HTML
You do more text formatting with HTML, including working with text alignment, rule lines, and character formatting. You'll also get an overview of the various HTML editors available to help you write HTML.

Day 4 Images and Backgrounds
Today covers everything you ever wanted to know about images, backgrounds, and using color on the Web.

Day 5 Multimedia on the Web: Animation, Sound, Video, and Other Files
You learn all about adding multimedia capabilities to your Web presentations: using images, sounds, and video to enhance your material.

Day 6   Designing Effective Web Pages

You get some hints for creating a well-constructed Web presentation, and you explore some examples of Web presentations to get an idea of what sort of work you can do.

Day 7   Advanced HTML Features: Tables and Frames

You learn about some of the advanced features of HTML available in Netscape and other browsers: tables and frames.

Bonus Day 1

On this day, you learn how to put your presentation up on the Web, and how to add image maps to your Web page.

Bonus Day 2

Today you learn to add interactive forms to your Web pages. In addition, you try your hand at CGI programming.

What You Need Before You Start

There are seemingly hundreds of books on the market about how to get connected to the Internet, and lots of books about how to use the World Wide Web. This book isn't one of them. I'm assuming that if you're reading this book, you already have a working connection to the Internet, that you have a World Wide Web browser such as Netscape, Mosaic, or Lynx available to you, and that you've used it at least a couple of times. You should also have at least a passing acquaintance with some other portions of the Internet such as electronic mail, Gopher, and Usenet news, because I may refer to them in general terms in this book. Although you won't need to explicitly use them to work through the content in this book, some parts of the Web may refer to these other concepts.

In other words, you need to have used the Web in order to provide content for the Web. If you have this one simple qualification, then read on!

Conventions Used in This Book

This book uses special typefaces and other graphical elements to highlight different types of information.

Special Elements

Four types of "boxed" elements present pertinent information that relates to the topic being discussed: Note, Tip, Warning, and New Term. Each item has a special icon associated with it.

Notes highlight special details about the current topic.

It's a good idea to read the tips because they present shortcuts or trouble-saving ideas for performing specific tasks.

Don't skip the warnings. They supply you with information to help you avoid making decisions or performing actions that can cause trouble for you.

Whenever I introduce a *new term*, I set it off in a box like this one and define it for you. I use italic for new terms.

HTML Input and Output Examples

Throughout the book, I present exercises and examples of HTML input and output. Here are the input and output icons.

 An input icon identifies HTML code that you can type in yourself.

 An output icon indicates what the HTML input produces in a browser such as Netscape or Lynx.

Special Fonts

Several items are presented in a monospace font, which can be plain or italic. Here's what each one means:

plain mono   Applied to commands, filenames, file extensions, directory names, Internet addresses, URLs, and HTML input. For example, HTML tags such as `<TABLE>` and `<P>` appear in this font.

mono italic   Applied to placeholders, which are generic items for which something specific is substituted as part of a command or as part of computer output. For instance, the term represented by *filename* would be the real name of the file, such as `myfile.txt`.

Teach Yourself Web Publishing: the Web Site

When you tire of reading, visit the Teach Yourself HTML Web site. This site contains updated information about where to find tools and hints and source code for many Web tools you might be interested in incorporating into your own presentations. The site is at `http://www.lne.com/Web/`—check it out!

DAY

1

Getting Started: The World Wide Web and You

Chapter 1

The World of the World Wide Web

A journey of a thousand miles begins with a single step, and here you are at Day 1, Chapter 1, of a journey that will show you how to write, design, and publish pages on the World Wide Web. Before beginning the actual journey, however, it helps to start simple, with the basics:

☐ What the World Wide Web is and why it's really cool

☐ Web browsers: what they do, and some popular ones to choose from

☐ What a Web server is and why you need one

☐ Some information about Uniform Resource Locators (URLs)

If you've spent even a small amount time exploring the Web, most, if not all, of this chapter will seem like old news. If so, feel free to skim this chapter and skip ahead to the next chapter, where you'll find an overview of things to think about when you design and organize your own Web documents.

What Is the World Wide Web?

I have a friend who likes to describe things with lots of meaningful words strung together in a chain so that it takes several minutes to sort out what he's just said.

If I were him, I'd describe the World Wide Web as a global, interactive, dynamic, cross-platform, distributed, graphical hypertext information system that runs over the Internet. Whew! Unless you understand each of those words and how they fit together, that isn't going to make much sense. (My friend often doesn't make much sense, either.)

So let's take each one of those words and see what they mean in the context of how you'll be using the Web as a publishing medium.

The Web Is a Hypertext Information System

If you've used any sort of basic online help system, you're already familiar with the primary concept behind the World Wide Web: hypertext.

The idea behind hypertext is that instead of reading text in a rigid, linear structure (such as a book), you can skip easily from one point to another. You can get more information, go back, jump to other topics, and navigate through the text based on what interests you at the time.

NEW TERM

> *Hypertext* enables you to read and navigate text and visual information in a nonlinear way based on what you want to know next.

Online help systems or help stacks such as those provided by Microsoft Windows Help or HyperCard on the Macintosh use hypertext to present information. To get more information on a topic, just click on that topic. That topic might be a link that takes you to a new screen (or window, or dialog box) which contains that new information. Perhaps there are links on words or phrases that take you to still other screens, and links on those screens that take you even further away from your original topic. Figure 1.1 shows a simple diagram of how that kind of system works.

Now imagine that your online help system is linked to another online help system on another application related to yours; for example, your drawing program's help is linked to your word processor's help. Your word processor's help is then linked to an encyclopedia, where you can look up any other concepts that you don't understand. The encyclopedia is hooked into a global index of magazine articles that enables you to get the most recent information on the topics that the encyclopedia covers. The article index is then also linked into information about the writers of those articles, and some pictures of their children (see Figure 1.2).

Figure 1.1.

A simple online help system.

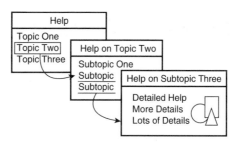

Figure 1.2.

A more complex online help system.

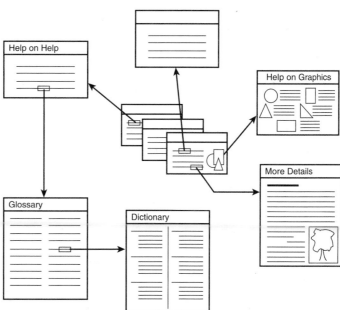

If you had all these interlinked help systems available with every program you bought, you'd rapidly run out of disk space. You might also question whether you needed all this information when all you wanted to know was how to do one simple thing. All that information could be expensive, too.

But if the information didn't take up much disk space, and if it were freely available, and you could get it reasonably quickly anytime you wanted, then things would be more interesting. In fact, the information system might very well end up more interesting than the software you bought in the first place.

That's just what the World Wide Web is: more information than you could ever digest in a lifetime, linked together in various ways, out there on the Net, available for you to browse whenever you want. It's big, and deep, and easy to get lost in. But it's also an immense amount of fun.

The Web Is Graphical and Easy To Navigate

One of the best parts of the Web, and arguably the reason it has become so popular, is its ability to display both text and graphics in full color on the same page. Before the Web, using the Internet involved simple text-only connections. You had to navigate the Internet's various services using typed commands and arcane tools. Although there was plenty of really exciting information on the Net, it wasn't necessarily pretty to look at.

The Web provides capabilities for graphics, sound, and video to be incorporated with the text, and newer software includes even more capabilities for multimedia and embedded applications. More importantly, the interface to all this is easily navigable—just jump from link to link, from page to page, across sites and servers.

NOTE

> If the Web incorporates so much more than text, why do I keep calling the Web a Hyper*text* system? Well, if you're going to be absolutely technically correct about it, the Web is not a hypertext system—it's a hyper*media* system. But, on the other hand, one could argue that the Web began as a text-only system, and much of the content is still text-heavy, with extra bits of media added in as emphasis. Many very educated people are arguing these very points at this moment, and presenting their arguments in papers and discursive rants as educated people like to do. Whatever. I prefer the term hypertext, and it's my book, so I'm going to use it. You know what I mean.

The Web Is Cross-Platform

If you can access the Internet, you can access the World Wide Web regardless of whether you're running on a low-end PC, a fancy expensive graphics workstation, or a multimillion-dollar mainframe. You can be using a simple text-only modem connection, a small 14-inch black and white monitor or a 21-inch full-color super gamma-corrected graphics-accelerated display system. If you think Windows menus and buttons look better than Macintosh menus and buttons, or vice versa (or if you think both Mac and Windows people are weenies), it doesn't matter. The World Wide Web is not limited to any one kind of machine, or developed by any one company. The Web is entirely cross-platform.

NEW TERM

> *Cross-platform* means that you can access Web information equally well from any computer hardware running any operating system using any display.

You gain access to the Web through an application called a *browser*, like Netscape's Navigator or Microsoft's Internet Explorer. There are lots of browsers out there for most existing computer systems. And once you've got a browser and a connection to the Internet, you've got it made. You're on the Web. (I explain more about what the browser actually does later in this chapter.)

> **NEW TERM**
> A *browser* is used to view and navigate Web pages and other information on the World Wide Web.

The Web Is Distributed

Information takes up an awful lot of space, particularly when you include images and multimedia capabilities. To store all the information that the Web provides, you'd need an untold amount of disk space, and managing it would be almost impossible. Imagine if you were interested in finding out more information about alpacas (a Peruvian mammal known for its wool), but when you selected a link in your online encyclopedia your computer prompted you to insert CD-ROM #456 ALP through ALR. You could be there for a long time just looking for the right CD!

The Web is successful in providing so much information because that information is distributed globally across thousands of Web sites, each of which contributes the space for the information it publishes. You, as a consumer of that information, go to that site to view the information. When you're done, you go somewhere else, and your system reclaims the disk space. You don't have to install it, or change disks, or do anything other than point your browser at that site.

> **NEW TERM**
> A *Web site* is a location on the Web that publishes some kind of information. When you view a Web page, your browser is connecting to that Web site to get that information.

Each Web site, and each page or bit of information on that site, has a unique address. This address is called a Uniform Resource Locator, or URL. When someone tells you to visit their site at `http://www.coolsite.com/`, they've just given you a URL. You can use your browser (with the `Open` command, sometimes called `Open URL` or `Go`) to enter in the URL (or just copy and paste it).

NEW TERM | A *Uniform Resource Locator (URL)* is a pointer to a specific bit of information on the Internet.

 NOTE | URLs are alternately pronounced as if spelled out "You are Ells" or as an actual word ("earls"). Although I prefer the former pronunciation, I've heard the latter used equally often.

You'll learn more about URLs later on in this chapter.

The Web Is Dynamic

Because information on the Web is contained on the site that published it, the people who published it in the first place can update it at any time.

If you're browsing that information, you don't have to install a new version of the help system, buy another book, or call technical support to get updated information. Just bring up your browser and check out what's up there.

If you're publishing on the Web, you can make sure your information is up to date all the time. You don't have to spend a lot of time rereleasing updated documents. There is no cost of materials. You don't have to get bids on number of copies or quality of output. Color is free. And you won't get calls from hapless customers who have a version of the book that was obsolete four years ago.

Take, for example, the development effort for a Web server called Apache. Apache is being developed and tested through a core of volunteers, has many of the features of the larger commercial servers, and is free. The Apache Web site at `http://www.apache.org/` is the central location for information about the Apache software, documentation, and the server software itself (Figure 1.3 shows its home page). Because the site can be updated any time, new releases can be distributed quickly and easily. Changes and bug fixes to the documentation, which is all online, can be made directly to the files. And new information and news can be published almost immediately.

Figure 1.3.
The Apache Web site.

NOTE

The pictures throughout this book are usually taken from a browser on the Macintosh (Netscape, most often), or using the text-only browser Lynx. The only reason for this is because I'm writing this book primarily on a Macintosh. If you're using Windows or a UNIX system, don't feel left out. As I noted earlier, the glory of the Web is that you see the same information regardless of the platform you're on. So ignore the buttons and window borders and focus on what's inside the window.

For some sites, the ability to update the site on the fly at any moment is precisely why the site exists. Figure 1.4 shows the home page for *The Nando Times*, an online newspaper that is updated 24 hours a day to reflect new news as it happens. Because the site is up and available all the time, it has an immediacy that neither hardcopy newspapers nor most television news programs can match. Visit *The Nando Times* at `http://www.nando.net/nt/nando.cgi`.

Figure 1.4.
The Nando
Times.

Web Browsers Can Access Many
Forms of Internet Information

If you've read any of the innumerable books on how to use the Internet, you're aware of the dozens of different ways of getting at information on the Net: FTP, Gopher, Usenet news, WAIS databases, Telnet, and e-mail. Before the Web became as popular as it is now, to get to these different kinds of information you had to use different tools for each one, all of which had to be installed and all of which used different commands. Although all these choices made for a great market for "How to Use the Internet" books, they weren't really very easy to use.

Web browsers change that. Although the Web itself is its own information system, with its own Internet protocol (HTTP, the HyperText Transfer Protocol), Web browsers can also read files from other Internet services. And, even better, you can create links to information on those systems just as you would create links to information on Web pages. It's all seamless and all available through a single application.

To point your browser to different kinds of information on the Internet, you use different kinds of URLs. Most URLs start with `http:`, which indicates a file at an actual Web site. To get to a file on the Web using FTP, you would use a URL that looks something like this:

ftp://name_of_site/directory/filename. You can also use an ftp: URL ending with a directory name, and your Web server will show you a list of the files, as in Figure 1.5. This particular figure shows a listing of files from SimTel, a repository of Windows software at ftp://ftp.coast.net/SimTel/win3/winsock/.

Figure 1.5.
The SimTel FTP archive.

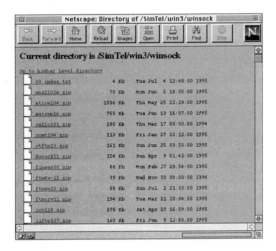

To use a Gopher server from a Web browser, use a URL that looks something like this: gopher://name_of_gopher_server/. For example, Figure 1.6 shows the Gopher server on the WELL, a popular Internet service in San Francisco. Its URL is gopher://gopher.well.com/. You'll learn more about different kinds of URLs in Chapter 4, "All About Links."

Figure 1.6.
The WELL's Gopher server.

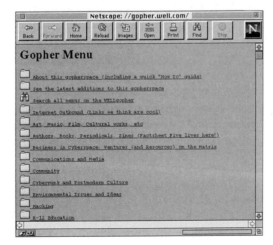

The Web Is Interactive

Interactivity is the ability to "talk back" to the Web server. More traditional media such as television isn't interactive at all; all you do is sit and watch as shows are played at you. Other than changing the channel, you don't have much control over what you see.

The Web is inherently interactive; the act of selecting a link and jumping to another Web page to go somewhere else on the Web is a form of interactivity. In addition to this simple interactivity, however, the Web also enables you to communicate with the publisher of the pages you're reading and with other readers of those pages.

For example, pages can be designed that contain interactive forms that readers can fill out. Forms can contain text-entry areas, radio buttons, or simple menus of items. When the form is "submitted," the information you typed is sent back to server where the pages originated. Figure 1.7 shows an example of an online form for a rather ridiculous census (a form you'll create later on in this book):

Figure 1.7.

The Surrealist Census form.

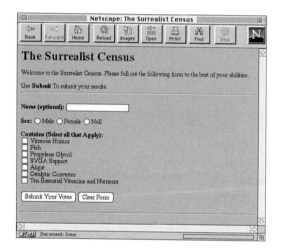

As a publisher of information on the Web, you can use forms for many different purposes, for example:

- ☐ To get feedback about your pages.
- ☐ To get information from your readers (survey, voting, demographic, or any other kind of data). You then can collect statistics on that data, store it in a database, or do anything you want with it.
- ☐ To provide online order forms for products or services available on the Web.
- ☐ To create "guestbooks" and conferencing systems that enable your readers to post their own information on your pages. These kinds of systems enable your readers to communicate not only with you, but with other readers of your pages as well.

In addition to forms, which provide some of the most popular forms of interactivity on the Web, advanced features of Web development provide even more interactivity. For example, capabilities such as Java and Shockwave enable you to include entire programs and games inside Web pages. Software can run on the Web to enable real-time chat sessions between your readers. And developments in 3D worlds enable you and your readers to browse the Web as if they were wandering through real three-dimensional rooms and meeting other people. As time goes on, the Web becomes less of a medium for people passively sitting and digesting information (and becoming "net potatoes") as it is a medium for reaching and communicating with other people all over the world.

Web Browsers

A Web browser, as I mentioned earlier, is the program you use to view pages on and navigate the World Wide Web. Web browsers are sometimes referred to as Web *clients* or other fancy names ("Internet navigation tools"), but Web browser is the most common term.

A wide array of Web browsers is available for just about every platform you can imagine, including graphical-user-interface-based systems (Mac, Windows, X11), and text-only for dial-up UNIX connections. Most browsers are freeware or shareware (try before you buy) or have a lenient licensing policy (Netscape allows you to evaluate its browser for some time, after which you are expected to buy it). Usually all you have to do to get a browser is download it from the Net.

If you get your Internet connection through a commercial online service such as America Online or CompuServe, you may have several browsers to choose from; try a couple and see what works best for you.

Currently the most popular browser for the World Wide Web is Netscape's Navigator, developed by Netscape Communications Corporation. Netscape has become so popular that using Netscape and using the Web have become synonymous to many people. However, despite the fact that Netscape has the lion's share of the market, it is not the only browser on the Web. This will become an important point later on when you learn how to design Web pages and learn about the different capabilities of different browsers. Assuming Netscape is the only browser in use on the Web, and designing your pages accordingly, will limit the audience you can reach with the information you want to present.

What the Browser Does

Any Web browser's job is twofold: given a pointer to a piece of information on the Net (a URL), it has to be able to access that information or operate in some way based on the contents of that pointer. For hypertext Web documents, this means that the browser must be able to communicate with the Web server using the HTTP protocol. Because the Web can also manage information contained on FTP and Gopher servers, in Usenet news postings, in e-mail, and so on, browsers can often communicate with those servers or protocols as well.

What the browser does most often, however, is deal with formatting and displaying Web documents. Each Web page is a file written in a language called HTML (HyperText Markup Language) that includes the text of the page, its structure, and links to other documents, images, or other media. (You'll learn all about HTML on Days 2 and 3, "Creating Simple Web Pages" and "Doing More with HTML 3.2," because you need to know it in order to write your own Web pages.) The browser takes the information it gets from the Web server and formats and displays it for your system. Different browsers may format and display the same file differently, depending on the capabilities of that system and the default layout options for the browser itself. You'll learn more about this tomorrow in Chapter 3, "The Basics of HTML 3.2."

Retrieving documents from the Web and formatting them for your system are the two tasks that make up the core of a browser's functionality. However, depending on the browser you use and the features it includes, you may also be able to play multimedia files, view and interact with Java applets, read your mail, or use other advanced features that a particular browser offers.

An Overview of Popular Browsers

This section describes a few of the more popular browsers on the Web at the time this book is being written. These are in no way all the browsers available, and if the browser you're using isn't here, don't feel that you have to use one of these. Whatever browser you have is fine as long as it works for you.

The browsers in this section can be used only if you have a direct Internet connection or a dial-up SLIP or PPP Internet connection. Getting your machine connected to the Internet is beyond the scope of this book, but plenty of books are out there to help you do so.

If your connection to the Internet is through a commercial online service (AOL, CompuServe, or Prodigy), you may have a choice of several browsers including the ones in this section and browsers that your provider supplies.

Finally, if the only connection you have to the Internet is through a dial-up text-only UNIX (or other) account, you are limited to using text-only browsers such as Lynx. You will not be able to view documents in color or view graphics online (although you usually can download them to your system and view them there).

Netscape

By far the most popular browser in use on the Web today is Netscape Navigator, from Netscape Communications Corporation. Netscape Navigator is most commonly just called Netscape. The Macintosh version of Netscape is shown in Figure 1.8.

Figure 1.8.
Netscape (for Macintosh).

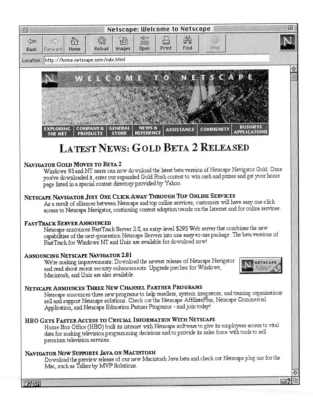

Netscape is available for Windows, Macintosh, and for many different versions of UNIX running the X Window System. It is well supported and provides up-to-the-minute features including an integrated news and mail reader, support for Java applets, and the ability to handle "plug-ins" for more new and interesting features yet to be developed.

The current version of Netscape is 2.02, which is available for downloading at Netscape's site at `http://www.netscape.com/`, or in boxes from your favorite computer software store.

If you're a student, faculty, or staff of an educational institution, or if you work for a charitable nonprofit organization, you can download and use Netscape for free. Otherwise, you're expected to pay for Netscape after an evaluation period (typically 90 days). If you buy Netscape from a store, you've already paid the license fee.

NCSA Mosaic

Only a short time ago, Mosaic had Netscape's place on the Web as the most popular browser. Indeed, Mosaic was the first of the full-color graphical browsers and is usually credited with making the Web as popular as it is today.

Mosaic is developed by NCSA at the University of Illinois, with several supported commercial versions available from companies such as Spry and Spyglass. NCSA Mosaic is free for personal use and comes in versions for Windows, Macintosh, and UNIX (the X Window System); each version is colloquially called WinMosaic, MacMosaic, and XMosaic, respectively. The current version of NCSA Mosaic is 2.01 on all platforms. You can find out more information and download a copy from `http://www.ncsa.uiuc.edu/SDG/Software/Mosaic/NCSAMosaicHome.html`.

Figure 1.9 shows NCSA Mosaic for the Macintosh.

Figure 1.9.

Mosaic (for Macintosh).

Lynx

Lynx ("links," get it?), originally developed by the University of Kansas and now by Foteos Macrides at the Worcester Foundation for Biological Research, is an excellent browser for text-only Internet connections such as dial-up UNIX accounts. It requires VT100 terminal emulation, which most terminal emulation programs should support. You can use arrow keys to select links in Web pages.

Because Lynx runs on systems that lack the ability to display graphics, viewing Web pages using Lynx gives you nothing but the text and the links. Designing pages that work equally well in Lynx and in graphical browsers is one of the more interesting challenges of Web page design (as you'll learn later on in this book).

Lynx should be available on the system where you have a dial-up account, or you can download it from `ftp://ftp2.cc.ukans.edu/pub/lynx`. The current version is 2.5. Figure 1.10 shows Lynx running on a UNIX system (from a terminal emulator).

Figure 1.10.

Lynx.

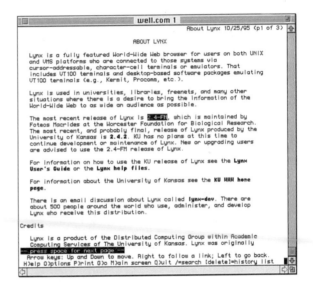

Microsoft Internet Explorer

New on the scene but expected to make a significant impact in the coming months is Microsoft's browser Internet Explorer, usually just called Explorer. Explorer runs on Windows 3.1, Windows 95, Windows NT, and Macintosh, and it is free for downloading from Microsoft's Web site (`http://www.microsoft.com/ie/`). No further license fee is required.

So far, Microsoft has been the only browser developer that has come close to keeping up with Netscape's pace of development, supporting many of Netscape's features and adding a few of its own. In addition, Microsoft has made significant deals with several commercial online services, which means its share of the browser market may be growing significantly in the future.

The current versions of Explorer are 2.0 for Windows 95, 1.5 for Windows NT, 1.6 beta for Windows 3.1, and 2.0 beta for Macintosh. An experimental developers-only version of the 3.0 version is also available in an alpha form. For more information about all these versions, see the Explorer home page.

Figure 1.11 shows Explorer 2.0b1 running on a Macintosh.

Figure 1.11.

Microsoft Internet Explorer (Mac-intosh).

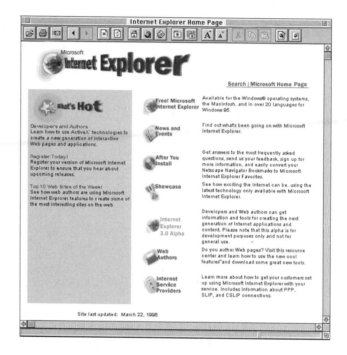

Web Servers

To view and browse pages on the Web, all you need is a Web browser. To publish pages on the Web, most of the time you'll need a Web server.

New Term

A *Web server* is the program that runs on a Web site and is responsible for replying to Web browser requests for files. You need a Web server to publish documents on the Web.

When you use a browser to request a page on a Web site, that browser is making a Web connection to a server (using the HTTP protocol). The server accepts the connection, sends the contents of the files that were requested, and then closes the connection. The browser then formats the information it got from the server.

On the server side, many different browsers may connect to the same server to get the same information. The Web server is responsible for handling all these requests.

Web servers do more than just deposit files. They are also responsible for managing form input and for linking forms and browsers with programs such as databases running on the server.

Just like with browsers, many different servers are available for many different platforms, each with many different features and each and ranging in cost from free to very expensive. For now, all you need to know is what the server is there for; you'll learn more about Web servers on Bonus Day 1.

Uniform Resource Locators (URLs)

As you learned earlier, a URL is a pointer to some bit of data on the Web, be it a Web document, a file on FTP or Gopher, a posting on Usenet, or an e-mail address. The URL provides a universal, consistent method for finding and accessing information, not necessarily for you, but mostly for your Web browser. (If URLs were for you, they would be in a format that would make them easier to remember.)

In addition to typing URLs directly into your browser to go to a particular page, you also use URLs when you create a hypertext link within a document to another document. So, any way you look at it, URLs are important to how you and your browser get around on the Web.

URLs contain information about how to get at the information (what protocol to use: FTP, Gopher, or HTTP), the Internet host name to look on (`www.ncsa.uiuc.edu`, or `ftp.apple.com`, or `netcom16.netcom.com`, and so on), and the directory or other location on that site to find the file. There are also special URLs for things such as sending mail to people (called mailto URLs), and for using the Telnet program.

You'll learn all about URLs and what each part of them means in Chapter 4.

Summary

In order to publish on the Web, you have to understand the basic concepts that make up the parts of the Web. In this chapter you learned three things. First, you learned about a few of the more useful features of the Web for publishing information. Second, you learned about Web browsers and servers and how they interact to deliver Web pages. Third, you learned about what a URL is and why it's important to Web browsing and publishing.

Q&A

Q **Who runs the Web? Who controls all these protocols? Who's in charge of all this?**

A No single entity "owns" or controls the World Wide Web. Given the enormous number of independent sites that supply information to the Web, it is impossible for any single organization to set rules or guidelines. There are two groups of organizations, however, that have a great influence over the look and feel and direction of the Web itself.

The first is the World Wide Web (W3) Consortium, based at MIT in the United States and INRIA in Europe. The W3 Consortium is an organization of individuals and organizations interested in supporting and defining the languages and protocols that make up the Web (HTTP, HTML, and so on). It also provides products (browsers, servers, and so on) that are freely available to anyone who wants to use them. The W3 Consortium is the closest anyone gets to setting the standards for and enforcing rules about the World Wide Web. You can visit the Consortium's home page at http://www.w3.org/.

The second group of organizations that influences the Web is the browser developers themselves, most notably Netscape Communications Corporation and Microsoft. The competition for most popular and technically advanced browser on the Web is fierce right now, with Netscape and Microsoft as the main combatants. Although both organizations claim to support and adhere to the guidelines proposed by the W3 Consortium, both also include their own new features in new versions of their software—features that often conflict with each other and with the work the W3 Consortium is doing.

Sometimes trying to keep track of all the new and rapidly changing developments feels like being in the middle of a war zone, with Netscape on one side, Microsoft on the other, and the W3 trying to mediate and prevent global thermonuclear war. As a Web designer, you're stuck in the middle, and you'll have to make choices about which side to support, if any, and how to deal with the rapid changes. But that's what the rest of this book is for!

Q **Why would anyone use a text-only browser such as Lynx when there are graphical browsers available?**

A You need a special Internet connection in order to use a graphical browser on the Web. If your machine isn't directly hooked up to the Internet (for example, on a network at work or school), you'll need to use a modem with a special account to make your system think it's on the Net or an account with a commercial online service. These special accounts can be quite expensive, even in areas where there are a lot of Internet service providers. Even then, unless you have a very fast modem,

Web pages can take a long time to load, particularly if there are lots of graphics on the page.

Lynx is the ideal solution for people who either don't have a direct Internet connection or don't want to take the time to use the Web graphically. It's fast and it enables you to get hold of just about everything on the Web; indirectly, yes, but it's there.

Q A lot of the magazine articles I've seen about the Web mention CERN, the European Particle Physics Lab, as having a significant role in Web development. You didn't mention them. Where do they stand in Web development?

A The Web was invented at CERN by Tim Berners-Lee, as I'm sure you know by now from all those magazine articles. And, for several years, CERN was the center for much of the development that went on. In late 1995, however, CERN passed its part in World Wide Web development to INRIA (the Institut National pour la Recherche en Informatique et Automatique), in France. INRIA today is the European leg of the W3 Consortium.

Chapter **2**

Get Organized

When you write a book, a paper, an article, or even a memo, you usually don't just jump right in with the first sentence and then write it through to the end. Same goes with the visual arts—you don't normally start from the top left corner of the canvas or page and work your way down to the bottom right.

A better way to write or draw or design a work is to do some planning beforehand—to know what it is you're going to do and what you're trying to accomplish, and to have a general idea or rough sketch of the structure of the piece before you jump in and work on it.

Just as with more traditional modes of communication, writing and designing Web pages takes some planning and thought before you start flinging text and graphics around and linking them wildly to each other—perhaps even more so, because trying to apply the rules of traditional writing or design to online hypertext often results in documents that are either difficult to understand and navigate online or that simply don't take advantage of the features that hypertext provides. Poorly organized Web pages are also difficult to revise or to expand.

In this chapter I describe some of the things you should think about before you begin developing your Web pages. Specifically, you

☐ Learn the differences between a Web presentation, a Web site, a Web page, and a home page.

☐ Think about the sort of information (content) you want to put on the Web.

☐ Set the goals for the presentation.

☐ Organize your content into main topics.

☐ Come up with a general structure for pages and topics.

After you have an overall idea of how you're going to construct your Web pages, you'll be ready to actually start writing and designing those pages tomorrow in Chapter 3, "The Basics of HTML 3.2." If you're anxious to get started, be patient! There will be more than enough HTML to learn over the next couple of days.

Anatomy of a Web Presentation

First, here's a look at some simple terminology I'll be using throughout this book. You need to know what the following terms mean and how they apply to the body of work you're developing for the Web:

☐ The Web presentation

☐ The Web site

☐ Web pages

☐ Home pages

A Web presentation consists of one or more Web pages linked together in a meaningful way, which, as a whole, describes a body of information or creates an overall consistent effect (see Figure 2.1).

Figure 2.1.

A Web presentation and pages.

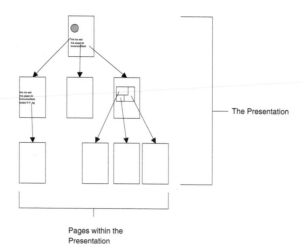

The Presentation

Pages within the Presentation

2

NEW TERM
> A *Web presentation* is a collection of one or more Web pages.

Each Web presentation is stored on a Web site, which is the actual machine on the Web that stores the presentation. Some people refer to the Web presentation and the Web site as the same thing; I like to keep them separate because a single Web site can contain many different presentations with very different purposes and developed by different people. Throughout the first week or so of this book you'll be learning how to develop Web presentations; in the bonus chapters you'll learn how to publish your presentation on an actual Web site.

NEW TERM
> A *Web site* is a system on the Internet containing one or more Web presentations.

A Web page is an individual element of a presentation in the same way that a page is a single element of a book or a newspaper (although, unlike a paper page, Web pages can be of any length). Web pages are sometimes called Web documents. Both terms refer to the same thing: A Web page is a single disk file with a single filename that is retrieved from a server and formatted by a Web browser.

NEW TERM
> A *Web page* is a single element of a Web presentation and is contained in a single disk file.

The terms *Web presentation*, *site*, and *page* are pretty easy to grasp, but the term "home page" is a little more problematic because it can have several different meanings.

If you are reading and browsing the Web, the home page is usually referred to as the Web page that loads when you start up your browser or when you choose the "Home" button. Each browser has its own default home page, which is often the same page for the site that developed the browser. (For example, the Netscape home page is at Netscape's Web site, and the Lynx home page is at the University of Kansas.)

Within your browser, you can change that default home page to start up any page you want—a common tactic I've seen many people use to create a simple page of links to other interesting places or pages that they visit a lot.

If you're publishing pages on the Web, however, the term home page has an entirely different meaning. The home page is the first or topmost page in your Web presentation—it's the entry point to the rest of the pages you've created and the first page your readers will see (see Figure 2.2).

Figure 2.2.

The home page.

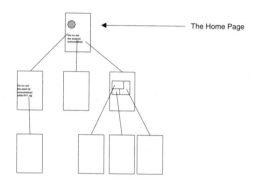

The home page usually contains an overview of the content in the presentation available from that starting point—for example, in the form of a table of contents or a set of icons. If your content is small enough, you may include everything on that single home page—making your home page and your Web presentation the same thing.

NEW TERM

The *home page* is the entry or starting point for the rest of your Web presentation.

What Do You Want To Do on the Web?

This may seem like a silly question. You wouldn't have bought this book if you didn't have some idea of what you want to put online already. But maybe you don't really know what it is you want to put up on the Web, or you have a vague idea but nothing concrete. Maybe it has suddenly become your job to put your company on the Web, and someone handed you this book and said, "Here, this will help." Maybe you just want to do something similar to some other Web page you've seen that you thought was particularly cool.

What you want to put on the Web is what I'll refer to throughout this book as your content. Content is a general term that can refer to text, or graphics, or media, or interactive forms, or anything. If you were to tell someone what your Web pages are "about," you would be describing your content.

NEW TERM

Your *content* is the stuff you're putting on the Web. Information, fiction, images, art, programs, humor, diagrams, games—all of this is content.

What sort of content can you put on the Web? Just about anything you want to. Here are some of the kinds of content that are popular on the Web right now:

- **Personal information.** You can create pages describing everything anyone could ever want to know about you and how incredibly marvelous you are—your hobbies, your resume, your picture, things you've done.

- **Hobbies or special interests.** A Web page could contain information about a particular topic, hobby, or something you're interested in, for example, music, *Star Trek*, motorcycles, cult movies, hallucinogenic mushrooms, antique ink bottles, or upcoming jazz concerts in your city.

- **Publications.** Newspapers, magazines, and other publications lend themselves particularly well to the Web, and they have the advantage of being more immediate and easier to update than their print counterparts.

- **Company profiles.** You could offer information about what a company does, where it is located, job openings, data sheets, white papers, marketing collateral, and whom to contact; such a page might even present demonstration software, if that's what the company does.

- **Online documentation.** The term "online documentation" can refer to everything from quick-reference cards to full reference documentation to interactive tutorials or training modules. And it doesn't have to refer to product documentation; anything task-oriented (changing the oil in your car, making a soufflé, creating landscape portraits in oil, learning HTML) could be described as online documentation.

- **Shopping catalogs.** If your company offers items for sale, making your lists available on the Web is a quick and easy way to let your customers know what you have available and your prices—and if prices change, you can just update your Web documents to reflect that. With interactive forms, you can even let your readers order your product online.

- **Polling and opinion gathering.** Interactivity and forms on the Web enable you to get feedback on nearly any topic from your readers, including opinion polls, suggestion boxes, comments on your Web pages or your products, and so on.

- **Anything else that comes to mind.** Hypertext fiction, online toys, media archives, collaborative art…anything!

The Web is limited only by what you want to do with it. In fact, if what you want to do with it isn't in this list or seems especially wild or half-baked, then that's an excellent reason to try it. The most interesting Web pages out there are the ones that stretch the boundaries of what the Web is supposed to be capable of.

If you really have no idea of what to put up on the Web, don't feel that you have to stop here, put this book away, and come up with something before continuing. Maybe by reading through this book you'll get some ideas (and this book will be useful even if you don't have ideas). I've personally found that the best way to come up with ideas is to spend an afternoon browsing the Web and exploring what other people have done.

Set Your Goals

What do you want people to be able to accomplish in your presentation? Are your readers looking for specific information on how to do something? Are they going to read through each page in turn, going on only when they're done with the page they're on? Are they just going to start at your home page and wander aimlessly around, exploring your "world" until they get bored and go somewhere else?

As an exercise, come up with a list of several goals that your readers might have for your Web pages. The clearer your goals, the better.

For example, say you were creating a Web presentation describing the company where you work. Some people reading that presentation may want to know about job openings. Others may want to know where you're actually located. Still others may have heard that your company makes technical white papers available over the Net, and they want to download the most recent version of a particular one. Each of these is a valid goal, and you should list each one.

For a shopping catalog Web presentation, you might have only a few goals: to allow your readers to browse the items you have for sale by name or by price and to order specific items once they're done browsing.

For a personal or special-interest presentation, you may have only a single goal: to allow your reader to browse and explore the information you've provided.

The goals do not have to be lofty ("this Web presentation will bring about world peace") or even make much sense to anyone except you. Still, coming up with goals for your Web documents prepares you to design, organize, and write your Web pages specifically to reach those goals. Goals also help you resist the urge to obscure your content with extra information.

If you're designing Web pages for someone else—for example, if you're creating the Web site for your company or if you've been hired as a consultant—having a set of goals for the site from your employer is definitely one of the most important pieces of information you should have before you create a single page. The ideas you have for the presentation may not be the ideas that other people have for the presentation, and you may end up doing a lot of work that has to be thrown away.

Break Up Your Content into Main Topics

With your goals in mind, now try to organize your content into main topics or sections, chunking related information together under a single topic. Sometimes the goals you came up with in the previous section and your list of topics will be closely related. For example, if you're putting together a Web page for a bookstore, the goal of being able to order books fits nicely under a topic called, appropriately, "Ordering Books."

You don't have to be exact at this point in development. Your goal here is just to try to come up with an idea of what, specifically, you'll be describing in your Web pages. You can organize things better later, as you write the actual pages.

For example, say you were designing a Web presentation about how to tune your car. This is a simple example since tune-ups consist of a concrete set of steps that fit neatly into topic headings. In this example, your topics might include

- ☐ Change the oil and oil filter
- ☐ Check and adjust engine timing
- ☐ Check and adjust valve clearances
- ☐ Check and replace the spark plugs
- ☐ Check fluid levels, belts, and hoses

Don't worry about the order of the steps or how you're going to get your reader to go from one section to another. Just list the things you want to describe in your presentation.

How about a less task-oriented example? Say you wanted to create a set of Web pages about a particular rock band because you're a big fan and you're sure there are other fans out there who would benefit from your extensive knowledge. Your topics might be

- ☐ The history of the band
- ☐ Biographies of each of the band members
- ☐ A "discography"—all the albums and singles the band has released
- ☐ Selected lyrics
- ☐ Images of album covers
- ☐ Information about upcoming shows and future products

You can come up with as many topics as you want, but try to keep each topic reasonably short. If a single topic seems too large, try to break it up into subtopics. If you have too many small topics, try to group them together into some sort of more general topic heading. For example, if you were creating an online encyclopedia of poisonous plants, having individual topics for each plant would be overkill. You could just as easily group each plant name under a letter of the alphabet (A, B, C, and so on) and use each letter as a topic. That's assuming, of course, that your readers will be looking up information in your encyclopedia alphabetically. If they want to look up poisonous plants using some other method, you would have to come up with different topics.

Your goal is to have a set of topics that are roughly the same size and that group together related bits of the information you have to present.

Ideas for Organization and Navigation

At this point you should have a good idea about what you want to talk about and a list of topics. The next step is to actually start structuring the information you have into a set of Web pages. But before you do that, consider some "standard" structures that have been used in other help systems and online tools. This section describes some of those structures, their various features, and some important considerations, including

- [ ] The kinds of information that work well for each structure
- [ ] How readers find their way through the content of each structure type to find what they need
- [ ] How to make sure readers can figure out where they are within your documents (context) and find their way back to a known position

Think, as you read this section, how your information might fit into one of these structures or how you could combine these structures to create a new structure for your Web presentation.

 NOTE

> Many of the ideas I describe in this section were drawn from a book called *Designing and Writing Online Documentation* by William K. Horton (John Wiley & Sons, 1994). Although Horton's book was written primarily for technical writers and developers working specifically with online help systems, it's a great book for ideas on structuring documents and for dealing with hypertext information in general. If you start doing a lot of work with the Web, you might want to pick up this book; it provides a lot of insight beyond what I have to offer.

Hierarchies

Probably the easiest and most logical way to structure your Web documents is in a hierarchical or menu fashion, illustrated in Figure 2.3. Hierarchies and menus lend themselves especially well to online and hypertext documents. Most online help systems, for example, are hierarchical. You start with a list or menu of major topics; selecting one leads you to a list of subtopics, which then leads you to discussion about a particular topic. Different help systems have different levels, of course, but most follow this simple structure.

Figure 2.3.

Hierarchical organization.

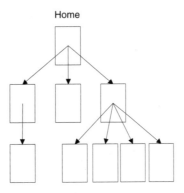

In a hierarchical organization, it's easy for readers to know their position in the structure; choices are to move up for more general information or down for more specific information. Providing a link back to the top level enables your reader to get back to some known position quickly and easily.

In hierarchies, the home page provides the most general overview to the content below it. The home page also defines the main links for the pages further down in the hierarchy.

For example, a Web presentation about gardening might have a home page with the topics shown in Figure 2.4.

Figure 2.4.

Gardening home page.

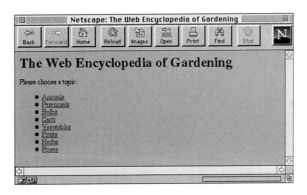

If you selected Fruits, you would then be linked "down" to a page about fruits (Figure 2.5). From there you can go back to the home page, or you can select another link and go further down into more specific information about particular fruits.

Figure 2.5.

Fruits.

Selecting Soft Fruits takes you to yet another menu-like page, where you have still more categories to choose from (Figure 2.6). From there you can go up to Fruits, back to the home page, or down to one of the choices in this menu.

Figure 2.6.

Soft fruits.

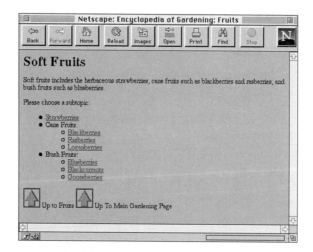

Note that each level has a consistent interface (up, down, back to index) and that each level has a limited set of choices for basic navigation. Hierarchies are structured enough that the chance of getting lost is minimal. (This is especially true if you provide clues about where "up" is; for example, a link that says "Up to Soft Fruits" as opposed to just "Up.") Additionally, if you organize each level of the hierarchy and avoid overlap between topics (and the content you have lends itself to a hierarchical organization), hierarchies can be an easy way to find particular bits of information. If that was one of your goals for your readers, using a hierarchy may work particularly well.

Avoid including too many levels and too many choices, however, because you can easily annoy your reader. Too many menu pages results in "voice-mail syndrome." After having to choose from too many menus, you forget what it was you originally wanted, and you're too annoyed to care. Try to keep your hierarchy two to three levels deep, combining information on the pages at the lowest levels (or endpoints) of the hierarchy if necessary.

Linear

Another way to organize your documents is to use a linear or sequential organization, much like printed documents are organized. In a linear structure, illustrated in Figure 2.7, the home page is the title, or introduction, and each page follows sequentially from that structure. In a strict linear structure, there are links that move from one page to another, typically forward and back. You may also want to include a link to "Home" that takes you quickly back to the first page.

Figure 2.7.
*Linear
organization.*

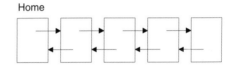

Context is generally easy to figure out in a linear structure simply because there are so few places to go.

A linear organization is very rigid and limits your readers' freedom to explore and your freedom to present information. Linear structures are good for putting material online when the information also has a very linear structure offline (such as short stories, step-by-step instructions, or computer-based training), or when you explicitly want to prevent your reader from skipping around.

For example, consider teaching someone how to make cheese using the Web. Cheese-making is a complex process that involves several steps that must be followed in a specific order.

Describing this process using Web pages lends itself to a linear structure rather well. When navigating a set of Web pages on this subject, you would start with the home page, which might have a summary or an overview of the steps to follow. Then, using the link for "forward," move on to the first step, "Choosing the Right Milk"; to the next step, "Setting and Curdling the Milk"; all the way through to the last step, "Curing and Ripening the Cheese." If you needed to review at any time, you could use the link for "back." Since the process is so linear, there would be little need for links that branch off from the main stem or links that join together different steps in the process.

Linear with Alternatives

You can soften the rigidity of a linear structure by allowing the reader to deviate from the main path. For example, you could have a linear structure with alternatives that branch out from a single point (see Figure 2.8). The offshoots can then rejoin the main branch at some point further down, or they can continue down their separate tracks until they each come to an "end."

Figure 2.8.
Linear with alternatives.

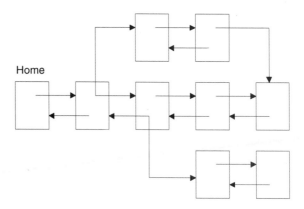

For example, say you had an installation procedure for a software package that was similar in most ways, regardless of the computer type, except for one step. At that point in the linear installation, you could branch out to cover each system, as shown in Figure 2.9.

Figure 2.9.
Different steps for different systems.

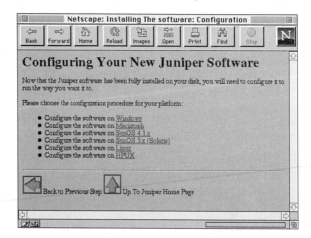

After the system-specific part of the installation, you could then link back to the original branch and continue on with the generic installation.

In addition to branching from a linear structure, you could also provide links that allow readers to skip forward or back in the chain if they need to review a particular step or if they already understand some content (see Figure 2.10).

Figure 2.10.

Skip ahead or back.

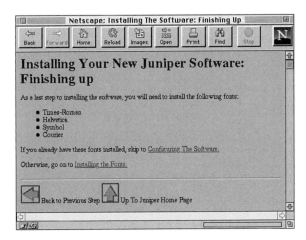

Combination of Linear and Hierarchical

A popular form of document organization on the Web is a combination of a linear structure and a hierarchical one, as shown in Figure 2.11. This structure occurs most often when very structured but linear documents are put online; the popular FAQ (Frequently Asked Questions) files use this structure.

Figure 2.11.

Combination of linear and hierarchical.

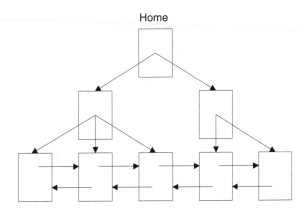

The combination of linear and hierarchical documents works well as long as there are appropriate clues regarding context. Because the reader can either move up and down or forward and back, it's easy to lose one's mental positioning in the hierarchy when one crosses hierarchical boundaries by moving forward or back.

For example, say you were putting the Shakespearean play *Macbeth* online as a set of Web pages. In addition to the simple linear structure that the play provides, you could create a hierarchical table of contents and summary of each act linked to appropriate places within the text, something like that shown in Figure 2.12.

Figure 2.12.
Macbeth hierarchy.

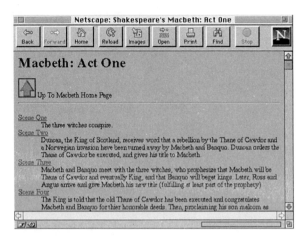

Because this is both a linear and hierarchical structure, on each page of the script you provide links to go forward, back, return to beginning, and up. But what is the context for going up?

If you've just come down into this page from an act summary, the context makes sense. "Up" means to go back to the summary you just came from.

But say you went down from a summary and then went forward, crossing an act boundary (say from Act 1 to Act 2). Now what does "up" mean? The fact that you're moving up to a page that you may not have seen before is disorienting given the nature of what you expect from a hierarchy. Up and down are supposed to be consistent.

Consider two possible solutions:

☐ Do not allow "forward" and "back" links across hierarchical boundaries. In this case, in order to read from Act 1 to Act 2 in *Macbeth*, you would have to move up in the hierarchy and then back down into Act 2.

☐ Provide more context in the link text. Instead of just "Up" or an icon for the link that moves up in the hierarchy, include a description as to where you're moving.

Web

A web is a set of documents with little or no actual overall structure; the only thing tying each page together is a link (see Figure 2.13). The reader drifts from document to document, following the links around.

Web structures tend to be free-flowing and allow the reader to wander aimlessly through the content. Web structures are excellent for content that is intended to be meandering or unrelated, or when you want to encourage browsing. The World Wide Web itself is, of course, a giant web structure.

Figure 2.13.

A web structure.

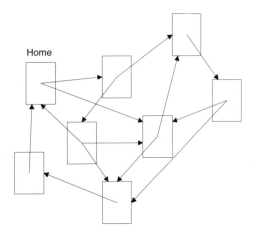

An example of content organized in a web structure might be a set of virtual "rooms" created using Web pages. If you've ever played an old text-adventure game like Zork or Dungeon, or if you've used a MUD (Multi-User Dungeon), you are familiar with this kind of environment.

In the context of a Web presentation, the environment is organized so that each page is a specific location (and usually contains a description of that location). From that location you can "move" in several different directions, exploring the environment much in the way you would move from room to room in a building in the real world (and getting lost just as easily). For example, the initial home page might look something like what's shown in Figure 2.14.

Figure 2.14.

The home page for a Web-based virtual environment.

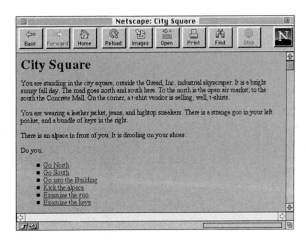

From that page you can then explore one of the links, say, to go into the building, which would take you to the page shown in Figure 2.15.

Figure 2.15.

Another page in the Web environment.

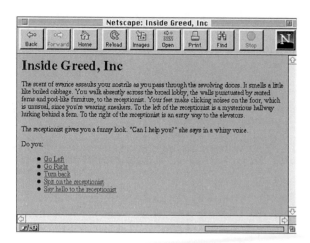

Each room has a set of links to each "adjacent" room in the environment. By following the links, you can explore the rooms in the environment.

The problem with web organizations is that it's too easy to get lost in them—just as you might in the "world" you were exploring in the example. Without any overall structure to the content, it's difficult to figure out the relationship between where you are and where you're going, and, often, where you've been. Context is difficult, and often the only way to find your way back out of a Web structure is to retrace your steps. Web structures can be extremely disorienting and immensely frustrating if you have a specific goal in mind.

To solve the problem of disorientation, you can use clues on each page. Two ideas:

☐ Provide a way out. "Return to home page" is an excellent link.

☐ Include a map of the overall structure on each page, with a "you are here" indication somewhere in the map. It doesn't have to be an actual visual map, but providing some sort of context will go a long way towards preventing your readers from getting lost.

Storyboarding Your Web Presentation

The next step in planning your Web presentation is to figure out what content goes on what page and to come up with some simple links for navigation between those pages.

If you're using one of the structures described in the previous section, much of the organization may arise from that structure, in which case this section will be easy. If you want to combine different kinds of structures, however, or if you have a lot of content that needs to be linked together in sophisticated ways, sitting down and making a specific plan of what goes where will be incredibly useful later on as you develop and link each individual page.

What Is Storyboarding and Why Do I Need It?

Storyboarding a presentation is a concept borrowed from filmmaking in which each scene and each individual camera shot is sketched and roughed out in the order in which it occurs in the movie. Storyboarding provides an overall structure and plan to the film that allows the director and his staff to have a distinct idea of where each individual shot fits into the overall movie.

The storyboarding concept works quite well for developing Web pages as well. The storyboard provides an overall rough outline of what the presentation will look like when it's done, including which topics go on which pages, the primary links, and maybe even some conceptual idea of what sort of graphics you'll be using and where they will go. With that representation in hand, you can develop each page without trying to remember exactly where that page fits into the overall presentation and its often complex relationships to other pages.

NEW TERM

> *Storyboarding*, borrowed from filmmaking, is the process of creating a rough outline and sketch of what your presentation will look like before you actually write any pages. Storyboarding helps you visualize the entire presentation and how it will look when it's complete.

In the case of really large sets of documents, a storyboard enables different people to develop different portions of the same Web presentation. With a clear storyboard, you can minimize duplication of work and reduce the amount of contextual information each person needs to remember.

For smaller or simpler Web presentations, or presentations with a simple logical structure, storyboarding may be unnecessary. But for larger and more complex projects, the existence of a storyboard can save enormous amounts of time and frustration. If you can't keep all the parts of your content and their relationships in your head, consider doing a storyboard.

So what does a storyboard for a Web presentation look like? It can be as simple as a couple of sheets of paper. Each sheet can represent a page, with a list of topics that each page will describe and some thoughts about the links that page will include. I've seen storyboards for very complex hypertext systems that involved a really large bulletin board, index cards, and string. Each index card had a topic written on it, and the links were represented by string tied on pins from card to card (see Figure 2.16).

The point of a storyboard is that it organizes your Web pages in a way that works for you. If you like index cards and string, work with it. If a simple outline on paper or on the computer works better, use that instead.

Figure 2.16.

A complex storyboard.

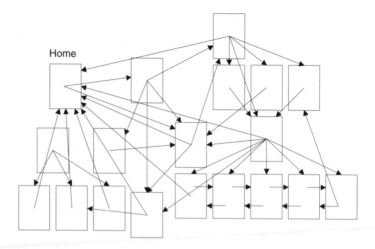

Hints for Storyboarding

Some things to think about when developing your storyboard are as follows:

☐ Which topics will go on each page?

A simple rule of thumb is to have each topic represented by a single page. But if you have a large number of topics, maintaining and linking them can be a daunting task. Consider combining smaller, related topics onto a single page instead. However, don't go overboard and put everything on one page; your reader still has to download your document over the Net. It's better to have several medium-sized pages (say, the size of two to 10 pages in your word processor) than to have one monolithic page or hundreds of little tiny pages.

☐ What are the primary forms of navigation between pages?

What links will you need for your reader to navigate from page to page? These are the main links in your document that enable your reader to accomplish the goals you defined in the first section. Links for forward, back, up, down, or home all fall under the category of primary navigation.

☐ What alternative forms of navigation are you going to provide?

In addition to the simple navigation links, some Web presentations contain extra information that is parallel to the main Web content, such as a glossary of terms, an alphabetical index of concepts, or a credits page. Consider these extra forms of information when designing your plan, and think about how you are going to link them into the main content.

☐ What will you put on your home page?

Since the home page is the starting point for the rest of the information in your presentation, consider what sort of information you're going to put on the home page. A general summary of what's to come? A list of links to other topics?

☐ Review your goals.

As you design the framework for your Web presentation, keep your goals in mind, and make sure you are not obscuring your goals with extra information or content.

Summary

Designing a Web presentation, like designing a book outline, a building plan, or a painting, can sometimes be a complex and involved process. Having a plan before beginning can help you keep the details straight and help you develop the finished product with fewer false starts. In this chapter, you've learned how to put together a simple plan and structure for creating a set of Web pages, including

☐ Deciding what sort of content to present

☐ Coming up with a set of goals for that content

☐ Deciding on a set of topics

☐ Organizing and storyboarding the presentation

With that plan in place, you can now move on to the next few chapters and learn the specifics of how to write individual Web pages, create links between them, and add graphics and media to enhance the presentation for your audience.

Q&A

Q This all seems like an awful lot of work. All I want to do is make something simple, and you're telling me I have to have goals and topics and storyboards.

A If you are doing something simple, then no, you won't need to do much, if any, of the stuff I recommend in this chapter. But once you're talking about two or three interlinked pages or more, it really helps to have a plan before you start. If you just dive in, you may discover that keeping everything straight in your head is too difficult. And the result may not be what you expected, making it hard for people to get the information they need out of your presentation as well as making it difficult for you to reorganize your page so that it makes sense. Having a plan before you start can't hurt, and it may save you time in the long run.

Q **You've talked a lot in this chapter about organizing topics and pages, but you've said nothing about the design and layout of individual pages.**

A I discuss that later in this book, after you've learned more about the sorts of layout HTML (the language used for Web pages) can do, and the stuff that it just can't do. There's a whole chapter and more about page layout and design on Day 6, in Chapter 11, "Writing and Designing Web Pages: Dos and Don'ts."

Q **What if I don't like any of the basic structures you talked about in this chapter?**

A Then design your own. As long as your readers can find what they want or do what you want them to do, there are no rules that say you *must* use a hierarchy or a linear structure. I presented those structures only as potential ideas for organizing your Web pages.

DAY 2

Creating Simple Web Pages

Chapter **3**

The Basics of HTML 3.2

After finishing up yesterday's discussion, with lots of text to read and concepts to digest, you're probably wondering when you're actually going to get to write a Web page. That is, after all, why you bought the book. Welcome to Day 2! Today you'll get to create Web pages, learn about HTML, the language for writing Web pages, and learn about the following things:

- [ ] What HTML is and why you have to use it
- [ ] What you can and cannot do when you design HTML pages
- [ ] HTML tags: what they are and how to use them
- [ ] Tags for overall page structure: `<HTML>`, `<HEAD>`, `<BODY>`
- [ ] Tags for titles and headings, and paragraphs: `<TITLE>`, `<H1>`...`<H6>`, `<P>`
- [ ] Tags for comments
- [ ] Tags for lists

What HTML Is...and What It Isn't

There's just one more thing to note before you dive into actually writing Web pages: you should know what HTML is, what it can do, and most importantly what it can't do.

HTML stands for HyperText Markup Language. HTML is based on SGML (Standard Generalized Markup Language), a much bigger document-processing system. To write HTML pages, you won't need to know a whole lot about SGML, but it does help to know that one of the main features of SGML is that it describes the general *structure* of the content inside documents, not that content's actual appearance on the page or on the screen. This will be a bit of a foreign concept to you if you're used to working with WYSIWYG (What You See is What You Get) editors, so let's go over this slowly.

HTML Describes the Structure of a Page

HTML, by virtue of its SGML heritage, is a language for describing the structure of a document, not its actual presentation. The idea here is that most documents have common elements—for example, titles, paragraphs, or lists. Before you start writing, therefore, you can identify and define the set of elements in that document and give them appropriate names (see Figure 3.1).

Figure 3.1.

*Document
elements.*

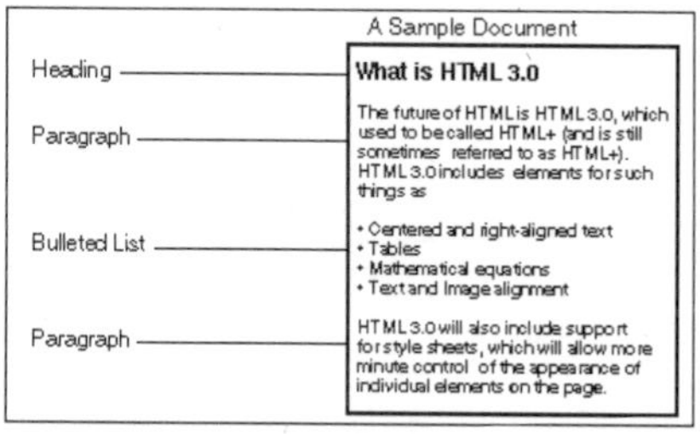

A Sample Document

Heading —————— **What is HTML 3.0**

Paragraph —————— The future of HTML is HTML 3.0, which used to be called HTML+ (and is still sometimes referred to as HTML+). HTML 3.0 includes elements for such things as

Bulleted List —————— • Centered and right-aligned text
• Tables
• Mathematical equations
• Text and Image alignment

Paragraph —————— HTML 3.0 will also include support for style sheets, which will allow more minute control of the appearance of individual elements on the page.

If you've worked with word processing programs that use style sheets (such as Microsoft Word) or paragraph catalogs (such as FrameMaker), then you've done something similar; each section of text conforms to one of a set of styles that are pre-defined before you start working.

HTML defines a set of common styles for Web pages: headings, paragraphs, lists, and tables. It also defines character styles such as boldface and code examples. Each element has a name and is contained in what's called a tag. When you write a Web page in HTML, you label the different elements of your page with these tags that say "this is a heading" or "this is a list item." It's like if you were working for a newspaper or a magazine where you do the writing but someone else does the layout; you might explain to the layout person that this line is the title, this line is a figure caption, or this line is a heading. It's the same way with HTML.

HTML Does Not Describe Page Layout

When you're working with a word processor or page layout program, styles are not just named elements of a page—they also include formatting information such as the font size and style, indentation, underlining, and so on. So when you write some text that's supposed to be a heading, you can apply the Heading style to it, and the program automatically formats that paragraph for you in the correct style.

HTML doesn't go this far. For the most part, HTML doesn't say anything about how a page looks when it's viewed. All HTML tags indicate is that an element is a heading or a list—they say nothing about how that heading or list is to be formatted. So, as with the magazine example and the layout person who formats your article, it's the layout person's job to decide how big the heading should be and what font it should be in—the only thing you have to worry about is marking which section is supposed to be a heading.

Web browsers, in addition to providing the networking functions to retrieve pages from the Web, double as HTML formatters. When you read an HTML page into a browser such as Netscape or Lynx, the browser reads, or parses, the HTML tags and formats the text and images on the screen. The browser has mappings between the names of page elements and actual styles on the screen; for example, headings might be in a larger font than the text on the rest of the page. The browser also wraps all the text so that it fits into the current width of the window.

Different browsers, running on different platforms, may have different style mappings for each page element. Some browsers may use different font styles than others. So, for example, one browser might display italics as italics, whereas another might use reverse text or underlining on systems that don't have italic fonts. Or it might put a heading in all capital letters instead of a larger font. What this means to you as a Web page designer is that the pages you create using HTML may look radically different from system to system and from browser to browser. The actual information and links inside those pages will still be there, but the appearance on the screen will change. You can design a Web page so that it looks perfect on your computer system, but when someone else reads it on a different system, it may look entirely different (and it may very well be entirely unreadable).

Why It Works This Way

If you're used to writing and designing on paper, this concept may seem almost perverse. No control over the layout of a page? The whole design can vary depending on where the page is viewed? This is awful! Why on earth would it work like this?

Remember in Chapter 1, "The World of the World Wide Web," when I mentioned that one of the cool things about the Web is that it is cross-platform and that Web pages can be viewed on any computer system, on any size screen, with any graphics display? If the final goal of Web publishing is for your pages to be readable by anyone in the world, you can't count on your readers having the same computer system, the same size screen, the same number of colors, or the same fonts as you. The Web takes into account all these differences and allows all browsers and all computer systems to be on equal ground.

The Web, as a design medium, is not a new form of paper. The Web is an entirely new medium, with new constraints and goals that are very different from working with paper. The number-one rule of Web page design, as I'll keep harping on throughout this book, is this:

☐ *Don't* design your pages based on what they look like on your computer system and on your browser. *Do* design your pages so they work in most browsers. *Do* focus on clear, well-structured content that is easy to read and understand.

Throughout this book I'm going to be showing you examples of HTML code and what they look like when displayed. In many examples, I'll give you a comparison of how a snippet of code looks in two very different browsers: Netscape, probably the most popular browser on the market today, and Lynx, a browser that works on text-only terminals which is less popular but still is in common use. Through these examples, you'll get an idea for how different the same page can look from browser to browser.

HTML Is a Markup Language

HTML is a *markup language*. Writing in a markup language means that you start with the text of your page and add special tags around words and paragraphs. If you've ever worked with other markup languages such as troff or LaTeX, or even older DOS-based word processors where you put in special codes for things such as "turn on boldface," this won't seem all that unusual.

The tags indicate the different parts of the page and produce different effects in the browser. You'll learn more about tags and how they're used in the next section.

HTML has a defined set of tags you can use. You can't make up your own tags to create new appearances or features. And, just to make sure things are really confusing, different browsers support different sets of tags.

The base set of HTML tags, the lowest common denominator, is referred to as HTML 2.0. HTML 2.0 is the current standard for HTML (there's a written specification for it that is developed and maintained by the W3 Consortium) and the set of tags that all browsers must support. For the next couple of chapters, you'll learn primarily about HTML 2.0 tags that you can use anywhere.

HTML 3 is considered the "next generation" of HTML and a catch-all for lots of new features that give you lots of flexibility over HTML 2.0 for how you design your pages. When a browser claims to support HTML 3, they usually mean it supports some HTML 3 features such as tables and backgrounds. HTML 3 is still in development, and there are many HTML 3 features that are not supported by any browsers yet. Like HTML 2.0, the HTML 3 standard is maintained by the W3 Consortium.

NOTE

> To be exactly correct about it, the HTML 3.0 standard no longer exists; the existing draft of the proposal has expired, and work on HTML 3.0 has broken into several smaller sub-groups, each handling a different aspect. Just announced is HTML 3.2, the brand-new W3 Consortium standard for HTML tags. HTML 3.2 is essentially HTML 2.0 plus some of the more common tags from HTML 3.0 in common use, including colors and tables. If you're interested in how HTML development is working, and just exactly what's going on at the W3 Consortium, check out the pages for HTML at the Consortium's site at `http://www.w3.org/pub/WWW/MarkUp/`.

In addition to the tags defined by HTML 2.0, 3.0, and 3.2, there are also browser-specific extensions to HTML that are implemented by an individual browser company and are proposed for inclusion in HTML 3.2. Netscape and Microsoft are particularly guilty of this, and they offer many new features unique to their browsers. However, many other browsers may also support other browser's extensions, to varying degrees; for example, NCSA Mosaic supports many of the Netscape extensions but none of Internet Explorer's.

Confused yet? You're not alone. Even Web designers with years of experience and hundreds of pages under their belts have to struggle with the problem of which set of tags to choose in order to strike a balance between wide support for a design (using HTML 2.0) or having more flexibility in layout but less consistency across browsers (HTML 3.2 or the browser extensions). Keeping track of all this can be really confusing. Throughout this book, as I introduce each tag, I'll let you know which version of HTML that tag belongs to, how widely supported it is, and how to use it to best effect in a wide variety of browsers. And later in this book, you'll get hints on how to deal with the different HTML tags to make sure that your pages are readable and still look good in all kinds of browsers.

But even with all these different tags to choose from, HTML is an especially small and simple-to-learn markup language—far smaller than other languages such as PostScript or troff on UNIX. Those languages are so large and complex that it often takes ages to learn enough to write even simple documents. With HTML, you can get started right away.

And with that note, let's get started.

What HTML Files Look Like

Pages written in HTML are plain text files (ASCII), which means they contain no platform- or program specific information—they can be read by any editor that supports text (which should be just about any editor—more about this later). HTML files contain two things:

- ☐ The text of the page itself
- ☐ HTML tags that indicate page elements, structure, formatting, and hypertext links to other pages or to included media

Most HTML tags look something like this:

```
<TheTagName> affected text </TheTagName>
```

The tag name itself (here, TheTagName) is enclosed in brackets (<>).

HTML tags generally have a beginning and an ending tag, surrounding the text that they affect. The beginning tag "turns on" a feature (such as headings, bold, and so on), and the ending tag turns it off. Closing tags have the tag name preceded by a slash (/).

NEW TERM

> *HTML tags* are the things inside brackets (<>) that indicate features or elements of a page.

Not all HTML tags have a beginning and an end. Some tags are only one-sided, and still other tags are "containers" that hold extra information and text inside the brackets. You'll learn about these tags as the book progresses.

All HTML tags are case-insensitive; that is, you can specify them in uppercase, lowercase, or in any mixture. So, <HTML> is the same as <html> is the same as <HtMl>. I like to put my tags in all caps (<HTML>) so I can pick them out from the text better. That's how I show them in the examples in this book.

Exercise 3.1: Take a look at HTML sources.

Before you actually start writing your own HTML pages, it helps to get a feel for what an HTML page looks like. Luckily, there's plenty of source material out there for you to look at—every page that comes over the wire to your browser is in HTML format. (You almost never see the codes in your browser; all you see is the final result.)

EXERCISE

3

Most Web browsers have a way of letting you see the HTML source of a Web page. You may have a menu item or a button for View Document Source or View HTML. In Lynx, the \ (backslash) command toggles between source view and formatted view.

 TIP

Some browsers do not have the capability to directly view the source of a Web page, but do allow you to save the current page as a file to your local disk. Under a dialog box for saving the file, there may be a menu of formats—for example, Text, PostScript, or HTML. You can save the current page as HTML and then open that file in a text editor or word processor to see the HTML source.

Try going to a typical home page and then viewing the source for that page. For example, Figure 3.2 shows the home page for Alta Vista, which is a popular search page at `http://www.altavista.digital.com/`:

Figure 3.2.

Alta Vista home page.

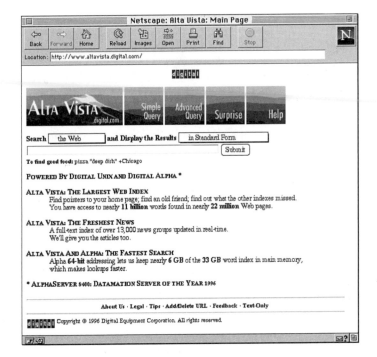

The HTML source of that page looks something like Figure 3.3.

Try viewing the source of your own favorite Web pages. You should start seeing some similarities in the way pages are organized and get a feel for the kinds of tags that HTML uses. You can learn a lot about HTML by comparing the text on the screen with the source for that text.

Figure 3.3.
Some HTML source.

Exercise 3.2: Create an HTML page.

EXERCISE

You've seen what HTML looks like—now it's your turn to create your own Web page. Let's start with a really simple example so you can get a basic feel for HTML.

To get started writing HTML, you're not going to need a Web server, a Web provider, or even a connection to the Web itself. All you really need is something to create your HTML files, and at least one browser to view them. You can write, link, and test whole suites of Web pages without even touching a network. In fact, that's what we're going to do for the majority of this book—I'll talk later about publishing everything on the Web so other people can see.

First, you'll need a text editor. A text editor is a program that saves files in ASCII format. ASCII format is just plain text, with no font formatting or special characters. On UNIX, vi, emacs, and pico are all text editors. On Windows, Notepad, Microsoft Write, and DOS edit are good basic text editors (and free with your system!); or, a shareware editor such as WED or WinEdit will work as well. On the Macintosh, you can use the SimpleText application that came with your system, or a more powerful text editor such as BBedit or Alpha (both of which are shareware).

If all you have is a word processor such as Microsoft Word, don't panic. You can still write pages in word processors just as you would in text editors, although it'll be more complicated to do so. When you use the Save or Save As command, there will be a menu of formats you can use to save the file. One of those should be "Text Only," "Text Only with Line Breaks," or "DOS Text." All these options will save your file as plain ASCII text, just as if you were using a text editor. For HTML files, if you have a choice between DOS Text and just Text, use DOS Text, and use the Line Breaks option if you have it.

NOTE

If you do choose to use a word processor for your HTML development, be very careful. Many recent word processors are including HTML modes or mechanisms for creating HTML code. The word processor may decide to take over your HTML coding for you, or mysteriously put you into that mode without telling you first. This may produce unusual results or files that simply don't behave as you expect. If you find that you're running into trouble with a word processor, try using a text editor and see if that helps.

What about the plethora of free and commercial HTML editors that claim to help you write HTML more easily? Most of them are actually simple text editors with some buttons that stick the tags in for you. If you've got one of those, go ahead and use it. If you've got a fancier editor that claims to hide all the HTML for you, put that one aside for the next couple of days and try using a plain-text editor just for a little while. I'll talk more about HTML editors after this example.

Open up that text editor, and type the following code. You don't have to understand what any of this means at this point. You'll learn about it later in this chapter. This is just a simple example to get you started:

```
<HTML><HEAD>
<TITLE>My Sample HTML Document</TITLE></HEAD>
<BODY>
<H1>This is an HTML Document</H1>
</BODY></HTML>
```

After you create your HTML file, save it to disk. Remember that if you're using a word processor, do Save As and make sure you're saving it as text only. When you pick a name for the file, there are two rules to follow:

☐ The filename should have an extension of .html (.htm on DOS or Windows systems that have only three-character extensions), for example, myfile.html or text.html or index.htm. Most Web software will require your files to have this extension, so get into the habit of using it now.

☐ Use small, simple names. Don't include spaces or special characters (bullets, accented characters)—just letters and numbers are fine.

Exercise 3.3: View the result.

Now that you have an HTML file, start up your Web browser. You don't have to be connected to the network since you're not going to be opening pages at any other site. Your browser or network connection software may complain about the lack of a network connection, but usually it will eventually give up and let you use it anyway.

TIP

If you're using a Web browser from Windows, using that browser without a network is unfortunately more complicated than on other systems. Most Windows browsers are unable to run without a network, preventing you from looking at your local files without running up online charges. Try starting up your browser while not online to see if this is the case. If your browser has this problem, there are several things you can try. Depending on your network software, you may be able to start your network package (Trumpet or Chameleon), but not actually dial the network. This often is sufficient for many browsers.

If this doesn't work, you'll have to replace the file `winsock.dll` in your windows directory with what's called a "null sock"—a special file that makes your system think it's on a network when it's not.

First, put your original `winsock.dll` in a safe place; you'll need to put everything back the way it was to get back onto the Web. Next, rename the null sock file to `winsock.dll` and copy it to your Windows directory. With the fake `winsock` file installed, you should be able to use your Windows browser without a network (it may still give you errors, but it should work).

Once your browser is running, look for a menu item or button labeled Open Local, Open File, or maybe just Open. It's a menu item that will let you browse your local disk. (If you're using Lynx, `cd` to the directory that contains your HTML file and use the command `lynx myfile.html` to start Lynx.) The Open File command (or its equivalent) tells the browser to read an HTML file from your disk, parse it, and display it, just as if it were a page on the Web. Using your browser and the Open Local command, you can write and test your HTML files on your computer in the privacy of your own home.

If you don't see something like what's in Figure 3.4 (for example, if parts are missing or if everything looks like a heading), go back into your text editor and compare your file to the example. Make sure that all your tags have closing tags and that all your < characters are matched by > characters. You don't have to quit your browser to do this; just fix the file and save it again under the same name.

Figure 3.4.

The sample HTML file.

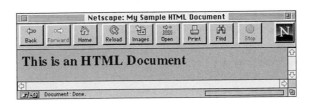

Then go back to your browser. There should be a menu item or button called Reload. (In Lynx, it's Control+R.) The browser will read the new version of your file, and voilà, you can edit and preview and edit and preview until you get it right.

If you're getting the actual HTML text repeated in your browser rather than what's shown in Figure 3.4, make sure your HTML file has a .html or .htm extension. This file extension is what tells your browser that this is an HTML file. The extension is important.

If things are going really wrong—if you're getting a blank screen or you're getting some really strange characters, something is wrong with your original file. If you've been using a word processor to edit your files, try opening your saved HTML file in a plain-text editor (again Notepad or SimpleText will work just fine). If the text editor can't read it or if the result is garbled, you haven't saved the original file in the right format. Go back into your original editor and try saving it as text only again, and then try it again in your browser until you get it right.

A Note About Formatting

When an HTML page is parsed by a browser, any formatting you may have done by hand—that is, any extra spaces, tabs, returns, and so on—are all ignored. The only thing that formats an HTML page is an HTML tag. If you spend hours carefully editing a plain text file to have nicely formatted paragraphs and columns of numbers, but you don't include any tags, when you read the page into an HTML browser, all the text will flow into one paragraph. All your work will have been in vain.

NOTE

There's one exception to this rule: a tag called <PRE>. You'll learn about this tag tomorrow in Chapter 5, "More Text Formatting with HTML 3.2."

The advantage of having all white space (spaces, tabs, returns) ignored is that you can put your tags wherever you want.

The following examples all produce the same output. (Try it!)

```
<H1>If music be the food of love, play on.</H1>

<H1>
If music be the food of love, play on.
</H1>

<H1>
If music be the food of love, play on.            </H1>

<H1>    If    music    be    the    food    of    love,
play    on. </H1>
```

Programs To Help You Write HTML

You may be thinking that all this tag stuff is a real pain, especially if you didn't get that small example right the first time. (Don't fret about it; I didn't get that example right the first time, and I created it.) You have to remember all the tags. And you have to type them in right and close each one. What a hassle.

Many freeware and shareware programs are available for editing HTML files. Most of these programs are essentially text editors with extra menu items or buttons that insert the appropriate HTML tags into your text. HTML-based text editors are particularly nice for two reasons: you don't have to remember all the tags, and you don't have to take the time to type them all.

I'll discuss some of the available HTML-based editors in Chapter 6, "HTML Assistants: Editors and Converters." For now, if you have a simple HTML editor, feel free to use it for the examples in this book. If all you have is a text editor, no problem; it just means you'll have to do a little more typing.

What about WYSIWYG editors? There are lots of editors on the market that purport to be WYSIWYG. The problem is, as you learned earlier in this chapter, that there's really no such thing as WYSIWYG when you're dealing with HTML because WYG can vary wildly based on the browser that someone is using to read your page. With that said, as long as you're aware that the result of working in those editors may vary, WYSIWYG editors can be a quick way to create simple HTML files. However, for professional Web development and for using many of the very advanced features, WYSIWYG editors usually fall short, and you'll need to go "under the hood" to play with the HTML code anyhow. Even if you intend to use a WYSIWYG editor for the bulk of your HTML work, I recommend you bear with me for the next couple of days and try these examples in text editors so you get a feel for what HTML really is before you decide to move on to an editor that hides the tags.

In addition to the HTML editors, there are also converters, which take files from many popular word-processing programs and convert them to HTML. With a simple set of templates, you can write your pages entirely in your favorite program then convert the result when you're done.

In many cases, converters can be extremely useful, particularly for putting existing documents on the Web as fast as possible. However, converters suffer from many of the same problems as WYSIWYG editors: the result can vary from browser to browser, and many newer or advanced features aren't available in the converters. Also, most converter programs are fairly limited, not necessarily by their own features, but mostly by the limitations in HTML itself. No amount of fancy converting is going to make HTML do things that it can't yet do. If a particular capability doesn't exist in HTML, there's nothing the converter can do to solve that (and it may end up doing strange things to your HTML files, causing you more work than if you just did all the formatting yourself).

Structuring Your HTML

HTML defines three tags that are used to describe the page's overall structure and provide some simple "header" information. These three tags identify your page to browsers or HTML tools. They also provide simple information about the page (such as its title or its author) before loading the entire thing. The page structure tags don't affect what the page looks like when it's displayed; they're only there to help tools that interpret or filter HTML files.

According to the strict HTML 2.0 definition, these tags are optional. If your page does not contain them, browsers will usually be able to read it anyway. However, it is possible that these page structure tags might become required elements in the future. It's also possible that tools may come along that need them. If you get into the habit of including the page structure tags now, you won't have to worry about updating all your files later.

<HTML>

The first page structure tag in every HTML page is the <HTML> tag. It indicates that the content of this file is in the HTML language.

All the text and HTML commands in your HTML page should go within the beginning and ending HTML tags, like this:

```
<HTML>
...your page...
</HTML>
```

\<HEAD>

The \<HEAD> tag specifies that the lines within the beginning and ending points of the tag are the prologue to the rest of the file. There generally are only a few tags that go into the \<HEAD> portion of the page (most notably, the page title, described later). You should never put any of the text of your page into the header.

Here's a typical example of how you would properly use the \<HEAD> tag (you'll learn about \</TITLE> later):

```
<HTML>
<HEAD>
<TITLE>This is the Title.</TITLE>
</HEAD>
....
</HTML>
```

\<BODY>

The remainder of your HTML page, including all the text and other content (links, pictures, and so on) is enclosed within a \<BODY> tag. In combination with the \<HTML> and \<HEAD> tags, this looks like:

```
<HTML>
<HEAD>
<TITLE>This is the Title. It will be explained later on</TITLE>
</HEAD>
<BODY>
....
</BODY>
</HTML>
```

You may notice here that each HTML tag is nested; that is, both \<BODY> and \</BODY> tags go inside both \<HTML> tags; same with both \<HEAD> tags. All HTML tags work like this, forming individual nested sections of text. You should be careful never to overlap tags (that is, to do something like this: \<HTML>\<HEAD>\<BODY>\</HEAD>\</BODY>\</HTML>); make sure whenever you close an HTML tag that you're closing the most recently opened tag (you'll learn more about this as we go on).

The Title

Each HTML page needs a title to indicate what the page describes. The title is used by your browser's bookmarks or hotlist program, and also by other programs that catalog Web pages. To give a page a title, use the \<TITLE> tag.

3

NEW TERM

The *title* indicates what your Web page is about and is used to refer to that page in bookmark or hotlist entries.

<TITLE> tags always go inside the page header (the <HEAD> tags) and describe the contents of the page, like this:

```
<HTML>
<HEAD>
<TITLE>The Lion, The Witch, and the Wardrobe</TITLE>
</HEAD>
<BODY>
....
</BODY>
</HTML>
```

You can have only one title in the page, and that title can contain only plain text; that is, there shouldn't be any other tags inside the title.

When you pick a title, try to pick one that is both short and descriptive of the content on the page. Additionally, your title should be relevant out of context. If someone browsing on the Web followed a random link and ended up on this page, or if they found your title in a friend's browser history list, would they have any idea what this page is about? You may not intend the page to be used independently of the pages you specifically linked to it, but because anyone can link to any page at any time, be prepared for that consequence and pick a helpful title.

Also, because many browsers put the title in the title bar of the window, you may have a limited number of words available. (Although the text within the <TITLE> tag can be of any length, it may be cut off by the browser when it's displayed.) Here are some other examples of good titles:

```
<TITLE>Poisonous Plants of North America</TITLE>
<TITLE>Image Editing: A Tutorial</TITLE>
<TITLE>Upcoming Cemetery Tours, Summer 1995</TITLE>
<TITLE>Installing The Software: Opening the CD Case</TITLE>
<TITLE>Laura Lemay's Awesome Home Page</TITLE>
```

And some not-so-good titles:

```
<TITLE>Part Two</TITLE>
<TITLE>An Example</TITLE>
<TITLE>Nigel Franklin Hobbes</TITLE>
<TITLE>Minutes of the Second Meeting of the Fourth Conference of the
Committee for the Preservation of English Roses, Day Four, After Lunch</TITLE>
```

The following examples show how titles look in both Netscape (Figure 3.5) and Lynx (Figure 3.6).

3

INPUT   `<TITLE>Poisonous Plants of North America</TITLE>`

OUTPUT

Figure 3.5.
*The output in
Netscape.*

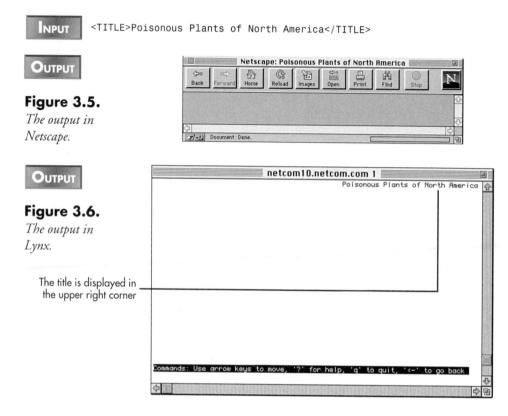

OUTPUT

Figure 3.6.
*The output in
Lynx.*

The title is displayed in
the upper right corner

Headings

Headings are used to divide sections of text, just like this book is divided. ("Headings," above, is a heading.) HTML defines six levels of headings. Heading tags look like this:

```
<H1>Installing Your Safetee Lock</H1>
```

The numbers indicate heading levels (H1 through H6). The headings, when they're displayed, are not numbered. They are displayed either in bigger or bolder text, or are centered or underlined, or are capitalized—something that makes them stand out from regular text.

Think of the headings as items in an outline. If the text you're writing has a structure, use the headings to indicate that structure, as shown in the next code lines. (Notice that I've indented the headings in this example to show the hierarchy better. They don't have to be indented in your page, and, in fact, the indenting will be ignored by the browser.)

```
<H1>Engine Tune-Up</H1>
    <H2>Change The Oil</H2>
    <H2>Adjust the Valves</H2>
    <H2>Change the Spark Plugs</H2>
        <H3>Remove the Old Plugs</H3>
```

```
    <H3>Prepare the New Plugs</H3>
       <H4>Remove the Guards</H4>
       <H4>Check the Gap</H4>
       <H4>Apply Anti-Seize Lubricant</H4>
       <H4>Install the Plugs</H4>
  <H2>Adjust the Timing</H2>
```

Unlike titles, headings can be any length, including many lines of text (although because headings are emphasized, having many lines of emphasized text may be tiring to read).

It's a common practice to use a first-level heading at the top of your page to either duplicate the title (which is usually displayed elsewhere), or to provide a shorter or less contextual form of the title. For example, if you had a page that showed several examples of folding bedsheets, part of a long presentation on how to fold bedsheets, the title might look something like this:

```
<TITLE>How to Fold Sheets: Some Examples</TITLE>
```

The top-most heading, however, might just say:

```
<H1>Examples</H1>
```

Don't use headings to display text in boldface type, or to make certain parts of your page stand out more. Although it may look cool on your browser, you don't know what it'll look like when other people use their browsers to read your page. Other browsers may number headings, or format them in a manner that you don't expect. Also, tools to create searchable indexes of Web pages may extract your headings to indicate the important parts of a page. By using headings for something other than an actual heading, you may be foiling those search programs and creating strange results.

The following examples show headings and how they appear in Netscape (Figure 3.7) and Lynx (Figure 3.8):

```
<H1>Engine Tune-Up</H1>
    <H2>Change The Oil</H2>
    <H2>Change the Spark Plugs</H2>
        <H3>Prepare the New Plugs</H3>
            <H4>Remove the Guards</H4>
            <H4>Check the Gap</H4>
```

OUTPUT

Figure 3.7.
The output in Netscape.

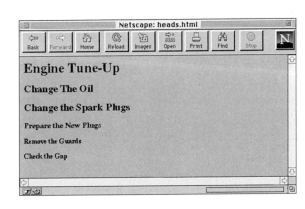

Figure 3.8.
The output in Lynx.

```
                                    ENGINE TUNE-UP


            Change The Oil


            Change the Spark Plugs


               PREPARE THE NEW PLUGS


                 Remove the Guards


                 Check the Gap
```

Paragraphs

Now that you have a page title and several headings, let's add some ordinary paragraphs to the page.

The first version of HTML specified the <P> tag as a one-sided tag. There was no corresponding </P>, and the <P> tag was used to indicate the end of a paragraph (a paragraph break), not the beginning. So paragraphs in the first version of HTML looked like this:

```
The blue sweater was reluctant to be worn, and wrestled with her as
she attempted to put it on. The collar was too small, and would not
fit over her head, and the arm holes moved seemingly randomly away
from her searching hands.<P>
Exasperated, she took off the sweater and flung it on the floor.
Then she vindictively stomped on it in revenge for its recalcitrant
behavior.<P>
```

Most browsers that were created early on in the history of the Web assume that paragraphs will be formatted this way. When they come across a <P> tag, these browsers start a new line and add some extra vertical space between the line they just ended and the one that they just began.

In the HTML 2.0 and HTML 3.2 specifications, and as supported by most current browsers, the paragraph tag has been revised. In these versions of HTML, the paragraph tags are two-sided (<P>...</P>), but <P> indicates the beginning of the paragraph. Also, the closing tag (</P>) is optional. So the sweater story would look like this in the newer versions of HTML:

```
<P>The blue sweater was reluctant to be worn, and wrestled with her as
she attempted to put it on. The collar was too small, and would not
fit over her head, and the arm holes moved seemingly randomly away
from her searching hands.</P>
<P>Exasperated, she took off the sweater and flung it on the floor.
Then she vindictively stomped on it in revenge for its recalcitrant
behavior.</P>
```

3

It's a good idea to get into the habit of using <P> at the start of a paragraph; this will become important when you learn how to align text left, right, or centered. Older browsers will accept this form of paragraphs just fine. Whether you use the </P> tag or not is up to you; it may help you remember where a paragraph ends, or it may seem unnecessary. I'll be using the closing </P> throughout this book.

Some people like to use extra <P> tags between paragraphs to spread out the text on the page. Once again, the cardinal reminder: Design for content, not for appearance. Someone with a text-based browser or a small screen is not going to care much about the extra space you so carefully put in, and some browsers may even collapse multiple <P> tags into one, erasing all your careful formatting.

The following example shows a sample paragraph and how it appears in Netscape (Figure 3.9) and Lynx (Figure 3.10):

```
<P>The sweater lay quietly on the floor, seething from its ill
treatment. It wasn't its fault that it didn't fit right. It hadn't
wanted to be purchased by this ill-mannered woman.</P>
```

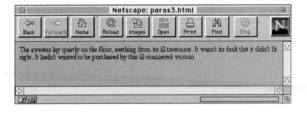

Figure 3.9.
The output in Netscape.

OUTPUT

The sweater lay quietly on the floor, seething from its ill treatment.
It wasn't its fault that it didn't fit right. It hadn't wanted to be
purchased by this ill-mannered woman.

Figure 3.10.
The output in Lynx.

Lists, Lists, and More Lists

In addition to headings and paragraphs, probably the most common HTML element you'll be using is the list. After this section, you'll not only know how to create a list in HTML, but how to create five different kinds of lists—a list for every occasion!

HTML defines five kinds of lists:

- ☐ Numbered, or ordered lists, typically labeled with numbers
- ☐ Bulleted, or unordered lists, typically labeled with bullets or some other symbol
- ☐ Glossary lists, in which each item in the list has a term and a definition for that term, arranged so that the term is somehow highlighted or drawn out from the text

- [ ] Menu lists, for lists of short paragraphs (typically one line)
- [ ] Directory lists, for lists of short items that can be arranged vertically or horizontally

List Tags

All the list tags have common elements:

- [ ] The entire list is surrounded by the appropriate opening and closing tag for the kind of list (for example, `<UL>` and `</UL>`, or `<MENU>` and `</MENU>`).
- [ ] Each list item within the list has its own tag: `<DT>` and `<DD>` for the glossary lists, and `<LI>` for all the other lists.

Although the tags and the list items can appear in any arrangement in your HTML code, I prefer to arrange the HTML for producing lists so that the list tags are on their own lines and each new item starts on a new line. This makes it easy to pick out the whole list as well as the individual elements. In other words, I find an arrangement like this

```
<P>Dante's Divine Comedy consists of three books:</P>
<UL>
<LI>The Inferno
<LI>The Purgatorio
<LI>The Paradiso
</UL>
```

easier to read than an arrangement like this, even though both result in the same output in the browser:

```
<P>Dante's Divine Comedy consists of three books:</P>
<UL><LI>The Inferno<LI>The Purgatorio<LI>The Paradiso</UL>
```

Numbered Lists

Numbered lists are surrounded by the `<OL>`...`</OL>` tags (`OL` stands for Ordered List), and each item within the list begins with the `<LI>` (List Item) tag.

The `<LI>` tag is one-sided; you do not have to specify the closing tag. The existence of the next `<LI>` (or the closing `</OL>` tag) indicates the end of that item in the list.

When the browser displays an ordered list, it numbers (and often indents) each of the elements sequentially. You do not have to do the numbering yourself, and if you add or delete items, the browser will renumber them the next time the page is loaded.

Ordered lists are lists in which each item is numbered.

So, for example, here's an ordered list of steps (a recipe) for creating nachos, with each list item a step in the set of procedures:

```
<P>Laura's Awesome Nachos</P>
<OL>
<LI>Warm up Refried beans with chili powder and cumin.
<LI>Glop refried beans on tortilla chips.
<LI>Grate equal parts Jack and Cheddar cheese, spread on chips.
<LI>Chop one small onion finely, spread on chips.
<LI>Heat under broiler 2 minutes.
<LI>Add guacamole, sour cream, fresh chopped tomatoes, and cilantro.
<LI>Drizzle with hot green salsa.
<LI>Broil another 1 minute.
<LI>Nosh.
</OL>
```

Use numbered lists only when you want to indicate that the elements are ordered; that is, that they must appear or occur in that specific order. Ordered lists are good for steps to follow or instructions to the reader. If you just want to indicate that something has some number of elements that can appear in any order, use an unordered list instead.

The following input and output examples show a simple ordered list and how it appears in Netscape (Figure 3.11) and Lynx (Figure 3.12):

```
<P>To summon the demon, use the following steps:</P>
<OL>1
<LI>Draw the pentagram
<LI>Sacrifice the goat
<LI>Chant the incantation
</OL>
```

Figure 3.11.
The output in Netscape.

Figure 3.12.
The output in Lynx.

Unordered Lists

Unordered lists are lists in which the elements can appear in any order. Unordered lists look just like ordered lists in HTML except that the list is indicated using `<UL>...</UL>` tags instead of `OL`. The elements of the list are separated by `<LI>`, just as with ordered lists. For example:

```
<P>Lists in HTML</P>
<UL>
<LI>Ordered Lists
<LI>Unordered Lists
<LI>Menus
<LI>Directories
<LI>Glossary Lists
</UL>
```

Browsers usually format unordered lists by inserting bullets or some other symbolic marker; Lynx inserts an asterisk (*).

NEW TERM

> *Unordered lists* are lists in which the items are bulleted or marked with some other symbol.

The following input and output example shows an unordered list and how it appears in Netscape (Figure 3.13) and Lynx (Figure 3.14):

INPUT

```
<P>The three Erinyes, or Furies, were:</P>
<UL>
<LI>Tisiphone
<LI>Megaera
<LI>Alecto
</UL>
```

OUTPUT

Figure 3.13.
The output in Netscape.

OUTPUT

Figure 3.14.
The output in Lynx.

```
The three Erinyes, or Furies, were:
    * Tisiphone
    * Megaera
    * Alecto
```

Glossary Lists

Glossary lists, sometimes called definition lists, are slightly different from other lists. Each list item in a glossary list has two parts:

- ☐ A term
- ☐ That term's definition

Each part of the glossary list has its own tag: <DT> for the term ("definition term"), and <DD> for its definition ("definition definition"). <DT> and <DD> are both one-sided tags, and they usually occur in pairs, although most browsers can handle single terms or definitions. The entire glossary list is indicated by the tags <DL>...</DL> ("definition list").

NEW TERM

Glossary lists are lists in which each list item has two parts: a term and a definition. Glossary lists are sometimes called definition lists.

Here's a glossary list example with a set of herbs and descriptions of how they grow:

```
<DL>
<DT>Basil<DD>Annual. Can grow four feet high; the scent of its tiny white
flowers is heavenly
<DT>Oregano<DD>Perennial. Sends out underground runners and is difficult
to get rid of once established.
<DT>Coriander<DD>Annual. Also called cilantro, coriander likes cooler
weather of spring and fall.
</DL>
```

Glossary lists are usually formatted in browsers with the terms and definitions on separate lines, and the left margins of the definitions are indented.

Glossary lists don't have to be used for terms and definitions, of course. They can be used anywhere that the same sort of list is needed. Here's an example:

```
<DL>
<DT>Macbeth<DD>I'll go no more. I am afraid to think of
what I have done; look on't again I dare not.
<DT>Lady Macbeth<DD>Infirm of purpose! Give me the daggers.
The sleeping and the dead are as but pictures. 'Tis the eye
of childhood that fears a painted devil. If he do bleed, I'll
gild the faces of the grooms withal, for it must seem their
guilt. (Exit. Knocking within)
<DT>Macbeth<DD>Whence is that knocking? How is't with me when
every noise apalls me? What hands are here? Ha! They pluck out
mine eyes! Will all Neptune's ocean wash this blood clean from
my hand? No. This my hand will rather the multitudinous seas
incarnadine, making the green one red. (Enter Lady Macbeth)
<DT>Lady Macbeth<DD>My hands are of your color, but I shame to
wear a heart so white.
</DL>
```

HTML also defines a "compact" form of glossary list in which less space is used for the list, perhaps by placing the terms and definitions on the same line and highlighting the term, or by lessening the amount of indent used by the definitions.

NOTE

Most browsers seem to ignore the COMPACT attribute and format compact glossary lists in the same way that normal glossary lists are formatted.

To use the compact form of the glossary list, use the COMPACT attribute inside the opening <DL> tag, like this:

```
<DL COMPACT>
<DT>Capellini<DD>Round and very thin (1-2mm)
<DT>Vermicelli<DD>Round and thin (2-3mm)
<DT>Spaghetti<DD>Round and thin, but thicker than vermicelli (3-4mm)
<DT>Linguine<DD>Flat, (5-6mm)
<DT>Fettucini<DD>Flat, (8-10mm)
</DL>
```

This input and output example shows how a glossary list is formatted in Netscape (Figure 3.15) and Lynx (Figure 3.16):

INPUT

```
<DL>
<DT>Basil<DD>Annual. Can grow four feet high; the scent
of its tiny white flowers is heavenly.
<DT>Oregano<DD>Perennial. Sends out underground runners
and is difficult to get rid of once established.
<DT>Coriander<DD>Annual. Also called cilantro, coriander
likes cooler weather of spring and fall.
</DL>
```

OUTPUT

Figure 3.15.

The output in Netscape.

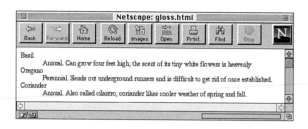

OUTPUT

Figure 3.16.

The output in Lynx.

Basil   Annual. Can grow four feet high; the scent of its tiny white
        flowers is heavenly

Oregano
        Perennial. Sends out underground runners and is difficult to
        get rid of once established.

Coriander
        Annual. Also called cilantro, coriander likes cooler weather of
        spring and fall.

Menu and Directory Lists

Menus are lists of items or short paragraphs with no bullets or numbers or other label-like things. They are similar to simple lists of paragraphs, except that some browsers may indent them or format them in some way differently from normal paragraphs. Menu lists are surrounded by <MENU> and </MENU> tags, and each list item is indicated using <LI>, as shown in this example:

```
<MENU>
<IL>Go left
<LI>Go right
<LI>Go up
<LI>Go down
</MENU>
```

Directory lists are for items that are even shorter than menu lists, and are intended to be formatted by browsers horizontally in columns—like doing a directory listing on a UNIX system. As with menu lists, directory lists are surrounded by <DIR> and </DIR>, with <LI> for the individual list items, as shown in this example:

```
<DIR>
<LI>apples
<LI>oranges
<LI>bananas
</DIR>
```

NEW TERM

Menu lists are used for short lists of single items. *Directory lists* are even shorter lists of items such as those you'd find in a UNIX or DOS directory listing.

NOTE

Although menu and directory lists exist in the HTML 2.0 specification, they are not commonly used in Web pages, and in HTML 3.2, they no longer exist (there are other available tags that produce the same effect). Considering that most browsers seem to format menus and directories in similar ways to the glossary lists (or as unordered lists), and not in the way they are described in the specification, it is probably best to stick with the other three forms of lists.

The following input and output example shows a menu list and a directory list and how they appear in Netscape (Figure 3.17) and Lynx (Figure 3.18):

3

INPUT

```
<MENU>
<LI>Canto 1: The Dark Wood of Error
<LI>Canto 2: The Descent
<LI>Canto 3: The Vestibule
<LI>Canto 4: Circle One: Limbo
<LI>Canto 5: Circle Two: The Carnal
</MENU>

<DIR>
<LI>files
<LI>applications
<LI>mail
<LI>stuff
<LI>phone_numbers
</DIR>
```

OUTPUT

Figure 3.17.
*The output in
Netscape.*

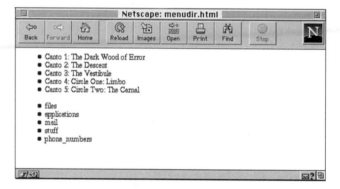

OUTPUT

Figure 3.18.
*The output in
Lynx.*

3

Nesting Lists

What happens if you put a list inside another list? This is fine as far as HTML is concerned; just put the entire list structure inside another list as one of its elements. The nested list just becomes another element of the first list, and it is indented from the rest of the list. Lists like this work especially well for menu-like entities in which you want to show hierarchy (for example, in tables of contents), or as outlines.

Indenting nested lists in HTML code itself helps show their relationship to the final layout:

```
<OL>
   <UL>
   <LI>WWW
   <LI>Organization
   <LI>Beginning HTML
   <UL>
      <LI>What HTML is
      <LI>How to Write HTML
      <LI>Doc structure
      <LI>Headings
      <LI>Paragraphs
      <LI>Comments
   </UL>
<LI>Links
<LI>More HTML
</OL>
```

Many browsers format nested ordered lists and nested unordered lists differently from their enclosing lists. For example, they might use a symbol other than a bullet for a nested list, or number the inner list with letters (a, b, c) instead of numbers. Don't assume that this will be the case, however, and refer back to "section 8, subsection b" in your text, because you cannot determine what the exact formatting will be in the final output.

Here's an input and output example of a nested list and how it appears in Netscape (Figure 3.19) and Lynx (Figure 3.20):

INPUT

```
<H1>Peppers</H1>
<UL>
<LI>Bell
<LI>Chile
    <UL>
    <LI>Serrano
    <LI>Jalapeno
    <LI>Habanero
    <LI>Anaheim
    </UL>
<LI>Szechuan
<LI>Cayenne
</UL>
```

Figure 3.19.
The output in Netscape.

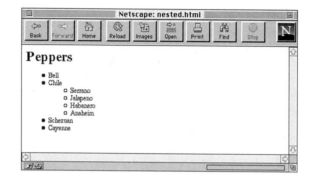

Figure 3.20.
The output in Lynx.

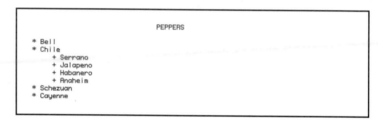

Comments

You can put comments into HTML pages to describe the page itself or to provide some kind of indication of the status of the page; some source code control programs can put page status into comments, for example. Text in comments is ignored when the HTML file is parsed; comments don't ever show up on screen—that's why they're comments. Comments look like this:

```
<!-- This is a comment -->
```

Each line of text should be individually commented, and it's usually a good idea not to include other HTML tags within comments. (Although this practice isn't strictly illegal, many browsers may get confused when they encounter HTML tags within comments and display them anyway.)

Here are some examples:

```
<!-- Rewrite this section with less humor -->
<!-- Neil helped with this section -->
<!-- Go Tigers! -->
```

Exercise 3.4: Creating a real HTML page.

At this point, you know enough to get started creating simple HTML pages. You understand what HTML is, you've been introduced to a handful of tags, and you've even tried browsing an HTML file. You haven't done any links yet, but you'll get to that soon enough, in the next chapter.

This exercise shows you how to create an HTML file that uses the tags you've learned about up to this point. It will give you a feel for what the tags look like when they're displayed on-screen and for the sorts of typical mistakes you're going to make. (Everyone makes them, and that's why it's often useful to use an HTML editor that does the typing for you. The editor doesn't forget the closing tags, or leave off the slash, or misspell the tag itself.)

So, create a simple example in that text editor of yours. It doesn't have to say much of anything; in fact, all it needs to include are the structure tags, a title, a couple of headings, and a paragraph or two, Here's an example:

```
<HTML>
<HEAD>
<TITLE>Company Profile, Camembert Incorporated</TITLE>
</HEAD>
<BODY>
<H1>Camembert Incorporated</H1>
<P>"Many's the long night I dreamed of cheese -- toasted, mostly."
-- Robert Louis Stevenson</P>
<H2>What We Do</H2>
<P>We make cheese. Lots of cheese; more than eight tons of cheese
a year.</P>
<H2>Why We Do It</H2>
<P>We are paid an awful lot of money by people who like cheese.
So we make more.</P>
<H2>Our Favorite Cheeses</H2>
<UL>
<LI>Brie
<LI>Havarti
<LI>Camembert
<LI>Mozzarella
</UL>
</BODY>
</HTML>
```

Save your example to an HTML file, open it in your browser, and see how it came out.

If you have access to another browser on your computer or, even better, one on a different computer, I highly recommend opening the same HTML file there so you can see the differences in appearance between browsers. Sometimes the differences can surprise you; lines that looked fine in one browser might look strange in another browser.

Here's an illustration for you: The cheese factory example looks like Figure 3.21 in Netscape (the Macintosh version) and like Figure 3.22 in Lynx.

Figure 3.21.

The cheese factory in Netscape.

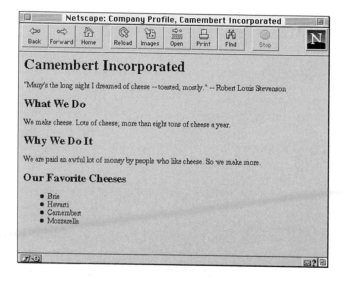

Figure 3.22.

The cheese factory in Lynx.

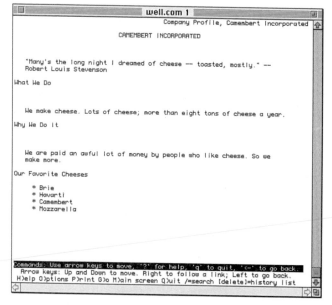

See what I mean?

Summary

HTML, a text-only markup language used to describe hypertext pages on the World Wide Web, describes the structure of a page, not its appearance.

In this chapter, you've learned what HTML is and how to write and preview simple HTML files. You've also learned about the HTML tags shown in Table 3.1.

Table 3.1. HTML tags from this chapter.

Tag	Use
`<HTML> ... </HTML>`	The entire HTML page.
`<HEAD> ... </HEAD>`	The head, or prologue, of the HTML page.
`<BODY> ... </BODY>`	All the other content in the HTML page.
`<TITLE> ... </TITLE>`	The title of the page.
`<H1> ... </H1>`	First-level heading.
`<H2> ... </H2>`	Second-level heading.
`<H3> ... </H3>`	Third-level heading.
`<H4> ... </H4>`	Fourth-level heading.
`<H5> ... </H5>`	Fifth-level heading.
`<H6> ... </H6>`	Sixth-level heading.
`<P> ... </P>`	Paragraph.
`<OL>...</OL>`	An ordered (numbered) list. Items in the list each begin with `<LI>`.
`<UL>...</UL>`	An unordered (bulleted or otherwise-marked) list. Items in the list each begin with `<LI>`.
`<MENU>...</MENU>`	A menu list (a list of short items or paragraphs).
`<DIR>...</DIR>`	A list of especially short (1–2 word) items. Directory lists are not often used in most HTML files.
`<LI>`	Individual list items in ordered, unordered, menu, or directory lists.
`<DL>...</DL>`	A glossary or definition list. Items in the list consist of pairs of elements: a term and its definition.
`<DT>`	The term part of an item in a glossary list.
`<DD>`	The definition part of an item in a glossary list.
`<!-- ... -->`	Comment.

Q&A

Q Can I do *any* formatting of text in HTML?

A You can do some formatting to strings of characters; for example, making a word or two bold. And the Netscape extensions allow you to change the font size and color of the text in your Web page (for readers using Netscape). You'll learn about these features tomorrow, in Chapters 5 and 6.

Q I'm using Windows. My word processor won't let me save a text file with an extension that's anything except `.txt`. If I type in `index.html`, it saves the file as `index.html.txt`. What can I do?

A You can rename your files after you've saved them so they have an `html` or `htm` extension, but this can be annoying with lots of files. Consider using a text editor or HTML editor for your Web pages.

Q I've noticed in many Web pages that the page structure tags (`<HTML>`, `<HEAD>`, `<BODY>`) aren't used. Do I really need to include them if pages work just fine without them?

A You don't need to, no. Most browsers will handle plain HTML without the page structure tags. But including the tags will allow your pages to be read by more general SGML tools and to take advantage of features of future browsers. And, it's the "correct" thing to do if you want your pages to conform to true HTML format.

Q I've seen comments in some HTML files that look like this:

```
<!-- this is a comment>
Is that legal?
```

A That's the old form of comments that was used in very early forms of HTML. Although many browsers may still accept it, you should use the new form (and comment each line individually) in your pages.

Q My glossaries came out formatted really strangely! The terms are indented farther in than the definitions!

A Did you mix up the `<DD>` and `<DT>` tags? The `<DT>` tag is always used first (the definition term), and then the `<DD>` follows (the definition). I mix these up all the time. There are too many D tags in glossary lists.

Q I've seen HTML files that use `<LI>` outside of a list structure, alone on the page, like this:

```
<LI>And then the duck said, "put it on my bill"
```

A Most browsers will at least accept this tag outside a list tag and will format it either as a simple paragraph or as a non-indented bulleted item. However, according to the true HTML definition, using an `<LI>` outside a list tag is illegal, so "good" HTML pages shouldn't do this. And because we are all striving to write good HTML (right?), you shouldn't do this either. Always put your list items inside lists where they belong.

Chapter 4

All About Links

After finishing the last chapter, you have a couple pages that have some headings, text, and lists in them. This is all well and good, but rather boring. The real fun starts when you learn how to do hypertext links and link up all your pages to the Web, and in this chapter, you'll learn just that. Specifically, you'll learn

- [ ] All about the HTML link tag (<A>) and its various parts
- [ ] How to link to other pages on your local disk using relative and absolute pathnames
- [ ] How to link to other pages on the Web using URLs
- [ ] Using links and anchors to link to specific places inside pages
- [ ] All about URLs: the various parts of the URL and the kinds of URLs you can use

Creating Links

To create a link in HTML, you need two things:

- ☐ The name of the file (or the URL of the file) you want to link to
- ☐ The text that will serve as the "hot spot"—that is, the text that will be highlighted in the browser, which your readers can then select to follow the link

Only the second part is actually visible on your page. When your reader selects the text that points to a link, the browser uses the first part as the place to "jump" to.

The Link Tag <A>

To create a link in an HTML page, you use the HTML link tag <A>...</A>. The <A> tag is often called an anchor tag, as it can also be used to create anchors for links. (You'll learn more about creating anchors later in this chapter.) The most common use of the link tag, however, is to create links to other pages.

Unlike the simple tags you learned about in the previous chapter, the <A> tag has some extra features: the opening tag, <A>, includes both the name of the tag (A) and extra information about the link itself. The extra features are called *attributes* of the tag. So instead of the opening <A> tag having just a name inside brackets, it looks something like this:

```
<A NAME="Up" HREF="../menu.html" TITLE="Ostrich Care">
```

NEW TERM

> *Attributes* are extra parts of HTML tags that contain options or other information about the tag itself.

The extra attributes (in this example, NAME, HREF, and TITLE) describe the link itself. The attribute you'll probably use most often is the HREF attribute, short for "Hypertext REFerence." The HREF attribute is used to specify the name or URL of the file where this link points.

Like most HTML tags, the link tag also has a closing tag, </A>. All the text between the opening and closing tags will become the actual link on the screen and be highlighted, underlined, or colored blue or red when the Web page is displayed. That's the text you or your reader will click on (or select, in browsers that don't use mice) to jump to the place specified by the HREF attribute.

Figure 4.1 shows the parts of a typical link using the <A> tag, including the HREF, the text of the link, and the closing tag:

4

Figure 4.1.
An HTML link using the <A> tag.

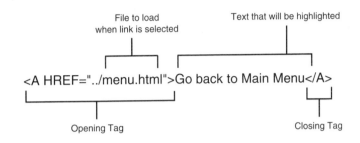

File to load
when link is selected

Text that will be highlighted

<A HREF="../menu.html">Go back to Main Menu</A>

Opening Tag

Closing Tag

The following two examples show a simple link and what it looks like in Netscape (Figure 4.2) and Lynx (Figure 4.3).

 INPUT

```
Go back to <A HREF="../menu.html">Main Menu</A>
```

OUTPUT

Figure 4.2.
The output in Netscape.

4

OUTPUT

Figure 4.3.
The output in Lynx.

Exercise 4.1: Link two pages.

EXERCISE

Let's try a really simple example, with two HTML pages on your local disk. You'll need your text editor and your Web browser for this, but since both the pages you'll be fooling with are on your local disk, you won't need to be connected to the network. (Be patient; you'll get to do network stuff in the next section of this chapter.)

First, create two HTML pages, and save them in separate files. Here's the code for the two HTML files I created for this section, which I called menu.html and feeding.html. It really doesn't matter what your two pages look like or what they're called, but make sure you put in your own filenames if you're following along with this example.

The first file is called `menu.html`, and it looks like this:

```
<HTML>
<HEAD>
<TITLE>How To Care For Your Ostrich</TITLE>
</HEAD><BODY>
<H1>Caring for Your New Ostrich</H1>
<P>Your new ostrich is a delicate and sensitive creature. This document
describes how to care for your ostrich so that he can be a happy and healthy
ostrich and give you hours of fun and friendship.</P>
<UL>
<LI>Feeding Your Ostrich
<LI>Grooming Your Ostrich
<LI>Cleaning Up After Your Ostrich
<LI>Taunting Your Ostrich
</UL>
</BODY>
</HTML>
```

The list of menu items ("Feeding Your Ostrich," "Grooming Your Ostrich," and so on) will be links to other pages. For now, just type them as regular text; you'll turn them into links later.

The second file, `feeding.html`, looks like this:

```
<HTML>
<HEAD>
<TITLE>How To Care For Your Ostrich: Feeding Your Ostrich</TITLE>
</HEAD><BODY>
<H1>Feeding Your Ostrich</H1>
<P>This section describes what, how often, and how to feed your ostrich
</P>
<H2>What to Feed Your Ostrich</H2>
Ostriches benefit best from a balanced diet such as that provided by United
Bird Food's Ostrich Kibble 102. We recommend feeding your ostrich a cup of
kibbles once a day, with ample water.
<H2>How to Feed Your Ostrich</H2>
<P>To feed your ostrich, leave the ostrich kibbles in a container by the
edge of the ostrich's pen.</P>
<P>NOTE: Ostriches do not like being watched while eating, and may attack
you if you stand too close. We recommend leaving your ostrich to eat in peace.
</P>
<P>Go back to Main Menu</P>
</BODY>
</HTML>
```

Make sure both your files are in the same directory or folder, and if you haven't called them `menu.html` and `feeding.html`, make sure that you take note of the names because you'll need them later.

First, let's create a link from the menu file to the feeding file. Edit the `menu.html` file, and put the cursor at the line that says `<LI>Feeding Your Ostrich`.

Link tags do not define the format of the text itself, so leave in the list item tags and just add the link inside the item. First, put in the link tags themselves (the `<A>` and `</A>` tags) around the text that you want to use as the link:

```
<LI><A>Feeding Your Ostrich</A>
```

Now add the name of the file you want to link to as the HREF part of the opening link tag. Enclose the name of the file in quotes (straight quotes ["], not curly or typesetter's quotes ["]), with an equals sign between HREF and the name. Note that uppercase and lowercase are different, so make sure you type the filename exactly as you saved it (Feeding.html is not the same file as feeding.html; it has to be exactly the same case). Here I've used feeding.html; if you used different files, use those different filenames.

```
<LI><A HREF="feeding.html">Feeding Your Ostrich</A>
```

Now, start up your browser, select Open File (or its equivalent in your browser), and open the menu.html file. The paragraph that you used as your link should now show up as a link that is in a different color, underlined, or otherwise highlighted. Figure 4.4 shows how it looked when I opened it in the Macintosh version of Netscape:

Figure 4.4.

The menu.html *file with link.*

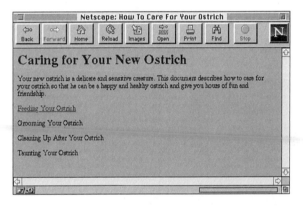

And now, when you click on the link, your browser should load in and display the feeding.html page, as shown in Figure 4.5.

Figure 4.5.

The feeding.html *page.*

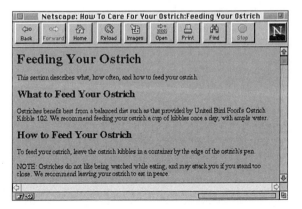

If your browser can't find the file when you choose the link, make sure that the name of the file in the HREF part of the link tag is the same as the name of the file on the disk, that uppercase and lowercase match, and that both of the files are in the same directory. Remember to close your link, using the </A> tag, at the end of the text that serves as the link. Also, make sure that you have quotes at the end of the filename (sometimes it's easy to forget) and that both quotes are ordinary straight quotes. All of these things can confuse the browser and make it not find the file or display the link properly.

Now, let's create a link from the feeding page back to the menu page. There is a paragraph at the end of the feeding.html page intended for just this purpose:

```
<P>Go back to Main Menu</P>
```

Add the link tag with the appropriate HREF to that line, like this, where menu.html is the original menu file:

```
<P><A HREF="menu.html">Go back to Main Menu</A></P>
```

NOTE

When you include tags inside other tags, make sure that the closing tag closes the tag that you most recently opened. That is, do this:

```
<P> <A> ... </A> </P>
```

instead of this:

```
<P> <A> ... </P> </A>
```

Some browsers may become confused if you overlap tags in this way, so it's best to always make sure that you close the most recently opened tag first.

Now when you reload the "feeding" file, the link will be active, and you can jump between the menu and the feeding file by selecting those links.

Linking Local Pages Using Relative and Absolute Pathnames

The example in the previous section shows how to link together pages that are contained in the same folder or directory on your local disk (local pages). This section continues that thread, linking pages that are still on the local disk but may be contained in different directories or folders on that disk.

NOTE

Folders and directories are the same thing, but they're called different things depending on whether you're on Mac, Windows, DOS, or UNIX. I'll call them simply directories from now on to make things easier.

When you specify just the pathname of a linked file within quotes, as you did earlier, the browser looks for that file in the same directory as the current file. This is true even if both the current file and the file being linked to are on a server somewhere else on the Net; both files are contained in the same directory on that server. This is the simplest form of a relative pathname.

Relative pathnames can also include directory names, or they can point to the path you would take to navigate to that file if you started at the current directory or folder. A pathname might include directions, for example, to go up two directory levels, and then go down two other directories to get to the file.

NEW TERM

Relative pathnames point to files based on their locations relative to the current file.

To specify relative pathnames in links, use UNIX-style pathnames regardless of the system you actually have. This means that directory or folder names are separated by forward slashes (/) and that you use two dots to refer generically to the directory above the current one (..).

Table 4.1 shows some examples of relative pathnames and what they mean.

Table 4.1. Relative pathnames.

Pathname	Means
HREF="file.html"	file.html is located in the current directory.
HREF="files/file.html"	file.html is located in the directory (or folder) called files (and the files directory is located in the current directory).
HREF="files/morefiles/file.html"	file.html is located in the morefiles directory, which is located in the files directory, which is located in the current directory.

continues

Table 4.1. continued

Pathname	Means
HREF="../file.html"	file.html is located in the directory one level up from the current directory (the "parent" directory).
HREF="../../files/file.html"	file.html is located two directory levels up, in the directory files.

If you're linking files on a personal computer (Mac or PC) and you want to link to a file on a different disk, use the name or letter of the disk as just another directory name in the relative path.

On the Macintosh, the name of the disk is used just as it appears on the disk itself. Assume you have a disk called Hard Disk 2, and your HTML files are contained in a folder called HTML Files. If you wanted to link to a file called jane.html in a folder called Public on a shared disk called Jane's Mac, you could use the following relative pathname:

HREF="../../Jane's Mac/Public/jane.html"

On DOS systems, the disks are referred to by letter, just as you would expect them to be, but instead of being c:, d:, and so on, substitute a vertical bar (¦) for the colon (the colon has a special meaning in link pathnames), and don't forget to use forward slashes like in UNIX. So, if the current file is located in C:\FILES\HTML\ and you want to link to D:\FILES.NEW\HTML\MORE\INDEX.HTM, the relative pathname to that file would be:

HREF="../../d¦/files.new/html/more/index.htm"

In most instances you'll never use the name of a disk in relative pathnames, but I've included it here for completeness. Most of the time you'll be linking between files that are reasonably close (only one directory or folder away) in the same presentation.

Absolute Pathnames

You can also specify the link to another page on your local system using an absolute pathname. Relative pathnames point to the page you want to link to by describing its location relative to the current page. Absolute pathnames, on the other hand, point to the page by starting at the top level of your directory hierarchy and working downward through all the intervening directories to reach the file.

NEW TERM

> *Absolute pathnames* point to files based on their absolute location on the file system.

Absolute pathnames always begin with a slash, which is the way they are differentiated from relative pathnames. Following the slash are all directories in the path from the top level to the file you are linking.

NOTE

"Top" has different meanings depending on how you're publishing your HTML files. If you're just linking to files on your local disk, the top is the top of your file system (/ on UNIX, or the disk name on a Mac or PC). When you're publishing files using a Web server, the top may or may not be the top of your file system (and generally isn't). You'll learn more about absolute pathnames and Web servers on Bonus Day 1.

Table 4.2 shows some examples of absolute pathnames and what they mean.

Table 4.2. Absolute pathnames.

Pathname	Means
HREF="/u1/lemay/file.html"	file.html is located in the directory /u1/lemay (typically UNIX).
HREF="/d¦/files/html/file.htm"	file.htm is located on the D: disk in the directories files/html (DOS systems).
HREF="/Hard Disk 1/HTML Files/file.html"	file.html is located on the disk Hard Disk 1, in the folder HTML Files (typically a Macintosh).

Should You Use Relative or Absolute Pathnames?

To link between your own pages, most of the time you should use relative pathnames instead of the absolute pathnames. Using absolute pathnames may seem easier for complicated links between lots of pages, but absolute pathnames are not portable. If you specify your links as absolute pathnames and you move your files elsewhere on the disk, or rename a directory or a disk listed in that absolute path, then all your links will break, and you'll have to laboriously edit all your HTML files and fix them all. Using absolute pathnames also makes it very difficult to move your files to a Web server when you decide to actually make them available on the Web.

Specifying relative pathnames enables you to move your pages around on your own system and to move them to other systems with little or no file modifications to fix the links. It's much easier to maintain HTML pages with relative pathnames, so the extra work of setting them up initially is often well worth the effort.

Links to Other Documents on the Web

So now you have a whole set of pages on your local disk, all linked to each other. In some places in your pages, however, you would like to refer to a page somewhere else on the Net; for example, to the Palo Alto Zoo home page for more information on the socialization of ostriches. You can also use the link tag to link those other pages on the Net, which I'll call remote pages.

NEW TERM

> *Remote pages* are pages contained somewhere on the Web other than the system you're currently working on.

The HTML code you use to link pages on the Web looks exactly the same as the code you used for links between local pages. You still use the <A> tag with an HREF attribute and include some text to serve as the link on your Web page. But instead of a filename or a path in the HREF, use the URL of that page on the Web, as Figure 4.6 shows.

Figure 4.6.

Link to remote files.

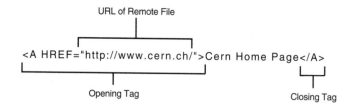

Exercise 4.2: Linking your ostrich pages to the Web.

Let's go back to those two pages you linked together earlier in this chapter, the ones about ostriches. The menu.html file contained several links to other local pages that described how to take care of your ostrich.

Now say you want to add a link to the bottom of the menu file to point to the ostrich archives at the Palo Alto Zoo (the world's leading authority on the care of ostriches), whose URL is http://www.zoo.palo-alto.ca.us/ostriches/home.html.

NOTE

I'm making most of this up as I go along. Although the city of Palo Alto, California, has a Web page (URL `http://www.city.palo-alto.ca.us/home.html`), Palo Alto doesn't have a zoo with ostriches (they do have a small petting zoo, however). For the purposes of this example, just pretend that there's a Web page for the Palo Alto Zoo.

First, add the appropriate text for the link to your menu page:

```
<P>The Palo Alto Zoo has more information on ostriches</P>
```

What if you don't know the URL of the home page for the Palo Alto Zoo (or the page you want to link to), but you do know how to get to it by following several links on several different people's home pages? Not a problem. Use your browser to find the home page for the page you want to link to. Figure 4.7 shows what the home page for the Palo Alto Zoo might look like, if it existed.

Figure 4.7.

The Palo Alto Zoo home page.

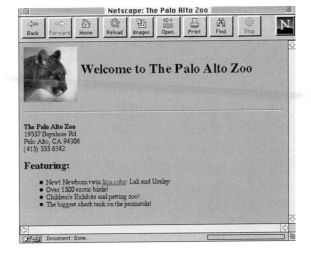

NOTE

If you set up your system (in the previous chapter) so that it would not connect to the network, you might want to put it back now to follow along with this example.

Most browsers display the URL of the file they're currently looking at in a box somewhere near the top of the page (in Netscape, this box may be hidden; choose Show Location from the Options menu to see it). This makes it particularly easy for you to link to other pages; all you have to do is go to the page you want to link to with your browser, copy the URL from the window, and paste it into the HTML page you're working on. No typing!

Once you have the URL of the zoo, you can construct a link tag in your menu file and paste the appropriate URL into the link:

```
<P>The <A HREF="http://www.zoo.palo-alto.ca.us/ostriches/
home.html">Palo Alto Zoo<A>
has more information on ostriches</P>
```

Of course, if you already know the URL of the page you want to link to, you can just type it into the HREF part of the link. Keep in mind, however, that if you make a mistake, your browser won't be able to find the file on the other end. Most URLs are a little too complex for normal humans to be able to remember them; I prefer to copy and paste whenever I can to cut down on the chances of typing them incorrectly.

Figure 4.8 shows how the menu.html file, with the new link in it, looks when it is displayed by Netscape.

Figure 4.8.

The Palo Alto Zoo link.

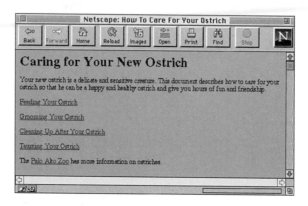

Exercise 4.3: Creating a link menu.

Now that you've learned how to do lists in this chapter and links in the last chapter, you can create what is called a link menu. Link menus are links on your Web page that are arranged in list form or in some other short, easy-to-read, and easy-to-understand format. Link menus are terrific for pages that are organized in a hierarchy, for tables of contents, or for navigation among several pages. Web pages that consist of nothing but links often organize those links in menu form.

NEW TERM

Link menus are short lists of links on Web pages that give your readers a quick, easy-to-scan overview of the choices they have to jump to from the current page.

The idea of a link menu is that you use short, descriptive terms as the links, with either no text following the link or with further description following the link itself. Link menus look best in a bulleted or unordered list format, but you can also use glossary lists or just plain paragraphs. Link menus let your reader scan the list of links quickly and easily, something that may be difficult to do if you bury your links in body text.

In this exercise, you'll create a Web page for a set of restaurant reviews. This page will serve as the index to the reviews, so the link menu you'll create is essentially a menu of restaurant names.

Start with a simple page framework: a first-level head and some basic explanatory text:

```
<HTML>
<HEAD>
<TITLE>Laura's Restaurant Guide</TITLE>
</HEAD><BODY>
<H1>Laura's Restaurant Reviews</H1>
<P>I spend a lot of time in restaurants in the area, having lunches or dinners
with friends or meeting with potential clients. I've written up several reviews
of many of the restaurants I frequent (and a few I'd rather not go back to).
Here are reviews for the following restaurants:</P>
</BODY></HTML>
```

Now add the list that will become the links, without the link tags themselves. It's always easier to start with link text and then attach actual links afterwards. For this list, we'll use a tag to create a bulleted list of individual restaurants. You could use a <MENU> tag here just as easily, but the <OL> tag wouldn't be appropriate, because the numbers would imply that you were ranking the restaurants in some way. Here's the HTML list of restaurants; Figure 4.9 shows the page in Netscape as it currently looks with the introduction and the list.

```
<UL>
<LI>Szechuan Supreme
<LI>Mel's Pizza
<LI>Tomi
<LI>The Summit Inn
<LI>Cafe Milieu
</UL>
```

Figure 4.9.

A list of restaurants.

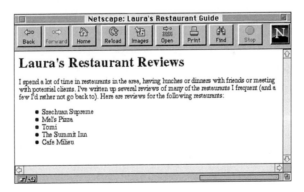

Now, modify each of the list items so that they include link tags. You'll need to keep the `<LI>` tag in there because it indicates where the list items begin. Just add the `<A>` tags around the text itself. Here we'll link to filenames on the local disk in the same directory as this file, with each individual file containing the review for the particular restaurant:

```
<UL>
<LI><A HREF="schezuan.html">Szechuan Supreme</A>
<LI><A HREF="mels.html">Mel's Pizza</A>
<LI><A HREF="tomi.html">Tomi</A>
<LI><A HREF="summitinn.html">The Summit Inn</A>
<LI><A HREF="millieu.html">Cafe Milieu</A>
</UL>
```

The menu of restaurants looks fine, although it's a little sparse. Your reader doesn't know what kinds of food each restaurant serves (although some of the restaurant names indicate the kind of food they serve) or if the review is good or bad. An improvement would be to add some short explanatory text after the links to provide a hint of what is on the other side of the link:

```
<UL>
<LI><A HREF="schezuan.html">Szechuan Supreme</A>. Chinese food. Prices are
excellent, but service is slow
<LI><A HREF="mels.html">Mel's Pizza</A>. Thin-crust New York style pizza.
Awesome, but loud.
<LI><A HREF="tomi.html">Tomi</A>. Sushi. So-so selection, friendly chefs.
<LI><A HREF="summitinn.html">The Summit Inn</A>. California food. Creative
chefs, but you pay extra for originality and appearance.
<LI><A HREF="millieu.html">Cafe Milieu</A>. Lots of atmosphere, sullen
postmodern waitrons, but an excellent double espresso none the less.
</UL>
```

The final list then looks like Figure 4.10.

Figure 4.10.

The final menu listing.

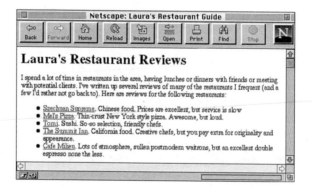

We'll use link menus similar to this one throughout this book.

Linking to Specific Places Within Documents

The links you've created so far in this chapter have been from one point in a page to another page. But what if, instead of linking to that second page in general, you wanted to link to a specific place within that page, for example, to the fourth major section down?

You can do this in HTML by creating an anchor within the second page. The anchor creates a special thing inside the page which you can link to. The link you create in the first page will contain both the name of the file you're linking to and the name of that anchor. Then, when you follow the link with your browser, the browser will load the second page and then scroll down to the location of the anchor (Figure 4.11 shows an example).

Figure 4.11.

Links and anchors.

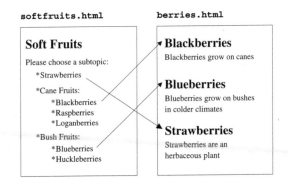

> *Anchors* are special places inside documents that can be linked to. Links can then jump to those special places inside the page as opposed to jumping just to the top of the page.

NEW TERM

You can also use links and anchors within the same page so that if you select one of those links, you jump to different places within that same page.

Creating Links and Anchors

You create an anchor in nearly the same way that you create a link, using the <A> tag. If you had wondered why the link tag uses an <A> instead of an <L>, now you know: A actually stands for Anchor.

When you specified links using <A>, there were two parts of the link: the HREF attribute in the opening <A> tag and the text between the opening and closing tags that served as a hot spot for the link.

Anchors are created in much the same way, but instead of using the HREF attribute in the <A> tag, you use the NAME attribute. The NAME attribute takes a keyword (or words) that will be used to name that anchor. Figure 4.12 shows the parts of the <A> tag when used to indicate an anchor.

Figure 4.12.

The <A> tag and anchors.

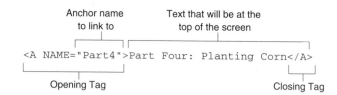

Anchors also require some amount of text between the opening and closing <A> tags, even though they usually point to a single-character location. The text between the <A> tags is used by the browser when a link that is attached to this anchor is selected. The browser scrolls the page to the text within the anchor so that it is at the top of the screen. Some browsers may also highlight the text inside the <A> tags.

So, for example, to create an anchor at the section of a page labeled Part 4, you might add an anchor called Part4 to the heading, like this:

```
<H1><A NAME="Part4">Part Four: Grapefruit from Heaven</A></H1>
```

Unlike links, anchors do not show up in the final displayed page. Anchors are invisible until you follow a link that points to them.

To point to an anchor in a link, you use the same form of link that you would when linking to the whole page, with the filename or URL of the page in the HREF attribute. After the name of the page, however, include a hash sign (#) and the name of the anchor exactly as it appears in the NAME attribute of that anchor (including the same uppercase and lowercase characters!), like this:

```
<A HREF="mybigdoc.html#Part4">Go to Part 4</A>
```

This link tells the browser to load the page mybigdoc.html and then to scroll down to the anchor name Part4. The text inside the anchor definition will appear at the top of the screen.

Exercise 4.4: Link sections between two pages.

Let's do an example with two pages. These two pages are part of an online reference to classical music, where each Web page contains all the references for a particular letter of the alphabet (A.html, B.html, and so on). The reference could have been organized such that each section was its own page. Organizing it that way, however, would have involved an awful lot of pages to manage, as well as an awful lot of pages the reader would have to load if they were exploring the reference. It's more efficient in this case to bunch the related sections together under lettered groupings. (Chapter 11, "Writing and Designing Web Pages: Dos and Don'ts," goes into more detail about the trade-offs between short and long pages.)

The first page we'll look at is the one for M, the first section of which looks like this in HTML (Figure 4.13 shows how it looks when it's displayed):

```
<HTML>
<HEAD>
<TITLE>Classical Music: M</TITLE>
</HEAD>
<BODY>
<H1>M</H1>
<H2>Madrigals</H2>
<UL>
<LI>William Byrd, <EM>This Sweet and Merry Month of May</EM>
<LI>William Byrd, <EM>Though Amaryllis Dance</EM>
<LI>Orlando Gibbons, <EM>The Silver Swan</EM>
<LI>Roland de Lassus, <EM>Mon Coeur se Recommande &agrave; vous</EM>
<LI>Claudio Monteverdi, <EM>Lamento d'Arianna</EM>
<LI>Thomas Morley, <EM>My Bonny Lass She Smileth</EM>
<LI>Thomas Weelkes, <EM>Thule, the Period of Cosmography</EM>
<LI>John Wilbye, <EM>Sweet Honey-Sucking Bees</EM>
</UL>
<P>Secular vocal music in four, five and six parts, usually a capella.
15th-16th centuries.</P>
<P><EM>See Also</EM>
Byrd, Gibbons, Lassus, Monteverdi, Morley, Weelkes, Wilbye</P>
</BODY>
</HTML>
```

Figure 4.13.
Part M of the Online Music Reference.

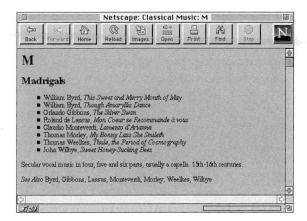

In that last line (the See Also), it would be useful to link those composer names to their respective sections elsewhere in the reference. If you used the procedure you learned previously in this chapter, you'd create a link here around the word Byrd to the page B.html. When your readers selected the link to B.html, the browser would drop them at the top of the Bs. Those hapless readers would then have to scroll down through all the composers that start with B (and there are lots of them: Bach, Beethoven, Brahms, Bruckner) to get to Byrd, a lot of work for a system that claims to link information so that you can find what you want quickly and easily.

What you want is to be able to link the word Byrd in M.html directly to the section for Byrd in B.html. Here's the relevant part of B.html you want to link (I've deleted all the Bs before Byrd to make this file shorter for this example. Pretend they're still there).

```
<HTML>
<HEAD>
<TITLE>Classical Music: B</TITLE>
</HEAD>
<BODY>
<H1>B</H1>
<!-- I've deleted all the Bs before Byrd to make things shorter -->
<H2>Byrd, William, 1543-1623</H2>
<UL>
<LI>Madrigals
<UL>
<LI><EM>This Sweet and Merry Month of May</EM>
<LI><EM>Though Amaryllis Dance</EM>
<LI><EM>Lullabye, My Sweet Little Baby</EM>
</UL>
<LI>Masses
<UL>
<LI><EM>Mass for Five Voices</EM>
<LI><EM>Mass for Four Voices</EM>
<LI><EM>Mass for Three Voices</EM>
</UL>
<LI>Motets
<UL>
<LI><EM>Ave verum corpus a 4</EM>
</UL>
</UL>
<P><EM>See Also</EM>
Madrigals, Masses, Motets</P>
</BODY>
</HTML>
```

What you'll need to do here is to create an anchor at the section heading for Byrd. You can then link to that anchor from the See Alsos in the file for M.

As I described in the previous section, you need two things for each anchor: an anchor name and the text inside the link to hold that anchor (which may be highlighted in some browsers). The latter is easy; the section heading itself works well, as that's the thing you're actually linking to.

For the anchor name, you can choose any name you want, but each anchor in the page must be unique. (If you had two or more anchors with the name fred in the same page, how would the browser know which one to choose when a link to that anchor is selected?) A good unique anchor name for this example would be simply Byrd because there's only one place Byrd could appear in the file, and this is it.

With the two parts decided on, you can create the anchor itself in your HTML file. Add the <A> tag to the William Byrd section heading, but be careful here. If this were normal text within a paragraph, you'd just surround the whole line with <A>. But when you're adding an anchor to a big section of text that is also contained within an element—such as a heading or paragraph—always put the anchor inside the element. In other words, do this:

```
<H2><A NAME="Byrd">Byrd, William, 1543-1623</A></H2>
```

But not this:

```
<A NAME="Byrd"><H2>Byrd, William, 1543-1623</H2></A>
```

The second example could confuse your browser. Is it an anchor, formatted just like the text before it, with mysteriously placed heading tags, or is it a heading that also happens to be an anchor? If you use the right code in your HTML file, with the anchor inside the heading, you solve the confusion.

It's easy to forget about this, especially if you're like me and you create text first and then add links and anchors. It makes sense to just surround everything with an <A> tag. Think of it this way: If you were linking to just one word and not to the entire element, you'd put the <A> tag inside the <H2>. Working with the whole line of text isn't any different. Keep this rule in mind, and you'll get less confused.

NOTE If you're still confused, Appendix B, "HTML 3.2 Language Reference," has a summary of all the HTML tags and rules for which tags can and cannot go inside each one.

4

So you've added your anchor to the heading, and its name is Byrd. Now go back to your M.html file, to the line with See Also.

```
<P><EM>See Also</EM>
Byrd, Gibbons, Lassus, Monteverdi, Morley, Weelkes, Wilbye</P>
```

You're going to create your link here around the word Byrd, just as you would for any other link. But what's the URL? As you learned in the previous section, pathnames to anchors look like this:

```
page_name#anchor_name
```

If you were creating a link to the B.html page itself, the HREF would be this:

```
<A HREF="B.html">
```

Because you're linking to a section inside that page, add the anchor name to link that section, so that it looks like this:

```
<A HREF="B.html#Byrd">
```

Note the capital B in Byrd. Anchor names and links are case sensitive; if you put #byrd in your HREF, the link might not work properly. Make sure that the anchor name you used in the NAME attribute and the anchor name in the link after the # are identical.

TIP | A common mistake is to put a hash sign in both the anchor name and in the link to that anchor. The hash sign is used only to separate the page and the anchor in the link; anchor names should never have hash signs in them.

So, with the new link to the new section, the See Also line looks like this:

```
<P><EM>See Also</EM>
<A HREF="B.html#Byrd">Byrd</A>,
Gibbons, Lassus, Monteverdi, Morley, Weelkes, Wilbye</P>
```

And, of course, you could go ahead and add anchors and links to the other parts of the reference for the remaining composers.

With all your links and anchors in place, test everything. Figure 4.14 shows the Madrigals section with the link to Byrd ready to be selected.

Figure 4.15 shows what pops up when you select the Byrd link.

Figure 4.14.

The Madrigals *section with link.*

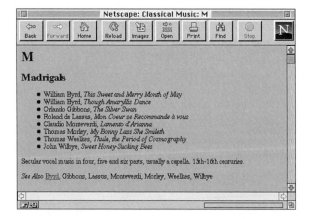

Figure 4.15.

The Byrd *section.*

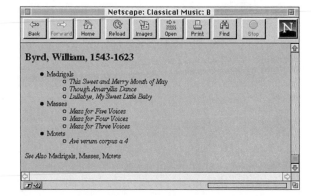

4

Linking to Anchors in the Same Document

What if you have only one large page, and you want to link to sections within that page? You can use anchors for this, too, and for larger pages this can be an easy way to jump around within sections. All you need to do to link to sections is to set up your anchors at each section the way you usually would. Then, when you link to those anchors, leave off the name of the page itself, but include the hash sign and the name of the anchor. So, if you were linking to an anchor name called Section5 in the same page as the link, the link would look like this:

```
Go to <A HREF=#Section5>The Fifth Section</A>
```

When you leave off the page name, the browser assumes you are linking with the current page and will scroll to the appropriate section.

Anatomy of a URL

So far in this book you've encountered URLs twice—in Chapter 1, "The World of the World Wide Web," as part of the introduction to the Web, and in this chapter, when you created links to remote pages. If you've ever done much exploring on the Web, you've encountered URLs as a matter of course. You couldn't start exploring without a URL.

As I mentioned in Chapter 1, URLs are Uniform Resource Locators. URLs are effectively street addresses for bits of information on the Internet. Most of the time, you can avoid trying to figure out which URL to put in your links by simply navigating to the bit of information you want with your browser and then copying and pasting the long string of gobbledygook into your link. But it's often useful to understand what a URL is all about and why it has to be so long and complex. Also, when you put your own information up on the Web, it'll be useful to know something about URLs so that you can tell people where your Web page is.

In this section, you'll learn what the parts of a URL are, how you can use them to get to information on the Web, and the kinds of URLs you can use (HTTP, FTP, Mailto, and so on).

Parts of URLs

Most URLs contain (roughly) three parts: the protocol, the host name, and the directory or filename (see Figure 4.16).

Figure 4.16.

URL parts.

The protocol is the way in which the page is accessed; that is, the type of protocol or program your browser will use to get the file. If the browser is using HTTP to get to the file, the protocol part is http. If the browser uses FTP, it's ftp. If you're using Gopher, it's gopher, and so on. The protocol matches an information server that must be installed on the system for it to work. You can't use an FTP URL on a machine that does not have an FTP server installed, for example.

The host name is the system on the Internet where the information is stored, such as www.netcom.com, ftp.apple.com, or www.aol.com. You can have the same host name but have different URLs with different protocols, like this:

```
http://mysystem.com
ftp://mysystem.com
gopher://mysystem.com
```

Same machine, three different information servers, and the browser will use different methods of connecting to that same machine. As long as all three servers are installed on that system and available, there's not a problem.

The host-name part of the URL may include a port number. The port number tells your browser to open a connection of the appropriate protocol on a specific network port other than the default port. The only time you'll need a port number in a URL is if the server handling the information has been explicitly installed on that port.

If a port number is necessary, it goes after the host name but before the directory, like this:

```
http://my-public-access-unix.com:1550/pub/file
```

Finally, the directory is the location of the file or other form of information on the host. The directory may be an actual directory and filename, or it may be another indicator that the protocol uses to refer to the location of that information. (For example, Gopher directories are not explicit directories.)

Special Characters in URLs

A *special character* in a URL is anything that is not an upper- or lowercase letter, a number (0–9), or the following symbols: dollar sign ($), dash (·), underscore (_), period (.), or plus sign (+). Any other characters may need to be specified using special URL escape codes to keep them from being interpreted as parts of the URL itself.

4

URL escape codes are indicated by a percent sign (%) and a two-character hexadecimal symbol from the ISO-Latin-1 character set (a superset of standard ASCII). For example, `%20` is a space, `%3f` is a question mark, and `%2f` is a slash.

Say you had a directory named `All My Files`, probably on a Macintosh since there are spaces in the filename. Your first pass at a URL with that name in it might look like this:

```
http://myhost.com/harddrive/All My Files/www/file.html
```

If you put this URL in quotes in a link tag, it might work (but only if you put it in quotes). Because the spaces are considered special characters to the URL, though, some browsers may have problems with them and not recognize the pathname correctly. For full compatibility with all browsers, use `%20`:

```
http://myhost.com/harddrive/All%20My%20Files/www/file.html
```

Most of the time, if you make sure your file and directory names are short and use only alphanumeric characters, you won't need to include special characters in URLs. Keep this in mind as you write your own pages.

Kinds of URLs

There are many kinds of URLs defined by the Uniform Resource Locator specification. (See Appendix A, "Sources for Further Information," for a pointer to the most recent version.) This section describes some of the more popular URLs and some things to look out for when using them.

HTTP

HTTP URLs are the most popular form of URL on the World Wide Web. HTTP stands for HyperText Transfer Protocol and is the protocol that World Wide Web servers use to send HTML pages over the Net.

HTTP URLs follow the basic URL form:

```
http://www.foo.com/home/foo/
```

If the URL ends in a slash, the last part of the URL is considered to be a directory name. The file that you get using a URL of this type is the "default" file for that directory as defined by the HTTP server, usually a file called `index.html`. (If the Web page you are designing is the top-level file for all the files in a directory, it's a good idea to call it `index.html`.)

You can also specify the filename directly in the URL. In this case, the file at the end of the URL is the one that is loaded.

```
http://www.foo.com/home/foo/index.html
http://www.foo.com/home/foo/homepage.html
```

It's also usually acceptable to use HTTP URLs like this, where foo is a directory:

```
http://www.foo.com/home/foo
```

In this case, because foo is a directory, this URL should have a slash at the end. Most Web servers are able to figure out that you meant this to be a directory and will "redirect" to the appropriate file. Some older servers, however, may have difficulties resolving this URL, so it's a good idea to always identify directories and files explicitly and to make sure that a default file is available if you are indicating a directory.

Anonymous FTP

FTP URLs are used to point to files located on FTP servers—and usually anonymous FTP servers; that is, those which you can log into using anonymous as the login ID and your e-mail address as the password. FTP URLs also follow the "standard" URL form.

```
ftp://ftp.foo.com/home/foo
ftp://ftp.foo.com/home/foo/homepage.html
```

Because you can retrieve either a file or a directory list with FTP, the restrictions on whether you need a trailing slash at the end of the URL are not the same as with HTTP. The first URL above retrieves a listing of all the files in the foo directory. The second URL retrieves and parses the file homepage.html in the foo directory.

 NOTE

> Navigating FTP servers using a Web browser can often be much slower than navigating them using FTP itself, because the browser does not hold the connection open. Instead, it opens the connection, finds the file or directory listing, displays it, and then closes down the FTP connection. If you select a link to open a file or another directory in that listing, the browser will construct a new FTP URL from the items you selected, re-open the FTP connection using the new URL, get the next directory or file, and close it again. For this reason, FTP URLs are best when you know exactly which file you want to retrieve, rather than for browsing an archive.

Although your browser uses FTP to fetch the file, you still can get an HTML file from that server just as if it were an HTTP server, and it will parse and display just fine. Web browsers don't care how they get a hypertext file. As long as they can recognize it as HTML, either by the servers telling them it's an HTML file (as with HTTP—you'll learn more about this later), or by the extension to the filename, they will parse and display that file as an HTML file. If they don't recognize it as an HTML file, it's not a big deal; the browser can either display it if it knows what kind of file it is, or just save it to disk.

Non-anonymous FTP

All the FTP URLs in the previous section were used for anonymous FTP servers. You can also specify an FTP URL for named accounts on an FTP server, like this:

```
ftp://username:password@ftp.foo.com/home/foo/homepage.html
```

In this form of the URL, the username part is your login ID on the server, and password is that account's password. Note that no attempt is made to hide that password in the URL. Be very careful that no one is watching you when you are using URLs of this form—and don't put them into a link that someone else can find!

File

File URLs are intended to reference files contained on the local disk. In other words, they refer to files that are located on the same system as the browser. For local files, file URLs take one of these two forms: the first with an empty host name (see the three slashes instead of two?) or with the host name as localhost:

```
file:///dir1/dir2/file
file://localhost/dir1/dir2/file
```

Depending on your browser, one or the other will usually work.

File URLs are very similar to FTP URLs, and in fact, if the host part of a file URL is not empty or localhost, your browser will try to find the given file using FTP. Both of the following URLs result in the same file being loaded in the same way:

```
file://somesystem.com/pub/dir/foo/file.html
ftp://somesystem.com/pub/dir/foo/file.html
```

Probably the best use of file URLs is in start-up pages for your browser (which are also called "home pages"). In this instance, because you will almost always be referring to a local file, a file URL makes sense.

The problem with file URLs is that they reference local files, where "local" means on the same system as the browser that is pointing to the file—not the same system that the page was retrieved from! If you use file URLs as links in your page and then someone from elsewhere on the Net encounters your page and tries to follow those links, their browser will attempt to find the file on their local disk (and generally will fail). Also, because file URLs use the absolute pathname to the file, if you use file URLs in your page, you will not be able to move that page elsewhere on the system or to any other system.

4

If your intention is to refer to files that are on the same file system or directory as the current page, use relative pathnames instead of file URLs. With relative pathnames for local files and other URLs for remote files, there's no reason why you should need to use a file URL at all.

Mailto

The Mailto URL is used to send electronic mail. If the browser supports Mailto URLs, when a link that contains one is selected, the browser will prompt you for a subject and the body of the mail message, and send that message to the appropriate address when you're done.

Some browsers do not support `mailto` and produce an error if a link with a Mailto URL is selected.

The Mailto URL is different from the standard URL form. It looks like this:

```
mailto:internet_email_address
```

For example:

```
mailto:lemay@lne.com
```

> **NOTE**
>
> If your e-mail address includes a percent sign (%), you'll have to use the escape character `%25` instead. Percent signs are special characters to URLs.

Gopher

Gopher URLs use the standard URL file format up to and including the host name. After that, they use special Gopher protocols to encode the path to the particular file. The directory in Gopher does not indicate a directory pathname as HTTP and FTP URLs do and is too complex for this chapter. See the URL specification if you're really interested.

Most of the time you'll probably be using a Gopher URL just to point to a Gopher server, which is easy. A URL of this sort looks like this:

```
gopher://gopher.myhost.com/
```

If you really want to point directly to a specific file on a Gopher server, probably the best way to get the appropriate URL is not to try to build it yourself. Instead, navigate to the appropriate file or collection using your browser, and then copy and paste the appropriate URL into your HTML page.

Usenet

Usenet news URLs have one of two forms:

```
news:name_of_newsgroup
news:message-id
```

The first form is used to read an entire newsgroup, such as `comp.infosystems.www.authoring.html` or `alt.gothic`. If your browser supports Usenet news URLs (either directly or through a newsreader), it will provide you with a list of available articles in that newsgroup.

The second form enables you to retrieve a specific news article. Each news article has a unique ID, called a message ID, which usually looks something like this:

```
<lemayCt76Jq.CwG@netcom.com>
```

To use a message ID in a URL, remove the angle brackets and include the `news:` part:

```
news:lemayCt76Jq.CwG@netcom.com
```

Be aware that news articles do not exist forever—they "expire" and are deleted—so a message ID that was valid at one point may become invalid a short time later. If you want a permanent link to a news article, it is best to just copy the article to your Web presentation and link it as you would any other file.

Both forms of URL assume that you are reading news from an NNTP server. Both can be used only if you have defined an NNTP server somewhere in an environment variable or preferences file for your browser. Because of this, news URLs are most useful simply for reading specific news articles locally, and not necessarily for using in links in pages.

NOTE

News URLs, like Mailto URLs, might not be supported by all browsers.

Summary

In this chapter, you learned all about links. Links are the things that turn the Web from a collection of unrelated pages into an enormous, interrelated information system (there are those big words again).

To create links, you use the `<A>...</A>` tag, called the link or anchor tag. The anchor tag has several attributes for indicating files to link to (the HREF attribute) and anchor names (the NAME attribute).

When linking pages that are all stored on the local disk, you can specify their pathnames in the HREF attribute as relative or absolute paths. For local links, relative pathnames are preferred because they let you move those local pages more easily to another directory or to another system. If you use absolute pathnames, your links will break if you change anything in that hard-coded path.

To link to a page on the Web (a remote page), the value of the HREF attribute is the URL of that page. You can easily copy the URL of the page you want to link. Just go to that page using your favorite Web browser, and then copy and paste the URL from your browser into the appropriate place in your link tag.

To create links to specific parts of a page, first set an anchor at the point you want to link to, use the <A>...</A> tag as you would with a link, but instead of the HREF attribute, you use the NAME attribute to name the anchor. You can then link directly to that anchor name using the name of the page, a hash sign (#), and the anchor name.

Finally, URLs (Uniform Resource Locators) are used to point to pages, files, and other information on the Internet. Depending on the type of information, URLs can contain several parts, but most contain a protocol type and location or address. URLs can be used to point to many kinds of information but are most commonly used to point to Web pages (http), FTP directories or files (ftp), information on Gopher servers (gopher), electronic mail addresses (mailto), or Usenet news (news).

Q&A

Q My links aren't being highlighted in blue or purple at all. They're still just plain text.

A Is the filename in an HREF attribute rather than in a NAME? Did you remember to close the quotes around the filename you're linking to? Both of these things can prevent links from showing up as links.

Q I put a URL into a link, and it shows up as highlighted in my browser, but when I click on it, the browser says "unable to access page." If it can't find the page, why did it highlight the text?

A The browser highlights text within a link tag whether or not the link is valid. In fact, you don't even need to be online for links to still show up as highlighted links, even though there's no way to get to them. The only way you can tell if a link is valid is to select it and try to view the page that the link points to.

As to why the browser couldn't find the page you linked to—make sure you're connected to the network and that you entered the URL into the link correctly. Make sure you have both opening and closing quotes around the filename and that those quotes are straight quotes. If your browser prints link destinations in the status bar when you move the mouse over a link, watch that status bar and see if the URL that appears is actually the URL you want.

Finally, try opening that URL directly in your browser and see if that works. If directly opening the link doesn't work either, there might be several reasons why. Two common ones are

☐ The server is overloaded or is not on the Net.

Machines go down, as do network connections. If a particular URL doesn't work for you, perhaps there's something wrong with the machine or the network. Or maybe it's a popular site, and too many people are trying to access it at once. Try again later or during non-peak hours for that server. If you know the people who run the server, you can try sending them electronic mail or calling them.

☐ The URL itself is bad.

Sometimes URLs become invalid. Because a URL is a form of absolute pathname, if the file to which it refers moves around or if a machine or directory name gets changed, the URL won't be any good any more. Try contacting the person or site you got the URL from in the first place. See if they have a more recent link.

Q Can I put any URL in a link?

A You bet. If you can get to a URL using your browser, you can put that URL in a link. Note, however, that some browsers support URLs that others don't. For example, Lynx is really good with Mailto URLs (URLs that allow you to send electronic mail to a person's e-mail address). When you select a Mailto URL in Lynx, it prompts you for a subject and the body of the message. When you're done, it sends the mail.

Other browsers, on the other hand, may not handle Mailto URLs and insist that a link containing the Mailto URL is invalid. The URL itself may be fine, but the browser can't handle it.

Q Can I use images as links?

A Yup. You'll learn how to do this in Chapter 7, "Using Images, Color, and Backgrounds."

Q You've only described two attributes of the <A> tag: HREF and NAME. Aren't there others?

A Yes; the <A> tag has several attributes including REL, REV, URN, METHODS, and TITLE. However, most of those attributes can be used only by tools that automatically generate links between pages, or by browsers that can manage links better than most of those now available. Because 99 percent of you reading this book won't care about (or ever use) those links or browsers, I'm sticking to HREF and NAME and ignoring the other attributes.

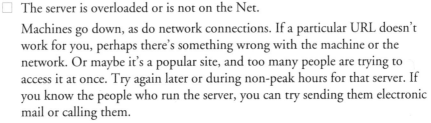

Q **My links are not pointing to my anchors. When I follow a link, I'm always dropped at the top of the page instead of at the anchor. What's going on here?**

A Are you specifying the anchor name in the link after the hash sign the same way that it appears in the anchor itself, with all the uppercase and lowercase letters identical? Anchors are case-sensitive, so if your browser cannot find an anchor name with an exact match, it may try to select something else in the page that is closer. This is dependent on browser behavior, of course, but if your links and anchors aren't working, it's usually because your anchor names and your anchors do not match. Also, remember that anchor names don't contain hash signs—only the links to them do.

Q **It sounds like file URLs aren't overly useful. Is there any reason you'd want to use them?**

A I can think of two. The first one is if you have many users on a single system (for example, on a UNIX system) and you want to give those local users (but nobody else) access to files on that system. By using file URLs you can point to files on the local system, and anyone on that system can get to them. Readers from outside the system won't have direct access to the disk and won't be able to get to those files.

A second good reason for using file URLs is that you actually want to point to a local disk. For example, you could create a CD full of information in HTML form, and then create a link from a page on the Web to a file on the CD using a file URL. In this case, because your presentation depends on a disk your readers must have, using a file URL makes sense.

Q **Is there any way to indicate a subject in a Mailto URL?**

A Not at the moment. According to the current Mailto URL definition, the only thing you can put in a Mailto URL is the address to mail to. If you really need a subject or something in the body of the message, consider using a form instead (you'll learn more about forms on Bonus Day 2).

DAY 3

Doing More with HTML 3.2

Chapter **5**

More Text Formatting with HTML 3.2

Yesterday you learned the basics of HTML, including several basic page elements and links. With that background you're ready to learn more about what HTML can do in terms of text formatting and layout. This chapter describes most of the remaining tags in HTML that you'll need to know to construct pages, including both tags in standard HTML 2.0 and HTML 3.2 as well as HTML extensions in individual browsers. Today you'll learn how to

☐ Specify the appearance of individual characters (bold, italic, typewriter)

☐ Include special characters (characters with accents, copyright and registration marks, and so on)

☐ Create preformatted text (text with spaces and tabs retained)

☐ Align text left, right, justified, and centered

☐ Change the font and font size

☐ Create other miscellaneous HTML text elements, including line breaks, rule lines, addresses, and quotations

In addition, you'll learn the differences between standard HTML and HTML extensions, and when to choose which tags to use in your pages. At the end of this chapter, you'll create a complete Web page that uses many of the tags presented in this chapter as well as the information from the previous four chapters.

This is a long chapter, covering tags and options, and it's all going to be a bit overwhelming. But don't worry about remembering everything now; just get a grasp of what sorts of formatting you can do in HTML, and then you can look up the specific tags later. In the next chapter, we'll take a significant break and look at some of the tools and programs you can use to help you write HTML so you don't have to remember everything while you're still learning how to put pages together.

Character Styles

When you use an HTML tag for paragraphs, headings, or lists, those tags affect that block of text as a whole, changing the font, changing the spacing above and below the line, or adding characters (in the case of bulleted lists). Character styles are tags that affect words or characters within other HTML entities and change the appearance of that text so it is somehow different from the surrounding text—making it bold or underline, for instance.

To change the appearance of a set of characters within text, you can use one of two kinds of tags: logical styles or physical styles.

Logical Styles

Logical style tags indicate how the given highlighted text is to be used, not how it is to be displayed. This is similar to the common element tags for paragraphs or headings. They don't indicate how the text is to be formatted, just how it is to be used in a document. Logical style tags might, for example, indicate a definition, a snippet of code, or an emphasized word.

> *Logical style* tags indicate the way text is used (emphasis, citation, definition).

When you use logical style tags, the browser determines the actual presentation of the text, be it in bold, italic, or any other change in appearance. You cannot guarantee that text highlighted using these tags will always be bold or always be italic (and, therefore, you should not depend on it, either).

Each character style tag has both opening and closing sides, and affects the text within those two tags. There are eight logical style tags in standard HTML:

<EM>   Indicates that the characters are to be emphasized in some way; that is, they are formatted differently from the rest of the text. In graphical browsers, <EM> is typically italic. For example:

```
<P>We'd all get along much better if you'd stop being so
<EM>silly.</EM></P>
```

<STRONG>   The characters are to be more strongly emphasized than with <EM>. <STRONG> text is highlighted differently from <EM> text, for example, in bold. For example:

```
<P>You <STRONG>must </STRONG> open the can before drinking</P>
```

<CODE>   A code sample (a fixed-width font such as Courier in graphical displays):

```
<P><CODE>#include "trans.h"</CODE></P>
```

<SAMP>   Example text, similar to <CODE>:

```
<P>The URL for that page is <SAMP>http://www.cern.ch/</SAMP></P>
```

<KBD>   Text intended to be typed by a user:

```
<P>Type the following command:
<KBD>find . -name "prune" -print</KBD></P>
```

<VAR>   The name of a variable, or some entity to be replaced with an actual value. Often displayed as italic or underline, for example:

```
<P><CODE>chown </CODE><VAR>your_name the_file</VAR></P>
```

<DFN>   A definition. <DFN> is used to highlight a word that will be defined or has just been defined:

```
<P>Styles that are named after how they are actually used are
called
<DFN>logical character styles</DFN></P>
```

<CITE>   A short quote or citation:

```
<P>Eggplant has been known to cause nausea in many unsuspecting
people<CITE> (Lemay, 1994)</CITE></P>
```

5

NOTE

Of the tags in this list, all except <DFN> are part of the official HTML 2.0 specification. <DFN> is part of HTML 3.2 but is commonly supported by most browsers, so I've included it here.

Got all those memorized now? Good! There will be a pop quiz at the end of the chapter. The following code snippets demonstrate each of the logical style tags, and Figures 5.1 and 5.2 illustrate how all eight tags are displayed in Netscape and Lynx.

INPUT
```
<P>We'd all get along much better if you'd stop being so
<EM>silly.</EM>
<P>You <STRONG>must</STRONG> open the can before drinking</P>
<P><CODE>#include "trans.h"</CODE></P>
<P>Type the following command:
<KBD>find . -name "prune" -print</KBD></P>
<P><CODE>chown </CODE><VAR>your_name the_file</VAR></P>
<P>The URL for that page is <SAMP>http://www.cern.ch/</SAMP></P>
<P>Styles that are named on how they are used are called
<DFN>character styles</DFN></P>
<P>Eggplant has been known to cause extreme nausea in many
unsuspecting people<CITE> (Lemay, 1994)</CITE></P>
```

OUTPUT

Figure 5.1.

*The output in
Netscape.*

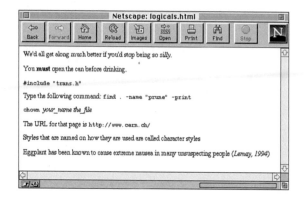

OUTPUT

Figure 5.2.

*The output in
Lynx.*

```
We'd all get along much better if you'd stop being so silly.

You must open the can before drinking.

#include "trans.h"

Type the following command: find . -name "prune" -print

chown your_name the_file

The URL for that page is http://www.cern.ch/

Styles that are named on how they are used are called character styles

Eggplant has been known to cause extreme nausea in many unsuspecting
people (Lemay, 1994)
```

Physical Styles

In addition to the tags for style in the previous section, there is also a set of tags that change
the actual presentation style of the text—to make it bold, italic, or monospace.

NEW
TERM

Physical style tags indicate exactly the way text is to be formatted (bold,
underline).

5

Like the character style tags, each formatting tag has a beginning and ending tag. Standard HTML 2.0 defines three physical style tags:

`<B>`	Bold
`<I>`	Italic
`<TT>`	Monospaced typewriter font

HTML 3.2 defines several other physical style tags, including:

`<U>`	Underline
`<S>`	Strike through
`<BIG>`	Bigger print than the surrounding text
`<SMALL>`	Smaller print
`<SUB>`	Subscript
`<SUP>`	Superscript

If you choose to use the physical style tags, particularly the newer HTML 3.2 tags, be forewarned that if a browser cannot handle one of the physical styles, it may substitute another style for the one you're using, or ignore that formatting altogether.

You can nest character tags—for example, use both bold and italic for a set of characters—like this:

```
<B><I>Text that is both bold and italic</I></B>
```

However, the result on the screen, like all HTML tags, is browser-dependent. You will not necessarily end up with text that is both bold and italic. You may end up with one or the other.

This input and output example shows some of the physical style tags and how they appear in Netscape (Figure 5.3) and Lynx (Figure 5.4).

INPUT

```
<P>In Dante's <I>Inferno</I>, malaboge was the eighth circle of hell,
and held the malicious and fraudulent.</P>
<P>All entries must be received by <B>September 26, 1996</B>.</P>
<P>Type <TT>lpr -Pbirch myfile.txt</TT> to print that file.</P>
<P>Sign your name in the spot marked <U>Sign Here</U>:</P>
<P>People who wear orange shirts and plaid pants <S>have no taste</S>
are fashion-challenged.</P>
<P>RCP floor mats give you <BIG>BIG</BIG> savings over the competition!
</P>
<P>Then, from the corner of the room, he heard a <SMALL>tiny voice</
SMALL>.</P>
<P>In heavy trading today, Consolidated Orange Trucking
rose <SUP>1</SUP>/<SUB>4</SUB>
points on volume of 1,457,900 shares.</P>
```

5

Figure 5.3.
*The output in
Netscape.*

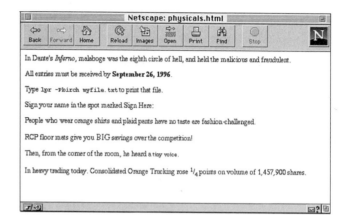

Figure 5.4.
*The output in
Lynx.*

Preformatted Text

Most of the time, text in an HTML file is formatted based on the HTML tags used to mark up that text. As I mentioned in Chapter 3, "The Basics of HTML 3.2," any extra white space (spaces, tabs, returns) that you put in your text are stripped out by the browser.

The one exception to this rule is the preformatted text tag <PRE>. Any white space that you put into text surrounded by the <PRE> and </PRE> tags is retained in the final output. With

5

the `<PRE>` and `</PRE>` tags, you can format the text the way you want it to look, and it will be presented that way.

The catch is that preformatted text is also displayed (in graphical displays, at least) in a monospaced font such as Courier. Preformatted text is excellent for things such as code examples, where you want to indent and format lines appropriately. Because you can also use the `<PRE>` tag to align text by padding it with spaces, you can also use it for simple tables. However, the fact that those tables are presented in a monospaced font may make them less than ideal (you'll learn how to do real tables in Chapter 13, "Tables"). Here's an example of a table created with `<PRE>`. (Figure 5.5 shows how it looks in Netscape.)

```
<PRE>
           Diameter   Distance    Time to     Time to
           (miles)    from Sun    Orbit       Rotate
                      (millions
                      of miles)

- - - - - - - - - - - - - - - - - - - - - - - - - - - - - - - - - - - - - - -
Mercury    3100          36       88 days     59 days
Venus      7700          67       225 days    244 days
Earth      7920          93       365 days    24 hrs
Mars       4200         141       687 days    24 hrs 24 mins
Jupiter    88640        483       11.9 years  9 hrs 50 mins
Saturn     74500        886       29.5 years  10 hrs 39 mins
Uranus     32000       1782       84 years    23 hrs
Neptune    31000       2793       165 days    15 hrs 48 mins
Pluto      1500        3670       248 years   6 days 7 hrs
</PRE>
```

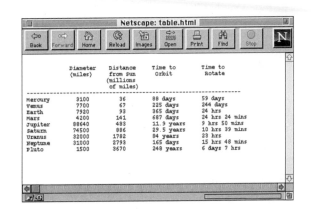

Figure 5.5.
A table created using `<pre>`, *shown in Netscape.*

When creating text for the `<PRE>` tag, you can use link tags and character styles, but not element tags such as headings or paragraphs. Break your lines using a return , and try to keep your lines at 60 characters or less. Some browsers may have limited horizontal space in which to display text, and since browsers cannot reformat preformatted text to fit that space, you should make sure you stay within the boundaries to prevent your readers from having to scroll from side-to-side.

Be careful with tabs in preformatted text. The actual number of characters for each tab stop varies from browser to browser. One browser may have tabs stops at every fourth character, whereas another may have them at every eighth character. If your preformatted text relies on tabs at a certain number of spaces, consider using spaces instead of tabs.

The <PRE> tag is also excellent for converting files that were originally in some sort of text-only form, such as mail messages or Usenet news postings, to HTML quickly and easily. Just surround the entire content of the article within <PRE> tags, and you have instant HTML, for example:

```
<PRE>
To: lemay@lne.com
From: jokes@lne.com
Subject: Tales of the Move From Hell, pt. 1
Date: Fri, 26 Aug 1994 14:13:38 +0800

I spent the day on the phone today with the entire household
services division of northern california, turning off services,
turning on services, transferring services and other such fun
things you have to do when you move.

It used to be you just called these people and got put on hold for
and interminable amount of time, maybe with some nice music, and
then you got a customer representative who was surly and hard of
hearing, but with some work you could actually get your phone
turned off.
</PRE>
```

The following HTML input and output example shows a simple ASCII art cow and how it appears in Netscape (Figure 5.6) and Lynx (Figure 5.7):

INPUT

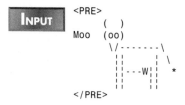

OUTPUT

Figure 5.6.
The output in Netscape.

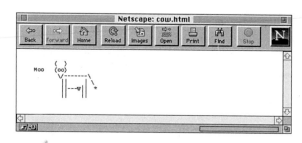

5

Figure 5.7.
The output in Lynx.

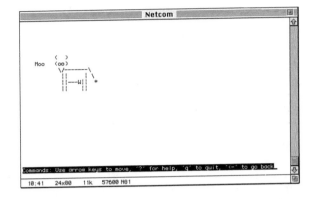

Horizontal Rules

The `<HR>` tag, which has no closing tag and no text associated with it, creates a horizontal line on the page. Rule lines are excellent for visually separating sections of the Web page; just before headings, for example, or to separate body text from a list of items. Figure 5.8 illustrates a rule line.

Figure 5.8.
A rule line.

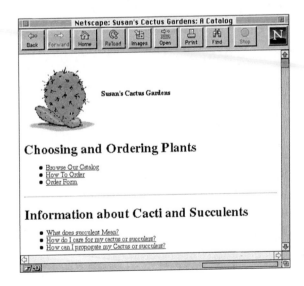

This input and output example shows a rule line and a list and how they appear in Netscape (Figure 5.9) and Lynx (Figure 5.10).

```
<HR>
<H2>To Do on Friday</H2>
<UL>
<LI>Do laundry
<LI>Send Fedex with pictures
<LI>Have lunch with Mollie
<LI>Read Email
<LI>Set up Ethernet
</UL>
<HR>
```

Figure 5.9.
*The output in
Netscape.*

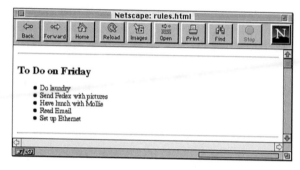

Figure 5.10.
*The output in
Lynx.*

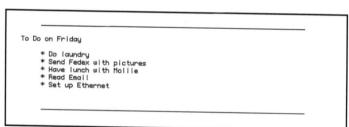

HTML 3.2 Extensions to the `<HR>` Tag

In HTML 2.0, the `<HR>` tag is just as you see it, with no closing tag or attributes. However, several HTML 3.2 extensions to the `<HR>` tag that are supported by several other browsers give you greater control over the appearance of the line drawn by `<HR>`.

The SIZE attribute indicates the thickness, in pixels, of the rule line. The default is 2, and this is also the smallest thickness that you can make the rule line. Figure 5.11 shows some sample rule line thicknesses.

The WIDTH attribute indicates the horizontal width of the rule line. You can specify either the exact width, in pixels, or the value as a percentage of the screen width (for example, 30 percent or 50 percent), which will change if you resize the window. Figure 5.12 shows some sample rule line widths.

Figure 5.11.

Examples of rule line thicknesses.

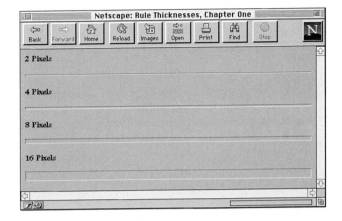

Figure 5.12.

Examples of rule line widths.

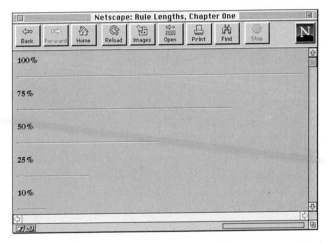

If you specify a WIDTH smaller than the actual width of the screen, you can also specify the alignment of that rule line with the ALIGN attribute, making it flush left (ALIGN=LEFT), flush right (ALIGN=RIGHT), or centered (ALIGN=CENTER). By default, rule lines are centered.

A popular trick used by Web designers who use these extensions is to create patterns with several small rule lines, as shown in Figure 5.13.

This is one of those instances in which using newer features of HTML in your pages looks awful in other browsers that don't support those features. When viewed in browsers without the SIZE attribute, each of the small rule lines now covers the entire width of the screen. If you must use these rule line patterns, consider using small images instead (which will work in other browsers).

Figure 5.13.

An example of patterns created with several small rule lines.

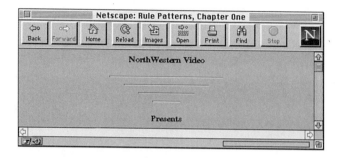

Finally, the NOSHADE attribute causes the browser to draw the rule line as a plain black line, without the three-dimensional shading, as shown in Figure 5.14.

Figure 5.14.

Rule lines without shading.

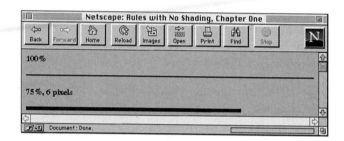

Line Break

The <BR> tag breaks a line of text at the point where it appears. When a Web browser encounters a <BR> tag, it restarts the text after the tag at the left margin (whatever the current left margin happens to be for the current element). You can use <BR> within other elements such as paragraphs or list items;
 will not add extra space above or below the new line or change the font or style of the current entity. All it does is restart the text at the next line. This example shows a simple paragraph where each line ends with a <BR>. Figures 5.15 and 5.16 show how it appears in Netscape and Lynx, respectively.

INPUT

```
<P>Tomorrow, and tomorrow, and tomorrow<BR>
Creeps in this petty pace from day to day<BR>
To the last syllable of recorded time;<BR>
And all our yesterdays have lighted fools<BR>
The way to dusty death. Out, out, brief candle!<BR>
Life's but a walking shadow, a poor player,<BR>
That struts and frets his hour upon the stage<BR>
And then is heard no more. It is a tale <BR>
Told by an idiot, full of sound and fury, <BR>
Signifying nothing.</P>
```

Figure 5.15.
The output in Netscape.

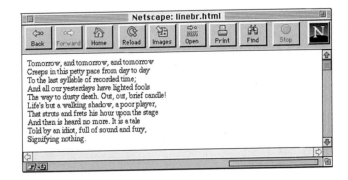

Figure 5.16.
The output in Lynx.

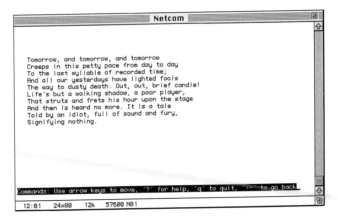

An HTML 3.2 extension to the `<BR>` tag is the `CLEAR` attribute, which is used with images that have text wrapped alongside them. You'll learn about this extension in Chapter 7, "Using Images, Color, and Backgrounds."

Addresses

The address tag `<ADDRESS>` is used for signature-like entities on Web pages. Address tags usually go at the bottom of each Web page and are used to indicate who wrote the Web page, who to contact for more information, the date, any copyright notices or other warnings, and anything else that seems appropriate. Addresses are often preceded with a rule line (`<HR>`), and the `<BR>` tag can be used to separate the lines, for example:

```
<HR>
<ADDRESS>
Laura Lemay lemay@lne.com <BR>
```

```
A service of Laura Lemay, Incorporated <BR>
last revised September 30 1994 <BR>
Copyright Laura Lemay 1994 all rights reserved <BR>
Void where prohibited. Keep hands and feet inside the vehicle at all times.
</ADDRESS>
```

Without an address or some other method of "signing" your Web pages, it becomes close to impossible to find out who wrote it, or who to contact for more information. Signing each of your Web pages using the <ADDRESS> tag is an excellent way to make sure that if people want to get in touch with you, they can.

This simple input and output example shows an address in Netscape (Figure 5.17) and Lynx (Figure 5.18).

```
<HR>
<ADDRESS>
lemay@lne.com Laura Lemay
</ADDRESS>
```

Figure 5.17.
The output in Netscape.

Figure 5.18.
The output in Lynx.

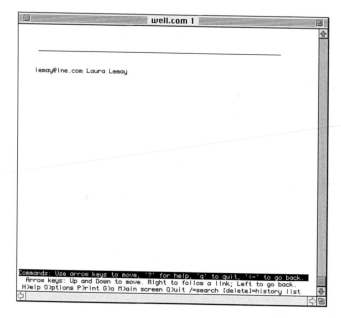

Quotations

The <BLOCKQUOTE> tag is used to create a quotation. (Unlike the <CITE> tag, which highlights small quotes, <BLOCKQUOTE> is used for longer quotations that should not be nested inside other paragraphs.) Quotations are generally set off from regular text by indentation or some other method. For example, the *Macbeth* soliloquy I used in the example for line breaks would have worked better as a <BLOCKQUOTE> than as a simple paragraph. Here's another example:

```
<BLOCKQUOTE>
"During the whole of a dull, dark, and soundless day in the autumn
of the year, when the clouds hung oppressively low in the heavens,
I had been passing alone, on horseback, through a singularly dreary
tract of country, and at length found myself, as the shades of evening
grew on, within view of the melancholy House of Usher."—Edgar Allen Poe
</BLOCKQUOTE>
```

As in paragraphs, you can separate lines in a <BLOCKQUOTE> using the line-break tag <BR>. This input and output example shows a sample of this, and how it appears in Netscape (Figure 5.19).

```
<BLOCKQUOTE>
Guns aren't lawful, <BR>
nooses give.<BR>
gas smells awful.<BR>
You might as well live.<BR>
—Dorothy Parker
</BLOCKQUOTE>
```

OUTPUT

Figure 5.19.

*The output in
Netscape.*

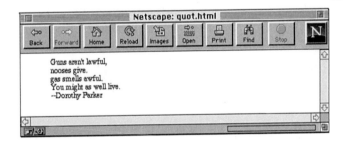

Special Characters

As you learned earlier in the week, HTML files are ASCII text and should contain no formatting or fancy characters. In fact, the only characters you should be putting in your HTML files are characters that are actually printed on your keyboard. If you have to hold down any key other than Shift, or type an arcane combination of keys to produce a single character, you can't use that character in your HTML file. That includes characters you may use every day, such as em dashes and curly quotes (and, if your word processor is set up to do automatic curly quotes, you should turn them off when you write your HTML files).

But wait a minute, I can hear you say. If I can type a character, like a bullet or an accented "a" on my keyboard using a special key sequence, include it in an HTML file, and my browser can display it just fine when I look at that file, what's the problem?

The problem is that the internal encoding your computer does to produce that character (which allows it to show up properly in your HTML file and in your browser's display) most likely will not translate to other computers. Someone else on the Net reading your HTML file with that funny character in it may very well end up with some other character, or garbage. Or, depending on how your page gets shipped over the Net, the character may be lost before it ever gets to the computer where the file is being viewed.

NOTE

In technical jargon, this means that the characters in HTML files must be from the standard (7-bit) ASCII character set, and cannot include any characters from "extended" (8-bit) ASCII, as every platform has a different definition of the characters that are included in the upper ASCII range. HTML browsers interpret codes from upper ASCII as characters in the ISO-Latin-1 (ISO-8859-1) character set, a superset of ASCII.

So what can you do? HTML provides a reasonable solution. It defines a special set of codes, called character entities, which you can include in your HTML files to represent the characters you want to use. When interpreted by a browser, these character entities are displayed as the appropriate special characters for the given platform and font.

Character Entities for Special Characters

Character entities take one of two forms: named entities and numbered entities.

Named entities begin with an ampersand (&) and end with a semicolon (;). In between is the name of the character (or, more likely, a shorthand version of that name like agrave for an "a" with a grave accent or reg for a registered trademark sign). The names, unlike other HTML tags, are case sensitive, so you should make sure to type them exactly. Named entities look something like this:

```
&quot;
&laquo;
&copy;
```

The numbered entities also begin with an ampersand and end with a semicolon, but instead of a name, they have a hash sign and a number. The numbers correspond to character positions in the ISO-Latin-1 (ISO 8859-1) character. Every character that you can type or use a named entity for also has a numbered entity. Numbered entities look like this:

```
&#130;
&#245;
```

You use either numbers or named entities in your HTML file by including them in the same place that the character they represent would go. So, to have the word "resumé" in your HTML file, you would use either:

```
resum&eacute;
```

or

```
resum&#233;
```

NOTE

> HTML's use of the ISO-Latin-1 character set allows it to display most accented characters on most platforms, but it has its limitations. For example, common characters such as bullets, em dashes, and curly quotes are simply not available in the ISO-Latin-1 character set. This means you cannot use these characters at all in your HTML files. Also, many ISO-Latin-1 characters may be entirely unavailable in some browsers depending on whether or not those characters exist on that platform and in the current font. Future versions of HTML will allow multiple character sets (including the Unicode character set, which includes most of the known characters and symbols in the world).

5

Character Entities for Reserved Characters

For the most part, character entities exist so you can include special characters that are not part of the standard ASCII character set. There are several exceptions, however, for the few characters that have special meaning in HTML itself. You must also use entities for these characters.

For example, say you wanted to include a line of code in an HTML file that looked something like this:

```
<P><CODE>if x < 0 do print i</CODE></P>
```

Doesn't look unusual, does it? Unfortunately, HTML cannot display this line as written. Why? The problem is with the < (less-than) character. To an HTML browser, the less-than character means "this is the start of a tag." Because in this context the less than character is not actually the start of a tag, your browser may get confused. You'll have the same problem with the greater than character (>) because it means the end of a tag in HTML, and with the ampersand (&), meaning the beginning of a character escape. Written correctly for HTML, the line of code above would look like this:

```
<P><CODE>if x &lt; 0 do print i</CODE></P>
```

HTML provides named escape codes for each of these characters, and one for the double-quote, as well, as shown in Table 5.1.

Table 5.1. Escape codes for characters used by tags.

Entity	Result
<	<
>	>
&	&
"	"

The double-quote escape is the mysterious one. Technically, to produce correct HTML files, if you want to include a double quote in text, you should be using the escape sequence and not typing the quote character. However, I have not noticed any browsers having problems displaying the double-quote character when it is typed literally in an HTML file, nor have I seen many HTML files that use it. For the most part, you are probably safe just using plain old " in your HTML files rather than the escape code.

Text Alignment

Text alignment is the ability to arrange a block of text such as a heading or a paragraph so that it is aligned against the left margin (left justification, the default), aligned against the right margin (right justification), or centered. In standard HTML 2.0, there are no mechanisms for aligning text; the browser is responsible for determining the alignment of the text (which means most of the time it's left-justified).

HTML 3.2 provides HTML extensions for text and element alignment, and these extensions have been incorporated into other browsers to varying degrees. In browsers that don't support some or all of the tags described in this section, you'll lose the alignment, and the text will appear aligned according to that browser's default rules. And, given the variety of support for

5

the different tags described in this section, this probably will happen to you at some point. Keep that in mind as you design your pages to take alignment into account.

Aligning Individual Elements

To align an individual heading or paragraph, use the ALIGN attribute to that HTML element. ALIGN, which is an HTML 3.2 extension, has one of three values: LEFT, RIGHT, or CENTER.

```
<H1 ALIGN=CENTER>Northridge Paints, Inc.</H2>
<P ALIGN=CENTER >We don't just paint the town red.</P>

<H1 ALIGN=LEFT>Serendipity Products</H1>
<H2 ALIGN=RIGHT><A HREF="who.html">Who We Are</A></H2>
<H2 ALIGN=RIGHT><A HREF="products.html">What We Do</A></H2>
<H2 ALIGN=RIGHT><A HREF="contacts.html">How To Reach Us</A></H2>
```

Browsers support this type of alignment to varying degrees. Netscape 2.0 supports all three, whereas Internet Explorer and other browsers support only ALIGN=CENTER. Many other browsers may not support alignment of this sort at all.

This input and output example shows simple alignment of several headings in Netscape (Figure 5.20 shows the results):

```
<H1 ALIGN=LEFT>Serendipity Products</H1>
<H2 ALIGN=RIGHT><A HREF="who.html">Who We Are</A></H2>
<H2 ALIGN=RIGHT><A HREF="products.html">What We Do</A></H2>
<H2 ALIGN=RIGHT><A HREF="contacts.html">How To Reach Us</A></H2>
```

Figure 5.20.
The output in Netscape.

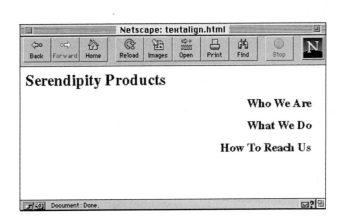

Aligning Blocks of Elements

A slightly more flexible method of aligning text elements is to use the <DIV> tag, an HTML 3.2 extension. <DIV> stands for division, and includes the ALIGN attribute just as headings and paragraphs do. Unlike using alignments in individual elements, however, <DIV> is used to surround a block of HTML tags of any kind, and it affects all the tags and text inside the opening and closing tags. There are two advantages of <DIV> over the ALIGN attribute:

- ☐ <DIV> needs to be used only once, rather than including ALIGN repeatedly in several different tags.
- ☐ <DIV> can be used to align anything (headings, paragraphs, quotes, images, tables, and so on); the ALIGN attribute is only available on a limited number of tags.

 NOTE

> Actually, according to the HTML 3.2 specification, all of the HTML elements have the ALIGN attribute, but in reality very few browsers support ALIGN on anything other than headings and paragraphs.

To align a block of HTML code, surround that code by opening and closing <DIV> tags, and then include the ALIGN attribute in the opening tag. As in other tags, ALIGN can have the values LEFT, RIGHT, or CENTER.

```
<H1 ALIGN=LEFT>Serendipity Products</H1>
<DIV ALIGN=RIGHT>
<H2><A HREF="who.html">Who We Are</A></H2>
<H2><A HREF="products.html">What We Do</A></H2>
<H2><A HREF="contacts.html">How To Reach Us</A></H2>
</DIV>
```

All the HTML between the two <DIV> tags will be aligned according to the value of the ALIGN attribute. If there are individual ALIGN attributes in headings or paragraphs inside the <DIV>, those values will override the global DIV setting.

Note that <DIV> is not itself a paragraph type. You still need regular element tags (<P>, <H1>, <UL>, <BLOCKQUOTE>, and so on) inside the opening and closing <DIV> tags.

At the moment, the only browser that supports <DIV> is Netscape 2.0, although other browsers will most likely follow suit.

In addition to <DIV>, there is also the centering tag <CENTER>, a Netscape extension that is not part of HTML 2.0 or 3.2 (and is unlikely to be part of a future version of HTML). The <CENTER> tag acts identically to <DIV ALIGN=CENTER>, centering all the HTML content inside the opening and closing tags. You put the <CENTER> tag before the text you want centered, and the </CENTER> tag after you're done, like this:

```
<CENTER>
<H1>Northridge Paints, Inc.</H2>
<P>We don't just paint the town red.</P>
</CENTER>
```

5

Although <CENTER> is far more limited than the <DIV> tag, it is also more widely supported by other browsers than <DIV>. However, given that <DIV> and the ALIGN attributes are more "correct" HTML than <CENTER> is, and because <CENTER> will be obsolete in the future, it's a good idea to move to the HTML 3.2 equivalents for alignment wherever you can.

Fonts and Font Sizes

The <FONT> tag, part of HTML 3.2, is used to control the characteristics of a given set of characters not covered by the character styles. Originally, <FONT> was used only to control the font size of the characters it surrounds, but it has since been extended to allow you to change the font itself and the color of those characters.

In this section, we'll discuss fonts and font sizes. On Day 4, "Images and Backgrounds," when we talk about color in general, you'll learn about changing the font color.

Changing the Font Size

The most common use of the <FONT> tag is to change the size of the font for a character, word, phrase, or on any range of text. The <FONT>...</FONT> tags enclose the text, and the SIZE attribute indicates the size to which the font is to be changed. The values of SIZE are 1 to 7, with 3 being the default size. Look at the following example:

```
<P>Bored with your plain old font?
<FONT SIZE=5>Change it.</FONT></P>
```

Figure 5.21 shows the typical font sizes for each value of SIZE.

Figure 5.21.

Font sizes in Netscape.

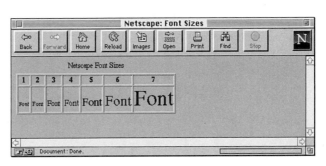

You can also specify the size in the <FONT> tag as a relative value using the + or - characters in the value for SIZE. Because the default size is 3, you can change relative font sizes from -3 to +4, like this:

```
<P>Change the <FONT SIZE=+2>Font</FONT> size again.</P>
```

Here, the word Font (inside the <FONT> tags) will be two size levels larger than the default font when you view that example in Netscape.

Relative font sizes are actually based on a value that you can define using the <BASEFONT> tag. The <BASEFONT> tag also has the required attribute SIZE. SIZE can have a value of 1 to 7. All relative font changes in the document after the <BASEFONT> tag will be relative to that value.

Try to avoid using the <FONT> tag to simulate the larger-font effect of the HTML content-based tags such as the heading tags (<H1>, <H2>, and so on), or to emphasize a particular word or phrase. If your documents are viewed in browsers other than Netscape, you'll lose the font sizes, and your text will appear as if it were any other paragraph. If you stick to the content-based tags, however, a heading is a heading regardless of where you view it. Try to limit your use of the FONT tag to small amounts of special effects.

Changing the Font Face

Netscape introduced the <FONT> tag to HTML with its 1.0 browser. Microsoft's Internet Explorer, playing the same game, extended the <FONT> tag to include the FACE attribute. FACE can be used to change the actual font of the text between the <FONT> tags.

FACE takes as its value a set of font names, surrounded by quotes and separated by commas. When a browser that supports FACE interprets a page with FACE in it, it will search the system for the given font names one at a time. If it can't find the first one, it'll try the second, and then the third, and so on, until it finds a font that is actually installed on the system. If it cannot find any of the listed fonts, the default font will be used instead. So, for example, the following text would be rendered in Futura. If Futura is not available, the browser will try Helvetica, and fall back on the default if Helvetica is not available.

```
<P><FONT FACE="Futura,Helvetica">Sans Serif fonts are fonts without
the small "ticks" on the strokes of the characters. </FONT></P>
```

Keep in mind if you use the FACE attribute that currently very few browsers support it, so it may be unavailable to most of your audience. Also, many fonts have different names on different systems; for example, plain old Times is Times on some systems, Times-Roman on others, and Times New Roman elsewhere. Because of the varying names of fonts and the lack of widespread support for the FACE attribute, changing the font name should only be used as an optional presentation-only feature rather than one to be relied on in your pages.

The Dreaded <BLINK>

You won't find the <BLINK> tag listed in Netscape's official documentation of its extensions. The capability to cause text to blink was included in Netscape as a hidden undocumented feature or Easter egg. Still, a good percentage of pages on the Web seem to use this feature.

5

The <BLINK>...</BLINK> tags cause the text between the opening and closing tags to have a blinking effect. Depending on the version of Netscape you are using, this can mean that the text itself vanishes and comes back at regular intervals or that an ugly gray or white block appears and disappears behind the text. Blink is usually used to draw attention to a portion of the page.

The problem with blink is that it provides too much emphasis. Because it repeats, the blink continues to drag attention to that one spot and, in some cases, can be so distracting that it can make it nearly impossible to absorb any of the other content of the page. The use of <BLINK> is greatly discouraged by most Web designers (including myself), because many people find it extremely intrusive, ugly, and annoying. Blink is the HTML equivalent of fingernails on a blackboard.

If you must use blink, use it very sparingly (no more than a few words on a page). Also, be aware that in some versions of Netscape, blinking can be turned off. If you want to emphasize a word or phrase, you should use a more conventional way of doing so, in addition to (or in place of) blink, because you cannot guarantee that blink will be available even if your reader is using Netscape to view your pages.

Other Extensions

This section is a catch-all for the remaining HTML extensions in common use in browsers and in pages on the Web today, including extensions to lists to change the numbering or bullet style, and tags for non-breaking text and word breaks.

Special List Formats

Normally, when you create lists in HTML, the browser determines the size and type of the bullet in an unordered list (the <UL> tag) or the numbering scheme in numbered lists (usually simply 1, 2, and so on for each item in the list). In HTML 3.2, several attributes to the list tags were added to allow greater control over how individual items are labeled.

For unordered lists (the <UL> tag), the TYPE attribute indicates the type of bullet used to mark each item. The possible values are as follows:

TYPE=DISC   A solid bullet (the default)
TYPE=CIRCLE   A hollow bullet
TYPE=SQUARE   A square bullet

For example, the following code shows a list with hollow squares as the labels. Figure 5.22 shows the result in Netscape.

```
<UL TYPE=SQUARE>
<LI>The Bald Soprano
<LI>The Lesson
<LI>Jack, or the Submission
<LI>The Chairs
</UL>
```

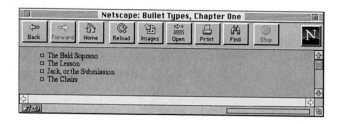

Figure 5.22.

*Bullet types in
Netscape.*

For ordered lists (the <OL> tag), the TYPE attribute also applies but has a different set of values that indicate the numbering scheme used for the list:

TYPE=1   The default; labels the list items with numbers (1, 2, 3)

TYPE=A   Orders the list items with uppercase letters (A, B, C, and so on)

TYPE=a   Orders the list items with lowercase letters (a, b, c, and so on)

TYPE=I   Labels the list items with uppercase Roman numerals (I, II, III, IV, and so on)

TYPE=i   Labels the list items with lowercase Roman numerals (i, ii, iii, iv, and so on)

For example, the following code numbers the outer list with Roman numerals (I, II, III), and the inner list with Arabic numerals (1, 2, 3). Figure 5.23 shows the result in Netscape.

```
<OL TYPE=I>
<LI>Income
     <OL TYPE=1>
     <LI>Wages, Salaries and other Earnings
     <LI>Interest and Dividend Income
     <LI>Gains and Losses
     </OL>
<LI>Itemized Deductions
<LI>Figuring your Tax
</OL>
```

5

Figure 5.23.
Numbered list types in Netscape.

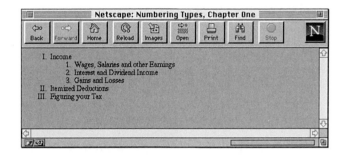

In addition, the START attribute indicates the number from which the list is to be started. The START attribute takes a number regardless of the TYPE. So, if you have an OL tag of TYPE=A with a START=3 attribute, the list starts from C and progresses through D, E, and so on.

Note that because other browsers ignore the START attribute, your lists might be numbered differently in browsers that don't support HTML 3.2. To prevent such renumbering, either avoid using START altogether, or don't refer to specific list items by number in your text.

Finally, each list item tag (<LI>) also has added attributes to control list labels within a single list. The TYPE attribute can take any of the same values that it had in <UL> and <OL>. If you use numbering types in a <UL> list or bullet types in an <OL>, they will be ignored. Changing the TYPE for a list item affects that list item and all the items following it.

Within ordered lists, the <LI> tag can also have the VALUE attribute, which sets the value of this item to a particular number. This also affects all list items after this one, enabling you to restart the numbering within a list at a particular value.

Both TYPE and VALUE are ignored in other browsers, so relying on the effect they produce (for example, to mark specific items within a list as different from other items in a list) is probably not a good idea, because you will lose that emphasis in browsers that don't support these extensions.

These examples show how use of the TYPE attribute to the <OL> tag appears in both Netscape (Figure 5.24) and MacWeb, which does not yet support these new list types (Figure 5.25).

```
<P>Planting Instructions:</P>
<OL>
    <UL TYPE=SQUARE>
    <LI>Bare root plants should be planted immediately,
    or submerged in water until planting
    <LI>Roses should be submerged in water for 4-6 hours
    <LI>Avoid letting other plants dry out
    </UL>
<LI>Dig appropriate-sized holes in planting location
<LI>Dust with fertilizer
<LI>Plant with crown level with soil surface, firming as the hole is
filled in
<LI>Water well and keep damp for the first week.
</OL>
```

Figure 5.24.

*The output in
Netscape.*

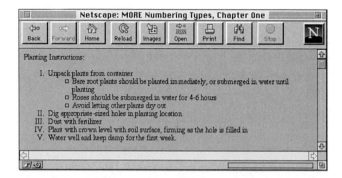

Figure 5.25.

*The output in
MacWeb.*

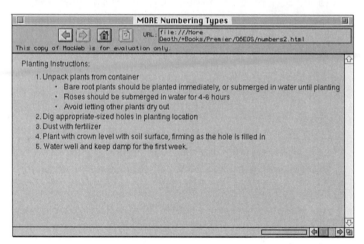

<NOBR> **and** <WBR>

The <NOBR>...</NOBR> tags are the opposite of the <BR> tag. The text inside the NOBR tags
always remains on one line, even if it would have wrapped to two more lines without the NOBR.
NOBR is used for words or phrases that must be kept together on one line, but be careful: long
unbreakable lines can look really strange on your page, and if they are longer than the page
width, they might extend beyond the right edge of the screen.

The <WBR> tag (word break) indicates an appropriate breaking point within a line (typically
one inside a <NOBR>...</NOBR> sequence). Unlike <BR>, which forces a break, <WBR> is only
used where it is appropriate to do so. If the line will fit on the screen just fine, the <WBR> is
ignored.

Exercise 5.1: Create a real HTML page.

EXERCISE

Here's your chance to apply what you've learned and create a real Web page. No more disjointed or overly silly examples. The Web page you'll create in this section is a real one, suitable for use in the real world (or the real world of the Web, at least).

Your task for this example: to design and create a home page for a bookstore called The Bookworm, which specializes in old and rare books.

Plan the Page

In Chapter 2, "Get Organized," I mentioned that planning your Web page before writing it usually makes things easier to build and to maintain. So first, consider the content you want to include on this page. Here are some ideas for topics for this page:

- ☐ The address and phone number of the bookstore
- ☐ A short description of the bookstore and why it is unique
- ☐ Recent titles and authors
- ☐ Upcoming events

Now, come up with some ideas for the content you're going to link from this page. Each title in a list of recently acquired books seems like a logical candidate. You can also create links to more information about the book, its author and publisher, its pricing, maybe even its availability.

The Upcoming Events section might suggest a potential series of links, depending on how much you want to say about each event. If you only have a sentence or two about each one, describing them on this page might make more sense than linking them to another page. Why make your reader wait for each new page to load for just a couple of lines of text?

Other interesting links may arise in the text itself, but for now, the basic link plan will be enough to start with.

Begin with a Framework

First, we'll create the framework that all HTML files must include: the document structuring commands, a title, and an initial heading. Note that the title is descriptive but short; you can save the longer title for the `<H1>` element in the body of the text.

```
<HTML>
<HEAD>
<TITLE>The Bookworm Bookshop</TITLE>
</HEAD>
<BODY>
<H1>The Bookworm: A Better Book Store</H1>
</BODY></HTML>
```

Add Content

Now begin adding the content. Since this is a literary endeavor, a nice quote about old books to start the page would be a nice touch. Because it's a quote, you can use the `<BLOCKQUOTE>` tag to make it stand out as such. Also, the name of the poem is a citation, so use `<CITE>` there, too.

```
<BLOCKQUOTE>
"Old books are best—how tale and rhyme<BR>
Float with us down the stream of time!"<BR>
- Clarence Urmy, <CITE>Old Songs are Best</CITE>
</BLOCKQUOTE>
```

The address of the bookstore is a simple paragraph, with the lines separated by line breaks:

```
<P>The Bookworm Bookshop<BR>
1345 Applewood Dr<BR>
Springfield, CA 94325<BR>
(415) 555-0034
</P>
```

After the address comes the description of the bookstore. I've arranged the description to include a list of features, to make the features stand out from the text better:

```
<P>Since 1933, The Bookworm Bookshop has offered
rare and hard-to-find titles for the discerning reader.
Unlike the bigger bookstore chains, the Bookworm offers:</P>
<UL>
<LI>Friendly, knowledgeable, and courteous help
<LI>Free coffee and juice for our customers
<LI>A well-lit reading room so you can "try before you buy"
<LI>Four friendly cats: Esmerelda, Catherine, Dulcinea and Beatrice
</UL>
```

Add one more note about the hours the store is open, and emphasize the actual numbers:

```
<P>Our hours are <STRONG>10am to 9pm</STRONG> weekdays,
<STRONG>noon to 7</STRONG> on weekends.</P>
```

Add More Content

After the description come the other major topics of this home page: the recent titles and upcoming events sections. Since these are topic headings, we'll label them with second-level head tags:

```
<H2>Recent Titles (as of 25-Sept-95)</H2>
<H2>Upcoming Events</H2>
```

The Recent Titles section itself is a classic link menu, as I described earlier on in this section. Here we'll put the list of titles in an unordered list, with the titles themselves as citations (the `<CITE>` tag):

```
<H2>Recent Titles (as of 25-Sept-95)</H2>
<UL>
```

```
<LI>Sandra Bellweather, <CITE>Belladonna</CITE>
<LI>Jonathan Tin, <CITE>20-Minute Meals for One</CITE>
<LI>Maxwell Burgess, <CITE>Legion of Thunder</CITE>
<LI>Alison Caine, <CITE>Banquo's Ghost</CITE>
</UL>
```

Now, add the anchor tags to create the links. How far should the link extend? Should it include the whole line (author and title), or just the title of the book? This is a matter of preference, but I like to link only as much as necessary to make sure the link stands out from the text. I prefer this approach to overwhelming the text. Here, I've linked only the titles of the books:

```
<UL>
<LI>Sandra Bellweather, <A HREF="belladonna.html">
<CITE>Belladonna</CITE></A>
<LI>Johnathan Tin, <A HREF="20minmeals.html">
<CITE>20-Minute Meals for One</CITE></A>
<LI>Maxwell Burgess, <A HREF="legion.html">
<CITE>Legion of Thunder</CITE></A>
<LI>Alison Caine, <A HREF="banquo.html">
<CITE>Banquo's Ghost</CITE></A>
</UL>
```

Note that I've put the `<CITE>` tag inside the link tag `<A>`. I could have just as easily put it outside the anchor tag; character style tags can go just about anywhere. But as I mentioned once before, be careful not to overlap tags. Your browser may not be able to understand what is going on. In other words, don't do this:

```
<A HREF="banquo.html"><CITE>Banquo's Ghost</A></CITE>
```

Next, let's move on to the Upcoming Events section. In the planning section we weren't sure if this would be another link menu, or if the content would work better solely on this page. Again, this is a matter of preference. Here, because the amount of extra information is minimal, it doesn't make much sense to create links for just a couple of sentences. So for this section we'll create a menu list (using the `<UL>` tag), which results in short paragraphs (bulleted in some browsers). I've boldfaced a few phrases near the beginning of each paragraph. Those phrases emphasize a summary of the event itself so that each paragraph can be scanned quickly and ignored if the reader isn't interested.

```
<H2>Upcoming Events</H2>
<UL>
<LI><B>The Wednesday Evening Book Review</B> meets, appropriately, on Wednesday
evenings at PM for coffee and a round-table discussion. Call the Bookworm for
information on joining the group and this week's reading assignment.
<LI><B>The Children's Hour</B> happens every Saturday at 1pm and includes
reading, games, and other activities. Cookies and milk are served.
<LI><B>Carole Fenney</B> will be at the Bookworm on Friday, September 16, to
read from her book of poems <CITE>Spiders in the Web.</CITE> <LI><B>The Bookworm
will be closed</B> October 1 to remove a family of bats that has nested in the
tower. We like the company, but not the mess they leave behind!
</UL>
```

5

Sign the Page

To finish off, sign what you have so your readers know who did the work. Here, I've separated the signature from the text with a rule line. I've also included the most recent revision date, my name as the "Webmaster" (cute Web jargon meaning the person in charge of a Web site), and a basic copyright (with a copyright symbol indicated by the numeric escape ©):

```
<HR>
<ADDRESS>
Last Updated: 25-Sept-95<BR>
WebMaster: Laura Lemay lemay@bookworm.com<BR>
&#169; copyright 1995 the Bookworm<BR>
</ADDRESS>
```

Review What You've Got

Here's the HTML code for the page, so far:

```
<HTML>
<HEAD>
<TITLE>The Bookworm Bookshop</TITLE>
</HEAD>
<BODY>
<H1>The Bookworm: A Better Book Store</H1>
<BLOCKQUOTE>
"Old books are best—how tale and rhyme<BR>
Float with us down the stream of time!"<BR>
- Clarence Urmy, <CITE>Old Songs are Best</CITE>
</BLOCKQUOTE>
<P>The Bookworm Bookshop<BR>
1345 Applewood Dr<BR>
Springfield, CA 94325<BR>
 (415) 555-0034
</P>
<P>Since 1933, The Bookworm Bookshop has offered rare
and hard-to-find titles for the discerning reader.
Unlike the bigger bookstore chains, the Bookworm offers:
<UL>
<LI>Friendly, knowledgeable, and courteous help
<LI>Free coffee and juice for our customers
<LI>A well-lit reading room so you can "try before you buy"
<LI>Four friendly cats: Esmerelda, Catherine, Dulcinea and Beatrice
</UL>
<P>Our hours are <STRONG>10am to 9pm</STRONG> weekdays,
<STRONG>noon to 7</STRONG> on weekends.</P>
<H2>Recent Titles (as of 25-Sept-95)</H2>
<UL>
<LI>Sandra Bellweather, <A HREF="belladonna.html">
<CITE>Belladonna</CITE></A>
<LI>Johnathan Tin, <A HREF="20minmeals.html">
<CITE>20-Minute Meals for One</CITE></A>
<LI>Maxwell Burgess, <A HREF="legion.html">
<CITE>Legion of Thunder</CITE></A>
```

```
<LI>Alison Caine, <A HREF="banquo.html">
<CITE>Banquo's Ghost</CITE></A>
</UL>
<H2>Upcoming Events</H2>
<UL>
<LI><B>The Wednesday Evening Book Review</B> meets, appropriately, on
Wednesday evenings at PM for coffee and a round-table discussion. Call
the Bookworm for information on joining the group and this week's
reading assignment.
<LI><B>The Children's Hour</B> happens every Saturday at 1pm and includes
reading, games, and other activities. Cookies and milk are served.
<LI><B>Carole Fenney</B> will be at the Bookworm on Friday, September 16,
to read from her book of poems <CITE>Spiders in the Web.</CITE>
<LI><B>The Bookworm will be closed</B> October 1 to remove a family
of bats that has nested in the tower. We like the company, but not
the mess they leave behind!
</UL>
<HR>
<ADDRESS>
Last Updated: 25-Sept-95<BR>
WebMaster: Laura Lemay lemay@bookworm.com<BR>
&#169; copyright 1995 the Bookworm<BR>
</ADDRESS>
</BODY></HTML>
```

So, now we have some headings, some text, some topics, and some links. This is the basis for an excellent Web page. At this point, with most of the content in, consider what else you might want to create links for, or what other features you might want to add to this page.

For example, in the introductory section, a note was made of the four cats owned by the bookstore. Although you didn't plan for it in the original organization, you could easily create Web pages describing each cat (and showing pictures), and then link them back to this page, one link (and one page) per cat.

Is describing the cats important? As the designer of the page, that's up to you to decide. You could link all kinds of things from this page if you had interesting reasons to link them (and something to link to). Link the bookstore's address to the local chamber of commerce. Link the quote to an online encyclopedia of quotes. Link the note about free coffee to the Coffee Home Page.

I'll talk more about good things to link (and how not to get carried away when you link) on Day 6, "Designing Effective Web Pages," when you learn about Dos and Don'ts for good Web pages. My reason for bringing this point up here is that once you have some content in place in your Web pages, opportunities for extending the pages and linking to other places may arise, opportunities you didn't think of when you created your original plan. So, when you're just about finished with a page, it's often a good idea to stop and review what you have, both in the plan and in your Web page.

5

For the purposes of this example, we'll stop here and stick with the links we've got. We're close enough to being done that I don't want to make this chapter longer than it already is!

Test the Result

Now that all the code is in place, you can preview the results in a browser. Figure 5.26 shows how it looks in Netscape. Actually, this is how it looks after you fix the spelling errors and forgotten closing tags and other strange bugs that always seem to creep into an HTML file the first time you create it. This always seems to happen no matter how good you get at it. If you use an HTML editor or some other help tool it will be easier, but there always seems to be mistakes. That's what previewing is for, so you can catch those problems before you actually make the document available to other people.

Figure 5.26.

The Bookworm home page, almost done.

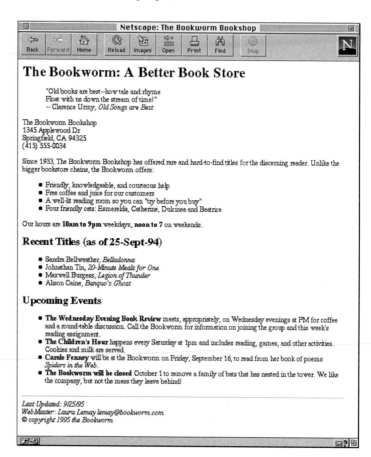

Looks good so far, but in the browsers I used to test it, the description of the store and the Recent Titles sections tend to run together; there isn't enough distinction between them (see Figure 5.27).

Figure 5.27.

A problem section.

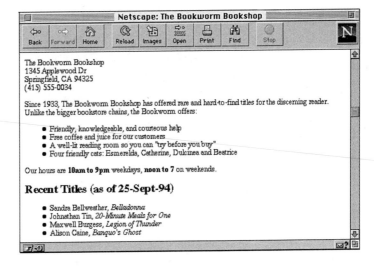

You have two choices for making them more distinct:

☐ Add rule lines (<HR>) in between sections.

☐ Change the <H2> tags to <H1> for more emphasis of the individual sections.

With design issues like this, it often comes down to a matter of preference and what looks the best in as many browsers as you can get your hands on. Either choice is equally correct, as both are visually interesting, and you haven't had to do strange things in HTML in order to get it to do what you want.

I settled on a single rule line between the description and the Recent Titles section. Figure 5.28 shows how it came out.

Get Fancy

Everything I've included on that page up to this point has been straight up HTML 2.0, so its readable in all browsers and will look pretty much the same in all browsers. Once I've got the page to this point, however, I can add HTML extensions that won't change the page for many readers, but might make it look a little fancier in browsers that do support these extensions.

5

Figure 5.28.

*The final Book-
worm home page.*

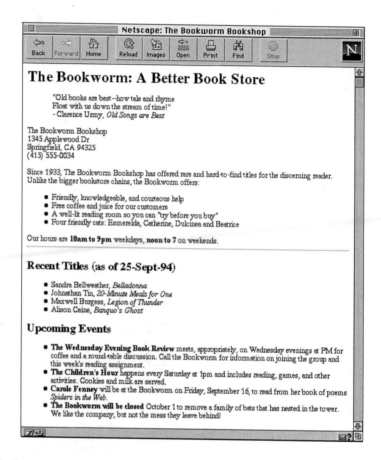

So what extensions shall we use? I picked two:

☐ Centering the title of the page, the quote, and the bookstore's address

☐ Making a slight font size change to the address itself

To center the topmost part of the page, we'll use the `<DIV>` tag around the heading, the quote, and the bookshop's address, like this:

```
<DIV ALIGN=CENTER>
<H1>The Bookworm: A Better Book Store</H1>
<BLOCKQUOTE>
"Old books are best—how tale and rhyme<BR>
Float with us down the stream of time!"<BR>
- Clarence Urmy, <CITE>Old Songs are Best</CITE>
</BLOCKQUOTE>
<P>The Bookworm Bookshop<BR>
1345 Applewood Dr<BR>
Springfield, CA 94325<BR>
(415) 555-0034
</P>
</DIV>
```

5

To change the font size of the address, add a `<FONT>` tag around the lines for the address:

```
<P><FONT SIZE=+1>The Bookworm Bookshop<BR>
1345 Applewood Dr<BR>
Springfield, CA 94325<BR>
(415) 555-0034
</FONT></P>
```

Figure 5.29 shows the final result, with extensions, in Netscape. Note that neither of these changes affect the readability of the page in browsers that don't support `<DIV>` or `<FONT>`; the page still works just fine without them. It just looks different.

Figure 5.29.

The final Book-worm home page, with extensions.

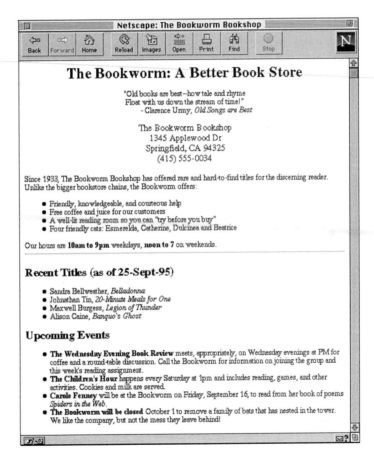

When should you use HTML extensions? The general rule that I like to follow is to use extensions only when using them will not interfere with other browsers. But just as with the type of content to provide, it's up to you to decide whether you'll use extensions, and if you do, which ones you'll use. You'll learn more about extensions and how to design well with them in Chapter 11, "Writing and Designing Web Pages: Dos and Don'ts."

Summary

Tags, tags, and more tags! In this chapter, you've learned about most of the remaining tags in the HTML 2.0 language for presenting text, quite of a few of the HTML extensions for additional text formatting and presentation, and put together a real-life HTML home page. You could stop now and create quite presentable Web pages. But there's more cool stuff to come, so don't put the book down yet.

Table 5.2 presents a quick summary of all the tags and extensions you've learned about in this chapter.

Table 5.2. HTML Tags from Chapter 5.

Tag	Attribute	Use
`<EM>...</EM>`		Emphasized text.
`<STRONG>...</STRONG>`		Strongly emphasized text.
`<CODE>...</CODE>`		A code sample.
`<KBD>...</KBD>`		Text to be typed in by the user.
`<VAR>...</VAR>`		A variable name.
`<SAMP>...</SAMP>`		Sample text.
`<DFN>...</DFN>`		A definition, or a term about to be defined.
`<CITE>...</CITE>`		A citation.
`<B>...</B>`		Bold text.
`<I>...</I>`		Italic text.
`<TT>...</TT>`		Text in typewriter font (a monospaced font such as Courier).
`<U>...</U>`		(HTML 3.2 extension) Underlined text.
`<S>...</S>`		(HTML 3.2 extension) Strikethrough text.
`<BIG>...</BIG>`		(HTML 3.2 extension) Text in a larger font than the text around it.
`<SMALL>...</SMALL>`		(HTML 3.2 extension) Text in a smaller font than the text around it.
`<SUB>...</SUB>`		(HTML 3.2 extension) Subscript text.
`<SUP>...</SUP>`		(HTML 3.2 extension) Superscript text.

5

Tag	Attribute	Use
`<PRE>...</PRE>`		Preformatted text; all spaces, tabs, and returns are retained. Text is also printed in a monospaced font.
`<HR>`		A horizontal rule line at the given position in the text.
	`SIZE`	(HTML 3.2 extension) The thickness of the rule, in pixels.
	`WIDTH`	(HTML 3.2 extension) The width of the rule, either in exact pixels or as a percentage of page width (for example, 50 percent).
	`ALIGN`	(HTML 3.2 extension) The alignment of the rule on the page. Possible values are `LEFT`, `RIGHT`, and `CENTER`.
	`NOSHADE`	(HTML 3.2 extension) Display the rule without three-dimensional shading.
` `		A line break; start the next character on the next line (but do not create a new paragraph or list item).
`<BLOCKQUOTE>...</BLOCKQUOTE>`		A quotation longer than a few words.
`<ADDRESS>...</ADDRESS>`		A "signature" for each Web page; typically occurs near the bottom of each document and contains contact or copyright information.
`<P>, <H1-6>`	`ALIGN=LEFT`	(HTML 3.2 extension) Left-justifies the text within that paragraph or heading.
	`ALIGN=RIGHT`	(HTML 3.2 extension) Right-justifies the text within that paragraph or heading.
	`ALIGN=CENTER`	(HTML 3.2 extension) Centers the text within that paragraph or heading.
`<DIV>...</DIV>`	`ALIGN=LEFT`	(HTML 3.2 extension) Left-justifies all the content between the opening and closing tags.

continues

5

Table 5.2. continued

Tag	Attribute	Use
	ALIGN=RIGHT	(HTML 3.2 extension) Right-justifies all the content between the opening and closing tags.
	ALIGN=CENTER	(HTML 3.2 extension) Centers all the content between the opening and closing tags.
<CENTER>...</CENTER>		(Netscape extension) Centers all the content between the opening and closing tags.
<FONT>...</FONT>	SIZE	(HTML 3.2 extension) The size of the font to change to, either from 1 to 7 (default is 3) or as a relative number using +N or -N. Relative font sizes are based on the value of <BASEFONT>.
	FACE	(HTML 3.2 extension) The name of the font to change to, as a list of fonts to choose from.
<BASEFONT>	SIZE	(HTML 3.2 extension) The default font size on which relative font size changes are based.
<BLINK>...</BLINK>		(Netscape extension) Causes the enclosed text to have a blinking effect.
<UL>	TYPE	(HTML 3.2 extension) The type of bullet to label the list items. Possible values are DISC, CIRCLE, and SQUARE.
<OL>	TYPE	(HTML 3.2 extension) The type of number to label the list items. Possible values are A, a, I, i, and 1.
	START	(HTML 3.2 extension) The number with which to start the list.
<LI>	TYPE	(HTML 3.2 extension) The type of bullet (in <UL> lists), or the type of number (in <OL> lists). TYPE has the same values as its <UL> or <OL> equivalent, and affects this item and all those following it.

5

Tag	Attribute	Use
	VALUE	(HTML 3.2 extension) (In `<OL>` lists only.) The number with which to label this item. Affects the numbering of all list items after it.
`<NOBR>...</NOBR>`		(extension) Do not wrap the enclosed text.
`<WBR>`		(extension) Wrap the text at this point only if necessary.

Q&A

Q If there are line breaks in HTML, can I also do page breaks?

A There is no page break tag in HTML. Consider what the term "page" means in a Web document. If each document on the Web is a single "page," then the only way to produce a page break is to split your HTML document into separate files and link them.

Even within a single document, browsers have no concept of a page; each HTML document simply scrolls by continuously. If you consider a single screen a page, you still cannot have what results in a page break in HTML. This is because the screen size in each browser is different, and is based on not only the browser itself but also the size of the monitor on which it runs, the number of lines defined, the font being currently used, and other factors that you cannot control from HTML.

When designing your Web pages, don't get too hung up on the concept of a "page" the way it exists in paper documents. Remember, HTML's strength is its flexibility for multiple kinds of systems and formats. Think instead in terms of creating small chunks of information and how they link together to form a complete presentation.

Q What about that pop quiz you threatened?

A OK, smarty. Without looking at Table 5.2, list all eight logical style tags and what they're used for. Explain why you should use the logical tags instead of the physical tags. Then create an HTML page that uses each one in a sentence, and test it in several browsers to get a feel for how it looks in each.

Q Why doesn't underlined text (the `<U>` tag) show up in Netscape 2.0? Netscape supports HTML 3.0, doesn't it?

A Netscape supports some of the old HTML 3.0 specification, now obsolete, and most of HTML 3.2. Underlined text is one of its omissions, presumably because underlined text looks too much like a link. Other browsers, for example, Internet Explorer, do support underlining.

5

Q **How can I include em dashes or curly quotes (typesetter's quotes) in my HTML files?**

A You can't. Neither em dashes nor curly quotes are defined as part of the ISO-Latin-1 character set, and therefore those characters are not available in HTML. The old HTML 3.0 specification defines special character entities for these characters, but as I write this, no browsers currently support them.

Q **"Blink is the HTML equivalent of fingernails on a blackboard"? Isn't that a little harsh?**

A I couldn't resist. :)

Many people absolutely detest blink and will tell you so at a moment's notice, with a passion usually reserved for politics and religion. There are people who might ignore your pages simply because you use blink. Why alienate your audience and distract from your content for the sake of a cheesy effect?

Chapter 6

HTML Assistants: Editors and Converters

After the bushel of tags and HTML information I've thrown at you over the last couple of chapters, you're probably just the smallest bit overwhelmed. You may be wondering how on earth you're supposed to remember all these tags and all their various attributes, remember which tag goes where and which ones have opening and closing tags, and a host of other details.

After you've written a couple thousand HTML pages, remembering everything isn't all that difficult. But until you do have that many pages under your belt, sometimes it can be rough, particularly if you're writing all your HTML files in a plain text editor.

This is where HTML editors and converters come in. Both HTML editors and converters make writing HTML files easier—or at least they help you get started and often take away a lot of the drudgery in composing HTML. In this chapter, I'll survey some of the more common editors and converters available that claim to make writing HTML easier. These tools fall into the following categories:

☐ Tag editors—text editors that help you create HTML files by inserting tags or managing links

☐ WYSIWYG and near-WYSIWYG editors

☐ Converters—programs that let you convert files created by popular word processing programs or other formats to HTML

This chapter is by no means a complete catalog of the available tools for HTML, only a sample of some of the more popular tools for various platforms. HTML tools sprout like weeds, and by the time you read this, it's likely that there will be newer, better, and more powerful tools for HTML development. For this reason, Appendix A, "Sources for Further Information," provides some pointers to lists of editors and filters. These lists are being constantly updated and are the best source for finding tools that may not be described in this chapter.

Many of the editors described in this section are also contained on the CD-ROM that comes with this book.

Do You Need an Editor?

As I mentioned early on in this book, you don't technically need a special HTML editor in order to do pages for the Web. In fact, it could be argued that one of the reasons the Web became so popular so quickly was that you didn't need any special equipment to publish on the Web. You didn't have to buy a lot of software or upgrade your computer system. Creating pages for publishing on the Web was, and still is, free.

But the Web has changed a lot. HTML itself has grown a great deal since those days, not only in the number of available tags, but also in complexity. If you're like me and you've been following it while it's been changing, it hasn't been that bad. But if you're just starting out now, you've got a lot of catching up to do.

Editors can help you get over the initial hurdles. They can help you keep track of the tags and create basic pages. If you're interested in learning HTML in depth, they can help teach you good HTML coding style and structure so that when you move on to more advanced forms of HTML, you have that baseline to build on. For this reason, you may find that investing a little cash in an editor may pay off in the long run.

Later on, once you've done a lot of pages and you understand how HTML works, you may find that the editor you're working in isn't quite as useful as it was when you were starting out. You may find it fine for simple pages or for the first initial pass of a page, but not quite as good for adding advanced stuff. At that time, you may end up working in a plain text editor after all.

Try out a couple of the editors in this chapter; all are available in trial versions for down-loading, so there's no cost or risk.

Tag Editors

Tag editor is a term I use to describe a simple stand-alone text editor or an extension to another editor. Tag editors help you write HTML documents by inserting the tags for you. They make no claim to being WYSIWYG—all they do is save you some typing, and they help you remember which tags are which. Instead of trying to remember whether which tag is which, or having to type both the opening and closing parts of a long tag by hand, tag editors usually provide windows or buttons with meaningful names that insert the tag into the text for you at the appropriate spot. You're still working with text, and you're still working directly in HTML, but tag editors take away a lot of the drudgery involved in creating HTML documents.

Most tag editors work best if you already have a document prepared in regular text with none of the tags. Using tag editors as you type a document is slightly more difficult; it's best to type the text and then apply the style after you're done.

HTML Assistant Pro (Windows)

HTML Assistant Pro (shown in Figure 6.1) by Harold Harawitz and distributed by Brooklyn North Software Works was one of the first HTML editors, and it continues to be one of the best and most popular. Using buttons from a tool bar and various menu commends, HTML Assistant allows you to insert HTML tags as you type and to preview the result with your favorite browser. The interface is simple and intuitive, with all the important tags available on a toolbar.

Figure 6.1.

HTML Assistant.

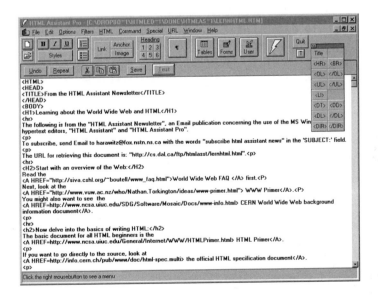

To get the most use out of HTML Assistant, you'll need to know at least the basics of HTML, and to preferably have a good idea of which tags go where and what they are used for. HTML Assistant supports all of HTML 2.0, including forms and many of the HTML extensions. If there is a tag HTML Assistant doesn't currently support, you can add it to a User Tools menu and then insert that tag with the click of a mouse button.

One of its best features is the capability to collect URLs from hotlists or bookmark files generated by Mosaic and Cello so you can create links to those URLs without having to retype them. I also like the table and forms assistants, although I found their interface less intuitive than the rest of the program. Once I figured it out, however, inserting sophisticated tables and forms became easy.

HTML Assistant comes in two versions: a freeware version with enough basic features for many HTML files, and a commercial version (HTML Assistant Pro 2, available for $99.95) that includes many more features (more HTML tags, a nice spell checker, a tool for automatic page creation, and other options), support, and a manual.

Visit the home page for HTML Assistant Pro at http://www.brooknorth.com/.

HotDog (Windows)

HotDog, from Sausage Software, is a full-featured HTML tag editor with support for just about every HTML feature, either existing or proposed, including HTML 2.0, tables, forms, all the Netscape extensions, and HTML 3.2. Like HTML Assistant, HotDog has two versions: a shareware standard version ($29.99), which should be fine for most people doing basic HTML work, and a professional version, HotDog Pro ($99.95) with more features (unlimited file sizes, more customization options, and a spell checker). Figure 6.2 shows the HotDog main window.

Using HotDog is quite intuitive, allowing you to insert most of the common tags through well-labeled buttons on a toolbar. Unlike HTML Assistant, one very nice feature is that when you start a new document, all the HTML structuring tags are inserted for you: <HTML>, <HEAD>, and <BODY>. Since I include these tags in all my HTML files, having them included by default saves some time over inserting them by hand. HotDog's linking feature is also quite nice, allowing you to build a URL from parts and showing you the result as you build it.

Also very nice is the tables editor, which builds the table using spreadsheet-like cells (you haven't learned about tables in HTML yet; you'll learn about them in Chapter 13, "Tables"). You enter your table data and headings into the table cells in the editor, and when you're done, HotDog inserts all the right HTML tags for the table.

Figure 6.2.
HotDog Pro.

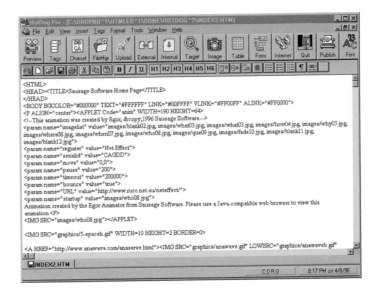

HotDog's biggest drawback is the fact that it tries to support everything nearly equally, from the basic HTML 2.0 tags to the advanced Netscape and Internet Explorer extensions to even the proposed HTML 3.2 features that have not yet been implemented in any browsers (not even Netscape). Unless you know exactly what you're doing and which tags you should be using, it's easy to become confused about what you can use and the results you expect to see in your favorite browser. Plus, there's that many more tags to search through for the one you really want even if you do know exactly which tags are supported where. The inclusion of all these extra tags may make HotDog very complete, but it complicates the use of an otherwise terrific editor.

You can get more information about both versions from Sausage Software's Web site at `http://www.sausage.com/`.

WebEdit (Windows)

Like HotDog, the shareware Ken Nesbitt's WebEdit (see Figure 6.3) purports to support the full suite of HTML 2.0, 3.2, and Netscape tags. Also like HotDog, this means dozens of tags and options and alternatives to choose from without any distinction of which tags are actually useful for real-life Web presentations, which needlessly complicates the use of the editor for creating simple pages.

Figure 6.3.
WebEdit.

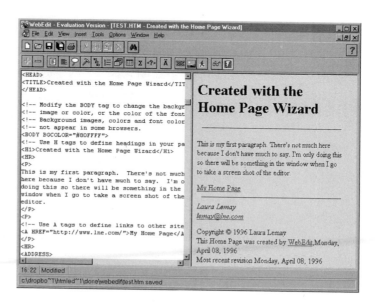

If you know which tags to ignore, however, WebEdit becomes a very nice editor to work in. The toolbar provides immediate access to each element, although I had some initial trouble figuring out which icon went with what set of tags. The template page is particularly nice, putting in not only the basic structuring tags but also the date and time and some initial text so you have something to start with.

WebEdit allows you to preview your work either in the browser of your choice or in a built-in previewer. The previewer is particularly interesting, as it allows you to edit the page on one side of the screen and view the immediate result on the other side. The previewer supports a subset of the tags available in the editor itself: all of HTML 2.0, and selected extensions.

WebEdit is available as a downloadable 30-day trial version, after which time you must pay for it. The cost is $39.99 for educational, non-profit, or home users, and $79.99 for commercial users, making it one of the more reasonable tag editors. Find out more about WebEdit from http://www.nesbitt.com/.

HTML.edit (Macintosh)

HTML.edit is a HyperCard-based HTML tag editor, but it does not require HyperCard to run. It provides menus and buttons for inserting HTML tags into text files, as well as features for automatic indexing (for creating those hyperlinked table-of-contents lists) and automatic conversion of text files to HTML. Figure 6.4 shows HTML.edit's editing page.

6

Figure 6.4.
HTML.edit.

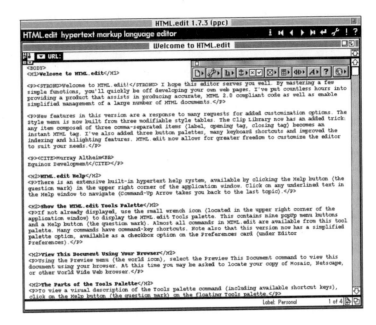

Its most interesting feature, however, is its Index page, which collects and organizes a set of related HTML documents, sort of like a project in THINK C or a book file in FrameMaker. Once a file is listed on the Index page, that file appears in a list of files that you can link between, and so you can create navigation links between related files quickly and easily. The Index page allows you to keep track of your entire presentation and the pages inside it.

I found the interface to HTML.edit somewhat confusing to figure out, but a quick read through the online help answered most of my questions. HTML.edit supports all of HTML 2.0, including forms and tables. Extensions are included as part of a custom tags menu which can be customized to include any new extensions.

HTML.edit runs on both 68K and PowerPC Macintoshes, and is freeware. Visit http://ogopogo.nttc.edu/tools/HTMLedit/HTMLedit.html for information about HTML.edit.

HTML Web Weaver and World Wide Web Weaver (Macintosh)

HTML Web Weaver and World Wide Web Weaver are similar programs with similar interfaces and philosophies. Both written by Robert C. Best, HTML Web Weaver is shareware ($25, with a 30-day evaluation period) and has fewer features than the commercial World Wide Web Weaver ($50 basic price, cheaper for education, free upgrades to newer versions). Figure 6.5 shows World Wide Web Weaver.

6

Figure 6.5.

World Wide Web Weaver.

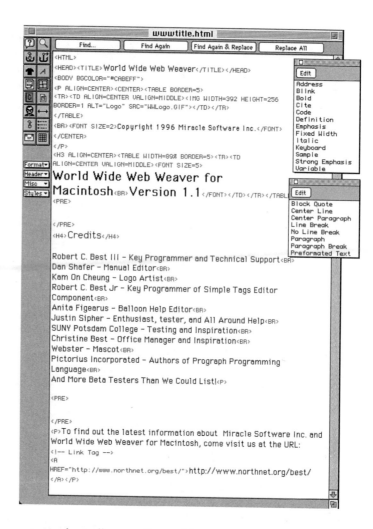

Both Web Weaver programs are basically tag editors with some WYSIWYG capabilities. Unlike other tag editors, in which all the text and tags are in the same font and size, the Web Weaver programs format the tags in a different color from the rest of the text, and format the text itself as well (for example, when you apply a heading to a line of text, the Web Weaver programs increase the font size of the heading). Both allow you to preview the result in your favorite browser.

Both Web Weaver Programs work best when you have a base of text to start with and you apply tags to various portions of the text. I found it difficult to apply tags as I was typing (and you don't get the formatting as easily that way, either).

HTML Web Weaver provides basic capabilities for standard HTML 2.0, including forms and images. World Wide Web Weaver has extensive other features including tables and even Netscape 2.0's frames capabilities as well as search and replace. The home page for both programs notes that few new features will be added to HTML Web Weaver, making World Wide Web Weaver most likely the better choice of the two. Get more information and download copies of each from `http://www.miracleinc.com/`.

HTML Extensions for Alpha and BBedit (Macintosh)

Alpha and BBedit are two of the more popular shareware text editors available for the Macintosh. Both provide mechanisms to add extensions for working in particular languages and writing text that conforms to a particular style. Extensions exist for both Alpha and BBedit to help with writing HTML pages.

There are significant advantages to using a standard text editor with extensions as opposed to using a dedicated HTML tag editor. For one thing, general text editors tend to provide more features for writing than a simple HTML text editor, including search and replace and spell-checking. Also, if you're used to working in one of these editors, being able to continue to use it for your HTML development means that you don't have to take the time to learn a new program to do your work.

If you use the Alpha editor, versions after 5.92b include the HTML extensions in the main distribution. You can get Alpha and its HTML extensions from `http://www.cs.umd.edu/~keleher/alpha.html`.

For BBedit, the BBedit HTML Extensions are available from most Mac shareware archives, or from `http://www.uji.es/bbedit-html-extensions.html`.

tkHTML (UNIX/X11)

tkHTML, by Liem Bahneman, is a simple freeware graphical HTML tag editor for the X11 Window System that uses the TCL language and the tk toolkit (you don't need to have either installed). Menu items allow you to insert tags into your text, either by inserting the tag and then typing, or by selecting text and choosing the tag that text should have. tkEdit easily allows you to convert existing text to HTML, and a Preview button automatically previews your HTML files using Netscape, Mosaic, or Lynx (Netscape is the default). Figure 6.6 shows tkHTML.

tkHTML supports all of HTML 2.0 and many extensions, including those for tables. Visit `http://www.ssc.com/~roland/tkHTML/tkHTML.html` for more information about tkHTML.

Figure 6.6.
tkHTML.

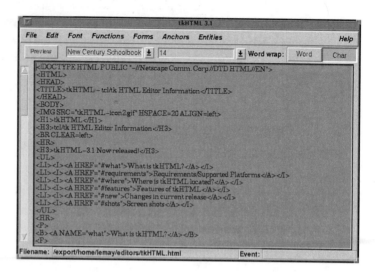

AsWedit (UNIX)

AsWedit (short for AdvaSoft's Web Editor, presumably, and shown in Figure 6.7), also for the X Window System running Motif and available for many different UNIX flavors, is a context-sensitive HTML editor. Context sensitive means that different tags and options are available depending on where you've put the cursor in the HTML code. So if the cursor is inside a list, the only choice you have is to include a list item, for example.

Figure 6.7.
AsWedit.

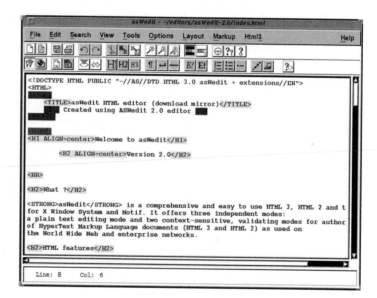

Context sensitivity makes editing using AsWedit interesting, as it forces you to use correct HTML style at all times. But it was confusing for me to figure out what was going on when I first tried using it, and if you don't already have a basic idea of what HTML can do and what tags are available in what context, it can be confusing to use.

AsWedit supports all of HTML 2.0, all of HTML 3.2, as well as most HTML extensions. It also provides an option to disable HTML 3.2 so that the only available tags are from the standard HTML 2.0 set.

There are two versions of AsWedit: a basic version, free for educational users and for evaluation by others, and a $149 commercial version with more features, support, and a manual. You can get information about both versions from AdvaSoft's home page at `http://www.advasoft.com/`.

HTML Tools for Emacs (UNIX)

If you prefer to work in Emacs, the popular text editor-slash-kitchen sink, you have several Emacs packages (modes) to choose from, including:

- html-mode, the original mode for writing HTML, available at `ftp://archive.cis.ohio-state.edu/pub/gnu/emacs/elisp-archive/modes/html-mode.el.Z`.
- html-helper-mode, an enhanced version of the above. You can get information about it at `http://www.santafe.edu/~nelson/tools/`.

If you use Emacs extensively, you might also want to look at William Perry's Emacs w3-mode, which turns Emacs into a fully featured Web browser with support for most advanced features of HTML. It includes support for quite a bit of HTML 3.2, many of the Netscape extensions, and just about anything else you can imagine. Get more information about w3-mode from `http://www.cs.indiana.edu/elisp/w3/docs.html`.

WYSIWYG and Near-WYSIWYG Editors

6

The concept of a true WYSIWYG (what you see it what you get) editor for HTML files is a bit of a fallacy, since (as I've harped on earlier) each browser formats HTML documents in different ways, for different size screens. However, for simple documents, with an understanding of what HTML can and cannot do, the editors described in this section can be just fine for creating simple pages and presentations.

I've made the distinction in this section between WYSIWYG and "near-WYSIWYG" editors. The former are editors that claim to allow you to write HTML files without ever seeing a single tag; everything you need to create an HTML page is available directly in the program.

"Near-WYSIWYG" editors provide a WYSIWYG environment without trying overly hard to hide the tags. They may allow you to toggle between a tag view and a WYSIWYG view, or you may be able to view the tags using a menu item.

Netscape Navigator Gold (Windows, Macintosh)

Netscape Navigator Gold is an enhanced version of the Netscape Navigator browser which included integrated WYSIWYG HTML editing capabilities.

If you're used to using Netscape as your browser (as most of you probably are), Navigator Gold will look quite familiar. In fact, except for the addition of an Edit button on the toolbar, it looks and behaves identically to the regular Netscape Navigator. When you choose Edit, the HTML editor window appears (as shown in Figure 6.8). In the edit windows, you can change the text, add new HTML elements, rearrange formatting, and change colors.

Figure 6.8.

Netscape Naviga-tor Gold (Editing Window).

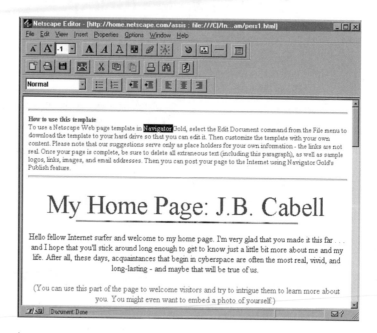

The Netscape HTML editor is very nicely done, with HTML elements all available through toolbar items with well-designed icons and an intuitive layout. The integration with the browser, including Netscape's file-upload features, means that in many cases you can view your pages on a server, make changes to them using the editor, and then upload them back to the server in a few easy steps.

Netscape Gold supports many common HTML tags, including, of course, the Netscape HTML extensions. New or unsupported tags can be entered by hand. Two obvious omissions from Gold's feature set, however, are forms and tables, and, even worse, if you edit an existing page with tables in it, Netscape Gold removes the table formatting entirely (forms are retained using the extra tag features). But for most basic uses of HTML, Netscape Gold is great for editing pages and creating new ones.

Netscape Navigator Gold is available for Windows 95, Windows NT, UNIX, and Macintosh. You can download it from Netscape site at http://home.netscape.com/. Gold has the same license agreement as Navigator does—it's free for educational and non-profit use, with an evaluation period for everyone else. Netscape Gold costs $79. If you own a license for Netscape Navigator, the upgrade to Netscape Gold is only $29.

Microsoft Internet Assistant (Windows)

Internet Assistant is a plug-in for Word for Windows 6.0 that allows you to create your HTML files directly in Word and then save them as HTML (see Figure 6.9). If you stick to the style sheet included with Internet Assistant and you understand HTML's limitations, this can make creating HTML documents almost easy.

Figure 6.9.

Internet Assistant.

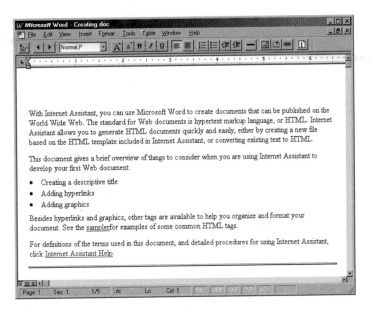

Internet Assistant also doubles as a Web browser, allowing you to visit sites on the Web from within Word. The browser support is quite slow in comparison to dedicated browsers such as Netscape or Mosaic, however.

You can get Internet Assistant from Microsoft's Web site, `http://www.microsoft.com/msword/Internet/IA/default.htm`, or by calling their support lines.

NOTE

> Microsoft has demonstrated a version of Internet Assistant for the Macintosh and promises a released version soon. At this time it has not yet been released, but may be available by the time you read this.

SoftQuad HoTMetaL Pro 2.0 (Windows, Macintosh, UNIX)

SoftQuad HoTMetaL Pro (see Figure 6.10) is a unique editor that allows very near-WYSIWYG capabilities without trying to hide the fact that you're still working very much in HTML. In HoTMetaL, the tags are represented by flag-type objects that can be inserted only in legal places on the page. So, for example, you can't put regular paragraphs into a <HEAD> section. This is a good thing; it means that if you use HoTMetaL, you cannot write an HTML document that does not conform to correct HTML style.

The text you type in between the HTML tag objects appears in a font roughly equivalent to what might appear on your screen in a graphical browser. You can also choose to hide the tags so that you can get a better idea of what it'll look like when you're done.

HoTMetaL comes in two versions, a freeware version and a "professional" commercial version. The freeware version (called, appropriately, HoTMetaL Free) has all the basic capabilities and support for HTML 2.0, HTML 3.2, and all the Netscape extensions. The commercial version, HoTMetaL Pro 2.0, for $195, has additional features for importing and converting files from word processors, a spell checker, free updates when new tags appear, a thesaurus, keyboard macros, and full support.

Information about HoTMetaL and SoftQuad's other SGML-based tools is available at `http://www.sq.com/`.

6

Figure 6.10.

HoTMetaL Pro 2.0.

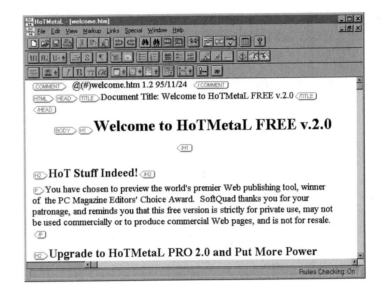

PageMill (Macintosh)

Adobe's PageMill, a commercial HTML editor costing $149, bills itself as "The easiest way to create pages for the World Wide Web." And, using PageMill is very easy indeed. The main window (shown in Figure 6.11) has a simple tool bar, with most of the main HTML styles (headings, paragraphs, addresses, plus character styles) available as menu items. You can enter text and apply styles to that text, or you can choose a style first, and then type in that style. For most simple HTML elements, PageMill is indeed WYSIWYG and very easy to use.

PageMill's handling of images and links is particularly nice, allowing you to drag and drop images into a page, and drag and drop between open pages to link between them. Double-clicking images brings up an image window with features for applying special image tricks such as transparency and interlacing (which you'll learn about in Chapter 8, "Creating Images for the Web").

PageMill supports much of HTML 2.0, plus several of the more common HTML extensions (centering, page backgrounds, and so on). It does not support tables or any of the newer Netscape 2.0 or Internet Explorer extensions, but you can enter any raw HTML tags onto the page in the appropriate places for those new features (which sort of defeats the purpose of being WYSIWYG, but at least you're not tied only to what PageMill supports).

One strange oddity with PageMill is the HTML it generates after you're done creating your pages. Remember the <P> tag, for paragraphs? PageMill doesn't use paragraph tags; it inserts

6

two line breaks (

) where the paragraph break should occur. This is not only incorrect HTML, but it prevents you from using paragraph alignments (<P ALIGN=CENTER>) without fixing all of your HTML in program other than PageMill.

Figure 6.11.

PageMill (editing Adobe's Product Pages).

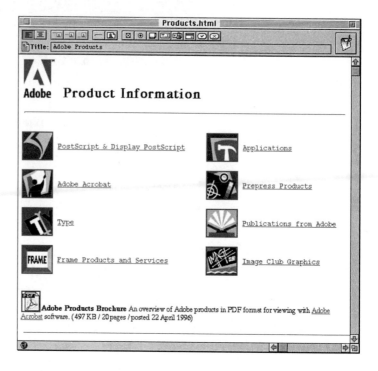

Overall, PageMill is a great program for simple HTML pages, or for putting together a simple program quickly and easily.

Microsoft FrontPage (Windows)

Microsoft's FrontPage, formerly by a company called Vermeer, is an integrated Web site construction and maintenance kit that includes a Web site administration tool, a Web server, and various other tools for administering the entire package. The Web page editor itself (FrontPage Editor as shown in Figure 6.12) is only a small part of the overall package.

The editor itself is easy to work with, although there are a few peculiarities. Although most of the editors let you either select an element and then type, or type first and then change the style, the FrontPage editor separates these two functions. This means you can either insert an element from a menu item and then type in it, or you can select text and change the style using a pull-down on the tool bar.

6

Figure 6.12.

FrontPage editor.

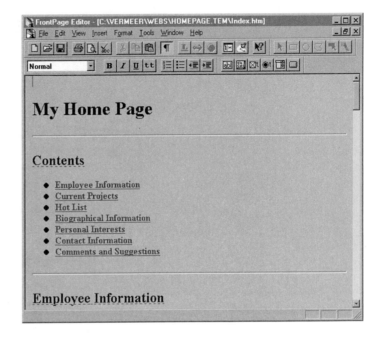

Besides that, inserting and adding elements is straightforward. Because the editor is tied closely to a browser and a server, linking between pages and loading files and images from the Web is fast and easy.

Part of the FrontPage package is an enormous set of templates and wizards for creating different kinds of Web pages, and so starting and building a Web page or entire presentation is fast and easy. Since I'm more used to working from scratch, sometimes the many different options were confusing to me, but for beginners, starting from templates might be easier than starting from a blank page.

The complete FrontPage package is available for Windows NT and Windows 95. Information about FrontPage is available at http://www.microsoft.com/frontpage.

GNNpress (Windows, Macintosh, UNIX)

GNNpress, formerly NaviPress, is an integrated browser and HTML editor much in the same vein as Netscape Gold. Using GNNpress (shown in Figure 6.13), you can browse to pages that interest you, edit them in the same window, and then, if you own those pages, save them back to the server where they came from.

Figure 6.13.
GNNpress.

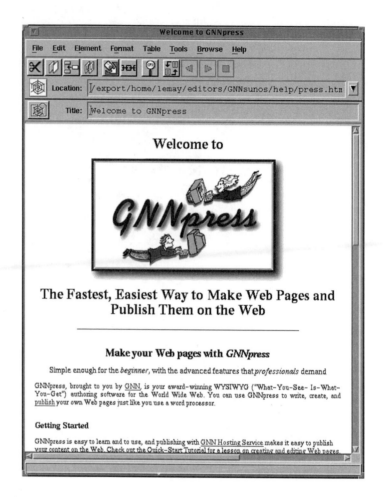

GNNpress is right up there with Netscape Gold in terms of ease of use, although the main HTML elements and features are all in menu items as opposed to on the tool bar (the tool bar itself had overly small and difficult-to-understand icons).

One interesting feature of GNNpress is the ability to create miniwebs, which are collections of related pages (what I've been calling Web presentations). When you create a miniweb, you can add pages and link between them fairly easily. A Miniweb window also lets you see a graphical representation of your collection of pages.

GNNpress supports HTML 2.0, many HTML extensions, and forms and tables. The forms editor is particularly nice, allowing you to insert form elements very quickly, and using a dotted line on the page to indicate the current form (very useful for pages with multiple forms).

GNNpress is the client half of an HTML publishing system, the other half being GNNserver. The combination of the two allows you to edit HTML pages anywhere on the Web and then save them back to the server (assuming you have the right access permissions, of course).

GNNpress is available for Windows, Macintosh, and many flavors of UNIX, and is free. Get more information about GNNpress and GNNserver, and GNN's Web site hosting services, at http://www.tools.gnn.com/.

HTML Editor (Macintosh)

HTML Editor is a shareware editor (see Figure 6.14) that lets you insert tags into your file and see the result in a WYSIWYG fashion—at the same time. The tags are shown in a lighter color than the surrounding text, and the text looks like it would look in Netscape or Mosaic, although you can change the appearance of any style and apply it throughout the document. There are options to hide the tags in your document to get the full effect, and you can also preview the document using your favorite browser.

Figure 6.14.
HTML Editor.

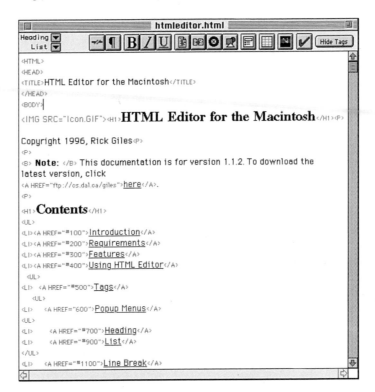

HTML Editor's current version is 1.0. It supports only the basic HTML 2.0 tags, not including forms. It does not include any of the Netscape extensions or HTML 3.2 tags. It has a feature for including custom tags, however, so you can customize the application to include these new tags.

The documentation for HTML Editor is available at `http://dragon.acadiau.ca/~giles/HTML_Editor/Documentation.html`. You can get the actual package from `ftp://cs.dal.ca/giles/HTML_Editor_1.1.4.sit.hqx`.

Converters

What if you'd prefer not to work in HTML at all—you have your own tool or language that you're familiar with, and you'd prefer to work in that? Many programs exist that will convert different formats into HTML. This section describes some of those converters.

If you use a commercial word processor, and you don't see a converter listed here or among the lists of converters in Appendix A, try calling the vendor of that word processor. Conversion to HTML has been a hot topic for most word processing and desktop publishing companies, and that company may have a converter available.

Lists of converters from many formats to HTML are also maintained at Yahoo! at `http://www.yahoo.com/Computers_and_Internet/Internet/World_Wide_Web/HTML_Converters/` and at NCSA at `http://union.ncsa.uiuc.edu/HyperNews/get/www/html/converters.html`.

Plain Text

In many cases, simple HTML editors can add HTML tags quickly to text files, or simply adding `<PRE>` tags to the beginning and end of a text file is a quick-and-dirty solution. Actual converter programs do, however, exist. For UNIX, two programs, both called text2html, will do the job. See either `http://www.seas.upenn.edu/~mengwong/txt2html.html` or `http://www.cs.wustl.edu/~seth/txt2html/` for more information.

For the Macintosh, two programs called HTML Markup and text2html will create HTML files by dragging and dropping a text file onto its icon. You can get either of these programs from various Mac shareware archives (try `http://www.shareware.com/`).

Microsoft Word

Microsoft's Internet Assistant, mentioned earlier in this chapter, can be used to easily convert Word documents to HTML. You can also use QuarterDeck's WebAuthor 2.0 as a conversion tool for Word for Windows files. Find out more information about WebAuthor from `http://arachnid.qdeck.com/qdeck/products/WebAuthr/`.

6

Microsoft Word can also export files in RTF (Rich Text Format), which can then be converted to HTML using various RTF converters (see the section on RTF later in this chapter).

WordPerfect

In addition to the Internet Publisher program I mentioned earlier in this chapter, other converters exist. WP2X ("WordPerfect to Anything") can convert WordPerfect 5.1 files to HTML. It runs under UNIX. Get information about it at `http://www.milkyway.com/People/Michael_Richardson/wp2x.html`.

RTF (Rich Text Format)

RTF format is output by many popular word processing and page layout programs, and in many cases it can be the easiest route from many programs to HTML. To convert RTF to HTML on Mac and UNIX, the terrific `rtftohtml` program is the most comprehensive tool to get. Find out more about it at `http://www.sunpack.com/RTF/rtftohtml_overview.html`. For Windows, a version of `rtftohtml` is promised but is not yet available at the time I write this. However, a package called Tag Perfect, available at most Windows shareware servers (try `http://www.shareware.com/`), also converts RTF to HTML.

Quark XPress

If you use Quark XPress, you can either use the RTF converter mentioned above, or export your Quark files to tagged text and then use the Macintosh or UNIX filter described at `http://the-tech.mit.edu/~jeremy/qt2www.html`.

PageMaker

PageMaker 6.0 itself allows you to create HTML files using its HTML plug-in. If you're using PageMaker, this may be the quickest way to convert your files to HTML.

There is also Mitch Cohen's PageMaker Websucker, which is a HyperCard stack that extracts the text from PageMaker files and turns it into HTML. Check out `http://www.msystems.com/mcohen/websucker.html` for more information.

FrameMaker

FrameMaker 5.0, on Macintosh, UNIX, and Windows, includes support for creating and exporting HTML files through the Quadralay WebWorks HTML filter. The version shipped with FrameMaker is a "lite" version; the complete package is available from Qualdralay and is described at `http://www.quadralay.com/Products/WWPub/wwpub.html`.

In addition, Harlequin's WebMaker, also available on Windows, Macintosh, and UNIX, provides sophisticated HTML conversion for FrameMaker files. See `http://www.harlequin.com/webmaker/2.0/`.

Working Directly in HTML versus Using a Converter

With all these converters from word processors to HTML, you can often do most of your HTML development in those programs and deal with converting the files to HTML at the last minute. For many projects, this may be the way to go.

Consider the advantages of using a converter:

- ☐ Authors do not have to keep track of tags. Having to memorize and know the rules of how tags work is a major issue if all one wants to do is write.

- ☐ Fewer errors end up in HTML documents (misspellings, missing close tags, overlapping tags). Because the HTML is automatically generated, there's less chance of "operator error" in the final output.

- ☐ Authors can use a tool they're familiar with. If they know MS Word and live and die by MS Word, they can work in MS Word.

On the other hand, working in a converter is not a panacea. There are pitfalls, which include the following:

- ☐ No tools can provide all the features of HTML, particularly with links to external documents. Some handworking of the final HTML files will generally be required after you convert.

- ☐ The split-source issue. Once you convert your files from their original form to HTML, you have two sources you are going to have to monitor. To make changes after you do the conversion, you will either have to change the original and regenerate the HTML (wiping out any hand-massaging you did to those files), or you'll have to make sure you make the change to *both* the original source and the HTML documents. For large projects, splitting the source at any time except the very last minute can create enormous headaches for everyone involved.

Working directly in HTML, for all its hideous text-only markup what-you-see-is-nothing-like-what-you-get glory, does have advantages, including these:

- ☐ All your work is done in one file; no extra step is required to generate the final version.

☐ HTML files are text only, making it possible for them to be filtered through programs that can easily do automatic tasks such as generating tables of contents of major headings (and hyperlinking them back to those headings), or testing for the validity of the links in those files. The files can also easily be put under source code control.

☐ You have the full flexibility of the HTML language, including the ability to code new features as they appear, rather than having to wait for the next revision of the converter.

Summary

To wind down, I've provided some simple lists of HTML editors and converters to help you in your HTML development. After everything you've learned so far, the prospect of tools to help you must come as a welcome relief. Consider using one or more of the tools mentioned in this chapter; they may be able to help you in producing HTML documents.

You know which HTML tag creates a level-three heading. I hope that somewhere along the line so far, you've picked up some ideas for designing and structuring your documents so they can be read and navigated quickly and easily and serve the demands of your readers.

Q&A

Q You, as an author of HTML books, probably know HTML pretty well. What HTML editor do you use?

A For the vast majority of my HTML work, I use a plain old text editor: Emacs on a UNIX system, or Alpha on a Macintosh. However, many of the editors I've reviewed in this chapter have impressed me, HotDog and Netscape Gold in particular, so I may start using an editor for some of the more basic pages. I don't think anything will entirely replace working directly with the tags, however; it's difficult for an editor to be able to keep up with the rapid changes in HTML technology and still be easy to use.

6

DAY 4

Images and Backgrounds

Chapter 7

Using Images, Color, and Backgrounds

If you've been struggling to keep up with all the HTML tags I've been flinging at you over the last couple of days, you can breathe easier: things will be easier today. In fact, today you're going to learn very few new HTML tags. The focus for today is on adding images and color to your Web pages. In this chapter you'll learn about the HTML codes for adding images, color, and backgrounds, in particular:

- ☐ The kinds of images you can use in Web pages
- ☐ How to include images on your Web page, either alone or alongside text
- ☐ How to use images as clickable links
- ☐ Using external images as a substitute for or in addition to inline images
- ☐ Providing alternatives for browsers that cannot view images
- ☐ Image dimensions and scaling, and providing image previews
- ☐ Changing the font and background colors in your Web page

☐ Using images for tiled page backgrounds

☐ How (and when) to use images in your Web Pages

After this chapter you'll know all there is to adding images to your Web pages. Chapter 8, "Creating Images for the Web," will teach you about the tricks you can do with the images themselves to create different effects on your Web pages.

Images on the Web

Images for Web pages fall into two general classes: inline images and external images. Inline images appear directly on a Web page among the text and links and are loaded automatically when you load the page itself—assuming, of course, that you have a graphical browser and that you have automatic image-loading turned on. External images are images that are not directly displayed when you load a page. They are downloaded only at the request of your reader, usually on the other side of a link. External images don't need a graphical browser to be viewed—you can download an image file just fine using a text-only browser and then use an image editor or viewer to see that image later on. You'll learn about how to use both inline and external images in this chapter.

NEW TERM

> *Inline* images appear on a Web page along with text and links, and are automatically loaded when the page itself is retrieved.

NEW TERM

> *External* images are stored separate from the Web page and are loaded only on demand, for example, as the result of a link.

Regardless of whether you're using inline or external images, those images must be in a specific format. For inline images, that image has to be in one of two formats: GIF or JPEG. GIF is actually the more popular standard, and more browsers can view inline GIF files than JPEG files. Support for JPEG is becoming more widespread but is still not as popular as GIF, and so sticking with GIF is the safest method of making sure your images can be viewed by the widest possible audience. You'll learn more about the difference between GIF and JPEG and how to create images in these formats in Chapter 8. You'll learn more about external images and the formats you can use for them later in this chapter.

For this chapter, let's assume you already have an image you want to put on your Web page. How do you get it into GIF or JPEG format so that your page can view it? Most image-editing programs such as Adobe Photoshop, Paint Shop Pro, CorelDRAW!, or XV provide ways to convert between image formats. You may have to look under an option for Save As or Export in order to find it. There are also freeware and shareware programs out there for most platforms that do nothing but convert between image formats.

To save files in GIF format, you're looking for an option called CompuServe GIF, GIF87, GIF89, or just plain GIF. Any of these will work. If you're saving your files as JPEG, usually the option will be simply JPEG.

Remember how your HTML files had to have a `.html` or `.htm` extension for them to work properly? Image files have extensions, too. For GIF files, the extension is `.gif`. For JPEG files, the extension is either `.jpg` or `.jpeg`; either will work fine.

NOTE

> Some image editors will try to save files with extensions in all caps (`.GIF`, `.JPEG`). Although these are the correct extensions, image names, like HTML file names, are case sensitive, and so GIF is not the same extension as gif. The case of the extension isn't important when you're testing on your local system, but it will be when you move your files to the server, so use lowercase if you possibly can.

Inline Images in HTML: The `<IMG>` Tag

After you have an image in GIF or JPEG format ready to go, you can include it in your Web page. Inline images are indicated in HTML using the `<IMG>` tag. The `<IMG>` tag, like the `<HR>` and `<BR>` tags, has no closing tag. It does, however, have many different attributes that allow different ways of presenting and handling inline images. Many of these attributes are newer extensions to HTML and may not be available in some browsers. I'll make note of those extensions as you learn about them.

The most important attribute to the `<IMG>` tag is SRC. The SRC attribute indicates the filename or URL of the image you want to include, in quotes. The pathname to the file uses the same pathname rules as the HREF attribute in links. So, for a GIF file named `image.gif` in the same directory as this file, you can use the following tag:

```
<IMG SRC="image.gif">
```

For an image file one directory up from the current directory, use

```
<IMG SRC="../image.gif">
```

And so on, using the same rules as for page names in the HREF part of the `<A>` tag.

Exercise 7.1: Try it!

Let's try a simple example. Here's the Web page for a local haunted house that happens every year at Halloween. Using all the excellent advice I've given you in the last six chapters, you should be able to create a page like this one pretty easily. Here's the HTML code for this HTML file, and Figure 7.1 shows how it looks so far.

```
<HTML>
<HEAD>
<TITLE>Welcome to the Halloween House of Terror</TITLE>
</HEAD><BODY>
<H1>Welcome to The Halloween House of Terror!!</H1>
<HR>
<P>Voted the most frightening haunted house three years in a row, the
<STRONG>Halloween House of Terror</STRONG> provides the ultimate in
Halloween thrills. Over <STRONG>20 rooms of thrills and excitement</STRONG> to
make your blood run cold and your hair stand on end!</P>
<P>The Halloween House of Terror is open from <EM>October 20 to November
1st</EM>, with a gala celebration on Halloween night. Our hours are:</P>
<UL>
<LI>Mon-Fri 5PM-midnight
<LI>Sat & Sun 5PM-3AM
<LI><STRONG>Halloween Night (31-oct)</STRONG>: 3PM-???
</UL>
<P>The Halloween House of Terror is located at:<BR>
The Old Waterfall Shopping Center<BR>
1020 Mirabella Ave<BR>
Springfield, CA 94532</P>
</BODY>
</HTML>
```

Figure 7.1.

The Halloween House home page.

So far, so good. Now, let's add an image to the page. I happen to have an image of a spider web kicking around in a clip art library (Figure 7.2) that would look excellent at the top of that Web page.

Figure 7.2.

The spider web image.

The image is called web.gif and is in GIF format, so it's ready to go into the Web page. Let's say we want to add it to this page on its own line so that the heading appears just below it. We'll add an <IMG> tag to the file inside its own paragraph, just before the heading. (Images, like links, don't define their own text elements, so the <IMG> tag has to go inside a paragraph or heading element.)

```
<P><IMG SRC="web.gif"></P>
<H1>Welcome to The Halloween House of Terror!!</H1>
```

And now, when you reload the halloween.html page, your browser should include the spider web image in the page, as shown in Figure 7.3.

If your image doesn't load (if your browser displays a funny-looking icon in its place), first make sure you've specified the name of the file properly in the HTML file. Image filenames are case-sensitive, so all the uppercase and lowercase letters have to be the same.

If that doesn't work, double-check the image file to make sure that it is indeed a GIF or JPEG image, and that it has the proper file extension.

Finally, make sure that you have image loading turned on in your browser. (The option is called Auto Load Images in both Netscape and Mosaic.)

If one spider is good, two would be really good, right? Try adding another <IMG> tag next to the first one and see what happens:

```
<P><IMG SRC="web.gif"><IMG SRC="web.gif"></P>
<H1>Welcome to The Halloween House of Terror!!</H1>
```

Figure 7.3.

The Halloween House home page, with spider.

Figure 7.4 shows how it looks in Netscape, with both images adjacent to each other, as you would expect.

Figure 7.4.

Multiple images.

And that's all there is to it! No matter what the image or how large or small it is, that's how you include it on a Web page.

Images and Text

In the previous exercise we put an inline image on a page in its own separate paragraph, with text below the image. You can also include an image inside a line of text. (In fact, this is what the phrase "inline image" actually means—in a line of text.)

To include images inside a line of text, just add the `<IMG>` tag at the appropriate point, inside an element tag (`<H1>`, `<P>`, `<ADDRESS>`, and so on):

```
<H1><IMG SRC="web.gif">The Halloween House of Terror!!</H1>
```

So, for example, Figure 7.5 shows the difference that putting the image inline with the heading makes. (I've also shortened the title itself.)

Figure 7.5.

The Halloween House page with image inside the heading.

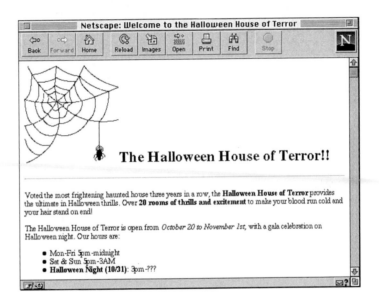

The image doesn't have to be large, and it doesn't have to be at the beginning of the text. You can include an image anywhere in a block of text:

```
<BLOCKQUOTE>
Love, from whom the world <IMG SRC="world.gif"> begun,<BR>
Hath the secret of the sun. <IMG SRC="sun.gif"> <BR>
Love can tell, and love alone,
Whence the million stars <IMG SRC="star.gif"> were strewn <BR>
Why each atom <IMG SRC="atom.gif"> knows its own. <BR>
--Robert Bridges
</BLOCKQUOTE>
```

Figure 7.6 shows how this looks.

7

Figure 7.6.

*Images can go
anywhere in text.*

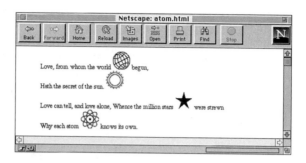

Text and Image Alignment

Notice that with these examples of including images in text the image was displayed so that
the bottom of the image and the bottom of the text matched up. The `<IMG>` tag also includes
an `ALIGN` attribute which allows you to align the image upwards or downwards with the
surrounding text or other images in the line.

Standard HTML 2.0 defines three basic values for `ALIGN`:

`ALIGN=TOP`	Aligns the top of the image with the topmost part of the line (which may be the top of the text or the top of another image).
`ALIGN=MIDDLE`	Aligns the center of the image with the middle of the line (usually the baseline of the line of text, not the actual middle of the line).
`ALIGN=BOTTOM`	Aligns the bottom of the image with the bottom of the line of text.

In addition to these values, there are several new values for `ALIGN` that provide greater control
over precisely where the image will be aligned within the line. These values are Netscape
extensions to HTML but are supported in many other popular browsers.

`ALIGN=TEXTTTOP`	Aligns the top of the image with the top of the tallest text in the line (whereas `ALIGN=TOP` aligns the image with the topmost item in the line).
`ALIGN=ABSMIDDLE`	Aligns the middle of the image with the middle of the largest item in the line. (`ALIGN=MIDDLE` usually aligns the middle of the image with the baseline of the text, not its actual middle.)
`ALIGN=BASELINE`	Aligns the bottom of the image with the baseline of the text. `ALIGN=BASELINE` is the same as `ALIGN=BOTTOM`, but `ALIGN=BASELINE` is a more descriptive name.
`ALIGN=ABSBOTTOM`	Aligns the bottom of the image with the lowest item in the line (which may be below the baseline of the text).

Figure 7.7 shows examples of all these alignment options. In each case, the line on the left
side and the text are aligned to each other, and the arrow varies.

Figure 7.7.

New alignment options.

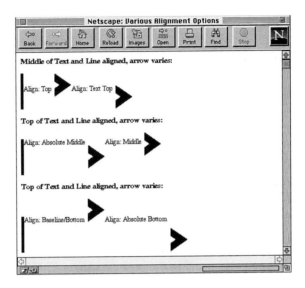

Wrapping Text Next to Images

Including an image inside a line works fine if you have only one line of text. One aspect of inline images I have sneakily avoided mentioning up to this point is that in HTML 2.0 all this works only with a single line of text. If you have multiple lines of text and you include an image in the middle of it, all the text around the image (except for the one line) will appear above and below that image—see Figure 7.8 for an example.

Figure 7.8.

Text does not wrap around images.

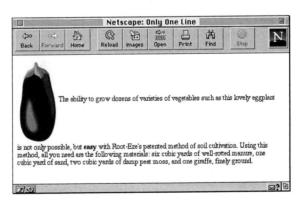

What if you want to wrap multiple lines of text next to an image so you have text surrounding all sides? Using HTML 2.0, you can't. You're restricted to just a single line of text on either side of the image, which limits the kinds of designs you can do.

7

To get around this limitation in HTML 2.0, Netscape defined two new values for the ALIGN attribute of the <IMG> tag—LEFT and RIGHT. These new values have been incorporated into HTML 3.2 and are supported now by many browsers other than Netscape.

ALIGN=LEFT and ALIGN=RIGHT

The ALIGN=LEFT aligns an image to the left margin, and ALIGN=RIGHT aligns an image to the right margin. But using these attributes also causes any text following the image to be displayed in the space to the right or left of that image, depending on the margin alignment. Figure 7.9 shows an image with some text aligned next to it.

Figure 7.9.

Text and images aligned.

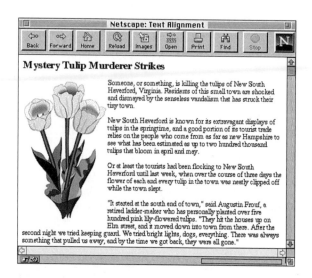

You can put any HTML text (paragraphs, lists, headings, other images) after an aligned image, and the text will be wrapped into the space between the image and the margin (or you can also have images on both margins and put the text between them). The browser fills in the space with text until the bottom of the image, and then continues filling in the text beneath the image.

Stopping Text Wrapping

What if you want to stop filling in the space and start the next line underneath the image? A normal line break won't do it—it'll just break the line to the current margin alongside the image. A new paragraph will also continue wrapping the text alongside the image. To stop wrapping text next to an image, use a line break tag (<BR>) with the new attribute CLEAR. With the CLEAR attribute you can break the line so that the next line of text begins after the end of the image (all the way to the margin). See Figure 7.10 for an example (I've used a smaller image here than the one in the previous example so that the line break is more visible).

7

Figure 7.10.

Line break to a clear margin.

The CLEAR attribute can have one of three values:

LEFT   Break to an empty left margin, for left-aligned images

RIGHT   Break to an empty right margin, for right-aligned images

ALL   Break to a line clear to both margins

So, for example, this code snippet shows a picture of a tulip with some text wrapped next to it. A line break with CLEAR=LEFT breaks the text wrapping and restarts the text after the image.

```
<P><IMG ALIGN=LEFT SRC="tulipsmall.gif">
<H2>Mystery Tulip Murderer Strikes</H2>
<P>Someone, or something, is killing the tulips of New South Haverford,
Virginia.  Residents of this small town are shocked and dismayed by the
senseless vandalism that has struck their tiny town.</P>
<BR CLEAR=LEFT>
<P>New South Haverford is known for its extravagant displays of tulips
in the springtime, and a good portion of its tourist trade relies on the
people who come from as far as new Hampshire to see what has been estimated
as up to two hundred thousand tulips that bloom in April and may.</P>
```

Text Wrapping in Older Browsers

Given that ALIGN=LEFT and ALIGN=RIGHT are newer features to HTML, it's interesting to take note about what happens if a page that includes these features is viewed in a browser that doesn't support left and right alignment.

Usually you'll just lose the formatting; the text will appear below the image rather than next to it. However, because the first line of text will still appear next to the image, the text may break in odd places. Something as simple as putting a <BR> after the image (which does little in Netscape or other browsers that support text wrapping, but pushes all the text after the image on other browsers) can create an effect that works well both in the browsers that support image and text wrapping and those that don't. Be sure to test your pages in multiple browsers so you know what the effect will be.

For example, the following input and output example shows the HTML code for a page for Papillon Enterprises, a fictional company that designs Web pages. Figure 7.11 shows the result in Netscape, and Figure 7.12 shows the result in browser called MacWeb (which does not have image and text wrapping capabilities).

INPUT

```
<H1><IMG SRC="butterfly.gif" ALIGN=RIGHT ALIGN=MIDDLE>
Papillon Enterprises</H1>
<P>Design, Writing, Illustration, and Programming for the
<B>World Wide Web</B></P>
<P>Specializing in:</P>
<UL>
<LI>HTML and Web Page Design
<LI>Illustration
<LI>Forms Design and Programming
<LI>Complete Web Server Installation
</UL>
<HR>
```

OUTPUT

Figure 7.11.
*The output in
Netscape.*

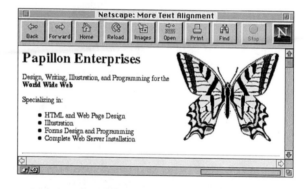

OUTPUT

Figure 7.12.
*The output in
MacWeb (no
image alignment).*

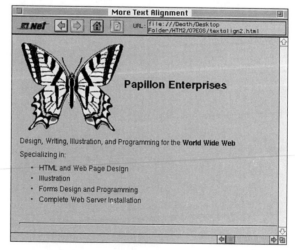

Adjusting the Space Around Images

With the ability to wrap text around an image, you may also want to adjust the amount of space around that image. The VSPACE and HSPACE attributes (also a Netscape and HTML 3.2

feature) allow you to do this. Both take a value in pixels; VSPACE controls the space above and below the image, and HSPACE controls the space to the left and the right.

For example, the following HTML code produces the effect shown in Figure 7.13:

```
<P><IMG SRC="eggplant.gif" VSPACE=30 HSPACE=30 ALIGN=LEFT>
This is an eggplant. We intend to stay a good ways away from it,
because we really don't like eggplant very much.</P>
```

Figure 7.13.
Image spacing.

Images and Links

Can an image serve as a link? Sure it can! If you include an <IMG> tag inside the opening and closing parts of a link tag (<A>), that image serves as a clickable hot spot for the link itself:

```
<A HREF="index.html"><IMG SRC="uparrow.gif"></A>
```

If you include both an image and text in the anchor, the image and the text become hot spots pointing to the same page:

```
<A HREF="index.html"><IMG SRC="uparrow.gif">Up to Index</A>
```

By default in HTML 2.0, images that are also hot spots for links appear with a border around them to distinguish them from ordinary nonclickable images, as Figure 7.14 shows.

Figure 7.14.
Images that are also links.

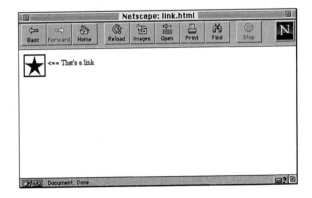

You can change the width of the border around that image using the BORDER attribute to <IMG>. The BORDER attribute, a Netscape extension now part of HTML 3.2, takes a number, which is the width of the border in pixels. BORDER=0 hides the border entirely.

Be very careful when setting BORDER to 0 (zero) for images with links. The border provides a visual indication that the image is also a link. By removing that border, you make it difficult for the reader to know which are plain images and which are hot spots without them having to move the mouse around to find them. Make sure, if you must use borderless image links, that your design provides some indication that the image is selectable and isn't just a plain image. For example, you might design your images so they actually look like buttons (see Figure 7.15).

Figure 7.15.

Images that look like buttons.

Exercise 7.2: Navigation icons.

Let's create a simple example of using images as links. When you have a set of related Web pages among which the navigation takes place in a consistent way (for example, moving forward, or back, up, home, and so on), it makes sense to provide a menu of navigation options at the top or bottom of each page so that your readers know exactly how to find their way through your pages.

This example shows you how to create a set of icons that are used to navigate through a linear set of pages. You have three icons in GIF format: one for forward, one for back, and a third to enable the reader to jump to a global index of the entire page structure.

First, we'll write the HTML structure to support the icons. Here, the page itself isn't all that important, so I'll just include a shell page. Figure 7.16 shows how the page looks to begin with.

```
<HTML>
<HEAD>
<TITLE>Motorcycle Maintenance: Removing Spark Plugs</TITLE></HEAD>
<BODY>
<H1>Removing Spark Plugs</H1>
<P>(include some info about spark plugs here)</P>
<HR>
</BODY>
</HTML>
```

Now, at the bottom of the page, add your images using IMG tags (Figure 7.17 shows the result).

```
<IMG SRC="arrowright.gif">
<IMG SRC="arrowleft.gif">
<IMG SRC="arrowup.gif">
```

7

Figure 7.16.

The basic page, no icons.

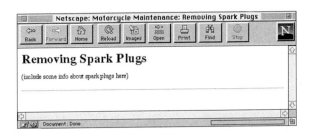

Figure 7.17.

The basic page with icons.

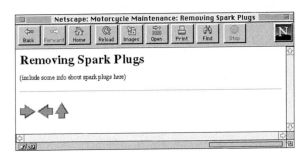

Now, add the anchors to the images to activate them. Figure 7.18 shows the result.

```
<A HREF="replacing.html"><IMG SRC="arrowright.gif"></A>
<A HREF="ready.html"><IMG SRC="arrowleft.gif"></A>
<A HREF="index.html"><IMG SRC="arrowup.gif"></A>
```

Figure 7.18.

The basic page with iconic links.

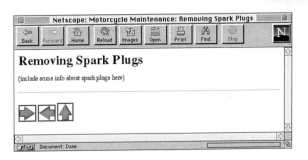

When you click on the icons now, the browser jumps to the page in the link just as it would have if you had used text links.

Speaking of text, are the icons usable enough as they are? How about adding some text describing exactly what is on the other side of the link? You can add the text inside or outside the anchor, depending on whether you want the text to be a hot spot for the link as well. Here, we'll include it outside the link so that only the icon serves as the hot spot. We'll also align the bottoms of the text and the icons using the ALIGN attribute of the <IMG> tag. Finally, because the extra text causes the icons to move onto two lines, we'll arrange each one on its own line instead. See Figure 7.19 for the final menu.

```
<P>
<A HREF="replacing.html"><IMG SRC="arrowright.gif" ALIGN=BOTTOM></A>
On to "Gapping the New Plugs"<BR>
<A HREF="ready.html"><IMG SRC="arrowleft.gif" ALIGN=BOTTOM></A>
Back to "When You Should Replace your Spark Plugs"<BR>
<A HREF="index.html"><IMG SRC="arrowup.gif" ALIGN=BOTTOM></A>
Up To Index
</P>
```

Figure 7.19.

The basic page with iconic links and text.

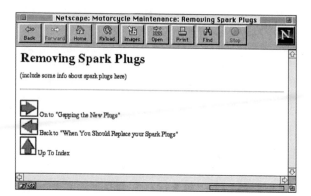

Using External Images

Unlike inline images, external images don't actually appear on your Web page; instead, they're stored separate from the page and linked from that page in much the same way that other HTML pages are.

The reason external images are worth mentioning in this chapter is that external images often can serve a complementary role to inline images. For example:

☐ Most Web browsers support inline GIF images, and many of them support inline JPEG images as well. However, most browsers support a much wider array of image formats through the use of external image files and helper applications. So, by using external images, you can use many other image formats besides GIF and JPEG, for example, BMP (Windows bitmaps) or PICT (Macintosh bitmaps).

☐ Text-only browsers can't display images inline with Web pages, but you can download external images with a text-only browser and view them with an image-editing or viewing program.

☐ You can combine a small inline image on your Web page that loads quickly with a larger, more detailed external image so that if readers want to see more, they can choose to load the image themselves.

To use external images, you create the image as you would an inline image and then save it with an appropriate filename. As with other files on the Web, the file extension is important. Depending on the image format, use one of the extensions listed in Table 7.1.

Table 7.1. Image formats and extensions.

Format	Extension
GIF	`.gif`
JPEG	`.jpg`, `.jpeg`
XBM	`.xbm`
TIFF	`.tiff`, `.tif`
BMP	`.bmp`
PICT	`.pict`

Once you have an external image, all you have to do is create a link to it, the same way you would a link to another HTML page, like this:

```
<P>I grew some really huge <A HREF="bigtomatos.jpeg">tomatoes</A> in
my garden last year</P>
```

For this next exercise, you'll use inline and external images together.

Exercise 7.3: Linking to external GIF and JPEG files.

A common practice in Web pages is to provide a very small GIF image (a "thumbnail") inline on the page itself. You can then link that image to its larger external counterpart. This has two major advantages over including the entire image inline:

- ☐ It keeps the size of the Web page small so that the page can be downloaded quickly.
- ☐ It gives your readers a "taste" of the image so they can choose to download the entire thing if they want to see more or get a better view.

In this simple example, you'll set up a link between a small image and an external, larger version of that same image. The large image is a photograph of some penguins in GIF format, called `penguinsbig.gif` (shown in Figure 7.20).

First, create a thumbnail version of the penguins photograph in your favorite image editor. The thumbnail can be a scaled version of the original file, a clip of that file (say, one penguin out of the group), or anything else you want to indicate the larger image.

Here, I've created a picture of one penguin in the group to serve as the inline image. (I've called it `penguinslittle.gif`.) Unlike the large version of the file, which is 100K, the small picture is only 3K. Using the `<IMG>` tag, I'll put that image directly on a nearly content-free Web page:

```
<HTML>
<HEAD>
<TITLE>Penguins</TITLE>
```

EXERCISE

7

```
</HEAD><BODY>
<H1>Penguins</H1>
<IMG SRC="penguinslittle.gif">
</BODY></HTML>
```

Figure 7.20.

Penguins.

Now, using a link tag, you can link the small icon to the bigger picture by enclosing the `<IMG>` tag inside an `<A>` tag:

```
<A HREF="penguinsbig.gif"><IMG SRC="penguinslittle.gif"></A>
```

The final result of the page is shown in Figure 7.21. Now, if you click on the small penguin image, the big image will be downloaded and viewed either by the browser itself or by the helper application defined for GIF files for that browser.

Figure 7.21.

The Penguins home page with link.

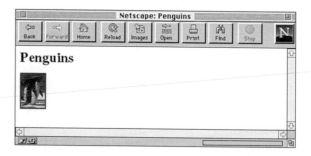

An alternative to linking the small image directly to the larger image is to provide the external image in several different formats and then create plain text links to the various different external versions (you might want to do this for readers who have software for one format but not another). Next, I'll link to a JPEG version of that same penguins file.

To create the JPEG version of the penguin photograph, you need to use your image editor or converter again to convert the original photograph. Here, I've called it penguinsbig.jpg.

To provide both GIF and JPEG forms of the penguin photo we'll convert the link on the image into a simple link menu to the GIF and JPEG files, providing some information about file size (the result is shown in Figure 7.22).

```
<P><IMG SRC="penguinslittle.gif"></P>
<UL>
<LI>Penguins (<A HREF="pengiunsbig.gif">100K GIF file</A>)
<LI>Penguins (<A HREF="pengiunsbig.jpg">25K JPEG file</A>)
</UL>
```

Figure 7.22.
The Penguins link menu.

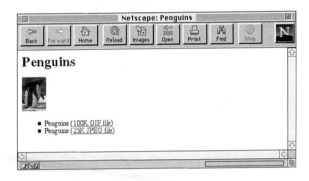

NOTE

Images are not the only types of files you can store externally to your Web page. Sound files, video, zip archives—just about anything can be linked as an external file. You'll learn more about this in Chapter 9, "External Files, Multimedia, and Animation."

Providing Alternatives to Images

Images can turn a simple text-only Web page into a glorious visual feast. But what happens if someone is reading your Web page from a text-only browser, or what if he or she has image-loading turned off so that all your careful graphics appear as plain generic icons? All of a sudden that glorious visual feast isn't looking as nice. And, worse, if you haven't taken these possibilities into consideration while designing your Web page, your work could be unreadable and unusable by that portion of your audience.

There is a simple solution to one of these problems. The ALT attribute of the <IMG> tag provides a way for you to substitute something meaningful in place of the image on browsers that cannot display that image.

Usually, in text-only browsers such as Lynx, graphics that are specified using the <IMG> tag in the original file are "displayed" as the word IMAGE with square brackets around it like this: [IMAGE]. (An example is shown in Figure 7.23.) If the image itself was a link to something else, that link is preserved.

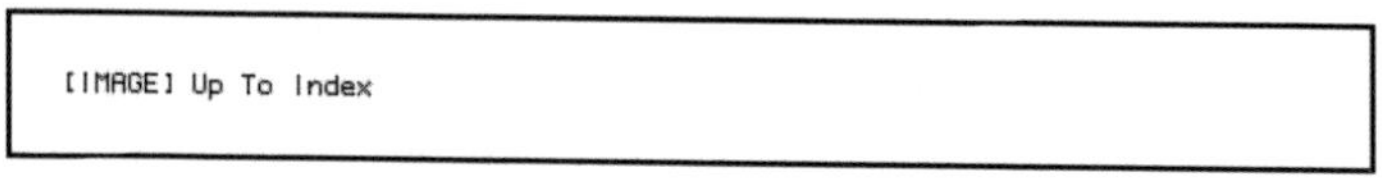

Figure 7.23.

"Images" in Lynx.

```
[IMAGE] Up To Index
```

The ALT attribute in the <IMG> tag provides a more meaningful text alternative to the blank [IMAGE] for your readers who are using text-only Web browsers. The ALT attribute contains a string with the text you want to substitute for the graphic:

```
<IMG SRC="myimage.gif" ALT="[a picture of a cat]">
```

Note that most browsers will interpret the string you include in the ALT attribute as a literal string; that is, if you include any HTML tags in that string, they will be printed as typed instead of being parsed and displayed as HTML code. This means you can't use whole blocks of HTML code as a replacement for an image—just a few words or phrases.

For example, remember in Exercise 7.2, where you used arrow icons for navigation between pages? Here are two ideas for providing text-only alternatives for those icons:

- Use text-only markers to replace the images (see Figure 7.24). Here's the code:

```
<P>
<A HREF="replacing.html"><IMG SRC="arrowright.gif" ALIGN=BOTTOM
ALT="[NEXT]"></A>
On to "Gapping the New Plugs"<BR>
<A HREF="ready.html"><IMG SRC="arrowleft.gif" ALIGN=BOTTOM
ALT="[PREVIOUS]"></A>
Back to "When You Should Replace your Spark Plugs"<BR>
<A HREF="index.html"><IMG SRC="arrowup.gif" ALIGN=BOTTOM ALT="[UP]"></A>
Up To Index</P>
```

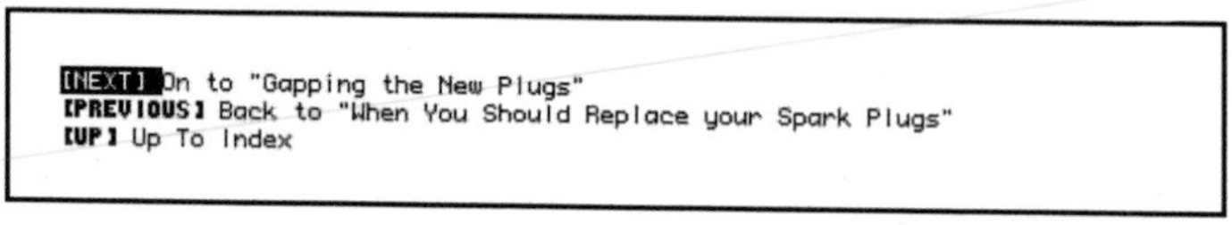

Figure 7.24.

Text markers to replace images.

```
[NEXT] On to "Gapping the New Plugs"
[PREVIOUS] Back to "When You Should Replace your Spark Plugs"
[UP] Up To Index
```

- Hide the images altogether and make the text the anchor instead (see Figure 7.25). Here's the code:

```
<P>
<A HREF="replacing.html"><IMG SRC="arrowright.gif" ALIGN=BOTTOM ALT="">
On to "Gapping the New Plugs"</A><BR>
<A HREF="ready.html"><IMG SRC="arrowleft.gif" ALIGN=BOTTOM ALT="">
Back to "When You Should Replace your Spark Plugs"</A><BR>
<A HREF="index.html"><IMG SRC="arrowup.gif" ALIGN=BOTTOM ALT="">
Up To Index</A></P>
```

Figure 7.25.

Hide the images.

```
On to "Gapping the New Plugs"
Back to "When You Should Replace your Spark Plugs"
Up To Index
```

TIP

A sneaky trick I've seen used for the ALT attribute is to include an ASCII art picture (a picture made up of characters, like the cow in Day 3, "Doing More with HTML 3.2") in the ALT attribute, which then serves as the "picture" in text-only browsers such as Lynx (unfortunately, it doesn't seem to work in graphical browsers with images turned off). To accomplish this trick, you'll need the ASCII art prepared ahead of time. Then, in your HTML code, include the entire <IMG> tag inside <PRE>...</PRE> tags, and put the ASCII art inside the ALT attribute, like this:

```
<PRE>
<IMG SRC="cow.gif" ALT="
          (  )
Moo      (oo)
          \/------\
           ||     | \
           ||.    |  \
           ||----W||  *
           ||     ||
           ||     ||
">
</PRE>
```

In this code, the original image (cow.gif) will be replaced by the text version, neatly formatted, in text-only browsers. Note that because the <PRE> tags are outside the <IMG> tag itself (to get around the fact that you can't put HTML code inside the ALT attribute), this trick works best when the image is alone on a line; that is, there is no text on the line before or after it.

Other Neat Tricks with Images

Now that you've learned about inline and external images, images as links, and how to wrap text around images, you know the majority of what most people do with images in Web pages—and you know everything that HTML 2.0 can do with images. But there are a few newer tricks to play with, and that's what this section is all about.

All the attributes in this section were originally Netscape extensions that have since been incorporated into HTML 3.2.

7

Image Dimensions and Scaling

Two Netscape extensions to the <IMG> tag, HEIGHT and WIDTH, specify the height and width of the image, in pixels. Both are now part of the HTML 3.2 specification.

If you use the actual height and width of the image in these values (which you can find out in most image editing programs), your Web pages will appear to load and display much faster in some browsers than if you did not include these values.

Why? Normally when a browser is parsing the HTML code in your file, it has to load and test each image to get its width and height before proceeding so that it can format the text appropriately. This usually means that it loads and formats some of your text, waits for the image to load, formats around the image when it gets the dimensions, and then moves on for the rest of the page. If the width and height are already specified in the HTML code itself, the browser can just make a space for the image of the appropriate size and keep formatting all the text around it. This way, your readers can continue reading the text while the images are loading rather than having to wait. And, because WIDTH and HEIGHT are just ignored in other browsers, there's no reason not to use them for all your images. They neither harm nor affect the image in browsers that don't support them.

TIP

If you test your page with images in it in Netscape, try choosing Document Info from the View menu. You'll get a window listing all the images in your page. By selecting each image in turn, you'll get information about that image—including its size, which you can then copy into your HTML file.

If the values for WIDTH and HEIGHT are different from the actual width and height of the image, your browser will automatically scale the image to fit those dimensions. Because smaller images take up less disk space than larger images, and therefore take less time to transfer over the network, this is a sneaky way to get away with large images on your pages without the additional increase in load time—just create a smaller version, and then scale it to the dimensions you want on your Web page. Note, however, that the pixels will also be scaled, so the bigger version may end up looking grainy or blocky. Experiment with different sizes and scaling factors to get the right effect.

NOTE

Don't do reverse scaling—create a large image and then use WIDTH and HEIGHT to scale it down. Smaller file sizes are better because they take less time to load. If you're just going to display a small image, make it smaller to begin with.

More About Image Borders

You learned about the BORDER attribute to the <IMG> tag as part of the section on links, where setting BORDER to a number or to zero determined the width of the image border (or hid it entirely).

Normally, plain images don't have borders; only images that hold links do. But you can use the BORDER attribute with plain images to draw a border around the image, like this:

```
<P>Frame the image <IMG SRC="monalisa.gif" BORDER=5></P>
```

Figure 7.26 shows an example of an image with a border around it.

Figure 7.26.
An image border.

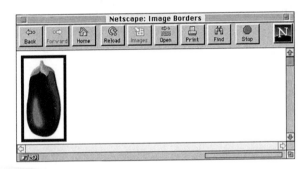

Image Previews

One completely optional Netscape extension to images is the use of the LOWSRC attribute to <IMG>, which provides a sort of preview for the actual image on the page. LOWSRC is used just like SRC is, with a pathname to another image file:

```
<IMG SRC="wall.gif" LOWSRC="wallsmall.gif">
```

When a browser that support LOWSRC encounters a LOWSRC tag, it loads in the LOWSRC image first, in the first pass for the overall page layout. Then, after all the layout and LOWSRC images are done loading and displaying, the image specified in SRC is loaded and fades in to replace the LOWSRC image.

Why would you want this? The image in LOWSRC is usually a smaller or lower resolution preview of the actual image, one that can load very quickly and give the reader an idea of the overall effect of the page (make sure your LOWSRC image is indeed a smaller image, otherwise there's no point to including it). Then, after all the layout is done, the reader can scroll around and read the text while the better images are quietly loaded in the background.

Using LOWSRC is entirely optional; it's simply ignored in browsers other than Netscape.

Using Color

One way to add color to your Web pages is to add images; images can provide a splash of color amongst the black and gray and white. Several Netscape extensions to HTML, however, enable you also to change the colors of the page itself, including changing the background color of the page, changing the color of the text and links on that page, and to add "spot color" to individual characters on that page. In this section you'll learn how to do all these things.

NOTE | You'll learn a whole lot about color and color theory tomorrow. Today you'll just learn how to change colors in HTML.

Naming Colors

Before you can change the color of any part of an HTML page, you have to know what color you're going to change it to. There are two ways to specify colors using the color extensions to HTML:

- ☐ Using a hexadecimal number representing that color
- ☐ Using one of a set of predefined color names

The most flexible and most widely supported method of indicating color involves finding out the numeric value of the color you want to use. Most image-editing programs have what's called a color picker—some way of choosing a single color from a range of available colors. Most color pickers, in turn, will tell you the value of that color in RGB form, as three numbers (one for red, one for green, and one for blue—that's what RGB stands for). Each number is usually 0 to 255, with 0 0 0 being black and 255 255 255 being white.

Once you have your colors as three numbers from 0 to 255, you have to convert those numbers into hexadecimal. You can use any scientific calculator that converts between ASCII and hex to get these numbers. A slew of freeware and shareware color pickers for HTML are available as well, including HTML Color Reference and ColorFinder for Windows, and ColorMeister and ColorSelect for the Macintosh. Alternately, you can use rgb.html, a form that will do the conversion for you, which you'll learn how to implement later in this book. For now, you can try out the rgb.html form at http://www.lne.com/rgb.html, which will give you the hex for any three numbers. So, for example, the RGB values 0 0 0 convert to 00 00 00, and the RGB values for 255 255 255 convert to FF FF FF.

The final hex number you need is all three numbers put together with a pound sign (#) at the beginning, like this:

```
#000000
#DE04E4
#FFFF00
```

The second way of indicating colors in HTML is much easier to deal with. Instead of using arcane numbering schemes, you just pick a color name: Black, White, Green, Maroon, Olive, Navy, Purple, Gray, Red, Yellow, Blue, Teal, Lime, Aqua, Fuchsia, or Silver (these colors come from the Windows color palette, which allows only 16 colors).

Although color names are easier to remember and to figure out than the numbers, they do offer less flexibility in the kinds of colors you can use (you have only 16 colors to choose from, as opposed to millions), and names are not as widely supported in browsers as the color numbers (although both Netscape and Internet Explorer do support color names). Keep that in mind if you do choose to use color names because you may lose the colors in other browsers.

Once you have a color name or number in hand, you can go on and apply that color to various parts of your HTML page.

Changing the Background Color

To change the color of the background on a page, decide what color you want and then add an attribute to the <BODY> tag called BGCOLOR. The <BODY> tag, in case you've forgotten, is the tag that surrounds all the content of your HTML file. <HEAD> contains the title, and <BODY> contains almost everything else. BGCOLOR is an HTML 3.2 extension.

To use color numbers for backgrounds the value of the BGCOLOR attribute to <BODY> is the hexadecimal number you found out in the previous section in quotes. It looks like this:

```
<BODY BGCOLOR="#FFFFFF">
<BODY BGCOLOR="#934CE8">
```

To use color names, simply use the name of the color as the value to BGCOLOR:

```
<BODY BGCOLOR=white>
<BODY BGCOLOR=green>
```

NOTE Internet Explorer also allows you to indicate color numbers without the leading pound sign (#). Although this may seem more convenient, given that it is incompatible with many other browsers, the inclusion of the one other character does not seem like that much of a hardship.

Changing Text Colors

When you can change the background colors, it makes sense also to change the color of the text itself. More HTML extensions supported by Netscape, Internet Explorer, and HTML 3.2 allow you to globally change the color of the text in your pages.

7

To change the text and link colors, you'll need your color names or numbers just as you did for changing the backgrounds. With a color in hand, you can then add any of the following attributes to the <BODY> tag with either a color number or color name as their values:

TEXT   Controls the color of all the page's body text that isn't a link, including headings, body text, text inside tables, and so on.

LINK   Controls the color of normal, unfollowed links in the page (the ones that are usually blue by default).

VLINK   Controls the color of links you have visited (the ones that are usually purple or red by default).

ALINK   Controls the color of a link that has had the mouse button pressed on it but not released (an activated link). These are often red by default.

For example, to create a page with a black background, white text, and bright purple unfollowed links, you might use the following <BODY> tag:

```
<BODY BGCOLOR="#000000" TEXT="#FFFFFF" LINK="#9805FF">
```

For Internet Explorer, using the following color names would produce the same effect:

```
<BODY BGCOLOR=black TEXT=white LINK=purple>
```

Both of these links would produce a page that looks something like the one shown in Figure 7.27.

Figure 7.27.

Background and text colors.

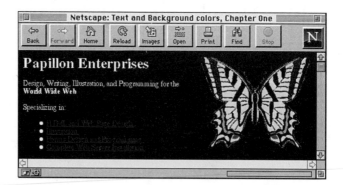

Spot Color

When you change the text colors in a page using attributes to the <BODY> tag, that change affects all the text on the page. Spot color is the ability to change the color of individual characters inside your page, which you can use instead of or in addition to a global text color.

Yesterday you learned about using the HTML 3.2 extension <FONT> for setting the font size and font name. A third, and even newer attribute to <FONT>, COLOR, lets you change the color of individual words or phrases. The value of COLOR is either a color name or number:

```
<P>When we go out tonight, we're going to paint the town
<FONT COLOR="#FF0000">RED</FONT>.
```

You can, of course, use font spot colors in addition to font names and sizes.

Image Backgrounds

One last topic for this chapter is the ability to use an image as a background for your pages rather than simply a solid colored background. When you use an image for a background, that image is "tiled"—that is, the image is repeated in rows to fill the browser window.

To create a tiled background, you'll need an image to serve as the tile. Usually when you create an image for tiling, you'll need to make sure that the pattern flows smoothly from one tile to the next. You can usually do some careful editing of the image in your favorite image-editing program to make sure the edges line up. The goal is to have the edges meet cleanly so there isn't a "seam" between the tiles after you've laid them end to end. (See Figure 7.28 for an example of tiles that don't line up very well.) You can also try clip-art packages for wallpaper or tile patterns that are often designed specifically to be tiled in this fashion.

Figure 7.28.

Tiled images with "seams."

When you have an image that can be cleanly tiled, all you need to create a tiled image background is the BACKGROUND attribute, part of the <BODY> tag. The value of BACKGROUND is a filename or URL that points to your image file, as in the following example:

```
<BODY BACKGROUND="tiles.gif">
<BODY BACKGROUND="backgrounds/rosemarble.gif">
```

Figure 7.29 shows the result of a simple tiled background.

Figure 7.29.

*A tiled background
in Netscape.*

Internet Explorer offers a twist on the tiled background design: a fixed tile pattern they call a *watermark*. The idea here is that when you scroll a page, instead of everything on the page including the background scrolling by, only the page foreground (text and images) scrolls. The tiles in the background stay rooted in one place. To create this effect, use the BGPROPERTIES=FIXED attribute to the body tag:

```
<BODY BACKGROUND="backgrounds/rosemarble.gif" BGPROPERTIES=FIXED>
```

Hints for Better Use of Images

The use of images in Web pages is one of the bigger arguments among users and providers of Web pages. For everyone who wants to design Web pages with more, bigger, and brighter images to take full advantage of the graphical capabilities of the Web, there is someone on a slow network connection who is begging for fewer images so that his or her browser doesn't take three hours to load a page.

As a designer of Web pages, you should consider both of these points of view. Balance the fun of creating a highly visual, colorful Web page with the need to get your information to everyone you want to have it—and that includes people who may not have access to your images at all.

This section offers some hints and compromises you can make in the design of your Web pages so that you can make everyone happy (or everyone unhappy, depending on how you look at it).

Do You Really Need This Image?

For each image you put inline on your Web page, consider why you are putting it there. What does that image add to the design? Does it provide information that could be presented in the text instead? Is it just there because you like how it looks?

7

Try not to clutter your Web page with pretty but otherwise unnecessary images. A simple Web page with only a few iconic images is often more effective than a page that opens with an enormous graphic and continues the trend with flashy 3D buttons, drop-shadow bullets, and psychedelic line separators.

Keep Your Images Small

A smaller image takes less time to transfer over the Net; therefore, using smaller images makes your Web page load faster and causes less frustration for people trying to read it over a slow link. What could be easier?

To create small images, you can reduce their actual physical dimensions on the screen. You can also create smaller file sizes for your images by reducing the number of colors in an image. Your goal is to reduce the file size of the image so that it transfers faster, but a four-inch by four-inch black-and-white image (two colors) may be smaller in file size than a $^1/_2$ inch by $^1/_2$ inch full-color photographic image. With most image-processing programs, you can reduce the number of colors and touch up the result so it looks good even with fewer colors.

A good rule to follow is that you should try to keep your inline images somewhere under 20K. That may seem small, but a single 20K file takes nearly that many seconds to download over a 14.4Kbps SLIP connection. Multiply that by the number of images on your Web page, and it may take a substantial amount of time for that page to load (even if you're using a browser that can load multiple images at once. The pipe is only so wide). Will someone care about what you have in your Web page if they have had to go off and have lunch while it's loading?

NOTE   The small icons that I used for the arrows in the navigation examples are 300 bytes apiece—less than a third of a K. The spider web image in the Halloween example is slightly larger than 1K. Small does not mean the image isn't useful.

Reuse Images as Often as Possible

In addition to keeping individual images small, try to reuse the same images as often as you can, on single pages and across multiple pages; for example, if you have images as bullets, use the same image for all the bullets rather than different ones. Reusing images has two significant advantages over using different images:

☐ Reusing images provides a consistency to your design across pages, part of creating an overall "look" for your site.

□ Even more importantly, reusing images means that your browser has to download it only once. Once it has the image in memory, it can simply draw it multiple times without having to make lots of connections back to the server.

To reuse an image, you don't have to do anything special; just make sure you refer to each image by the same URL each time you use it. The browser will take care of the rest.

Provide Alternatives to Images

If you're not using the ALT attribute in your images, you should be. The ALT attribute is extremely useful for making your Web page readable by text-only browsers. But what about people who turn off images in their browser because they have a slow link to the Internet? Most browsers do not use the value of ALT in this case. And sometimes ALT isn't enough; because you can specify text only inside an ALT string, you can't substitute HTML code for the image.

To get around all these problems while still keeping your nifty graphical Web page, consider creating alternative text-only versions of your Web pages and putting links to them on the full-graphics versions of that same Web page, like this:

```
<P>A <A HREF="TextVersion.html">text-only</A>
version of this page is available.</P>
```

The link to the text-only page takes up only one small paragraph on the "real" Web page, but it makes the information much more accessible. It's a courtesy that readers with slow connections will thank you for, and it still allows you to load up your "main" Web page with as many images as you like for those with fast connections.

Summary

One of the major features that makes the World Wide Web stand out from other forms of Internet information is that pages on the Web can contain full-color images. It was arguably the existence of those images that allowed the Web to catch on so quickly and to become so popular in so short a time.

To place images on your Web pages, those images must be in GIF or JPEG format (GIF is more widely supported) and small enough that they can be quickly downloaded over a potentially slow link. The HTML tag <IMG> allows you to put an image on the Web page, either inline with text or on a line by itself. The `<IMG>` tag has three primary attributes supported in standard HTML:

SRC   The location and filename of the image to include.

ALIGN   How to position the image vertically with its surrounding text. `ALIGN` can have one of three values: `TOP`, `MIDDLE`, or `BOTTOM`.

ALT   A text string to substitute for the image in text-only browsers.

You can include images inside a link tag (`<A>`) and have those images serve as hot spots for the links, same as text.

In addition to the standard attributes, several new attributes to the `<IMG>` tag provide greater control over images and layout of Web pages. Those new attributes, most of which are now part of the HTML 3.2 specification, include the following:

ALIGN=LEFT   Place the image against the appropriate margin, allowing all
ALIGN=RIGHT   following text to flow into the space alongside the image. In
                addition, an HTML 3.2 extension to `<BR>`, `CLEAR`, allows you to
                stop wrapping text alongside an image. `CLEAR` can have three
                values: `LEFT`, `RIGHT`, and `ALL`.

ALIGN=TEXTTOP   (Netscape) Allow greater control over the alignment of an
ALIGN=ABSMIDDLE inline image and the text surrounding it.
ALIGN=BASELINE
ALIGN=ABSBOTTOM

VSPACE   Define the amount of space between an image and the text
HSPACE   surrounding it.

BORDER   Defines the width of the border around an image (with or
                without a link). `BORDER=0` hides the border altogether.

LOWSRC   (Netscape only) Defines an alternate, lower-resolution image
                that is loaded before the image indicated by `SRC`.

In addition to images, you can also add color to the background and to the text of a page using attributes to the `<BODY>` tag, or add color to individual characters using the `COLOR` attribute to `<FONT>`. Finally, you can also add patterned or tiled backgrounds to images using the `BACKGROUND` attribute to `<BODY>` with an image for the tile.

7

Q&A

Q **How can I create thumbnails of my images so that I can link them to larger external images?**

A You'll have to do that with some kind of image-editing program; the Web won't do it for you. Just open up the image and scale it down to the right size.

Q **Can I put HTML tags in the string for the ALT attribute?**

A That would be nice, wouldn't it? Unfortunately, you can't. All you can do is put an ordinary string in there. Keep it simple, and you should be fine.

Q **You discussed a technique for including LOWSRC images on a page that are loaded in before regular images are. I've seen an effect on Web pages where an image seems to load in as a really blurry image and then become clearer as time goes on. Is that a LOWSRC effect?**

A No, actually, that's something called an interlaced GIF. There's only one image there, it just displays as it's loading differently from regular GIFs. You'll learn more about interlaced GIFs in the next chapter.

LOWSRC images load in just like regular images (with no special visual effect).

Q **I've seen some Web pages where you can click on different places in an image and get different link results, such as a map of the United States where each state has a different page. How do you do this in HTML?**

A That's called an image map, and it's an advanced form of Web page development. It involves writing code on the server side to interpret the mouse clicks and send back the right result. I describe image maps in Chapter 16, "Image Maps."

7

Chapter 8

Creating Images for the Web

You might have thought that I explained everything about images on the Web in the previous chapter. Well, although I did explain how to use images in HTML in that chapter, you might have noticed that I said very little about the images themselves. And in Web page design, a lot of the technique in working with images doesn't have anything to do with HTML at all, but instead with features and tricks you can do with the images before you even put them onto the page. In this chapter, I'll explain a bit more about basic image concepts on and off the Web, including the following:

- [ ] Image formats used on the Web: GIF and JPEG
- [ ] Color: HSB, RGB, bit depth, color tables, and how colors are used
- [ ] Image compression and how it affects file size and image quality
- [ ] Transparency and interlacing in GIF and JPEG files
- [ ] Ideas for creating and using images
- [ ] The future: PNG

Image Formats

I mentioned earlier in this book that GIF is the only format available on the Web that is guaranteed to be *cross-platform*, meaning that it could be viewed on any computer system. Your choice of image formats has doubled since the first edition of this book appeared: JPEG files have been growing in support on the Web and should be widely available on the Web by the time you read this. In this section, I'll give a quick overview of both formats, and the rest of this chapter will explain some of the advantages and disadvantages of each so that you can make the decision about which format to use for your images.

GIF

GIF, or CompuServe GIF, is the most widely used graphics format on the Web today. GIF stands for Graphics Interchange Format and was developed by CompuServe to fill the need for a cross-platform image format. You should be able to read GIF files on just about any computer with the right software.

NOTE

> GIF is pronounced *jiff,* like the peanut butter, not GIF with a hard G as in *gift.* Really. It says so in the early documentation of GIF tools.

The GIF format is actually two very similar image formats: GIF87, the original format; and GIF89a, which has enhancements for transparency, interlacing, and for multi-frame GIF images that you can use for simple animations. You'll learn about interlacing and transparency in this chapter, and about multi-frame GIFs in Chapter 9, "External Files, Multimedia, and Animation."

GIF files are great for logos, icons, line art, and other simple images. They don't work as well for highly detailed images because the GIF format is limited to only 256 colors. Photographs in GIF format, for example, tend to look grainy and blotchy.

The biggest problem with GIF at the moment has nothing to do with its technical aspects. The problem is that the form of compression it uses, LZW, is patented. UniSys, the owner of the patent, has requested that developers who use the GIF format after 1994 pay a per-copy royalty for the use of LZW. That includes Web browser developers and the people who write image-editing programs. Because of the problems with the patent on LZW, the GIF format may fade from view in the future and be replaced on the Web with some other, more freely available platform-independent format.

JPEG

The most obvious candidate for the format likely to replace GIF for the time being is JPEG, which stands for Joint Photographic Experts Group (the group that developed it). JPEG is actually more of a compression type that several other file formats can use. But the file format for which it is known is also commonly called JPEG. JPEG is pronounced *jay-peg*.

JPEG was designed for the storage of photographic images. Unlike GIF images, JPEG images can have any number of colors, and the style of compression (the compression algorithm) works especially well for photographic patterns, and so the file sizes it creates from photographs are considerably smaller than those that GIF can produce. On the other hand, the compression algorithm isn't nearly as good for line art and images with large blocks of color. It also uses *lossy* compression, which means that it throws out bits of the image to make the image smaller.

JPEG files have just begun to be widely supported by browsers on the World Wide Web, but most of the major browser makers already have JPEG support, and more are sure to follow.

Color

If I had a whole book to talk about color theory, I could go into the half-dozen or so common models for describing color. But this is a book about the Web, and this chapter is specifically about images that will be displayed on the Web, so I don't need to be so verbose (and boring). Instead, I'll talk about the two major color models: the model for how you and I perceive color, which is called HSB (Hue, Saturation, and Brightness), and the model for how your computer handles color, which is called RGB (Red, Green, and Blue). With a basic understanding of how these two color models work, you should be able to understand most of the color issues you'll encounter when dealing with images on the Web.

Hue, Saturation, and Brightness (HSB)

The Hue, Saturation, and Brightness model is sometimes called *subjective* or *perceptive* color, because this model intuitively describes how we perceive color and changes from one color to another. Under the HSB model, each color is represented by three numbers indicating hue, saturation, and brightness.

HSB stands for Hue, Saturation, and Brightness and is a way of representing individual colors based on how they are subjectively seen by humans.

Hue is the actual color you're working with. Think of it as being like the tubes of paint that an artist uses: red, blue, yellow, orange, violet, and so on are all hues. But so are orange-yellow or bluish-green. The hue encompasses all the colors in the spectrum and is measured from 0 to 360 in degrees around a color wheel, starting with red at 0 and 360, yellow at 120 degrees, blue at 240, and all the other colors in between (see Figure 8.1).

NEW TERM | *Hue* is the actual shade of color you're working with: for example, red, blue, or greenish-yellow. Hue values are from 1 to 360.

Figure 8.1.
Hues.

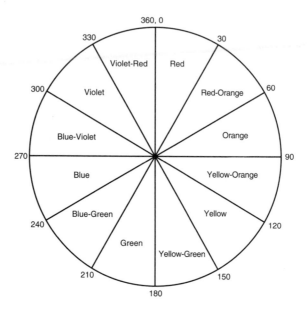

Brightness is how light or dark the color is. When you mix white or black paint in with the main color you're using, you increase or decrease the brightness. Brightness is measured as a percentage, with 0 being white and 100 being black (see Figure 8.2).

NEW TERM | *Brightness* is how light or dark the color is. Brightness can be made darker by adding more black, or lighter by adding more white. Brightness numbers are from 1 (white) to 100 (black).

Figure 8.2.
Brightness.

Saturation is the intensity of the color you're using—how much color there is in the mix. If you had a sky blue, which was a little blue paint and a little white paint, you could add more blue paint to increase the saturation and make it more blue. Saturation is also measured as a percentage, with 0 as no color and 100 as full color (see Figure 8.3).

Saturation is the amount of color. Less saturation creates pastel colors; more saturation creates more vibrant colors. Saturation numbers are from 1 (no color) to 100 (full color).

Figure 8.3.
Saturation.

You can represent any color you can see using the HSB model, and more importantly, you can represent any color you're using by simply using the three HSB numbers. Also, modifying colors is easy using the HSB model. When you seek to "make a color lighter" or "make it more purplish-blue," these correspond neatly to modifications to brightness and hue, respectively. In fact, if you've ever used a color picker on your computer, such as the one from Adobe Photoshop (shown in Figure 8.4), usually the user interface for that picker is based on the HSB model (or one similar with a different name such as "HSL: Hue Saturation and Lightness").

Figure 8.4.
An HSB color picker in Photoshop.

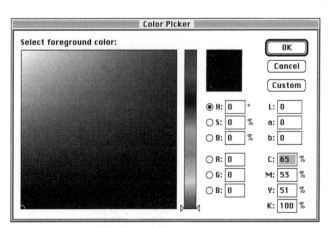

Red, Green, and Blue (RGB)

Now that I've spent all that time explaining color in terms of HSB, I'm going to mess it all up: Most of the time when you deal with colors in image-editing programs and on the Web, you don't describe a color in HSB. Most image programs indicate color as RGB (Red, Green, and Blue) values instead.

RGB is the way computer monitors display color. If you get really close to your monitor, you'll see what look like individual dots, which are actually combinations of red, green, and blue dots that are produced by the red, green, and blue electron guns in your monitor. It's the combination of those dots in varying intensities that creates a single color on your screen. Color values in RGB, as you learned in the previous chapter, are indicated using three numbers (one each for red, blue, and green) that range from 0 to 255. 0 0 0 is black, 255 255 255 is white, and the full range of colors (more than 16.7 million, which is more than the human eye can distinguish) is represented in the middle.

NEW TERM

> *RGB* stands for Red, Green, and Blue, and is a way of representing color based on color from light sources (display monitors, for example). RGB values have three 0-to-255 values (one each for red, green, and blue).

NOTE

> Although you can specify any of the 16.7 million colors as an RGB value in this way, your monitor or display system might not be able to display the color entirely accurately. The 16.7 million colors you can represent using the three RGB values is called 24-bit color (the RGB values are three eight-bit numbers, therefore, 24 bits total). If your display can handle only eight-bit or 16-bit color (256 and 65,536 colors, respectively), it will try to match the color you asked for as closely as it can to the colors it has, or it will create a pattern for the missing color. Don't worry about the differences in your display's capability to display colors and the image's colors; displays with more colors will just give finer gradations of color, usually not the wrong color altogether.

Note that you can still get the full range of colors using both RGB and HSB. They're not different sets of color; they're just different ways of describing color mathematically. The same color can be given in RGB numbers or HSB numbers, and if you convert one to the other, you'll still get the same color. It's like measuring your height in inches, centimeters,

8

cubits, or cans of Spam: Each one is a different measurement scale, but you stay the same height regardless of how you measure it.

So why did I go on for so long about HSB if RGB is much more common? Because it's easier to think about changes in color using HSB than it is in RGB. You usually won't say, "I need to increase the green level in that image" (which, in the RGB model, results in a more orangy red, believe it or not). So when you're working with images, go ahead and think in HSB to create the colors you want. But keep in mind that when a program asks you for a color, it is asking for the RGB values for that color. Fortunately, most color pickers and editing tools will give you color values in both RGB and HSB.

Image Formats and Color Maps

Both the GIF and JPEG formats can represent color as three 0 to 255 RGB values. The major difference between the two formats, however, is that images stored in a GIF file can have only 256 total colors, whereas JPEG images can store any number of colors.

The GIF format stores its colors in an *indexed color map*. A color map is like a series of slots, each one holding a single RGB color. The colors for each pixel in the image point to a slot in the color map. If you change a color in the map, all the pixels in the image that pointed to that slot will be changed (see Figure 8.5).

NEW TERM

A *color map* is a table of all the colors in the image, with each pixel in the image pointing to a slot in the color map.

Figure 8.5.
Color maps in GIF images.

The GIF format has a 256-color color map, which means that you can store a maximum of 256 colors in the image. When you convert an image to GIF format, you usually also have to reduce the number of colors in the image to 256 (and if your image-editing program is powerful enough, you'll have some options for controlling which colors are discarded and how). Of course, if you want to use fewer than 256 colors, that's an excellent idea. The fewer colors you use, the smaller the file.

NOTE

> Color maps are called by a great variety of names, including color table, indexed color, palette, color index, or Color LookUp Table (CLUT or LUT). They're all the same thing—a table of the available colors in the image. Your image-editing program should give you a way of looking at the color map in your image. Look for a menu item with one of these names.

JPEG, on the other hand, can represent any number of RGB colors, allowing you to choose from millions of colors. Reducing the number of colors won't help you much in JPEG because JPEG file sizes are determined primarily by the amount of compression, not by the number of colors.

Exercise 8.1: Reducing colors in a GIF image.

EXERCISE

When I first started working with images on the Web, someone told me that if I reduced the number of colors in my image, the file size would be smaller. Okay, I thought, that makes sense. But how does one reduce the number of colors? For simple icons I could just paint with only a few colors, but for more sophisticated images such as photographs or scanned art, trying to reduce the existing number of colors seemed like an incredibly daunting task.

With the help of some image-editing friends, I figured it out. In this exercise, we'll go through the process I use when I need to reduce the number of colors in an image so that you can see what is involved.

NOTE

> I'm going to be using Adobe Photoshop for this procedure. If you do a lot of image editing, Photoshop is by far the best tool you can use and is available for Macintosh, Windows, Sun, and SGI platforms. If you're using another editor, check the documentation for that editor to see whether it provides a similar procedure for reducing the number of colors in an image.

The image we'll start with is an RGB drawing of a pink rose (see Figure 8.6), with many shades of pink and green. (You can't see the pink and green here, but you can get the idea.)

The first step is to try converting the image to indexed color in preparation for making it into a GIF file. If we're lucky, there won't be more than 256 colors to begin with, in which case the job is easy.

8

Figure 8.6.
The pink rose.

In Photoshop, selecting Indexed Color from the Mode menu gives you the dialog box you see in Figure 8.7.

Figure 8.7.

The Indexed Color dialog box in Photoshop.

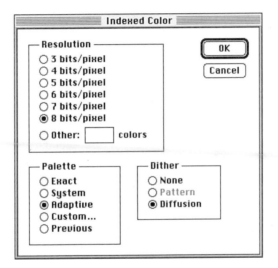

If the image contains fewer than 256 colors, the actual number of colors is listed in the Other part of the Resolution section. If your image already contains fewer than 256 colors, by all means use those colors. Otherwise, you'll have to cut some of them out. In the pink rose image, we didn't get lucky: Because there's nothing in the Other box, we've got more than 256 colors in the image. Darn.

To reduce the number of colors, choose one of the radio buttons in the Resolution section. The smaller the bits per pixel, the fewer colors you have. Look at Table 8.1 for a quick reference.

Table 8.1. Number of colors.

Choice	Colors
3 bits/pixel	8 colors
4 bits/pixel	16 colors
5 bits/pixel	32 colors
6 bits/pixel	64 colors
7 bits/pixel	128 colors
8 bits/pixel	256 colors

Remember that each of the colors you have is still a full RGB color, so you aren't restricted in the set of colors from which you can choose—just in the total number of colors you can have. So you could have an image with 256 colors, all of them varying shades of pink, if you wanted it.

Because fewer colors is better, let's try going for the minimum—three bits per pixel, or eight total colors. When you're reducing the number of colors, Photoshop also asks you which palette (Photoshop's name for the color map) you want to use and which Dithering option. Dithering is a way of reducing colors in an image by creating patterns of available colors that, when viewed together, look like the original color (for example, a black-and-white checker-board to approximate a gray color). Most of the time, you'll want to use an Adaptive Palette (which weights the colors in the palette based on how frequently they're used in the original image) and a Diffusion dither (which provides the most uniform dithering of missing colors).

NOTE

If you were lucky enough to have fewer than 256 colors in the image, use the Exact palette instead of the Adaptive palette.

After you select OK, the colors are converted and dithered, and the new image is created. In Figure 8.8, I've put the original image on the right so you can compare.

Figure 8.8.

The new image (3 bits per pixel).

With only eight colors, much of the detail that was in the original image is gone. The veins in the leaves are no longer visible, and the rose is primarily a pink blob with some black and white highlights.

But all is not lost. Just undo the mode change and go back to RGB color. Don't convert back to RGB using the Mode menu; when you converted to eight colors, you lost the original data. Use Undo instead.

Try converting to Indexed Color again, this time using four bits per pixel, slowly moving up in colors until the image quality is where you want it to be. Obviously, for the highest-quality image, you should use eight bits per pixel, but you might be able to get away with five or six and still have close to the same image to work with.

For this rose, I eventually ended up using five bits per pixel, which gave me 32 colors to choose from. The image still looks a little dithered, but the quality is quite good. Figure 8.9 shows the result (with the original image on the right for comparison).

Figure 8.9.
*The final image
(five bits per pixel).*

You might be interested in the actual file sizes before and after, for comparison purposes. The rose image, using 256 colors, was about 10.5K. The version with only eight colors was all the way down to 3K. The final version—the one with 32 colors—is a nice happy medium at 6K. Although the difference in three or four kilobytes may seem incredibly trivial, if you use multiple images on your pages, the total space saved can mean your page loads that much faster.

Color Allocation

Even if you manage to reduce the colors on your GIF images to a point at which the image quality is pretty good, or if you use JPEG images so you don't have to worry about reducing your colors, on some platforms and some pages, you might be in for a nasty surprise. Some of your images could come out looking horrible or in all the wrong colors. What's going on here?

This is most likely a problem with color allocation with the platform on which you're viewing the page. On some systems, the video card or display system might be limited to a single color map for everything on the system. That's only a certain number of colors (usually 256) for every application running on the system. And slots in the table for colors are allocated (assigned) on a first-come, first-served basis.

So let's assume that you have two images on your Web page: one that uses a 256-color map of predominantly pink hues and another (also 256 colors) that uses predominantly blue hues. Your Web browser has only 256 slots, but your images require 512 total colors. What can the browser do? Depending on the browser, it might display the first image fine and then try to use the remaining slots, if any, for the second image. Or it might try to merge the two color maps into something in the middle (a sort of lavender for both images). It might just apply the first color map to the second image (turning the second image pink). At any rate, the more images and more colors you use on a page, the more likely it is that people using systems with limited color maps are going to run into problems.

However, there are two ways to work around color-allocation problems and increase your chances of getting the colors correct.

One way is to make sure that the total colors in all the combined images in your page do not go over 256 colors. For example, if you have four images of equal size with 50 colors each, you can take only up 200 colors. Use the procedure you learned in the previous exercise to reduce the number of colors in each image.

Alternatively, you can use a single color map for all the images you want to put on the page. You can do this in Photoshop by using the following method:

1. Create one large document, copying all the images you want on your page onto that canvas.

2. Convert the large document to indexed color using as many colors as you need (up to 256). Use the procedure you learned in the previous exercise to reduce the number of colors.

3. Choose Color Table from the Mode menu. You'll see the color map for the larger document, which is also the combined color map for all the smaller images.

4. Save that color map.

5. Open each individual image and convert the image to indexed color (the number of colors isn't important).

6. Choose Color Table from the Mode menu, and load your saved global color table.

7. Save each image with the new global color map.

Image Compression

If you described a 24-bit color bitmap image as a list of pixels starting from the top of the image and working down to the bottom line by line, with each pixel represented by the three numbers that make up an RGB value, you would end up with an awful lot of numbers and a very large file size. The larger the file size, the harder it is to store and handle the image. This is where image compression comes in. Compression, as you might expect, makes an image smaller (in bulk, not in dimensions on the screen). Therefore, it takes up less space on your disk, is less difficult to process, and (for Web images) takes less time to transfer over the network. In this section, you'll learn about how the GIF and JPEG files handle compression and the best kinds of files for each file format.

Compression Basics

Most common image formats have some sort of compression built in so that you don't have to stuff or zip the images yourself. It's all handled for you as part of the image format and the programs that read or write that image format. Different image formats use different methods of compression, which have varying amounts of success in squeezing a file down as far as it can go, based on the kind of image you have. One form of compression might be really good for images that have few colors and lots of straight lines, but not so good for photographs. Another form of compression might do just the opposite.

Some forms of compression manage to get really small file sizes out of images by throwing out some of the information in the original image. They don't just randomly toss out pixels. (Imagine what this book would be like if you threw out every other word, and you can imagine the effect on an image using that method of compression.) *Lossy compression*, as it's called, is based on the theory that there are details and changes in color in an image that are smaller than the human eye can see. And if you can't tell the difference between two portions of an image, you don't need to keep both of them around in the file; just keep one and note that there were originally two of them. Lossy compression usually results in very small file sizes, but because you're losing some information when you compress it, the overall image quality might not be as good.

New Term

> *Lossy compression* discards parts of the image that the compression program deems unimportant. Lossy compression results in a degradation of image quality.

The reverse of lossy compression is *lossless compression*, which never throws out any information from the actual file. With lossy compression, if you have two identical images and you compress and then decompress one of them, the resulting two images will not be the same. With lossless compression, if you compress and decompress one of the images, you'll still end up with two identical images.

Lossless compression compresses without discarding any information from the original image. Lossless compression is less effective than lossy compression, but with no image degradation.

Compression in GIF and JPEG Files

That's all well and good, you say. You can now impress your friends at parties with your knowledge of lossless and lossy compression. But what does this mean for your image files and the World Wide Web?

GIF and JPEG use different forms of compression that work for different kinds of images. Based on the image you're using and how concerned you are with the quality of that image versus the size you want it to be, you might want to pick one format over the other.

GIF images use a form of lossless compression called LZW, named after its creators, Lempel, Ziv, and Welch. LZW compression works by finding repeated pixel patterns within an image (pixels that have the same color next to each other). The more repetition, the better the compression. So images with large blocks of color such as icons or line art images are great as GIF files because they can be compressed really well. Scanned images such as photographs, on the other hand, have fewer consistent pixel patterns and, therefore, don't compress as well.

JPEG has a reputation for being able to create smaller files than GIF, and for many images, that might be true. JPEG files use the JPEG compression algorithm, which examines groups of pixels for the variation between them and then stores the variations rather than the pixels themselves. For images with lots of pixel variations, such as photographs, JPEG works especially well; for images with large portions of similar colors, it doesn't work so well (and, in fact, it can introduce variations in formerly solid blocks of color). So, the rule that JPEG files are smaller than GIFs isn't entirely true. GIF is better for icons, logos, and files with few colors.

JPEG is also a form of lossy compression, as I noted earlier, which means that it discards some of the information in the image. When you save an image to JPEG, you can choose how lossy you want the compression to be, from lossless to extremely lossy. The more lossy the compression, the smaller the resulting file size but also the greater the degradation of the image. Extremely compressed JPEG files can come out looking blotchy or grainy, which might not be worth the extra space you saved.

If you're using the JPEG format for your image files, try several levels of compression to see what the optimum level is for the image quality you want.

Displaying Compressed Files

A compressed file can't be displayed until it is decompressed. Programs that read and display image files, such as your image editor or your Web browser, decompress your image and display it when that image is opened or when it is received over the network. How long it takes to decompress the image is a function of the type of compression that was originally used and how powerful your computer is.

In general, JPEG files take significantly longer to decompress and display than GIF files do because JPEG is a much more complicated form of compression. If you have a fast computer, this might not make much of a difference. But keep that in mind for the readers of your Web pages. You might have saved some file space (and loading time) by using the JPEG format over GIF, but decompressing and displaying a JPEG image can use up those time savings on a slower computer.

Exercise 8.2: Different formats and different compressions.

All this compression stuff is rather theoretical, and you might not be able to grasp exactly what it means to you. Let's try a couple of examples with some real images so you can compare the difference between GIF and JPEG compression firsthand. In this example, I'll use two images: one of a logo with only a few colors, and the other of a photograph with thousands of colors. Both are the same size and resolution (100×100 pixels at 72 dpi), and when saved as *raw* data (an uncompressed list of pixels, each one with an RGB value), both are 109,443 bytes (110K).

Let's work with the logo first. I'm going to use Photoshop as my image editor again; your image editor might work slightly differently than the one described in this example. Figure 8.10 shows the original logo I started with, a sort of blue flower-like thing.

Figure 8.10.

The original logo.

First, I had to convert the image to indexed color before I could save it, but it had only seven colors, so converting it was easy. When it is saved as a GIF image, the file is a mere 2,944 bytes (3K, down from 110K)! We've managed to compress the file over 97 percent. In compression lingo, that's about a 30:1 compression ratio, meaning that the original file size was 30 times larger than the compressed file size. Because LZW compression looks for repeating patterns (and there are lots of them in this image, with the big blocks of color), a good amount of compression was to be expected. And because GIF uses lossless compression, the GIF file is identical to the original logo.

Now, let's try JPEG. When you save the logo as a JPEG image, Photoshop gives you a dialog box for how much compression you want (see Figure 8.11).

Figure 8.11.

JPEG compression in Photoshop.

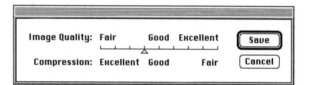

I saved the image as JPEG three times with varying amounts of compression and image quality—one at either end of the scale, and one in the middle.

The first image was saved with excellent compression and fair image quality. With this setting, the resulting file size was 6K, a 95 percent gain (about a 20:1 compression ratio), but it still was not as good as with GIF (of course, the difference between 3K and 6K isn't that significant). The second JPEG file was saved with good compression and good image quality, and the last with fair compression and excellent image quality. The resulting file sizes were 19K (an 83 percent gain, 7:1) and 60K (a 45 percent gain, 2.5:1), respectively—both hardly even worth the effort compared to GIF.

Checking out the image quality proved to be even more enlightening, particularly with that first JPEG file. Figure 8.12 shows the result of all three images.

Figure 8.12.

The logo as JPEG images.

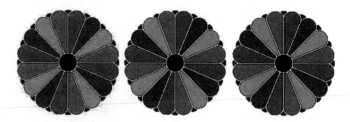

The first image I tried, on the left, the one that approached the space savings of GIF, is barely usable. The JPEG compression produced a grainy, smeared image with strange patterns outside the image itself. As a logo, it's unusable.

The other two images (the images on the middle and the right, the ones I saved at good and excellent image quality, respectively) look much better. But GIF, which is the smallest file and doesn't lose any information, is the clear winner here.

Now let's try the photograph—my favorite penguin picture (see Figure 8.13). Just like the logo, this file is 191×191 pixels, and the raw data is 109,443 bytes (about 110K).

Figure 8.13.
The original photograph.

To convert the image to a GIF file, I first have to change it to an indexed color image. Because of the number of colors in this image, I'll save the maximum number of colors (eight bits per pixel, or 256 colors), which will fill up the color map with the most common colors in the image, dithering the remaining colors.

The resulting GIF file is 26,298 bytes (26K), a 76 percent gain, and a 4:1 compression ratio. It's not nearly as good as the logo but not horrible either.

Now on to the JPEG, which should provide significantly better results. Once again, I created three files with varying amounts of compression and image quality, which resulted in the following file sizes:

☐ Excellent compression/fair image quality: 4K (97 percent gain, 25:1)

☐ Good compression/good image quality: 12K (89 percent gain, 9:1)

☐ Fair compression/excellent image quality: 21K (80 percent gain, 5:1)

Even the JPEG image with excellent image quality, which discards very little information, creates a smaller file than the GIF file of the same image. JPEG really becomes an advantage in photographs and images with lots of colors and detail.

Let's look at the resulting images to compare image quality (see Figure 8.14).

Figure 8.14.
The photograph as JPEG images.

Although the difference between the three is noticeable, the one with fair image quality is still quite usable. Because you can get a smaller file with a less noticeable degradation in the image (in the case of the middle one), either the middle or right image would be a good choice, and all three would be better (in terms of file sizes) than using GIF.

You should try this experiment with your own images to see what savings you get with each format.

Image Interlacing and Transparent Backgrounds

In addition to the color and compression features of GIF and JPEG images, there are several additional optional features of GIF and JPEG files that provide different effects when those images are displayed on your Web pages, including transparent backgrounds and interlaced images.

Transparency

Transparent GIF images have an invisible background so that the color (or pattern) of the page background shows through, giving the image the appearance of floating on the page. Figure 8.15 illustrates the difference between normal and transparent GIFs.

Figure 8.15.

Normal and transparent backgrounds.

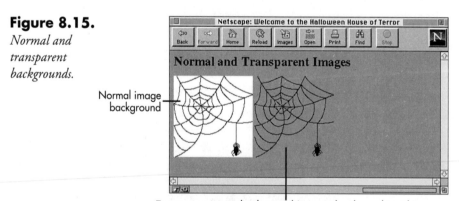

Transparency is a feature of newer GIF files (called GIF89a format). It is not available in JPEG files or in GIF files in the earlier GIF87 format. In order to create a GIF file with a transparent background, you'll need an image tool or program that can create transparent backgrounds. I discuss programs to do that later in this chapter.

8

**NEW
TERM**

Tranparency is a feature of GIF files that allows the background of an image to have no color; the color or pattern that the image is displayed over shows through the transparent parts of the image.

8

Before you can convert the image, however, you need an image with an appropriate background. The easiest images to convert have transparent backgrounds or are icons or other simple art in which the image and the background are distinct (see Figure 8.16). Although you can have photographs with transparent backgrounds, the results might not be as nice if the defining line between the image and the background is not clear.

Figure 8.16.

Good and bad images for transparent backgrounds.

The goal is to make sure that your background is all one color. If that background consists of several colors that are sort of close to each other (as they might be in a photograph), only one of those colors will be transparent.

You can isolate the background of your image using any image-editing program. Simply edit the pixels around the image so they are all one color. Also, be careful that the color you're using for the background isn't also used extensively in the image itself because the color will become transparent there, too.

NOTE

Even if you have a GIF image in the proper format with a transparent background, some browsers that do not understand GIF89 format may not be able to display that image or may display it with an opaque background. Transparent GIFs are still a new phenomenon, and full support for them in browsers has not yet become commonplace.

GIF Interlacing

Unlike transparency, interlacing a GIF image doesn't change the appearance of the image on the page. Instead, it affects how the image is saved and its appearance while it is being loaded. As the image comes in over the network, it may have the appearance either of fading in gradually or of coming in at a low resolution and then gradually becoming clearer. To create this effect, you have to both save your GIF files in an interlaced format and have a Web browser such as Netscape that can display files as they are being loaded.

NEW TERM

> *GIF interlacing* is a way of saving a GIF file so that it displays differently from regular GIF files. Interlaced GIFs appear to gradually fade in rather than displaying from top to bottom.

Normally, a GIF file is saved in a file one line at a time (the lines are actually called *scan lines*), starting from the top of the image and progressing down to the bottom (see Figure 8.17). If your browser can display GIFs as they are being loaded (as Netscape can), you'll see the top of the image first and then more of the image line by line as it arrives over the wire to your system.

Figure 8.17.

GIF files saved normally.

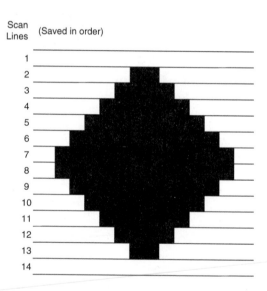

Interlacing saves the GIF image in a different way. Instead of saving each line linearly, an interlaced GIF file is saved in several passes: A first pass saves every eighth row starting from the first, followed by a second pass which saves every eighth row starting from the fourth, followed by a third pass which saves every fourth row starting from the third, and then the remaining rows (see Figure 8.18).

When the interlaced GIF file is displayed, the rows are loaded in as they were saved: The first set of lines appears, and then the next set, and so on. Depending on the browser, this can create a "venetian blind" effect. Or (as in Netscape) the missing lines might be filled in with the information with the initial lines, creating a blurry or blocky effect (as you can see in Figure 8.19), which then becomes clearer as more of the image appears.

Figure 8.18.

GIF files saved as interlaced.

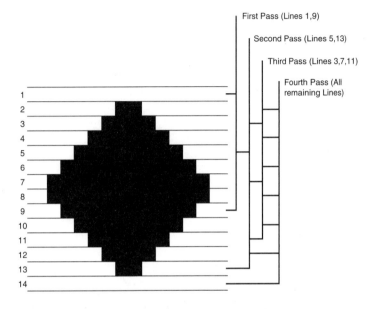

First Pass (Lines 1,9)

Second Pass (Lines 5,13)

Third Pass (Lines 3,7,11)

Fourth Pass (All remaining Lines)

Figure 8.19.

Interlaced GIF files being loaded.

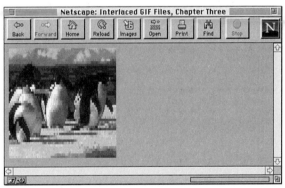

If your browser doesn't support interlaced GIF files, or if it waits until the entire image is loaded before displaying it, you won't get the interlaced effect, but your image will still display just fine. Interlacing doesn't break the GIF for other browsers; it just changes how it's loaded for browsers that can take advantage of it.

Interlacing is great for large images that may take some time to load. With the interlacing effect, your readers can get an idea of what the image looks like before it's finished—which then allows them to stop loading it if they're not interested or, if the image is an image map, to click on the appropriate spot and move on.

On the other hand, interlacing isn't as important for smaller files such as icons and small logos. Small images load quickly enough that the interlacing effect is lost.

Progressive JPEG

The concept of progressive JPEG files is very similar to that of GIF interlacing. Progressive JPEG files are saved in a special way so that they display in a progressively detailed fashion as they're loaded. And, like interlaced GIF files, you need special tools to create progressive JPEG files.

The most significant difference between progressive JPEG and interlaced GIF is in older browsers and tools. Unlike interlaced GIF files, which are still readable in older browsers or browsers that support the older GIF87 format, progressive JPEGs are not backward compatible. Although a quick survey of browsers shows few that cannot display progressive JPEGs at all, the possiblity is there nevertheless. If you do decide to use progressive JPEG files, keep this incompatibility in mind.

Tools for Creating Interlaced and Transparent Images

Many image-editing programs allow you to save GIF files as interlaced or with transparent backgrounds, or both, and JPEG files as progressive JPEGs. If your favorite program doesn't, you might try contacting its author or manufacturer—with these new features becoming more popular on the Web, a new version of your favorite tool may be out that provides these features.

On Windows, LView Pro is a great shareware image-editing program that you can get from just about any site that distributes shareware software (I like http://www.shareware.com/). LView Pro enables you to create GIF images with both transparency and interlacing, and the newest version (1.C) enables you to create progressive JPEG files. (Note that 1.B runs only on Windows 3.1; 1.C runs only on Windows 95 and NT.)

On the Mac, the shareware program GraphicConverter can create both transparent and interlaced GIF images as well as progressive JPEG files (and it reads files from Photoshop). You can get GraphicConverter from one of the many Sumex-AIM mirrors (I like http://hyperarchive.lcs.mit.edu/HyperArchive.html).

For UNIX, a program called GIFTool enables you to create both interlaced and transparent images, and it can also batch-convert a whole set of GIF files to interlaced format (great for converting whole directories at once!). You can get information, binaries for several common UNIX platforms, and source for GIF tools from http://www.homepages.com/tools/.

8

Also for UNIX and the X Window System is ImageMagick, which supports a vast variety of image formats and can handle all these options. See `http://www.wizards.dupont.com/cristy/ImageMagick.html` for details about ImageMagick.

Creating and Using Images

Now, with a firm grasp of image formats, compression, color, and other cool features, you should be all set to go out and create lots of images for your Web pages. Right? Here are some ideas for where to get them.

Design Your Own

If you've got even a small amount of artistic talent, consider drawing or painting your own images for the Web. Your own images will always have more of an impact on pages than the images everyone else is using, and with many image-editing programs there's a lot you can do even if you can't draw a straight line (the computer can do that for you).

Consider looking into scanners if drawing directly on the computer isn't your cup of tea. For flexibility in the sorts of images you can create, scanners are enormously powerful and great fun. Besides the obvious capability to scan in whole photographs (voilà—instant image), you can scan in drawings you've made on paper, patterns from paper or from other objects (leaves, wood, skin), or anything else you can stuff under the lid, and combine everything into an interesting pattern or image.

Flatbed scanners have come down enormously in price over the last couple of years, and you don't need a really high-quality scanner to do images for the Web. Remember, most monitors are only 72dpi, so you don't need a scanner that can do 1200, 2400, or more dpi. A basic 300dpi scanner will do just fine.

If you can't afford a flatbed scanner, hand-held scanners are good for flat images if you have a calm hand and some extra time. Alternatively, your local printing or copying shop might have scanning services, and you could bring your art in and scan it on their machines. Check around. If you're serious about images on the Web, you'll find scanning to be an enormous asset.

WARNING

Scanning is fun, but don't get carried away. Images you find in books and magazines are copyrighted, and scanning them is a form of stealing. Depending on how Net-savvy the company is that owns the copyright, you could find yourself in a lot of trouble. When scanning, be careful that you don't scan anyone else's work.

Commercial Clip Art

Not artistically inclined? Don't feel confident enough to draw your own images, or can't use scanned images? Sometimes the best source of images for your Web pages are the several thousand clip-art packages available on the market. You can get disks and CDs full of clip art from any store or mail-order vendor that sells software for your platform. Look in the back of your favorite computer magazine for dealers.

You should be careful with clip art, however, making sure that you have a right to put the image on the Web. Read the license that comes with the clip art carefully. You're looking for words such as *public domain* and *unlimited distribution*. If the license says something to the effect of "you may not publish the computer images as computer images," you do not have a right to put the images on the Web. The Web counts as publishing, and it counts as computer images.

When in doubt, ask. Most clip-art packages have a Technical Support or Customer Service line. Call them up and ask them.

Clip Art on the Web

With the demand for images, clip art, and icons on the Web, several sites have sprung up that archive freely available GIF files that you can use on your own Web pages. Here are some that I particularly like.

Barry's Clip Art Server has hundreds of images. Some of them require a donation to the author, but most are public domain. Sorting through this page can keep you busy for hours. Check it out at `http://www.barrysclipart.com`.

If you're looking specifically for icons, try Anthony's Icon Library at `http://www.cit.gu.edu.au/~anthony/icons/index.html`.

Also, there are several Web indexes that have topics for clip art and icons. My favorite is Yahoo, which has a whole section for icons on the Web at `http://www.yahoo.com/Computers/World_Wide_Web/Programming/Icons/`, and one for general clip art and image archives at `http://www.yahoo.com/Computers/Multimedia/Pictures/`.

Other Images on the Web

Say you've been wandering around on the Web, and you find a page in which the author has created really awesome 3D arrows for his navigation buttons that you haven't seen before. You really like those icons, and you'd like to use them in your own pages.

What do you do? You can copy the files over to your own server. Because they've been published on the Web, you can get them as easily as finding their names (they're in the source for the page) and then loading them into your browser and saving them. But taking the images from someone else's pages and using them on your own is ethically, if not legally, wrong. Someone might have worked hard on those images, and although copyright law for the Web has yet to be ironed out, you're certainly walking close to the illegal line by stealing the images.

The second idea you might have is to just put the URL of that image in your page, so you're not technically copying anything—you're just including a reference to those images on your page. The artist may very well find this worse than copying. The problem with just creating a reference to an image on a different site is that every time someone loads your page they retrieve the image from the original server, creating traffic for that server that it may not want. So putting in a reference can sometimes be worse than directly copying the image.

The neighborly thing to do if you're interested in using someone else's images is to ask permission to use them on your site. You might find out that the images are freely available already, in which case there isn't a problem. Or the artist might ask you simply to give credit for the original work. At any rate, a quick e-mail to the person who owns the pages will cover all the bases and diminish the potential for trouble.

Coming Soon: PNG

After the end of 1994, when the controversy over the GIF file format and its patented algorithm made the news, there was a scramble among graphics companies and organizations to come up with an image format that would replace GIF. Several image formats were proposed, including TIFF and a modified GIF format with a different compression, but there were disadvantages to all the formats that made them unsuitable for the demanding environment that the Web provides. In particular, the new image format needed to have the following:

☐ A nonpatented compression algorithm. This was obviously at the top of everyone's list. Also, the compression algorithm would have to be lossless

☐ Support for millions of 24-bit colors, as JPEG does

☐ Hardware and platform independence, as both GIF and JPEG have

☐ The capability for interlacing and transparency, as GIF has (JPEG is unlikely to have either feature in the near future)

As of early spring 1995, one new format proposal seemed to be standing out from the others. PNG, the Portable Network Graphics format, was designed by graphics professionals and Web developers to meet many of the needs of images that are intended to be used and displayed in a network environment. PNG is primarily intended as a GIF replacement, not as a general all-purpose graphics format. For photographs and other images where a slight loss in image quality is acceptable, JPEG is still the best choice.

PNG (which is pronounced *ping*) provides all the features listed in the preceding requirements, plus the following:

- [ ] An option for color map-based images, as with the GIF format
- [ ] A compression method that works equally well with photographand logo-type images
- [ ] Comments and other extra information that can be stored within the image file (the GIF89a format had this capability)
- [ ] An alpha channel, which allows for sophisticated effects such as masking and transparency
- [ ] Adjustment for gamma correction, which can compensate for differences in intensity and brightness in different kinds of monitors

A significant boost for the support of PNG has been from CompuServe, which published the original specification for GIF and has been caught in the middle between UniSys's patent and the huge array of angry graphics developers. CompuServe was originally going to propose its own replacement format, called GIF24, but announced its support for PNG instead.

At the time this book is being written, PNG is still in the specification stage. You can get the current technical information about PNG from `http://www.boutell.com/boutell/png/` or from the PNG home page at `http://quest.jpl.nasa.gov/PNG/`. You can also send mail to `png-info@uunet.uu.net` for more information.

For More Information

In a chapter of this size, I can barely scratch the surface of computer graphics and image theory, and it has not been my intent to provide more than a basic overview of the features of JPEG and GIF and how to best use them for the Web. For more information on any of the topics I've covered in this chapter, there are several FAQ (Frequently Asked Questions) files available on the Web, as well as several books on the subject. Here is partial list of the resources that helped me with this chapter:

- [ ] The `comp.graphics` FAQ at `http://www.primenet.com/~grieggs/cg_faq.html` is a great place to start, although it is oriented toward computer graphics developers. John Grieggs (`grieggs@primenet.com`) is its author and maintainer.
- [ ] The Colorspace FAQ, posted to `comp.graphics` periodically or available from `ftp://rtfm.mit.edu/pub/usenet/news.answers/graphics/colorspace-faq`, describes all the various color models and how they relate to each other. It also gets into more of the mathematical and physical aspects of color.

☐ *Computer Graphics: Secrets and Solutions*, by John Corrigan, from Sybex Publishing. Besides being extremely readable, it's a great introduction to graphics image formats, color, compression, and other digital image concepts.

☐ *The Desktop Multimedia Bible*, by Jeff Burger, from Addison Wesley, has a big section on graphics technology, color theory, image formats, and image processing. This is a big, meaty book that will also come in handy in the next chapter when we talk about sound and video.

☐ *Encyclopedia of Graphics File Formats*, by James D. Murray and William Van Ryper, from O'Reilly and Associates, is extremely complete and comes with a CD of image software.

Summary

Until recently, it was easy to pick an image format for the images you wanted to put on the Web, one that would work on all platforms. You could pick any format you wanted to, as long as it was GIF. Now, with JPEG support becoming more popular, there is a choice, and things are complicated. Both GIF and JPEG have advantages for different kinds of files and for different applications. Based on the type of images you want to put on your pages, you can pick one or the other, or mix them. In this chapter, I've explained a few of the issues and how the different formats handle them; I hope I've provided some ideas for how to choose.

Table 8.2 shows a summary of the features and merits of GIF and JPEG at a glance.

Table 8.2. A summary of GIF versus JPEG.

Format	Availability in Browsers	Colors	Interlacing and Transparency	Compression Type	Compression of Logos/Icons	Compression of Photos
GIF	Excellent	256	Both	Lossless	Excellent	Fair
JPEG	Good	Millions	Progressive	Lossy	Poor	Excellent

Q&A

Q What about image resolution?

A If you were creating images for printing in newsletters or books, you'd be more concerned about getting the image resolution right because printed images need a great deal of fidelity (600–1200dpi and up). But for the Web, your images are usually going to be viewed on a regular monitor, in which case the resolution is almost never greater than 72dpi. If you scan and create all your images at 72dpi, you should be fine.

Q You didn't talk much about bit depth. You didn't talk at all about halftones, resampling, or LAB color. You didn't talk about alpha channels or gamma correction.

A I only had so many pages. I focused on what I thought were the most important topics for people designing images for the Web—and halftoning and gamma correction aren't as important as understanding color maps and lossy compression. My apologies if I didn't cover your pet topic.

Q My clip-art packages say the images are "royalty free." Does that mean the same thing as public domain?

A All "royalty free" means is that you don't have to pay the author or the company anything if you use the image as they intended you to use it. It says nothing about how you can use the image. The images might be royalty free for use in printed material, but you might not be able to publish them as computer images at all. Again, read your license, and contact the company if you have any questions.

Q You talked about HSB and RGB, but the other one I keep seeing is CMYK. What's that?

A CMYK stands for Cyan, Magenta, Yellow, and Black (B is already taken by Blue). The CMYK color model is used in the printing industry. If you've heard of four-color printing, CMYK are the four colors. The color model is actually CMY, and various combinations of the three produce all the colors you'll ever need to print on paper. Full amounts of the three combined are supposed to add up to black, but because of variations in ink quality, they rarely do (you usually end up with a dark brown or green). For this reason, true black ink is usually added to the model so that the blacks can really be black.

Because CMYK is used for printing, and not for images that are designed for display, I ignored it in this chapter. If you're really interested, feel free to look at the books and FAQs I mentioned in the section "For More Information," earlier in this chapter.

DAY 5

Multimedia on the Web: Animation, Sound, Video, and Other Files

Chapter 9

External Files, Multimedia, and Animation

Multimedia is a bit of a high-powered word these days, bringing up images of expensive CD-ROMs with lots of integrated sound and video, textured ray-traced 3D virtual environments, and Doom-like fast-paced action. Multimedia on the Web, primarily because of limitations in network speeds and cross-platform file formats, isn't nearly that much fun. Multimedia on the Web has the potential for being very interesting, but at the present time it consists mostly of small sound and video files and simple animation. Yesterday you learned about images and, in particular, about the differences between external and inline images. You can make that same distinction between external and inline multimedia on the Web, and in this chapter, I will.

This chapter consists of two main parts. The first part describes external media files, which are the standard way of doing multimedia on the Web that all browsers support. In this first half of the chapter you'll learn the following:

☐ What external media means

☐ How browsers, servers, and helper applications work together to handle external media

☐ How to use external sound and video files

☐ How to use external media for things other than multimedia

In the second part of this chapter, I'll get fancy and talk about the newer advances in browsers to support inline animation and multimedia, including:

☐ Inline sound and video

☐ GIF animation

☐ Marquees

☐ Animation with Java

☐ Netscape's server push and client pull

☐ Notes about inline multimedia yet to come

What Is External Media?

Yesterday you learned about the difference between inline and external images—inline images appear directly on a Web page, whereas external images are stored, well, externally, and loaded by choosing a link in an HTML Web page. This same distinction between inline and external applies to many other kinds of media besides images. In its most general form, external media is defined as any file that cannot be automatically loaded, played, or displayed by a Web browser on a Web page.

Whereas when you use inline media you're limited to which kinds of files you can use (and, for most browsers, that means only GIF and JPEG images), external files can include just about any kind of file you can create: non-inline GIF files, MPEG video, PostScript files, zipped applications—just about anything you can put on a computer disk can be considered external media.

Using External Media in HTML

To point to an external media file from a Web page, you link to that file just as you would any other document, by using the <A> tag and the HREF attribute. The path to the external file is a pathname or URL just as you would use if the file were another HTML document, and the text inside the link describes the file you're linking to. Here's an example:

```
<A HREF="some_external_file">A media file.</A>
```

So what happens when you click on a link to one of these external files? For some files, such as images or text files, your browser may be able to load the file itself into the current browser window. In many cases, however, your browser will download the file and then pass it to some other application on your system which is designed to read and handle that file. These other applications are called helper applications, or sometimes viewers, and you can configure your browser to handle different external media types with different applications. If the browser can't figure out what kind of file the external media file is, it'll usually pop up a dialog asking you what to do (save the file, choose an application, or some other choice).

NEW TERM

A *helper application* is a program on your disk designed to read files that are not directly supported by your browser, for example, unusual image formats, movie formats, compressed or zipped applications, and so on. You can configure your browser to use different helper applications for different files.

How It Works

How does the browser figure out whether a given file is readable by the browser itself or if it needs to be passed on to a helper application? How the browser treats a file is determined by one of two things: the extension to the filename or the content-type of that file. You've seen the file extension quite a bit up to this point—HTML files must have extensions of `.html` or `.htm`, GIF files must have `.gif` extensions, and so on. When your browser reads and views local files on your disk, it uses the file extension to figure out what kind of file it is.

The content-type comes in when your browser gets files from a Web server. The Web server doesn't send the filename—in some cases, the data it sends back may be automatically generated and not have a filename at all. What it does send back is a special code called the content-type which tells the browser what kind of file it is sending. Content-types look something like this: `text/html`, `image/gif`, `video/mpeg`, `application/msword`, and so on.

NEW TERM

A *content-type* is a special code that Web servers use to tell the browser what kind of file they are sending.

Both browser and server have lists in their configuration or preferences which map file extensions to content-types. The server uses this list to figure out which content-type to send to the browser with a given file. The browser, in turn, has an additional list which maps content-types to helper applications on the local system (see Figure 9.1 for Netscape's Helper

Applications menu). In this way, regardless of where the browser gets a file, it can figure out what to do with almost every file it receives.

Figure 9.1.

Netscape's Helper applications.

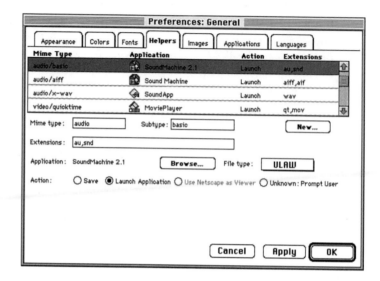

Allowing helper applications to deal with most external files works well for browsers, as it means that the browser can remain small and fast (no need to deal with every arcane file format that might be produced on the Web), and it's also configurable for new and better helper applications as they are written—or new and better file formats.

With that background in mind, let's actually create some Web pages that link to external media files.

External Sound, Video, and Other Files

Sound and video files are ideal for external media files on a Web page. You can use sound on your Web page for optional annotations to existing text, welcome messages from you or someone important in your organization, or extra information that words and pictures cannot convey. Video can be used to provide even more information that static pictures cannot convey (where the term *video* refers to any digitally encoded motion picture—both animation as well as "real" video files).

Sound Files

To include a link to an external sound on your Web page, you must have that sound file in the right format, just as you would for an image. You'll learn all about the various kinds of sound formats you can use in Chapter 10, "Sound and Video Files," but here's a quick summary. Currently, the only fully cross-platform sound file format for the Web is Sun Microsystems's AU format. AU allows several different kinds of sound sample encoding, but the most popular one is eight-bit μ-law (that funny character is the greek letter mu, so μ-law files are pronounced "mew-law"). For this reason, AU files are often called simply μ-law files. AU files are of only barely acceptable quality, as the eight-bit sampling causes them to sound a bit like they are being transmitted over a telephone.

You can use other better quality sound formats for specific platforms. The most popular are AIFF for the Macintosh and WAVE (WAV) for Windows, or MPEG audio, which is more cross-platform but even less popular.

Finally, the RealAudio format was developed specifically for playing audio files on the Internet and the World Wide Web. Unlike most audio files where you wait for the entire file to download before you can hear it, RealAudio uses streaming, which means that it can play at the same time it's being downloaded; there's only a small pause as the initial data first arrives on your machine. The one drawback of using RealAudio is that you need to set up a special server to deliver real audio files, and linking to them involves a slightly different process than linking to regular audio files. For both these reasons, I'm going to postpone talking about RealAudio until later in this book, after you're used to working with servers.

In order for a browser to recognize your sound file, the file must have the appropriate extension for its file type. Common formats and their extensions are listed in Table 9.1.

Table 9.1. Sound formats and extensions.

Format	Extension
AU/μ-law	.au
AIFF/AIFC	.aiff, .aif
WAVE/WAV	.wav
MPEG Audio	.mp2

After you have a file in the right format and with the right extension, you can link to it from your Web page like any other external file:

```
<P>Laurence Olivier's <A HREF="olivier_hamlet.au">"To Be or
Not To Be"</A> soliloquy from the film of the play Hamlet (AIFF
format, 357K)</P>
```

Video Files

Video files, like sound files, must be in one of a handful of formats to be able to be read by the current crop of Web browsers. Again, I'll talk extensively about video in the next chapter, but here's a quick format rundown.

For video files that can be read across platforms, the current standard on the Web is MPEG, but both Microsoft's Video for Windows (AVI) and Apple's QuickTime format have been gaining ground as players become more available. QuickTime and AVI files also have the advantage of being able to include an audio track with the video; although MPEG video files can have audio tracks, few existing players can play it.

The file extensions for each of these video files are listed in Table 9.2.

Table 9.2. Video formats and extensions.

Format	Extension
MPEG	`.mpeg, .mpg`
QuickTime	`.mov`
AVI	`.avi`

Then, simply link the file into your Web page as you would any other external file:

```
<P><A HREF="dumbo3.mov">The "pink elephant" scene</A> from
Disney's <CITE>Dumbo</CITE>.</P>
```

Using External Media for Other Files

External media isn't limited to actual media like sound, video, and images. Any file you can put on your disk with an extension on it can be used as an external media file: text files, PostScript files, MS Word files, ZIP files, Macintosh HQX files, and so on. As long as that file has the right extension and your browser has been configured to be able to handle that file type, you can create links to those files which will download that file when the link is selected.

Or at least, that's the theory. For many file types you may also need to configure your server to do the right thing, or when you try to download the file, you'll get gibberish or nothing at all.

Hints on Using External Media in HTML

If you're going to make use of links to external media files in your Web pages, a very helpful tip for your readers is to include information in the body of the link (or somewhere nearby) about the format of the media (is it AU or AIFF or AVI or MPEG or a ZIP file?) and the file size. All the examples I've used up to this point include this information.

Remember, your readers have no way of knowing what's on the other side of the link. So if they go ahead and select it, it may take some time for the file to download—and they may discover after waiting all that time that their system can't handle the file. By telling your readers what it is they're selecting, they can make the decision whether it's worth it to try downloading the file.

Simply adding a few words as part of the link text is all you really need:

```
<A HREF="bigsnail.jpeg">A 59K JPEG Image of a snail</A>
<A HREF="tacoma.mov">The Fall of the Tacoma Narrows Bridge </A>
 (a 200K QuickTime File)
```

Another useful trick if you use lots of media files on a page is to use small icon images of different media files to indicate a sound or a video clip (or some other media). Figure 9.2 shows some examples. Be sure to include a legend for which formats you're using, and don't forget to include the file sizes.

```
<A HREF="cranes.au"><IMG SRC="earicon.gif"
ALT="[sound]">Whooping Cranes (AU, 36K)</A>
```

Figure 9.2.
Media icons.

Exercise 9.1: Creating a media archive.

One of the common types of pages available on the Web is that of a media archive. A media archive is a Web page that serves no purpose other than to provide quick access to image or other media files for viewing and downloading.

Before the Web became popular, media such as images, sounds, and video were stored in FTP or Gopher archives. The text-only nature of these sorts of archives makes it difficult for people to find what they're looking for, as the filename is usually the only description they have of the content of the file. Even reasonably descriptive filenames, such as red-bird-in-green-tree.gif or verdi-aria.aiff, aren't all that useful when you're talking about images or sounds. It's only through actually downloading the file itself that people can really decide whether or not they want it.

By using inline images and icons and splitting up sound and video files into small clips and larger files, you can create a media archive on the Web that is far more usable than any of the text-only archives.

EXERCISE

NOTE

> Keep in mind that this sort of archive, in its heavy use of inline graphics and large media files, is optimally useful in graphical browsers attached to fast networks. However, the Web does provide advantages in this respect over FTP or Gopher servers, even for text-only browsers, simply because there is more room available to describe the files on the archive. Rather than having only the filename to describe the file, you can use as many words as you need. For example:
>
> ```
> <P>A <A HREF="orangefish.jpeg">34K JPEG file</A> of
> an orange fish with a bright yellow eye, swimming in
> front of some very pink coral.
> ```

In this exercise, you'll create a simple example of a media archive with several GIF images, AU sounds, and MPEG video.

First, start with the framework for the archive, which includes some introductory text, some inline images explaining the kind of files, and headings for each file type as in the following code. Figure 9.3 shows how it looks so far.

```
<HTML>
<HEAD>
<TITLE>Laura's Way Cool Image Archive</TITLE>
</HEAD>
<BODY>
<H1>Laura's Way Cool Image Archive</H1>
<P>Select an image to download the appropriate file.</P>
<P><IMG SRC="penguinslittle.gif">Picture icons indicate GIF images</P>
<P><IMG SRC="earicon.gif">This icon indicates an AU Sound file</P>
<P><IMG SRC="film.gif">This icon indicates an MPEG Video File</P>
<HR>
<H2>Images</H2>
<H2>Sound Files</H2>
<H2>Video Files</H2>
</BODY>
</HTML>
```

Figure 9.3.

The framework for the media archive.

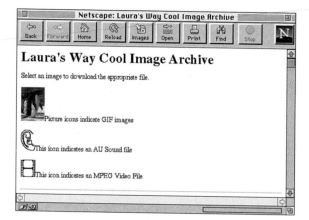

For the archive, we have four large GIF images:

- ☐ A drawing of a pink orchid
- ☐ A photograph full of jelly beans
- ☐ The cougar from the Palo Alto Zoo home page
- ☐ A biohazard symbol

Using your favorite image editor, you can create thumbnails of each of these pictures to serve as the inline icons, and then insert <IMG> links in the appropriate spots in your archive file:

```
<H2>Images</H2>
<IMG SRC="orchidsmall.gif" ALT="a drawing of a pink orchid">
<IMG SRC="jellybeansmall.gif" ALT="a photograph of some jellybeans">
<IMG SRC="cougarsmall.gif" ALT="a photograph of a cougar">
<IMG SRC="biohazardsmall.gif" ALT="a biohazard symbol">
```

Note that I included values for the ALT attribute to the <IMG> tag, which will be substituted for the images in browsers that cannot view those images. Even though you may not intend for your Web page to be seen by nongraphical browsers, it's polite to at least offer a clue to people who stumble onto it. This way, everyone can access the media files you are offering on this page.

Now, link the thumbnails of the files to the actual images (Figure 9.4 shows the result):

```
<A HREF="orchid.gif">
<IMG SRC="orchidsmall.gif" ALT="a drawing of a pink orchid"></A>
<A HREF="jellybean.gif">
<IMG SRC="jellybeansmall.gif" ALT="a photograph of some jellybeans"> </A>
<A HREF="cougar.gif">
<IMG SRC="cougarsmall.gif" ALT="a photograph of a cougar"> </A>
<A HREF="biohazard.gif">
<IMG SRC="biohazardsmall.gif" ALT="a biohazard symbol"> </A>
```

Figure 9.4.

Image links to larger images.

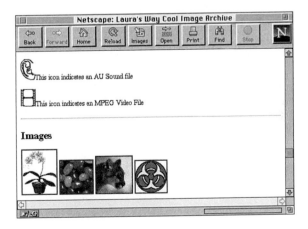

If I leave the archive like this, it looks nice, but I'm breaking one of my own rules: I haven't noted how large the files are. Here, you have several choices for formatting. You could just put the size of the file inline with the image and let the images wrap on the page however they want as follows (Figure 9.5 shows the result):

```
<H2>Images</H2>
<A HREF="orchid.gif">
<IMG SRC="orchidsmall.gif" ALT="a drawing of a pink orchid"></A>(67K)
<A HREF="jellybean.gif">
<IMG SRC="jellybeansmall.gif" ALT="a photograph of some jellybeans"></A>(39K)
<A HREF="cougar.gif">
<IMG SRC="cougarsmall.gif" ALT="a photograph of a cougar"></A>(122K)
<A HREF="biohazard.gif">
<IMG SRC="biohazardsmall.gif" ALT="a biohazard symbol"></A>(35K)
```

Figure 9.5.

Images with text.

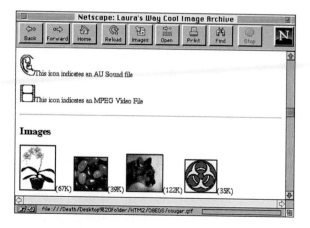

Or you could put inline breaks after each image to make sure they line up along the left edge of the page. I prefer the first method, as it allows a more compact layout of images.

Now, moving on to the sound and video files. You have three sound files and two videos. Because these files can't be reduced to a simple thumbnail image, we'll describe them in the text in the archive (including the huge sizes of the files):

```
<H2>Sound and Video Files</H2>
<P>A five-part a capella renaissance madrigal
called "Flora Gave me Fairest Flowers" (650K)</P>
<P>Some lovely wind-chime sounds (79K) </P>
<P>Chicken noises (112K)</P>
<P>The famous Tacoma Narrows bridge accident
(where the bridge twisted and fell down in the wind)(13Meg)</P>
<P>A three-dimensional computer animation of a
flying airplane over a landscape (2.3Meg)</P>
```

Now, add the icon images to each of the descriptions—the ear icon to the sounds and the filmstrip icon to the videos. Here we'll also include a value for the ALT attribute to the <IMG> tag, this time providing a simple description that will serve as a placeholder for the link itself in text-only browsers. Note that because we're using icons to indicate what kind of file each one is, you don't have to include text descriptions of that file format in addition to the icon.

And finally, just as you did in the image part of the example, link the icons to the external files. Here is the HTML code for the final list (Figure 9.6 shows how it looks):

```
<H2>Sound and Video Files</H2>
<P><A HREF="flora.au">
<IMG SRC="earicon.gif" ALT="[madrigal sound]"> A five-part a capella
renaissance madrigal called "Flora Gave me Fairest Flowers" (650K)</A></P>
<P><A HREF="windchime.au">
<IMG SRC="earicon.gif" ALT="[windchime sound]"> Some
lovely wind-chime sounds (79K)</A></P>
<P><A HREF="bawkbawk.au">
<IMG SRC="earicon.gif" ALT="[chicken sound]"> Chicken noises (112K)</A></P>
<P><A HREF="tacoma.mpeg">
<IMG SRC="film.gif" ALT="[tacoma video]"> The famous Tacoma
Narrows bridge accident (where the bridge twisted and fell
down in the wind) (13Meg)</A></P>
<P><A HREF="airplane.mpeg">
<IMG SRC="film.gif" ALT="[3D airplane]">A three-dimensional
computer animation of a flying airplane over a landscape (2.3Meg) </A></P>
```

Figure 9.6.

Sound and video files.

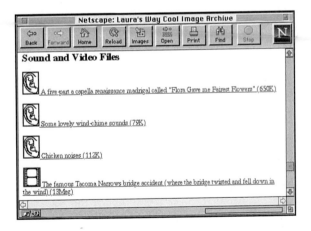

Et voilà, your media archive. It's simple with the combination of inline images and external files. And, with the use of the ALT attribute, you can even use it reasonably well in text-only browsers.

The State of Inline Multimedia on the Web

Until very recently, the only way you could distribute multimedia files over the Web was by using external files as described in the first half of this chapter. In recent months, however, both Netscape and Microsoft have made many interesting steps toward integrating multimedia more closely into Web pages, either through the use of new HTML tags, through advanced capabilities such as Java, or through the use of "plug-ins"—helper applications that are more closely integrated with the browser and with files viewed within that browser.

For the remainder of this chapter, I'll run down many of the newer innovations in inline media that different browsers are supporting, including inline sound and video, marquees, and simple animation using GIF files and Java. Keep in mind as you read through this half of the chapter that these capabilities are new and, at the moment, limited to their respective browsers. If you take advantage of these features, be aware that they may be unavailable for readers not using that particular browser.

Inline Video

One of the earlier mechanisms for handling inline animation was introduced with Microsoft's Internet Explorer browser. Internet Explorer includes an extension to the `<IMG>` tag that allows AVI (Video for Windows) files to be played inline on Web pages. This HTML extension, called DYNSRC (Dynamic Source), has not yet been supported by any other browsers, but since it is ignored by browsers that don't support it, the new extension does not affect the readability of the page in other browsers.

To include an AVI video file on a Web page using Internet Explorer, use the `<IMG>` tag with the DYNSRC attribute. The value of DYNSRC is the path to or URL of the AVI file:

```
<IMG DYNSRC="rainstorm.avi" SRC="rainstorm.gif" ALT="[a rainstorm]">
```

Note that you can still use all the other common attributes to the `<IMG>` tag for alignment and borders, and you can use them to place the AVI video on the page. Also note that the SRC attribute is still required; this image will be shown in lieu of the AVI file if it cannot be found or in browsers that do not support inline video using DYNSRC.

In addition to DYNSRC, Microsoft added several other attributes to the `<IMG>` tag to control how the AVI file is played:

☐ The CONTROLS attribute, if included in `<IMG>`, displays the AVI file with a set of simple controls beneath it for starting, stopping, and replaying the AVI file.

☐ The LOOP attribute, whose value is a number, determines how many times the video will play; for example, LOOP=5 will play the video five times. A LOOP value of -1 or INFINITE causes the video to play repeatedly until the reader leaves the page.

☐ The START attribute controls when the video will actually start playing. If START=FILEOPEN (the default), the video will begin playing as soon as the page and the video are loaded. If START=MOUSEOVER, the video will not start playing until the mouse has been moved over it.

Inline Sounds

In addition to the tags for inline video, Internet Explorer also added a tag for playing inline audio files. These sound files are loaded when the page is loaded without the reader having to press a button or follow a link to play the sound. To add an embedded background sound to a page, use the <BGSOUND> tag, like this:

```
<BGSOUND SRC="trumpet.au">
```

The browser, when it loads the page, will also load and play the background sound. The <BGSOUND> tag does not produce any visual effect on the page.

To repeat the sound multiple times, use the LOOP attribute. If the value of LOOP is a number, the sound is played that number of times. If LOOP is -1 or INFINITE, the sound will be repeated continually until the reader leaves the page.

Explorer supports three different formats for inline sounds: the popular Sun's AU (μ-law) format and Windows WAV files for sound samples, and MIDI files with a .mid extension.

When designing your Web pages, go easy with background sounds. If you must use one, play it only a short time and then stop. Continually playing sounds are distracting to many readers.

Animated Marquees

A marquee is a line of scrolling text that moves from one side of the Web page to the other. Although you can create marquees with just about any form of inline animation, Internet Explorer's <MARQUEE> tag allows you to create a marquee quickly and easily (and you don't need to download any other image or animation files). Figure 9.7 shows a scrolling marquee in Internet Explorer (in the process of scrolling).

Marquees are a new feature of Internet Explorer that are not yet supported in other browsers. Other browsers will still see the text itself; it just won't be animated.

Figure 9.7.
A scrolling marquee.

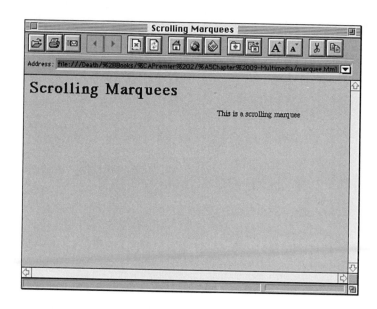

Creating a Marquee

To create a marquee, use the `<MARQUEE>` tag. The text between the opening and closing `<MARQUEE>` tags is the text that will scroll:

```
<MARQUEE>I'm scrolling!</MARQUEE>
```

By default, marquees appear on their own line, in the font and size of the enclosing element. So, for example, by enclosing the marquee inside a heading, you can get a heading-sized marquee:

```
<H1><MARQUEE>I'm scrolling, and large, too!</MARQUEE></H1>
```

This doesn't work with all HTML elements; you can't, for example, set the enclosing text to be `<FONT COLOR=yellow>`. Nor can you include HTML font changes inside the marquee itself—all HTML inside the marquee is ignored.

Changing the Behavior of the Marquee

When you create a simple marquee using just the plain `<MARQUEE>` tags, the marquee that is created scrolls from the right side of the page to the left, disappearing entirely before reappearing on the right again. It loops continually, just slowly enough for you to be able to read it.

You can change the behavior, direction, number of times to loop, and the speed of looping with different attributes to the `<MARQUEE>` tag:

☐ The BEHAVIOR attribute has three values: SCROLL, SLIDE, or ALTERNATE. The default is SCROLL. SLIDE causes the marquee to slide in from the right side of the screen and stop when the text hits the left margin (slide in and "stick"). ALTERNATE starts the text on the left side of the page and bounces it back and forth between the left and right margins.

☐ The DIRECTION attribute, which can have the values LEFT or RIGHT, affects only marquees of type SCROLL and determines which direction the marquee initially moves in. The default is RIGHT (it moves from the right side of the screen to the left); DIRECTION=LEFT reverses the directions.

☐ The value of the LOOP attribute determines how many times the marquee will scroll by, so, for example, LOOP=5 will scroll the marquee five times and stop. LOOP=-1 or LOOP=INFINITE will cause the marquee to scroll forever.

☐ Finally, the SCROLLAMOUNT and SCROLLDELAY attributes, which both have number values, determine the speed at which the marquee moves. SCROLLAMOUNT is the number of pixels between each step of the text in the marquee, that is, the number of pixels the text moves to the right or left each time. Higher numbers mean the marquee moves faster. SCROLLDELAY is the number of milliseconds between each step in the animation; higher numbers make the animation work more slowly and less smoothly. By experimenting with SCROLLAMOUNT and SCROLLDELAY you can find a marquee speed and smoothness that works for your presentation.

Changing the Appearance of the Marquee

Marquees take up a single vertical line of space on the Web page, and are transparent to the background color behind them. You can, however, change the appearance of the marquee on the page using several attributes:

☐ The BGCOLOR attribute determines the background color of the marquee's bounding box and, like all the color specifications in Internet Explorer, can take a hexadecimal RGB number or a color name.

☐ HEIGHT and WIDTH determine the size of the bounding box surrounding the marquee. Both HEIGHT and WIDTH can take a pixel number or a percentage of screen size (for example, HEIGHT=50% takes up half the vertical height of the screen).

☐ HSPACE and VSPACE determine the space between the edges of the marquee's bounding box and the surrounding text; HSPACE determines the space to either side of the marquee, and VSPACE determines the space above and below it.

☐ ALIGN, which can have the values TOP, MIDDLE, or BOTTOM, determines how the text surrounding the marquee will align with the marquee's bounding box (same as with images). It does not affect the placement of the scrolling text inside the bounding box, which is always aligned at the top.

Figure 9.8 shows the various parts of the marquee's appearance you can change with these attributes:

Figure 9.8.
Marquee parts.

Using Marquees

Marquees, like the <BLINK> tag, are a very intrusive way of getting the readers' attention. Marquees rivet your readers' attention to that one spot, distracting them from reading the rest of the page. As with <BLINK>, marquees should be used sparingly, if at all, and with a set number of loops (so the scrolling eventually stops). Small marquees are better than large ones, and marquees without background colors are more subtle than those with.

Animation Using GIF Files

Probably the simplest way to create basic animation is by using a feature of the GIF format that allows you to store multiple GIF images in a single GIF file. When these GIF images are loaded into a browser that understands this special format, the individual images are displayed one after the other, creating an animation. Depending on how the GIF file was originally saved, the animation can either play only once, play a number of times, or loop continuously.

Currently, Netscape 2.0 is the only browser that supports animated GIFs, and not very well at that (for example, there's no way to stop them from animating unless you leave the page they're on, which, depending on how irritating the animation is, can be a problem). However, given how quickly GIF animations have taken hold, it's likely that more browsers will support them by the time you read this.

What happens in browsers that don't support GIF animation? The good news is that they'll display only the first image in the series so that you won't lose the image altogether. The bad news is that storing several GIF images as a single animated GIF file means that the size of that file is the combination of all the individual GIF images, making your image files that much larger and more time-consuming to download. So there are definite trade offs to be considered when deciding whether or not to use GIF animation in your own Web pages.

To create a GIF animation, you'll need two things:

☐ The set of individual GIF files (frames) that make up your animation

☐ A program that can convert the individual files to an animated GIF file

For the first of those things, all you need to do is use your favorite image editor to create each individual frame of the animation. Depending on the complexity of the animation you want to create and how artistic you are, this can be relatively easy or very difficult (most impressive animations on the Web these days are done by professional artists).

When I set out to do a simple GIF animation, I used a black and yellow "Coming Soon" image I use on some of my Web pages and simply blocked out some of the lights around the edge for each of the frames (different ones for each frame, of course). The four frames I created are shown in Figure 9.9.

Figure 9.9.
Four Coming Soon frames.

 TIP

If you use Photoshop 3.0 for your animation, layers can be really useful; simply create a background that stays constant throughout the animation, and use different layers to do different frames of the animation. Then when you want to create the individual frames, save the Photoshop file somewhere safe, flatten the image to the background and one layer, and save it as a GIF file.

Once you have your frames, you'll need a program that can convert these images to the special animation format. Unfortunately, this special feature of the GIF format was used very little until the Web discovered it, so most GIF editors do not support it. There are small tools creeping up that do, however:

☐ For Windows, Alchemy Mindworks's GIF Construction Set is a shareware tool that can create GIF animations, as well as handle many other GIF features (transparency, interlacing, and so on). Find out more information from http://www.mindworkshop.com/alchemy/gifcon.html.

☐ For the Macintosh, GIFBuilder is a quick-and-dirty freeware tool that will take a series of GIF, PICT, or TIFF files and output an animated GIF file (as well as change lots of other GIF options as well). You can get GIFBuilder from most popular Macintosh archives (try `http://www.mid.net/INFO-MAC/`), or get more information from `http://iawww.epfl.ch/Staff/Yves.Piguet/clip2gif-home/GifBuilder.html`.

☐ For UNIX systems, the command-line `whirlgGIF` takes a series of GIF files and outputs an animated GIF. `WhirlGIF` has lots of options for different aspects of the animation. See `http://www.msg.net/utility/whirlgif/` for more information and the source code.

The GIF animation format allows you to specify several different features of the animation, including how many times to loop (`0` to `infinite`—only `infinite` is currently supported in Netscape) and the delay between individual frames.

Once you have an animated GIF file to play with, try it in Netscape or in some other tool that supports animated GIF files. In the case of my Coming Soon image, the "lights" around the edge of the box appear to blink on and off like a movie sign.

Animation Using Java

Java is a new feature on the Web that is getting a lot of people very excited. Java applets are little mini-programs that run on a Web page and can react to user input without having to constantly check back with a Web server (as forms need to do). And, indeed, there's a lot you can do with Java if you know how to program and you're willing to put in the work involved to learn how to use it (you'll learn more about Java later in this book, in fact). But even if you don't care about programming, you can use pre-built Java applets on your pages to create animation effects without touching a line of Java code. All you have to do is download the Java applet to your system, include a few lines of HTML on your page, and everything works just fine (assuming, of course, that you and your readers have a Java-enabled browser).

In this section you'll learn just enough about Java applets to set up animation on your Web page. Later in the week you'll learn more about Java.

Gathering the Pieces

One pre-built Java animation applet comes direct from Sun; it's called Animator. Animator can do simple animation with and without additional soundtracks, re-use frames, loop an animation, and control the time between each frame. To create animation using Java and the Animator applet, you'll need three things:

☐ A set of image files (GIF or JPEG) that make up your animation, each one usually named with a capital T plus a sequential number, like this: `T1.gif`, `T2.gif`, `T3.gif`, and so on. As I've mentioned before, case matters, so make sure you use a capital T.

(These are the default names the Animator applet uses; you can use different names if you want to, but you'll have to configure the applet differently to accept those names, so using the T names is the easiest way to go.)

☐ Sun's Animator classes. There are four of them: `Animator.class`, `ImageNotFoundException.class`, `ParseException.class`, and `DescriptionFrame.class`. You can download all these classes from the Animator page at `http://www.javasoft.com/applets/applets/Animator/index.html`.

☐ An HTML file that contains the Java applet.

The easiest way to create Java animations without knowing much about Java is to put all your files into the same directory: all the image files, all the class files, and your HTML file.

So, for example, let's say I have 12 GIF images of a pocket watch, each of which has the second hand in a different place on the dial. I've named them `T1.gif`, `T2.gif`, and so on, all the way up to `T12.gif`. Figure 9.10 shows the first few frames of the animation.

Figure 9.10.
The pocket watch animation.

After downloading the Animator class files, I put them and the image files into a single directory called `watch`. Now the last step is to create an HTML file which will contain that Java animation.

Adding the Applet to Your Web Page

To add Java animation (or any applet) to a Web page, you use the `<APPLET>` and `<PARAM>` tags. The `<APPLET>` tag contains the applet itself and determines how large the applet's bounding box will be on the page. So, for example, to include the Animator applet on your page in a box 100 pixels square, you would use these lines of code:

```
<APPLET CODE="Animator.class" WIDTH=100 HEIGHT=100>
...
</APPLET>
```

In my watch example, the size of the images is 129×166 pixels, so I'll use those values for the WIDTH and HEIGHT:

```
<APPLET CODE="Animator.class" WIDTH=122 HEIGHT=166>
...
</APPLET>
```

In between the opening and closing <APPLET> tags, there are several different <PARAM> tags, which indicate different parameters for the Animator applet itself to control the animation. Each <PARAM> tag has two attributes: NAME and VALUE. NAME is used for the parameter name and VALUE for its value. Using different <PARAM> tags, you can include different parameters to pass to the applet—and different applets will require different parameters. The Animator applet has a bunch of parameters to choose from, but I'll mention only a couple here.

STARTIMAGE is the image number to start from, usually 1. If your image filenames start from some other number, you'll use that number. ENDIMAGE, accordingly, is the number of the last image to use in the animation. My watch images are called T1.gif through T12.gif, so the value of STARTIMAGE would be 1 and the value of ENDIMAGE would be 12. Add these to your HTML file inside <PARAM> tags, which in turn go inside the <APPLET> tag:

```
<APPLET CODE="Animator.class" WIDTH=100 HEIGHT=100>
<PARAM NAME="STARTIMAGE" VALUE="1">
<PARAM NAME="ENDIMAGE" VALUE="12">
</APPLET>
```

The final parameter you'll usually want to include is PAUSE, which determines how many milliseconds the applet will wait between the images in the animation. By default, the pause is set to 3900 milliseconds (almost four seconds), which is a bit too much of a pause. You can experiment with the pause between frames until you get an animation you like (here I picked 1000 milliseconds, or an even second):

```
<APPLET CODE="Animator.class" WIDTH=100 HEIGHT=100>
<PARAM NAME="STARTIMAGE" VALUE="1">
<PARAM NAME="ENDIMAGE" VALUE="12">
<PARAM NAME="PAUSE" VALUE="1000">
</APPLET>
```

Finally, I'll include the REPEAT parameter, which tells the Animator applet to loop the image repeatedly (clicking on the animation will start and stop it):

```
<APPLET CODE="Animator.class" WIDTH=100 HEIGHT=100>
<PARAM NAME="STARTIMAGE" VALUE="1">
<PARAM NAME="ENDIMAGE" VALUE="12">
<PARAM NAME="PAUSE" VALUE="1000">
<PARAM NAME="REPEAT" VALUE="TRUE">
</APPLET>
```

With all that in place, you can save and load up the HTML file into your favorite Java-enabled browser. The Animator applet will be loaded, and it in turn loads and plays all the images in sequence.

NOTE

Testing Java applets in Netscape 2.0 can be difficult because Netscape sometimes refuses to reload the page after you've made changes to it. If this happens, try selecting Options | Network Preferences. Under the cache tag, select the buttons that say "Clear Memory Cache Now" and "Clear Disk Cache Now." Then Netscape will reload the new versions of everything properly.

I've mentioned only a couple of the Animator applet's parameters here in order to get you up and running. The Animator applet includes several other parameters to choose from, including parameters that let you change the location and name of the image files, add a background to the animation or a soundtrack, and control the order that frames are displayed. For more information about what you can do with the Animator applet, see the Animator page at `http://www.javasoft.com/applets/applets/Animator/index.html`.

Client Pull and Server Push

One of the earliest and most primitive forms of inline animation in Web pages were the Netscape capabilities for server push and client pull, which were introduced as part of Netscape 1.1. Client pull causes the browser to load the same page or a different page automatically after a certain amount of time has passed; server push keeps the connection between the server and the browser open and continues to feed data down the wire.

The concepts behind server push and client pull are similar: They allow a new page or portion of a page to be loaded automatically after a certain amount of time, without the reader having to select a link or move to a different page. In the case of client pull, this can be used for automatic slide shows or other slow-moving presentations. For server push, multiple images could load into a single page repeatedly, offering a sort of very basic animation.

Server push has fallen out of favor with the Web community, as it requires special setup programs on the server and is complex to set up. Newer forms of animation such as the GIF animation you learned about in this chapter have all but replaced the use of server push on the Web. I'll talk more about server push later in this book when you know more about servers.

Client pull, on the other hand, still has uses, not necessarily as an animation technique, but as a mechanism for pages to automatically reload after a certain amount of time has passed, or for a series of pages to automatically load themselves with a pause between them.

Client pull works on the idea that there is a special HTTP command (called an HTTP header) called `Refresh`. If a Web server sends the `Refresh` command to a browser along with a page's data, the browser is supposed to wait a certain amount of amount of time and then reload the page.

Normally, you would have to modify your server to send this special HTTP command with each page. But HTML provides (and Netscape supports) a special HTML tag that, when included inside a Web page, provides a way for the page to "fake" many HTTP headers as if they were sent by the server itself. That special HTML tag is called <META>, a general HTML 2.0 tag for providing information about an HTML page (meta-information). The attribute of the <META> tag that fakes the HTTP header is called HTTP-EQUIV, and its value for causing a page to reload is Refresh. To indicate the amount of time the browser should wait, use the attribute CONTENT. So, to put it all together, if you wanted the browser to reload the current page in four seconds, you would add this tag inside the <HEAD> section of your HTML page:

```
<META HTTP-EQUIV="Refresh" CONTENT=4>
```

If the value of CONTENT is 0, the page is refreshed as quickly as the browser can retrieve it (which may not be very fast at all, depending on how fast the connection is—certainly not fast enough for any kind of quality animation).

Note that once you've included this header inside your HTML page, the browser will continue to reload that page, repeatedly. To get it to stop, you'll have to provide a link on that page to somewhere else that doesn't have a client pull tag inside it.

Client pulls that repeatedly load the same page are useful for pages that are continually being updated—for example, for live data such as stock quotes or sports scores. Another use of client pull is to load a different page after a certain amount of time, instead of loading the same page over and over again, for example, to step automatically through a series of slides or instructions.

To use the <META HTTP-EQUIV> to load a different page from the current one, add the URL of the next page to the value of the CONTENT attribute for the current page, like this:

```
<META HTTP-EQUIV="Refresh"
CONTENT="4;URL=http://mysite.com/page2.html">
```

Note that the URL you put inside CONTENT has to be a full URL; that is, it cannot be a relative pathname. It has to start with http://.

Inside the second page, you can include a pointer to the next page in the series, and inside that page, a pointer to the next page. Using this method, you can have any number of pages load automatically in a sequence. However, just like with the pages that load repeatedly, it's a good idea to provide a link out of the automatic reloading, so that your readers won't be forced to sit through your presentation if they don't want to.

9

Notes on Shockwave and Other Netscape Plug-ins

Of all the new advances made in recent months to support more inline multimedia and animation on the Web, the one that will likely have the most significant effect over the long term is that of plug-ins.

Plug-ins are sort of like helper applications, except that instead of existing entirely separately from the browser, they add new capabilities to the browser itself. A video plug-in, for example, could allow video files to be played directly inline with the browser. A spreadsheet plug-in would allow editable spreadsheets to be included as elements inside a Web page. The plug-ins can allow links back to the browser as well—so, for example, that spreadsheet could theoretically have links in it that could be activated and followed from inside the plug-in.

Netscape introduced the concept of plug-ins with the 2.0 version of its browser. Plug-ins are already available for many forms of sound and video; in fact, the new version of Netscape includes sound and video plug-ins already installed.

The problem with plug-ins is that if you use plug-in capabilities in your Web pages, all your readers will need to have a browser that supports plug-ins (currently, only Netscape). They must also have that plug-in installed and available (readers that don't have your plug-in will get empty space or broken icons on your page where the media should be). And many plug-ins are available only for some platforms. For some forms of media, you may also need to configure your server to deliver that new media with the right content-type.

Plug-ins are an advanced Web feature. But because this is the multimedia and animation chapter, I do want to mention one significant plug-in for both these topics: Shockwave from Macromedia.

Shockwave is a plug-in that allows Macromedia Director movies to be played as inline media on a Web page. Macromedia Director is an extremely popular tool among professional multimedia developers for creating multimedia presentations, including synchronized sound and video as well as interactivity (in fact, many of the CD-ROMs you can buy today were developed using Macromedia Director). If you're used to working with Director, Shockwave provides an easy way to put Director presentations on the Web. Or, if you're looking to do serious multimedia work on the Web or anywhere else, Director is definitely a tool to check out.

Summary

In this chapter you learned about two main topics: external media files and inline multimedia and animation.

External media files are files that cannot be read directly by your Web browser. Instead, if you link to an external file, your browser starts up a "helper" application to view or play those files. In this chapter, you learned about how external media works, using sound and video files as external media, and some hints for designing external media files.

The second half of this chapter focused on inline multimedia in Netscape and Internet Explorer using new tags and capabilities of those browsers, including tags for inline sound and video, scrolling marquees, inline GIF animation, and Java applets. Table 9.3 shows a summary of the tags you learned about today.

Table 9.3. Tags for inline media.

Tag	Attribute	Use
<IMG>	DYNSRC	Include an AVI file instead of an image. If the AVI file cannot be found or played, the normal image (in SRC) is shown.
	CONTROLS	Shows a set of controls under the AVI movie.
	LOOP	The number of times to repeat the AVI movie. If LOOP is -1 or INFINITE, the movie loops indefinitely.
	START	If START=FILEOPEN, the AVI movie begins playing immediately. If START=MOUSEOVER, the movie starts playing when the reader moves the mouse over the movie.
<BGSOUND>		Plays a background sound.
	LOOP	The number of times to repeat the sound. If LOOP is -1 or INFINITE, the sound loops indefinitely.
<MARQUEE>...</MARQUEE>		Create a scrolling text marquee.
	BEHAVIOR	If BEHAVIOR=SCROLL, the marquee scrolls in from one side of the screen to the other side and then off. If BEHAVIOR=SLIDE, the marquee scrolls in from the right and stops at the left margin. If

9

Tag	Attribute	Use
		BEHAVIOR=ALTERNATE, the marquee bounces from one side of the screen to the other.
	DIRECTION	If BEHAVIOR=SCROLL, the direction the marquee scrolls in.
	LOOP	The number of times to repeat the marquee. If LOOP is -1 or INFINITE, the marquee loops indefinitely.
	SCROLLAMOUNT	The number of pixels to move for each step of the animation; higher numbers mean the marquee moves faster.
	SCROLLDELAY	The number of milliseconds between each step of the animation; higher numbers are slower.
	BGCOLOR	The background color of the marquee's bounding box (can be a color number or name).
	HEIGHT	The height of the marquee's bounding box.
	WIDTH	The width of the marquee's bounding box.
	HSPACE	The amount of space between the left and right edges of the marquee and its surrounding text.
	VSPACE	The amount of space between the upper and lower edges of the marquee and its surrounding text.
	ALIGN	The alignment of the marquee with the text before or after it. Possible values are TOP, MIDDLE, or BOTTOM.
<APPLET>...</APPLET>		Includes a Java applet on the Web page.
	CODE	The name of the applet's class.
	WIDTH	The width of the applet's bounding box.
	HEIGHT	The height of the applet's bounding box.

continues

Table 9.3. continued

Tag	Attribute	Use
<PARAM>...</PARAM>		Parameters to be passed to the applet.
	NAME	The name of the parameter.
	VALUE	The value of the parameter.
<META>		Meta-information about the page itself.
	HTTP-EQUIV	An HTTP header name.
	CONTENT	Generally, the value of any meta-information tags. For client pull, the number of seconds to wait before reloading the page; can also include a URL to load.

Q&A

Q My browser has a helper application for JPEG images listed in my helper applications list. But when I downloaded a JPEG file, it complained that it couldn't read the document. How can I fix this?

A Just because an application is listed in the helper application list (or initialization file) doesn't mean that you have that application available on your system. Browsers are generally shipped with a default listing of helper applications that are most commonly used for the common external file formats available on the Web. You have to locate and install each of those helper applications before your browser can use them. The fact that an application is listed isn't enough.

Q I've been using AU files for my sound samples, but there's an awful hiss during the quiet parts. What can I do?

A Some sound-editing programs can help remove some of the hiss in AU files, but because of the nature of AU encoding, you'll usually have some amount of noise. If sound quality is that important to you, consider using AIFF or, if you have the converters, MPEG audio.

Q Why don't my MPEG files have sound?

A Maybe they do! The MPEG standard allows for both video and audio tracks, but few players can handle the audio track at this time. You have two choices if you must have sound for your MPEG movies: Wait for better players (or bribe a programmer to write one), or convert your movies to QuickTime and show your readers how to install and use QuickTime players.

9

Q I'm using the Animator applet. I've got a bunch of Java animation that I want to put on different files, but if I put them all in the same directory I can't name them all T1, T2, and so on, without naming conflicts. What do I do?

A The Animator applet contains a lot of parameters I did not include in this chapter. One of them, IMAGESOURCE, takes a directory name relative to the current directory for images. So you can store your images in individual subdirectories and avoid naming problems. Using other Animator parameters you can also change the names from T1, T2, and so on. See the URL for the animator applet for details.

Chapter **10**

Sound and Video Files

After an afternoon of Web exploring, you've just reached a page that has a long list of movie samples you can download. Neat, you think, scanning over the list. The problem, however, is that beside the name of each file, there's a description, and it looks something like this:

```
'Luther's Banana' is a 1.2 megabyte AVI file with a CinePak codec and
an 8-bit 22Khz two-channel audio track.
```

If you understood that, you don't need this chapter. If, on the other hand, you're interested in learning about sound and video and how they relate to the Web, or if you've decided that you must know what all those strange words and numbers mean, read on.

In this chapter, I'll talk about digital audio and video: the basics of how they work, the common file formats in use on the Web and in the industry, and some ideas for obtaining sound and video and using it in your Web pages. Here are some of the things you'll learn in this chapter:

☐ Digital audio and video: what they are and how they work

☐ The common sound formats: μ-law, AIFF, WAVE, and RealAudio

☐ The common video formats: QuickTime, Video for Windows, and MPEG

☐ Video codecs: what they are and which ones are the most popular and useful

☐ Creating and modifying sound and video files for use on the Web

An Introduction to Digital Sound

Want to know something about how sound on the computer works? Want to create your own audio clips for the Web (be they music, voice, sound effects, or other strange noises)? You've come to the right place. In the first part of the chapter, you'll learn about what digital audio is and the sort of formats that are popular on the Web, and you'll have a quick lesson in how to get sound into your computer so you can put it on the Web.

Sound Waves

You might remember from high school physics that the basic definition of sound is that sound is created by disturbances in the air that produce waves. Those pressure waves are what is perceived as sound by the human ear. In its simplest form, a sound wave looks something like what you see in Figure 10.1.

Figure 10.1.
A basic sound wave.

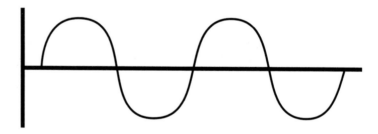

There are two important things to note about the basic sound wave. First, it has an amplitude, which is the distance between the middle line (silence) and the top or bottom of the wave crests. The greater the amplitude, the louder the sound.

It also has a frequency, which is the speed the wave moves (or, more precisely, the number of waves that move past a point during a certain amount of time). Higher frequencies (that is, faster waves moving past that point) produce high-pitched sounds, and lower frequencies produce low-pitched sounds.

Real sounds are much more complicated than that, of course, with lots of different complex wave forms making up a single sound as you hear it. With the combinations of lots of sound waves and different ways of describing them, there are many other words and concepts I could define here. But frequency and amplitude are the two most important ones, and are the ones that will matter most in the next section.

Converting Sound Waves to Digital Samples

An analog sound wave (the one you just saw in Figure 10.1) is a continuous line with an infinite number of amplitude values along its length. To convert it to a digital signal, your computer takes measurements of the wave's amplitude at particular points in time. Each measurement it takes is called a sample; therefore, converting an analog sound to digital audio is called sampling that sound. Figure 10.2 shows how values along the wave are sampled over time.

Figure 10.2.
Sampling a sound wave.

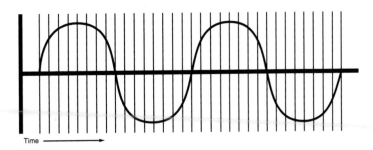

The more samples you take, the more amplitude values you have and the closer you are to capturing something close to the original sound wave. But because the original wave has an infinite number of values, you can never exactly re-create the original. With very high sampling rates, you can create a representation of the original sound wave so close that the human ear can't tell the difference.

The number of samples taken per second is called the sample rate and is usually measured in kilohertz (KHz). There are several different possible sample rates in use today, but the most popular are 11KHz, 22KHz, and 44KHz.

NOTE Those numbers are rounded off for simplicity. The actual numbers are usually 11.025KHz, 22.050KHz, and 44.1KHz.

In addition to the sample rate, you also have the sample size, sometimes called the sample resolution. There are generally two choices for sample resolutions, 8-bit and 16-bit. Think of sample resolution in terms of increments between the top and bottom of the wave form. The values don't actually change, but if you have 8-bit increments and 16-bit increments across that distance, the latter are smaller and provide finer detail (see Figure 10.3). It is much the same way that 8-bit versus 16- or 24-bit color works. You can get a much broader range of colors with the higher color resolution, but you always get close to the same color with each.

Figure 10.3.

Sample resolution.

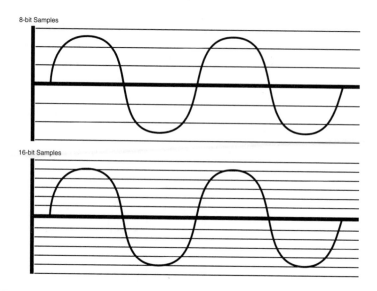

8-bit Samples

16-bit Samples

NEW TERM

The *sample rate* is the number of sound samples taken per second and is measured in KHz. The *sample size* is usually either 8-bit or 16-bit; 16-bit provides finer "details" in the sound.

When a sound sample is taken, the actual value of the amplitude is rounded off to the nearest increment (in audio jargon, the rounding off is called quantizing). If you're using a 16-bit sample, you're much more likely to get closer to the original value than in an 8-bit sample because the increments are smaller (see Figure 10.4).

The difference between the actual amplitude value and the rounded-off value is called quantization error (more audio jargon). Lots of quantization error results in a sort of hissing noise in the final sound file.

All this is a complicated way of saying that 16-bit is better than 8-bit. (So why didn't I just say that? Well, now you know why it's better.) The overall quality of a digital audio sound is loosely related to both its sample size and sample rate. However, because the human ear can pick up quantization errors more easily than errors in a low sample rate, it's always better to go with 16-bit over 8-bit. If you use 8-bit, use the highest possible sample rate to adjust for the errors.

10

Figure 10.4.

Taking a sample.

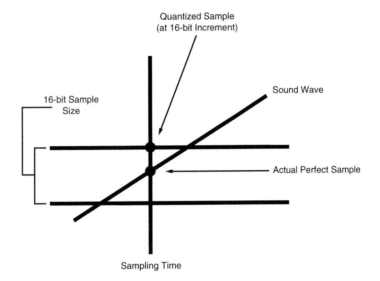

Finally, sounds can also have multiple channels, usually used for creating stereo effects. Typically, one channel is mono, two channels are stereo, four channels are quad, and so on, just as in your stereo.

The higher the sample rate and size, and the more channels, the better the quality of the resulting sound. For example, an 8-bit sound sample at 8KHz is about the quality you get over the telephone, whereas 16-bit stereo at 44KHz is CD-quality audio. Unfortunately, just as with image files, greater sound quality in your audio means larger file sizes. A minute of music at 22KHz with 8-bit sample resolution takes up 1.25MB on your disk, whereas a minute of CD-quality audio (16-bit, 44KHz) runs you 10MB. Stereo, of course, is twice the size of mono.

So what about compression? If these files take up so much room, why not do as the image folks have done and create compression algorithms that reduce the size of these files? Word from the experts is that audio is notoriously difficult to compress. (This makes sense. Unlike images, audio sound waves are incredibly complex, and there aren't the same sort of repeated patterns and consistent variations that allow images to be compressed so easily.) Only a few of the common sound file formats have built-in compression.

Digital Back to Analog

So now you have an analog sound encoded digitally on your computer, and you're going to play it. When you play a digital audio sound, the computer translates the digital samples back into an analog sound wave.

Because a digital sample relies on millions of single digits to represent the sound wave, each of which is held for the same amount of time as the sound was originally sampled, this can produce a jaggy sound wave and a funny-sounding sample (see Figure 10.5).

Figure 10.5.
A jaggy analog signal.

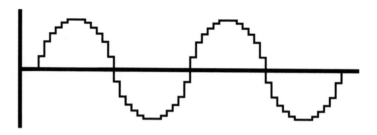

Analog filters are used to smooth out the jags in the wave (see Figure 10.6), which is then sent to your computer speakers.

Figure 10.6.
The jaggy wave smoothed out.

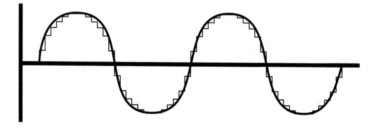

Common Sound Formats

Now that you know how digital sound works, let's go over how digital sound is stored. Unfortunately, even now there isn't a standard for audio on the Web that is similar to the way GIF and JPEG are standard now for images. It's still a hodgepodge of formats, all of them used at different times. This section will at least give you an idea of what's out there and what it means.

μ-law (Mu-law), AU

The most common and readily available sound format that works cross-platform is μ-law, pronounced myew-law (or sometimes you-law, because the Greek μ character looks like a *u*). Used by both Sun and NeXT for their standard audio format, μ-law format was designed for the telephone industry in the United States. Its European equivalent is called A-law and is, for the most part, the same format. μ-law also has several variations that all come under the same name, but all should be readable and playable by a player that claims to support μ-law. μ-law files are sometimes called AU files because of their .au filename extension.

Samples in μ-law format are mono, 8-bit, and 8KHz. But the encoding of the sample is different from most other formats, which allows μ-law to have a wider dynamic range (variation between soft and loud parts of a sound) than most sounds encoded with such a small sample size and rate. On the other hand, μ-law samples tend to have more hiss than other sound formats.

NOTE

> Some sound applications enable you to record μ-law samples at a higher sample rate than 8KHz. However, this might make them unplayable across platforms. If you're going to choose μ-law, stick with the standard 8-bit, 8KHz sample.

10

The only advantage of μ-law sound samples is their wide cross-platform support. Many sites providing sound samples in a more high-fidelity format such as AIFF or MPEG will provide a μ-law sample as well to reach a wider audience.

AIFF/AIFC

AIFF stands for Audio Interchange File Format. AIFF was developed by Apple and is primarily a Macintosh format, but SGI has adopted it as well. In terms of flexibility, AIFF is an excellent format, which allows for 8- or 16-bit samples at many sample rates, in mono or stereo. AIFF files have an .aiff or .aif filename extension.

AIFC is AIFF with compression built in. The basic compression algorithm is MACE (Macintosh Audio Compression/Expansion), with two variations, MACE3 (3-to-1 compression) and MACE6 (6-to-1 compression). Both are lossy compression schemes, so AIFC compressed files will lose some of the sound quality of the original. Most AIFF players also play AIFC, so using one over the other is only a question of file size or sound quality.

Macintosh SND Files

The SND format, sometimes called just plain Macintosh System Sounds, is the format used only on the Macintosh for many simple sounds such as the beeps and quacks that come with the system. SND files are actually files with SND resources (the Macintosh has a resource and data fork for many files) that can contain digital samples or a series of commands playable by the Macintosh Sound Manager. SND files are not widely used on the Web because they are limited to the Macintosh, but SND files are widely available and easily converted to other sound formats.

Windows WAVE

WAVE or RIFF WAVE format, sometimes called WAV from the .wav extension, was developed by Microsoft and IBM, and its inclusion in Windows 3.1 has made it the audio standard on the PC platform. WAVE and AIFF have much in common, mostly in their flexibility. WAVE files can also accommodate samples in any rate, size, and number of channels. In addition, WAVE files can include several different compression schemes.

MPEG Audio

MPEG stands for Moving Picture Experts Group, which is a standards committee interested primarily in compression for digital video. But, because video usually includes an audio track, the group considers issues in audio compression as well. The MPEG audio compression algorithm is far too complex to explain here (in other words, I don't understand it). However, you can get all the technical information you want from the MPEG FAQ, available at most sites that carry Usenet FAQs (one is listed at the end of this chapter).

MPEG audio has become popular on the Web mostly because of the Internet Underground Music Archive, which uses it for its sound samples (visit IUMA at http://www.iuma.com/ IUMA/). Using MPEG, you can get excellent sound quality without needing enormous amounts of disk space. The files are still rather large, but the quality is excellent. On the other hand, your readers (listeners) will also need an MPEG audio player for their platform and might need to configure their browser in order to properly use the samples.

RealAudio

RealAudio format, playable using the RealAudio player or plug-in and the RealAudio server, currently comes in two flavors: 14.4 format, playable over 14.4KB modems, provides "monophonic AM quality sound." The 28.8 format, playable over 28.8KB modems or faster connections, provides "monophonic near-FM quality sound."

Both 14.4 and 28.8 formats are highly compressed using a lossy compression algorithm of their own design. RealAudio files tend to be much smaller than their equivalent AIFF or WAVE equivalents, but the sound quality is not as good.

Getting Sound Files

Where can you get sound files to use on the Web? You can get them from a variety of sources:

☐ Some platforms with CD-ROM drives may allow you to record digital sounds directly off a standard audio CD; you'll need a CD-ROM drive that supports this, of course. Keep in mind if you go this route that most published audio material is copyrighted, and its owners may not appreciate your making their songs or sounds available for free on the Internet.

☐ Many Internet archives have collections of small, digitized samples in the appropriate format for the platform they emphasize (for example, SND format files for Macintosh archives, WAV format for Windows, AU for Sun's UNIX, and so on).

WARNING

> Keep in mind that, like images, sounds you find on the Net may be owned by someone who won't like your using them. Use caution when using "found" sounds.

☐ Commercial "clip sound" products are available, again, in appropriate formats for your platform. These sounds have the advantage of usually being public domain or royalty-free, meaning that you can use them anywhere without needing to get permission or pay a fee.

Sampling Sound

The most interesting sounds for your Web presentation, of course, are those you make yourself. As I mentioned earlier, the process of recording sounds to digital files is called sampling. In this section, you'll learn about the sort of equipment you can get and the software available to sample and save sounds.

NEW TERM

> *Sampling* is the process of encoding analog sound into a digital format.

Note that to get truly high-quality production digital audio for the Web or for any other use, you'll need to spend a lot of money on truly high-quality production equipment, and the choices are very broad. Also note that as time goes on, better technology becomes more widespread and cheaper, so the best I can hope to provide here is a general rundown of the technology. Shop your local computer store or magazines for more information.

Sampling on PCs

To sample sound on a PC, you'll need a sound card. Most sound cards can give you audio capabilities from 8-bit mono at 11 or 22KHz all the way up to 16-bit 44KHz stereo. Go for the 16-bit cards. Not only will you get better quality for the sounds you input, but more games and multimedia titles for the PC are taking advantage of 16-bit sound, and the better quality is much more impressive. Once you have a sound card, you can connect your tape deck or microphone to the line-in jacks on the card or just plug in a standard microphone. Then, it's a question of software.

Windows comes with a simple sound recorder called Sound Recorder (an apt choice for a name), which can record simple sounds in 8-bit mono at 11KHz. For very simple sound recordings such as voices and small sound effects, this might be all you need (see Figure 10.7).

Figure 10.7.

The Windows Sound Recorder.

Your sound card also should be packaged with sound tools that will enable you to record and edit sounds. The standard Sound Blaster card comes with several applications for capturing and editing sound, including the WaveEditor program (see Figure 10.8), which allows sound recording and editing across a broad range of rates and sizes.

Figure 10.8.

Sound Blaster's WaveEditor.

For serious sound editing and processing, you might want to check out Cool Edit. Cool Edit is a shareware sound editor with an enormous number of features. It supports full recording on most sound cards; it can read, convert, and save to a wide range of sound formats; and it even has built-in controls for your CD player. For $50 ($100 to receive all upgrades) with one free upgrade, it's a great deal if you're doing Windows sound editing. You can find out more about Cool Edit at http://www.netzone.com/syntrillium/.

If you're planning to work extensively with both sound and video, you might want to look into Adobe Premiere. Long the choice of multimedia developers for the Macintosh, Premiere provides a great deal of power over both audio and video capture and integration, and it works with most sound boards. It is more expensive, but it's one of the best tools out there.

Sampling on Macintoshes

Macintoshes have had sound capabilities built in for many years now, and most Macs are shipped with either a built-in microphone or a separate plug-in microphone. You can record directly into the microphone (for mono 22KHz, 8-bit sounds) or plug a standard stereo audio jack into the back of the computer. Most newer Macs are capable of recording 16-bit stereo at up to 48KHz (44KHz is CD quality, 48KHz is DAT [Digital Audio Tape] quality); check with the specifications for your model to see what it's capable of.

For basic 8-bit mono, 22KHz sounds that are under 10 seconds, you can record using the Sound control panel, which is part of the standard Mac system software. Just select Add and click the Record button (see Figure 10.9).

Figure 10.9.

Recording from the
Sound control
panel.

For more control over your sounds, you'll need different software. Lots of tools exist for recording sound on the Mac, from the excellent freeware SoundMachine (for recording and sound conversion) and the shareware SoundHack (for editing), to commercial tools that do both, such as MacroMedia's SoundEdit 16. As I mentioned in the Windows section, Adobe Premiere is also an excellent tool, particularly if you intend to do work with video as well (see Figure 10.10).

Figure 10.10.

Premiere's audio
options.

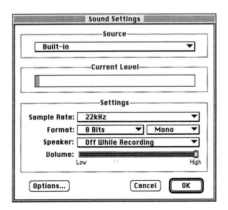

Sampling on UNIX Workstations

Most newer UNIX workstations come with built-in microphones that provide 16-bit sampling rates for audio. Check with your manufacturer for specifics.

Converting Sound Files

Once you have a sound file, it may not be in the right format—that is, the format you want it to be in. The programs mentioned in this section can read and convert many popular sound formats.

For UNIX and PC-compatible systems, a program called SOX by Lance Norskog can convert between many sound formats (including AU, WAV, AIFF, and Macintosh SND) and perform some rudimentary processing including filtering, changing the sample rate, and reversing the sample.

On DOS, WAVany by Bill Neisius converts most common sound formats (including AU and Macintosh SND) to WAV format.

Waveform Hold and Modify (WHAM), for Windows, is an excellent sound player, editor, and converter that also works really well as a helper application for your browser.

For the Macintosh, the freeware SoundApp by Norman Franke reads and plays most sound formats, and converts to WAV, Macintosh SND, AIFF, and NeXT sound formats (but mysteriously, not Sun AU). The freeware program Ulaw (yes, it's spelled with a U) will convert Macintosh sounds (SND) to AU format.

FTP sources for each of these programs are listed in Appendix A, "Sources for Further Information."

To convert any sound formats to RealAudio format, you'll need the RealAudio Encoder. It's available free with the RealAudio Server package, or you can download a copy from Real Audio's site at `http://www.realaudio.com/`.

Audio for the Web

Now that I've presented all the options you have for recording and working with audio, I should give some cautions for providing audio files on the Web.

Just as with images, you won't be able to provide as much as you would like on your Web pages because of limitations in your readers' systems and in the speed of their connections. Here are some hints for using audio on the Web:

- Few systems on the Web have 16-bit sound capabilities, and listening to 16-bit sounds on an 8-bit system can result in some strange effects. To provide the best quality of sound for the widest audience, distribute only 8-bit sounds on your Web page. Or, provide different sound files in both 8- and 16-bits.

- To provide the best quality of 8-bit sounds, record in the highest sampling rate and size you can, and then use a sound editor to process the sound down to 8-bit. A lot of sound converter programs and editors enable you to downsample the sound in this way. Check out, in particular, a package called SOX for UNIX and DOS systems that includes several filters for improving the quality of 8-bit sound.

☐ Try to keep your file sizes small by downsampling to 8-bit, using a lower sampling rate, and providing mono sounds instead of stereo.

☐ As I noted in the last chapter, always indicate on the page where you describe your sounds what format those sounds are in, whether it is WAVE, AIFF, or other format. Keep in mind that because there is no generic audio standard on the Web, your readers will be annoyed at you if they spend a lot of time downloading a sound and they don't have the software to play it. Providing the file size in the description is also a common politeness for your readers so they know how long they will have to wait for your sound.

☐ If you are very concerned about sound quality and you must provide large audio files on your Web page, consider including a smaller sound clip in μ-law format as a preview or for people who don't have the capabilities to listen to the higher-quality sample.

☐ Creating sounds for RealAudio format? Most of these same hints apply. However, you'll also want to check out the hints and suggestions RealAudio gives for getting the best sound quality out of RealAudio files at `http://www.realaudio.com/help/content/audiohints.html`.

An Introduction to Digital Video

Digital video is tremendously exciting to many in the computer industry at the moment, from hardware manufacturers to software developers (particularly of games and multimedia titles) to people who just like to play with cutting-edge technology. On the Web, digital video usually takes the form of small movie clips, usually in media archives.

I can't provide a complete overview of digital video technology in this book, partly because much of it is quite complicated, and mostly because the digital video industry is changing nearly as fast as the Web is. But for producing small, short videos for the purposes of publishing on the Web, I can provide some of the basics and hints for creating and using digital video.

Analog and Digital Video

Analog video, like analog audio, is a continuous stream of sound and images. In order to get an analog video source into your computer, you'll need a video capture board that samples the analog video at regular intervals to create a digital movie, just as the audio sampling board

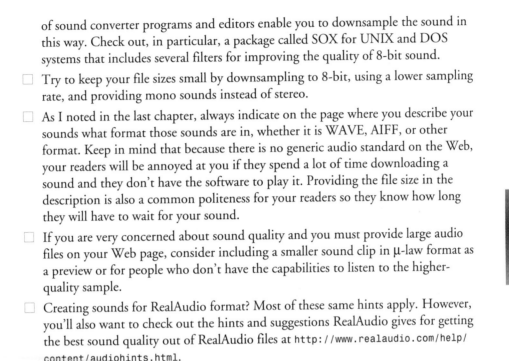

does for audio. At each interval, the capture board encodes an individual image at a given resolution called a frame. When the video is played back, the frames are played in sequence and give the appearance of motion. The number of frames per second—the speed at which the frames go by—is called the frame rate and is analogous to the sampling rate in digital audio. The better the frame rate, the closer you can get to the original analog source.

In addition to the frame rate, frame size (the actual size in pixels of the frame on your screen) is also important (see Figure 10.11).

Figure 10.11.

Frame rates and sizes.

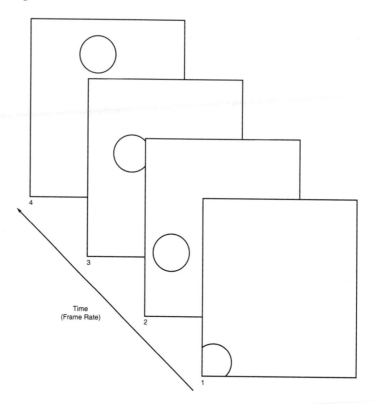

Time
(Frame Rate)

NEW TERM

A *frame* is an individual image in a video file. The *frame rate* is how many frames go by per second, and the *frame size* is the actual pixel dimension of each frame.

The frame rate of standard full-screen video, such as what you get on your VCR, is 30 frames per second. This frame rate is sometimes called full-motion video. Achieving full-screen, full-motion video—the sort of standard that is easy with a $700 camcorder—is the Holy Grail

10

for programmers and authors working with digital video. Most of the time, they must settle for significantly less in frame rates and frame sizes to get smooth playback.

Why? On an analog video source, 30 frames per second is no big deal. The frames go by, and they're displayed. With digital video, each frame must be read from disk, decompressed if necessary, and then spat onto the screen as fast as possible. Therefore, a lot of processing power, a fast hard drive, and an even faster graphics system in your computer are required in order for it to work correctly, even more so for larger frame sizes and faster frame rates.

So what happens if the movie is playing faster than your computer can keep up? Usually your computer will drop frames—that is, throw them away without displaying them. And when frames are being dropped, the frame rate goes down, creating jerkier motions or outright halts in the action. This is not a good situation for your video clip.

What you'll discover when you start playing with it is that producing digital video is often a series of compromises in order to fit into the constraints of the platform you are working with. You'll learn more about these compromises later in this section.

10

Compression and Decompression (Codecs)

Image and audio formats, as I've noted previously, take up an enormous amount of space. Now combine the two—hundreds, if not thousands, of images, plus an audio soundtrack—and you can begin to imagine how much disk space a digital video file can take up. The bigger the file, the harder it is for the computer system to process it with any amount of speed, and the more likely it is that playback quality will suffer. For these reasons, compression and decompression technology is especially important to digital video files, and lots of work has been done in this area.

In digital video, the algorithm for compression and decompression is usually referred to as a single thing called a codec (short for COmpression/DECompression, pronounced coh-deck). Unlike with image compression, video codecs are not tightly coupled with video file formats. A typical format can use many different kinds of codecs and can usually choose the right one on the fly when the video is played back.

NEW TERM

> A *video codec* is the algorithm used for compressing and decompressing that video file.

You'll learn more about codecs, how they work, and the popular kinds of codecs in use, later in this chapter in the section "Movie Compression."

Movie Formats

Digital video in a file ready to be played back on a computer is often referred to as a movie. A movie contains digital video data (just as a sound file contains digital audio data), but that data can be a live-action film or an animation; movie is simply a generic term to refer to the file itself.

Right now the Big Three movie formats on the Web and in the computer industry at large are QuickTime, Video for Windows (VfW), and MPEG.

QuickTime

Although QuickTime was developed by Apple for the Macintosh, QuickTime files are the closest thing the Web has to a standard cross-platform movie format (with MPEG a close second). The Apple system software includes QuickTime and a simple player (called MoviePlayer or SimplePlayer). For PCs, QuickTime files can be played through the QuickTime for Windows (QTfW) package, and the freely available Xanim program will play them under the X Window System and UNIX. QuickTime movies have the extension .qt or .mov.

QuickTime supports many different codecs, particularly CinePak and Indeo, both of which can be used cross-platform. See the "Codec Formats" section later in this chapter for more information on these formats.

NOTE

> If you produce your QuickTime videos on the Macintosh, you must make sure that they are flattened before they can be viewable on other platforms. See the section "Getting and Converting Video" later in this chapter for more information on programs that will flatten QuickTime files for you.

Video for Windows

Video for Windows (VfW) was developed by Microsoft and is the PC standard for desktop video. VfW files are sometimes called AVI files from the .avi extension (AVI stands for Audio/Video Interleave). VfW files are extremely popular on PCs, and hordes of existing files are available in AVI format. However, outside of the PC world, few players exist for playing AVI files directly, making VfW less suitable than QuickTime for video on the Web.

10

The MPEG Video Format

MPEG is both a file format and a codec for digital video. There are actually three forms of MPEG: MPEG video, for picture only; MPEG audio, which is discussed in the previous section; and MPEG systems, which includes both audio and video tracks.

MPEG files provide excellent picture quality but can be very slow to decompress. For this reason, many MPEG decoding systems are hardware-assisted, meaning that you need a board to play MPEG files reliably without dropping a lot of frames. Although software decoders definitely exist (and there are some very good ones out there), they tend to require a lot of processor power on your system and also usually support MPEG video only (they have no soundtrack).

A third drawback of MPEG video as a standard for the Web is that MPEG movies are very expensive to encode. You need a hardware encoder to do so, and the price ranges for encoders are in the thousands of dollars. As MPEG becomes more popular, those prices are likely to drop. But for now, unless you already have access to the encoding equipment or you're really serious about your digital video, a software-based format is probably the better way to go.

NOTE

> An alternative to buying encoding hardware is to contract a video production service bureau to do it for you. Some service bureaus may have the MPEG encoding equipment and can encode your video into MPEG for you, usually charging you a set rate per minute. Like the costs of MPEG hardware, costs for these service bureaus are also dropping and may provide you a reasonable option if you must have MPEG.

Movie Compression

As with images and audio, compression is very important for being able to store digital video data, perhaps even more so because movie files have so much data associated with them. Fortunately, lots of compression technologies exist for digital video, so you have lots to choose from.

As I mentioned early on in this section, video compression methods are called codecs, which include both compression and decompression as a pair. Compression generally occurs when a movie is saved or produced; decompression occurs on the fly when the movie is played back. The codec is not part of the movie file itself; the movie file can use one of several codecs, and you can usually choose which one you want to use for your movie when you create it. (When the movie is played, the right codec to decompress it is chosen automatically.)

In this section, I'll talk about methods of video compression and, in the next section, about specific codecs you have available for use in your own files.

Asymmetric and Symmetric Codecs

Codecs are often referred to as being symmetric or asymmetric (see Figure 10.12). These terms refer to balance of the speed of compression and speed of decompression. A symmetric codec takes the same amount of time to compress a movie as it does to decompress it, which is good for production time but not as good for playback. Asymmetric codecs usually take a very long time to compress, but make up for it by being fast to decompress (and remember, the faster it takes to decompress a movie, the better frame rate you can get, and so asymmetric codecs tend to be more desirable). Most codecs are at least a little asymmetric on the compression side; some are very much so.

NEW TERM

Symmetric codecs take as long to compress a digital video file as they do to compress it. With *asymmetric codecs* either the compression or the decompression takes longer than the other.

Figure 10.12.
Symmetric versus asymmetric codecs.

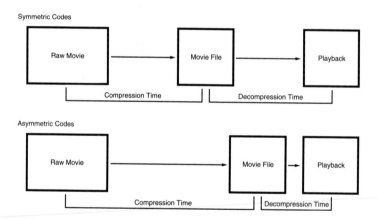

Frame Differencing

But how do codecs work for video? They can either work in much the same way image compressing works, with individual frames being compressed and then decompressed at playback, or they can support what is called frame differencing. Frame differencing is simply a method of movie compression that many codecs use; it is not a codec itself.

10

Much of the processing time required by digital video during playback is taken up in decompressing and drawing individual frames and then spitting them to the screen at the best frame rate possible. If the CPU gets behind in rendering frames, frames can get dropped, resulting in jerky motion. Frame differencing, therefore, is a way of speeding up the time it takes to decompress and draw a frame. Differenced frames do not have all the information that a standard frame has; instead, they have only the information that is different from that in the frame before it in the movie. Because the differences are usually a lot smaller than the full frame, that means your computer doesn't have to take as long to process it, which can help to minimize dropped frames. Of course, because a differenced frame is also a lot smaller in terms of information, the resulting file size of the movie is a lot smaller as well. Figure 10.13 shows a simple example of frame differencing.

NEW TERM | *Frame differencing* involves storing only the portions of frames that have changed since the previous frame, rather than storing the entire frame.

10

Figure 10.13.
Frame differencing.

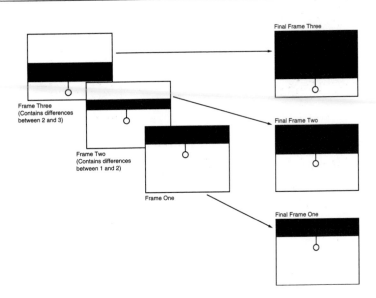

Frame differencing works best in what are called talking head movies: movies with a lot of static backgrounds, with only a small portion of the frame changing from frame to frame. For movies with a lot of change between frames, frame differencing might not work quite as well.

Key Frames

Frame differencing relies on the existence of what are called key frames in the movie file. Key frames are complete frames upon which the differences in differenced frames are based. Each time a differenced frame comes along, the differences are calculated from the frame before it, which is calculated from the frame before it, and so on, back to the key frame. Figure 10.14 shows how the differenced frames are created.

Figure 10.14.

Key frames and differencing.

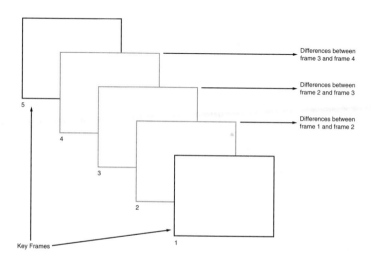

NEW TERM

Key frames are the frames that differenced frames are different from. Key frames are always complete frames and are inserted at appropriate intervals in the file.

Of course, the further away from the key frame you get, the more information will be different, the more information your computer has to keep track of with every frame, and the more likely it is that you'll start taking up too much processing time and dropping frames. So, having key frames at regular intervals is crucial to making sure that you get the best level of compression and that your movie plays smoothly and consistently. On the other hand, because key frames contain a lot more information than differenced frames, you don't want too many of them; key frames take longer to process in the first place. Usually, you can set the number of key frames in a movie in your movie-editing software. The general rule is to allow one key frame per second of video (or one every 15 frames for 15fps movies).

10

Hardware Assistance

As I stated earlier, because of the enormous amount of information that needs to be processed when a movie is captured, compressed, and played back, only very fast and powerful computers can handle good-quality video with a decent frame rate and size. Although software codecs exist and are popular for video with small frame rates and sizes, when you move toward the higher end of the technology, you'll usually want to invest in a hardware-assisted codec.

Hardware assistance usually takes the form of a video board you can plug into your computer that has special chips on it for processing digital video—usually files with the MPEG or JPEG codecs, as you'll learn about later in this chapter. In the future, video processing chips could very well be standard in many computers. But, for now, hardware assistance is rare in computers on the Web, and you should not rely upon it for the video you produce.

Codec Formats

There are several excellent codecs available for digital video today, both for software-only and for hardware-assisted recording and playback. The two biggest, CinePak and Indeo, are both cross-platform (Mac, Windows, and UNIX), but motion JPEG is quite popular as well, particularly with capture cards.

CinePak

CinePak, formerly called Compact Video, is the most popular codec for QuickTime files and is available in VfW as well. CinePak is a form of lossy compression, so if you use CinePak, you should make sure your original, uncompressed source is of the best quality possible.

CinePak supports frame differencing and is highly asymmetric, taking an enormous amount of time to compress. (I once saw a 15-second movie take an hour to compress.) On the other hand, when the compression is done, the playback is quite smooth and the file sizes are excellent.

Indeo

Second to CinePak, but catching up fast, is Indeo Video. Indeo was developed by Intel as part of the Intel Smart Video Recorder, an excellent video capture card. Indeo can be lossy or lossless, supports frame differencing, and is much less asymmetric than CinePak. However, it requires more processor time on decompression, making it more likely to drop frames on lower-end computers.

Indeo was initially available only for VfW files, but QuickTime 2.0 now supports it as well, making it a close second for the most popular codec for digital video, and it's catching up fast.

JPEG

JPEG Compression? Isn't that the image standard? Yes, it is, and it's exactly the same form of compression when it is used in digital video (where it's sometimes called motion JPEG). Remember, movies are a set of frames, and each one is an image—usually a photographic-quality image. Each of those images can be compressed quite well using JPEG compression.

There are two drawbacks to JPEG compression as a codec: lack of frame differencing, and slow decompression. Because JPEG is a compression method for still images, it treats each frame as if it were a still image and does no differencing between frames. For playback, this means that each frame must be individually decompressed and displayed, making it more likely that frames will be dropped and performance will degrade. With hardware assistance, however, JPEG decompression speeds can easily surpass those of software-only codecs with frame differencing, and with hardware assistance JPEG provides probably the best quality and the most widely available video format. But, as with all hardware-assisted codecs, few computers on the Web have JPEG capabilities, so producing JPEG files for the Web is probably not a good idea.

On the other hand, JPEG might be appropriate for video capture. Many video boards support JPEG compression for video capture. If you're planning on using CinePak as your final codec, capturing to JPEG first is an excellent first pass (if you have the disk space to store the movie before you finish compressing it).

The MPEG Codec

I'll mention MPEG here as well because MPEG is both a format and a codec. As I mentioned in the section on formats, MPEG provides excellent high-quality compression for digital video, but usually requires hardware assistance in order to decompress well. Also, MPEG encoders tend to be quite expensive, so creating MPEG movies is no small task. For Web purposes, you should probably go with a software codec such as CinePak or Indeo.

NOTE MPEG compression is extremely complicated and far beyond the scope of this book; if you have interest in MPEG and how it works, I highly recommend you look at the MPEG FAQ (referenced at the end of this chapter).

Digitizing Video

Getting fancy enough that you want to produce your own video for the Web? The process of actually capturing video into your computer, like audio capture, is pretty easy with the right equipment. You install a capture board, hook up your VCR or camera, start your software for doing captures, and off you go.

The specifics, of course, vary from platform to platform, and in recent months there has been an explosion of products available. In this section I'll provide a general overview of the technology; for more information on specific products, you may want to consult with your local computer store or look into reports in computer magazines.

Analog Video Signals and Formats

You won't need to know much about analog video itself unless you intend to get heavily involved in aspects of video production. But you should be aware of two analog video standards: the video signal and the broadcast format.

How you hook up your video equipment to your computer is determined by the video signal your equipment uses. There are two kinds of video signals: composite and S-video. Composite is the standard signal you get out of your TV, VCR, or camcorder, and, for basic video, it's probably the signal you're going to end up using. S-video, which uses a different cable, is a higher-end standard that separates color and brightness, providing a better-quality picture. If you can use S-video, your final movies will be of much better quality. But you'll have to buy special S-video equipment to do it.

After you have everything hooked up, you'll have to know what broadcast format you're sending to your computer. There are three standard formats in use: NTSC (National Television Standards Committee), which is used in most of North America and Japan; PAL (Phase alteration line), which is used in western Europe, the UK, and the Middle East; and SECAM (Systémé Électronic Pour Coleur Avec Mémoire), which is used in France and Russia.

Most video capture cards support NTSC and PAL, so most of the time you won't have to worry about the format you have in your camera or your VCR. If you're not sure what format you have, and you are in the United States, it's likely you have NTSC. Outside the United States, make sure you know what you have and if your video card can handle it.

Video on the PC

The market for low-cost desktop video capture cards on the PC has exploded recently. If you're interested in doing video on the PC, I strongly recommend that you check with the trade magazines to see what is currently out there and what is recommended.

On a very basic level of video production, an awesome tool for doing very simple video on the PC (and on the Mac) is the QuickCam from Connectix. This little $100 camera sits on your desktop, and can capture both audio and video or take video still pictures. It operates only in grayscale, and the frame rate is rather low for all but tiny pictures. For simple applications such as small files for the Web or video-conferencing, however, it's a great deal.

In terms of video software, VidCap and VidEdit come with the Video for Windows package. VidCap is used to capture video to VfW format (appropriately) and provide several options of codecs, and it can capture video stills as well. VidEdit (shown in Figure 10.15) is used to edit existing video clips. For example, you can change the frame rate, frame size, codec, or audio qualities, as well as cut, copy, and paste portions of the movie itself.

Figure 10.15.

VidEdit.

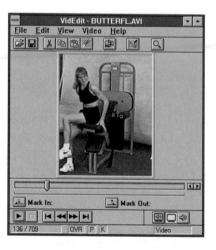

Also available is SmartVid from Intel, part of the Indeo Video system and the Intel Smart Video Recorder (see Figure 10.16). You can get a copy of SmartVid Beta (http:// www.intel.com./pc-supp/multimed/indeo/smartvid.htm) and use it for capturing, convert-ing, and editing video files. SmartVid also has the edge over VidCap for being able to capture to both VfW and QuickTime files using the Indeo codec.

Finally, there is Adobe Premiere, whose capture options for version 3.0 are shown in Figure 10.17 (version 4 is out). It is wildly popular on the Macintosh among video professionals, and if you plan on doing much video work, you should look into this application. It can capture and extensively edit both audio and video, combine the two from separate sources, add titles, and save files with varying key frames and codecs.

Figure 10.16.
Intel's SmartVid.

Figure 10.17.
Adobe Premiere.

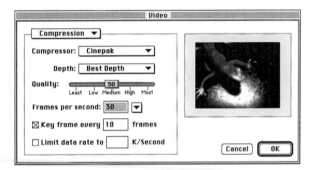

Video on the Mac

Many newer Macintoshes contain a built-in video card to which you can connect a composite video camera or VCR. In addition, you can spend between a couple hundred to several thousand dollars on video capture systems for the Macintosh as well.

The Connectix QuickCam, which I mentioned in the previous section, is also available for the Macintosh, and is of great use for very simple black-and-white video.

For software capturing and simple editing, FusionRecorder comes with many Macintoshes and can capture, edit, and save simple audio and video files. For more serious editing work, Adobe Premiere is (appropriately) the premier editing program for the Mac, and the one used by most professionals. Also available are Avid's VideoShop, which is cheaper and claims to be easier to use, and Radius's VideoFusion (which is also bundled with the Video Vision system).

Video on UNIX

Depending on your workstation, you may have video built into your box, or you may need to buy a third-party card. High-end SGI and Sun systems now come with video input jacks, video capture software, and sometimes even with small color video cameras. Again, check with your manufacturer for details.

Getting and Converting Video

Just as with images and sound, you can get video clips by making them yourself, downloading them from the Net, or purchasing royalty-free clips that you can read on your platform. Sometimes you may need to convert a video file from one format to another, or from one codec to another. For these sorts of operations, often the software you used to capture the original video is the best to use, but if you don't have that software, or if you got a video file from another source, you'll need simpler tools.

To convert video files between formats on Windows systems, a commercial program called XingCD enables you to convert AVI files to MPEG. AVI to QuickTime converters are also available; one is a program called SmartCap from Intel, which can convert between AVI and QuickTime files that use the Indeo compression method. To use AVI files, you'll need the Video for Windows package, available from Microsoft. To use QuickTime movies, you'll need the QuickTime for Windows package, available from Apple. You'll need both to convert from one format to the other.

To convert video files between formats on the Macintosh, you can use the freeware program Sparkle. Sparkle can read and play both MPEG and QuickTime files, and convert between them. In addition, the program AVI->Quick can convert AVI (Video for Windows) files to QuickTime format.

If you're using QuickTime for your movie files and you want that movie to be read on a platform other than the Macintosh, you will need to "flatten" that movie. On the Macintosh, files contain resource and data forks for different bits of the file. Flattening a QuickTime file involves moving all the data in the QuickTime file into the data fork so that other platforms can read it.

A small freeware program called FastPlayer will flatten QuickTime movies on the Mac; on Windows, try a program called Qflat. FTP locations and other information for these programs are in Appendix A.

Video for the Web

Using a basic desktop computer and simple video equipment you might have lying about, you're never going to get really high-quality video at a large frame rate and size. Even professional desktop video researchers are having trouble achieving that goal, and they're spending several thousands of dollars to get there.

What you can get with everyday household items, however, is a short video sample (less than a minute) in a small window with a high enough frame rate to avoid serious jerkiness. But, even then, the file sizes you'll end up with are pretty large. As I've emphasized time and time again, this is not a good thing over the Web where larger file sizes take longer to transmit over a network connection.

So plan to make some compromises now. The physical size of desktop video files depends on several factors:

☐ Frame size: The smaller the area of the video, the less space you take up on the disk. Shoot for 240×180, 160×120, or even smaller.

☐ Frame rate: The fewer frames per second, the less disk space the file takes; but the lower the frame rate, the jerkier the action. Frame rate tends to be one of the more important factors for good video, so when you have a choice, try to save space in areas other than the frame rate. 15fps is considered an excellent rate for digital video, but you can get down to 10fps before things start looking really bad.

☐ Color depth: Just as with images, the fewer colors in the movie, the smaller the file size.

☐ Audio soundtrack: All the hints that I mentioned in the previous section apply here. Or, avoid having a soundtrack altogether if you can.

☐ Compression algorithm: Some codecs are better than others for different kinds of video. Codecs that use frame differencing, for example, are better for movies in which the background doesn't change overly much. Most software programs let you play with different codecs and different key frames, so try several experiments to see what kind of file sizes you can get.

Of course, file size isn't the only consideration. Picture quality and speed of playback are both crucial factors that can affect some or all of these compromises. You might be willing to give up picture quality for smooth playback, or give up color for having audio as well as video.

In terms of actually producing the video, there are several hints for improving picture and sound quality and keeping the file sizes small so they can be more easily transferred over the Web:

☐ Record direct from a camera to the capture card instead of recording from tape. If you must use tape, use the best quality tape you can find.

10

☐ If you can get S-video equipment, use it.

☐ Record the audio track separately, using the hints in the audio section of this chapter, and then add it later using a video processing program.

☐ As with audio, capture the video at the highest possible quality, and then use software to shrink the frame size, frame rate, number of colors, and so on. The result will be better than if you sampled at the lower rate. Note that you might need a very large hard drive to store the file while you're processing it; multiple-gigabyte drives are not uncommon in the video-processing world.

☐ Do your compression last. Capture with JPEG compression if you can, at the highest quality possible. You can then compress the raw file later. Again, you'll need lots and lots of disk space for this.

For More Information

Alison Zhang's Multimedia File Formats on the Internet is an excellent resource for file formats and tools for playing both audio and video. Check it out at `http://ac.dal.ca/~dong/contents.htm`.

For information about audio formats, there are audio formats FAQs at the usual FAQ sites, including `ftp://rtfm.mit.edu/pub/usenet/news.answers/` and `ftp://ftp.uu.net/usenet/news.answers/`.

Finally, for a more technical introduction to digital audio and video and aspects of both, the *Desktop Multimedia Bible* by Jeff Burger, Addison Wesley, is exhaustive and covers all aspects of analog and digital audio and video, as well as audio and video production.

If you're interested in learning more about digital video and video production in general, I highly recommend a book called *How to Digitize Video*, by Nels Johnson with Fred Gault and Mark Florence, from John Wiley & Sons. This book is an extensive reference to all aspects of digital video, contains lots of information about hardware and software solutions, and includes a CD-ROM with Mac and Windows software you can use.

If you're interested in MPEG (which isn't covered very much in the previously mentioned book), your best source for information is probably the MPEG FAQ, which you can get anywhere that archives Usenet FAQs. One source is `http://www.cis.ohio-state.edu/hypertext/faq/usenet/mpeg-faq/top.html`.

For more information on QuickTime, definitely check out `http://quicktime.apple.com/`. This site has plenty of information on QuickTime itself as well as sample movies and the terribly excellent QuickTime FAQ, and you can even order the QuickTime software online from here.

10

Summary

Even though most audio and video files are stored offline in external files on the Web, sound and video can provide an extra bit of "oomph" to your Web presentation, particularly if you have something interesting to be played or viewed. And with many simple low-cost audio and video sampling tools available on the market today, creating sound and video is something you can accomplish even if you don't have an enormous amount of money or a background in audio and video production.

Here's a recap of topics covered in this chapter.

For digital audio files, there is no firm cross-platform standard. Files that are au can be played on the most platforms, but the sound quality is not very good. AIFF and WAVE are about equal in terms of sound quality, but neither is well supported outside its native platform (Mac and Windows, respectively). MPEG Audio has become more popular because of the Internet Underground Music Archive, but encoding MPEG audio is expensive. Finally, RealAudio can be used to play audio on the fly as it's being downloaded but requires extra software on both the server and browser side in order to work.

For digital video, QuickTime and MPEG are the most popular formats, with QuickTime drawing a greater lead because of its wide cross-platform support and software-based players. For QuickTime files, either the CinePak or Indeo Video codecs are preferred, although CinePak is slightly more supported, particularly on UNIX players.

For both audio and video, always choose the best recording equipment you can afford and record or sample at the best rate you can. Then use editing software to reduce the picture quality and size to a point at which the file sizes are acceptable for publishing on an environment such as the Web. Always keep in mind that because sound and video files tend to be large, you should always provide a good description of the file you are linking to, including the format it is in and the file size.

Q&A

Q I want to create one of those pages that has a spy camera that takes pictures of me, or the fish tank, or the toilet, or wherever, every couple of minutes. How can I do that?

A It depends, of course, on the system that you're working on and the capabilities of that system. When you have a camera attached to your computer that can take video stills, you'll need some way to take those pictures once every few minutes. On UNIX systems you can use cron; on Macs and PCs you'll have to look into macro recorders and programs that can capture your mouse and keyboard movements (or your video software might have a timer option, although I haven't seen any that do at the moment).

Then, when you have the image file, converting it to GIF or JPEG format and moving it automatically to your Web server might not be so easy. If your Web server is on the same machine as the camera, this isn't a problem. But if you're FTPing your regular files to your Web server, you'll have to come up with some system of automatically transferring those files to the right location.

Designing Effective
Web Pages

Chapter 11

Writing and Designing Web Pages: Dos and Don'ts

You won't learn about any HTML tags in this chapter, or how to convert files from one strange file format to another. You're mostly done with the HTML part of Web page design; next come the intangibles, the things that separate your pages from those of someone who just knows the tags and can fling text and graphics around and call it a presentation.

Armed with the information from the last five days, you could put this book down now and go off and merrily create Web pages to your heart's content. However, armed with both that information and what you'll learn today, you can create better Web pages. Do you need any more incentive to continue reading?

This chapter includes hints for creating well-written and well-designed Web pages, and highlights dos and don'ts concerning

☐ How to sort out the tangle of whether to use HTML 2.0 or HTML extensions or both

☐ How to write your Web pages so that they can be easily scanned and read

☐ Issues concerning design and layout of your Web pages

☐ When and why you should create links

☐ Using images effectively

☐ Other miscellaneous tidbits and hints

Using the HTML Extensions

In the past, before every browser company was introducing their own new HTML tags, being a Web designer was easy. The only HTML tags you had to deal with were those from HTML 2.0, and the vast majority of the browsers on the Web would be able to read your pages without a problem. Now being a Web designer is significantly more complicated. Now, you've got several groups of tags to work with:

☐ The HTML 2.0 tags

☐ HTML 3.2 tags such as tables, divisions, backgrounds, and color, which are supported by a few but not all browsers

☐ Browser-specific tags (from Netscape or Internet Explorer) which may or may not end up as part of the official HTML specification, and whose support varies from browser to browser

☐ Other proposed HTML 3.2 tags which few to no browsers support

If you're finding all of this rather mind-boggling, you're not alone. Authors and developers just like you are all trying to sort out the mess and make decisions based on how they want their pages to look. The HTML extensions do give you more flexibility with layout, but they limit the audience that can view those pages the way you want them to be viewed.

Choosing a strategy for using HTML extensions is one of the more significant design decisions you'll make as you start creating Web pages. It might be easier for you to look at the choices you have as a sort of continuum between the conservative and the experimental Web author (see Figure 11.1).

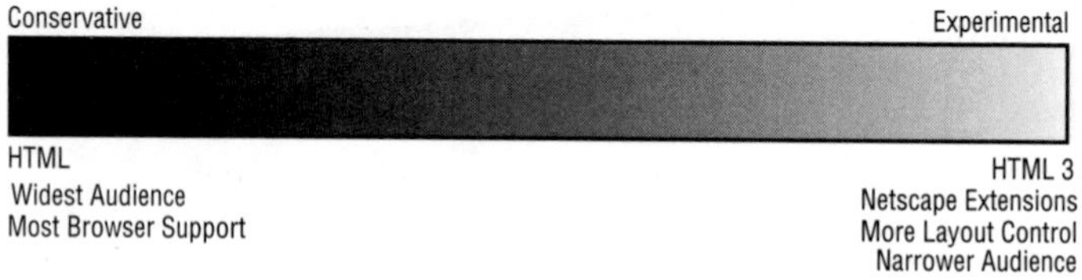

Figure 11.1.

The Web author continuum.

Conservative   Experimental

HTML
Widest Audience
Most Browser Support

HTML 3
Netscape Extensions
More Layout Control
Narrower Audience

11

NOTE

Don't think of these endpoints as value judgments; conservative isn't worse than experimental, or vice versa. There are advantages at both ends and significant advantages in the middle.

The conservative Web developer wants the widest possible audience for her Web pages. The conservative Web developer sticks to HTML 2.0 tags as defined by the standard. This is not to say that the conservative Web developer is boring. You can create magnificent Web content with the HTML 2.0 tags, and that content has the advantage over more experimental content in that it is supported without a hitch by the greatest number of browsers and, therefore, will reach the widest possible audience.

The experimental Web developer, on the other hand, wants the sort of control over layout that the more advanced tags gives him or her and is willing to shut out a portion of their audience to get it. The experimental Web developer's pages are designed for a single browser, tested only in a single browser, and might even have a big announcement on the pages that says, "These Pages Must Be Read Using Browser X." Using other browsers to read those pages may make the design unreadable or at least confusing—or it may be just fine.

Which kind of Web developer are you? Depending on the goals of your pages and the audience you're writing for, you may not need to think about this decision. If your readers are going to be seeing your pages only on an internal network using only Netscape 2.0, then that makes things easy for you; you can use all of the tags that Netscape 2.0 supports. If you're designing for an audience that may use different kinds of browsers, however (as you do for the global Internet), you'll have to come up with a strategy for which kinds of tags you'll be using.

For the latter situation, the best position in terms of choosing between interesting design and a wide audience is probably a balance between the two kinds of Web developers. With some knowledge beforehand of the effects that HTML extensions will have on your pages, both in browsers that support them and those that don't, you can make slight modifications to your design that will enable you to take advantage of both sides. Your pages are still readable and useful in older browsers over a wider range of platforms, but they can also take advantage of the advanced features in the newer browsers.

Throughout this book so far, I've explained which tags are part of HTML 2.0, which are extensions, and which tags are available in which major browsers. I've also noted for each tag the alternatives you can use in cases where a browser may not be able to view those tags. With this information in hand, you should be able to experiment with each tag in different browsers to see what the effect of each one is on your design.

The most important strategy I can suggest for using extensions while still trying to retain compatibility with other browsers is to test your files in those other browsers. Most browsers are free or shareware and available for downloading, so all you need to do is find them and

11

install them. If you have access to a UNIX account, it's likely that the Lynx software is installed so you can use it as well. By testing your pages you can get an idea of how different browsers interpret different tags, and eventually you'll get a feel for which extensions provide the most flexibility, which ones need special coding for alternatives in older browsers, and which tags can be used freely without complicating matters for other browsers.

Writing for Online

Writing on the Web is no different from writing in the real world. Even though the writing you do on the Web is not sealed in hardcopy, it is still "published" and is still a reflection of you and your work. In fact, because it is online, and therefore more transient to your reader, you'll have to follow the rules of good writing that much more closely because your readers will be less forgiving.

Because of the vast quantities of information available on the Web, your readers are not going to have much patience if your Web page is full of spelling errors or poorly organized. They are much more likely to give up after the first couple of sentences and move on to someone else's page. After all, there are several million pages out there. There isn't time to waste on bad pages.

This doesn't mean that you have to go out and become a professional writer to create a good Web page. But here are a few hints for making your Web page easier to read and understand.

Write Clearly and Be Brief

Unless you are writing the Great American Web Novel, your readers are not going to visit your page to linger lovingly over your words. One of the best ways you can make the writing in your Web pages effective is to write as clearly and concisely as you possibly can, present your points, and then stop. Obscuring what you want to say with extra words just makes it more difficult to figure out your point.

If you don't have a copy of Strunk and White's *The Elements of Style*, put this book down right now and go buy it and read it. And then reread it, memorize it, inhale it, sleep with it under your pillow, show it to all your friends, quote it at parties, and make it your life. There is no better guide to the art of good, clear writing than that book.

Organize Your Pages for Quick Scanning

Even if you write the clearest, briefest, most scintillating prose ever seen on the Web, chances are good your readers will not start at the top of your Web page and carefully read every word down to the bottom.

11

Scanning, in this context, is the first quick look your readers give to each page to get the general gist of the content. Depending on what your users want out of your pages, they may scan the parts that jump out at them (headings, links, other emphasized words), perhaps read a few contextual paragraphs, and then move on. By writing and organizing your pages for easy "scannability," you can help your readers get the information they need as fast as possible.

To improve the scannability of your Web pages:

- ☐ Use headings to summarize topics. Note how this book has headings and subheadings. You can flip through quickly and find the portions that interest you. The same thing applies to Web pages.

- ☐ Use lists. Lists are wonderful for summarizing related items. Every time you find yourself saying something like, "each widget has four elements," or "use the following steps to do this," the content after that phrase should be an ordered or unordered list.

- ☐ Don't forget link menus. As a form of list, link menus have all the advantages of lists for scannability, and they double as excellent navigation tools.

- ☐ Don't bury important information in text. If you have a point to make, make it close to the top of the page or at the beginning of a paragraph. Long paragraphs are harder to read and make it more difficult to glean information. The further into the paragraph you put your point, the less likely anybody will read it.

Figure 11.2 shows the sort of writing technique that you should avoid.

Figure 11.2.

A Web page that is difficult to scan.

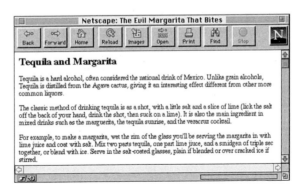

Because all the information on this page is in paragraph form, your readers have to read all three paragraphs in order to find out what they want and where they want to go next.

How would you improve this example? Try rewriting this section so that the main points can be better picked out from the text. Consider that

- ☐ There are actually two discrete topics in those three paragraphs.
- ☐ The four ingredients of the drink would make an excellent list.

Figure 11.3 shows what an improvement might look like.

Figure 11.3.

An improvement to the difficult Web page.

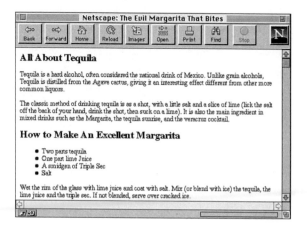

Make Each Page Stand on Its Own

Keep in mind as you write that your reader could jump into any of your Web pages from anywhere. For example, you may structure a page so section four distinctly follows section three and has no other links to it. Then, someone you don't even know might create a link to the page starting section four. From then on, a reader could very well find himself or herself on section four without even being aware that section three exists.

Be careful to write each page so that it stands on its own. These guidelines will help:

☐ Use descriptive titles. The title should provide not only the direct subject of this page, but its relationship to the rest of the pages in the presentation.

☐ If a page depends on the one before it, provide a navigational link back to the page before it (and preferably also one up to the top level).

☐ Avoid initial sentences like: "You can get around these problems by…," "After you're done with that, do…," and "The advantages to this method are…." The information referred to by "these," "that," and "this" are off on some other page. If those sentences are the first thing your readers see, they are going to be confused.

Be Careful with Emphasis

Use emphasis sparingly in your text. Paragraphs with a whole lot of boldface and italics or words in ALL CAPS are hard to read, both if you use any of them several times in a paragraph and if you emphasize long strings of text. The best emphasis is used only with small words (such as: AND, THIS, OR, BUT).

Link text is also a form of emphasis. Use single words or short phrases as link text. Do not use entire passages or paragraphs as links.

Figure 11.4 illustrates a particularly bad example of too much emphasis obscuring the rest of the text.

Figure 11.4.

Too much emphasis.

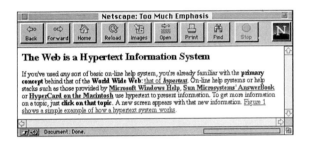

By removing some of the boldface and using less text for your links, you can considerably reduce the amount of distraction in the paragraph (Figure 11.5).

Figure 11.5.

Less emphasis.

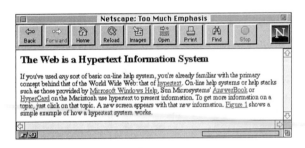

Be especially careful of emphasis that moves or changes such as marquees, blinking text, or animation on your pages. Unless the animation is the primary focus of the page, use movement and sound extremely sparingly to prevent distractions from the rest of your page.

Don't Use Browser-Specific Terminology

Avoid references in your text to specific features of specific browsers. For example, don't use wording like:

- ☐ "Click Here." What if your reader is using a browser without a mouse? A more generic phrase is "select this link." (Of course, you should avoid the "here" syndrome in the first place, which neatly gets around this problem as well.)

- ☐ "To save this page, pull down the File menu and select Save." Each browser has a different set of menus and different ways of accomplishing the same action. If at all possible, do not refer to specifics of browser operation in your Web pages.

- ☐ "Use the Back button to return to the previous page." As in the previous note, each browser has a different set of buttons and different methods for going "back." If you want your readers to have the ability to go back to a previous page, or to any specific page, link them.

Spell Check and Proofread Your Pages

Spell checking and proofreading may seem like obvious suggestions, but given the number of pages I have seen on the Web that have obviously not had either, it bears mentioning.

Designing a set of Web pages and making them available on the Web is like publishing a book, producing a magazine, or releasing a product. It is, of course, considerably easier to publish Web pages than books, magazines, or other products, but just because it is easy does not mean it can be sloppy.

Thousands of people may be reading and exploring the content you provide. Spelling errors and bad grammar reflect badly on your work, on you, and on the content you are describing. Poor writing may be irritating enough that your reader won't bother to delve any deeper than your home page, even if the subject you're writing about is fascinating.

Proofread and spell check each of your Web pages. If possible, have someone else read them— other people can often pick up errors that you, the writer, can't see. Even a simple edit can greatly improve many pages and make them easier to read and navigate.

Design and Page Layout

Although the design capabilities of HTML and the Web are quite limited, there's still a lot you can work with, and still quite a few opportunities for people without a sense of design to create something that looks simply awful.

Probably the best rule to follow at all times as far as designing each Web page is this: Keep the design as simple as possible. Reduce the number of elements (images, headings, rule lines), and make sure that the eye is drawn to the most important parts of the page first.

Keep that cardinal rule in mind as you read the next sections, which offer some other suggestions for basic design and layout of Web pages.

Use Headings as Headings

Headings are often rendered in graphical browsers in a larger or bolder font. Because of this, it's often tempting to use a heading tag to provide some sort of warning, note, or emphasis in regular text, as shown in Figure 11.6.

Headings work best when they're used as headings, because they stand out from the text and signal the start of a new topic. If you really want to emphasize a particular section of text, consider using a small image, a rule line, or some other way of emphasis instead. Figure 11.7 shows an example of the same text as in Figure 11.6 with a different kind of visual emphasis.

Figure 11.6.

*The wrong way
to use headings.*

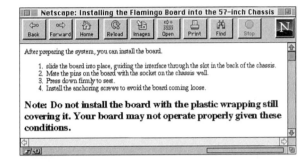

Figure 11.7.

*An alternative to
the wrong way to
use headings.*

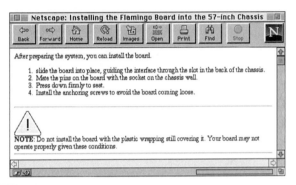

Group Related Information Visually

Grouping related information within a page is a task for both writing and design. By grouping related information under headings, as I suggested in the "Writing for Online" section earlier in this chapter, you improve the scannability of that information. Visually separating each section from the others helps to make each section distinct and emphasizes the relatedness of the information.

If a Web page contains several sections of information, find a way to visually separate those sections; for example, with a heading or with a rule line <HR> (see Figure 11.8).

Use a Consistent Layout

When you're reading a book or a magazine, each page, each section, usually has the same layout. The page numbers are where you expect them, and the first word on each page starts in the same place.

The same sort of consistent layout works equally well in Web pages. A single "look and feel" for each page in your Web presentation is comforting to your readers. After two or three pages, they will know what the elements of each page are and where to find them. With a consistent design, your readers can find the information they need and navigate through your pages without having to stop at every page and try to find where things are.

Figure 11.8.

*Separate sections
visually.*

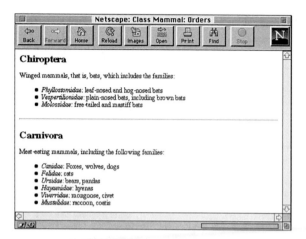

Consistent layout can include

- [ ] Consistent page elements. If you use second-level headings (<H2>) on one page to indicate major topics, use second-level headings for major topics on all your pages. If you have a heading and a rule line at the top of your page, use that same layout on all your pages.

- [ ] Consistent forms of navigation. Put your navigation menus in the same place on every page (usually the top or the bottom of the page), and use the same number of them. If you're going to use navigation icons, make sure you use the same icons in the same order for every page.

Using Links

Without links, Web pages would be really dull, and finding anything interesting on the Web would be close to impossible. The quality of your links, in many ways, can be as important as the writing and design of your actual pages. Here's some friendly advice on creating and using links.

Use Link Menus with Descriptive Text

As I've noted in this chapter and frequently in this book, link menus are a great way of organizing your content and the links on a page. By organizing your links into lists or other menu-like structures, your reader can scan their options for the page quickly and easily.

However, just organizing your links into menus often isn't enough. Make sure when you arrange your links into menus that you aren't too short in your descriptions. It's tempting to use menus of filenames or other marginally descriptive links in menus, like the menu shown in Figure 11.9.

11

Figure 11.9.

A poor link menu.

Well, that is a menu of links, and the links are descriptive of the actual page they point to, but they don't really describe the content of that page. How do readers know what's on the other side of that link, and how can they make a decision about whether they're interested in it or not from the limited information you've given them? Of these three links, only the last (`pesto.recipe.txt`) gives you a hint about what you will see when you jump to that file.

A better plan is either to provide some extra text describing the content of the file (Figure 11.10), or to avoid the filenames altogether (who cares?). Just describe the contents of the files in the menu, with the appropriate text highlighted (Figure 11.11).

Figure 11.10.

A better link menu.

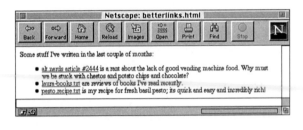

Figure 11.11.

Another better link menu.

Either one of these forms is better than the first; both give your reader more of a clue of what's on the other side of the link.

Using Links in Text

The best way to provide links in text is to first write the text without the links as if the text weren't going to have links at all, for example, if you were writing it for hardcopy. Then, highlight the appropriate words that will serve as the link text for links to other pages. Make sure you don't interrupt the flow of the page when you include a link. The idea of links in text is that the text should stand on its own. That way, links provide additional or tangential information that your readers can choose to ignore or follow based on their own whims.

Here's another example of using links in text (shown in Figure 11.12), but one in which the text itself isn't overly relevant—it's just there to support the links. If you're using text just to describe links, consider using a link menu instead of a paragraph. It'll be easier for your readers to find the information they want. Instead of having to read the entire paragraph, they can skim for the links that interest them.

Figure 11.12.

Links in text that don't work well.

Probably the easiest way to figure out if you're doing links within text properly is to print out the formatted Web page from your browser. In hardcopy, without hypertext, would the paragraph still make sense? If the page reads funny on paper, it'll read funny online as well. Some simple rephrasing of sentences can often help enormously in making the text on your pages more readable and more usable both online and when printed.

Avoid "Here" Syndrome

A common mistake that many Web authors make in creating links in body text is "here" syndrome. *Here syndrome* is the tendency to create links with a single highlighted word (here), and to describe the link somewhere else in the text. Here are a couple of examples (with underlining indicating link text):

```
Information about ostrich socialization is contained here.

Select this link for a tutorial on the internal combustion engine.
```

Because links are highlighted on the Web page, those links visually "pop out" more than the surrounding text (or "draw the eye" in graphic design lingo). Your reader will see the link first, before reading the text. Try it. Here's a picture of a particularly heinous example of "here" syndrome, in Figure 11.13. Close your eyes, and then open them quickly, pick a "here" at random, and see how long it takes you to find out what the "here" is for.

Now try the same thing with a well-organized link menu of the same information, shown in Figure 11.14.

Figure 11.13.

"Here" syndrome.

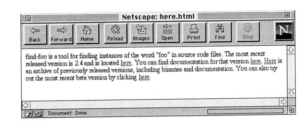

Figure 11.14.

The same page, reorganized.

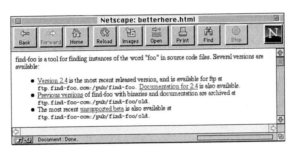

Since "here" says nothing about what the link is there for, your poor reader has to search the text before and after the link itself to find out just what is supposed to be "here." In paragraphs that have lots of "here" or other nondescriptive links, it becomes difficult to match up the links with what they are supposed to link to, forcing your reader to work harder to figure things out.

So instead of a link like this:

```
Information about ostrich socialization is contained here.
```

A much better choice of wording would be something like this:

```
The Palo Alto Zoo has lots of information about ostrich socialization.
```

or just

```
The Palo Alto Zoo has lots of information about ostrich socialization.
```

To Link or Not To Link

Just as with graphics, every time you create a link, consider why you are linking two pages or sections. Is the link useful? Will it give your readers more information or take them closer to their goal? Is the link relevant in some way to the current content?

Each link should serve a purpose. Link for relevant reasons. Just because you mention the word "coffee" deep in a page about some other topic, you don't have to link that word to the coffee home page. It may seem cute, but if a link has no relevance to the current content, it just confuses your reader.

This section describes some of the categories of links that are useful in Web pages. If your links do not fall into one of these categories, consider why you are including them in your page.

NOTE   Thanks to Nathan Torkington for his "Taxonomy of Tags," published on the www-talk mailing list, which inspired this section.

Explicit navigation links are links that indicate the specific paths one can take through your Web pages: forward, back, up, home. These links are often indicated by navigation icons (Figure 11.15).

Figure 11.15.

Explicit navigation links.

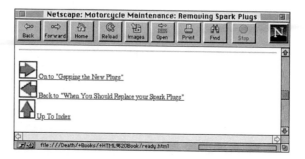

Implicit navigation links (Figure 11.16) are different from explicit navigation links in that the link text implies, but does not directly indicate, navigation between pages. Link menus are the best example of this; it is apparent from the highlighting of the link text that you will get more information on this topic by selecting the link, but the text itself does not necessarily say that. Note that the major difference between explicit and implicit navigation links is this: if you print a page containing both, you should no longer be able to pick out the implicit links.

Figure 11.16.

Implicit navigation links.

Implicit navigation links can also include table-of-contents-like structures or other overviews made up entirely of links.

Word or concept definitions make excellent links, particularly if you are creating large networks of pages that include glossaries. By linking the first instance of a word to its definition, you can explain the meaning of that word to readers who don't know what it means while not distracting those who do (Figure 11.17).

Figure 11.17.
Definition links.

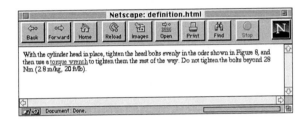

Finally, links to tangents and related information are valuable when the text content would distract from the main purpose of the page. Think of tangent links as footnotes or end notes in printed text (Figure 11.18). They can refer to citations to other works, or to additional information that is interesting but not necessarily directly relevant to the point you're trying to make.

Figure 11.18.
Footnote links.

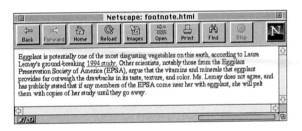

Be careful that you don't get carried away with definitions and tangent links. It's possible to create so many tangents that your readers spend so much time linking elsewhere that they can't follow the point of your original text. Resist the urge to link every time you possibly can, and link only to relevant tangents on your own text. And avoid duplicating the same tangent—for example, linking every instance of the letters "WWW" on your page to the WWW Consortium's home page. If you are linking twice or more to the same location on one page, consider removing most of the extra links. Your readers can make the effort to select one of the other links if they are interested in the information.

Using Images

On Day 4, "Images and Backgrounds," you learned all about creating and using images in Web pages. This section summarizes many of the hints you learned for using images.

Don't Overuse Images

Be careful about including lots of images on your Web page. Besides the fact that each image adds to the amount of time it takes to load the page, including too many images on the same page can make your page look busy and cluttered and distract from the point you are trying to get across (Figure 11.19).

Figure 11.19.

Too many images.

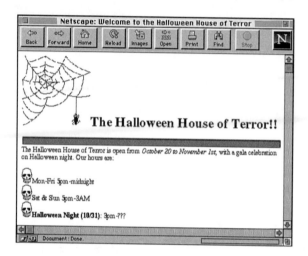

Remember the hints I gave you in Chapter 7, "Using Images, Color, and Backgrounds." Consider why you need to use each image before you put it on the page. If it doesn't directly contribute to the content, consider leaving it off.

Use Alternatives to Images

And of course, as soon as I mention images, I have to also mention that not all browsers can view those images. To make your pages accessible to the widest possible audience, you're going to have to take the text-only browsers into account when you design your Web pages. Here are two possible solutions that can help:

- ☐ Use the ALT attribute of the <IMG> tag to automatically substitute appropriate text strings for the graphics in text-only browsers. Use either a descriptive label to substitute for the default [image] that appears in the place of each inline image, or use an empty string ("") to ignore the image altogether.

- ☐ If providing a single-source page for both graphical and text-only browsers becomes too much work, and the result is not turning out to be acceptable, consider creating separate pages for each one: a page designed for the full-color full-graphical browsers, and a page designed for the text-only browsers. Then provide the option of choosing one or the other from your home page.

Keep Images Small

Keep in mind if you use images that each image is a separate network connection and takes time to load over a network, meaning that each image adds to the total time it takes to view a page. Try to reduce the number of images on a page, and keep your images small both in file size and in actual dimensions. In particular, keep the following hints in mind:

☐ A good rule of thumb for large images is that at a 14.4Kbps modem connection, your page will load at an average of 1K per second. The entire page (text and images) should not take more than 30 seconds to load, or you risk annoying your readers and having them move on without reading your page. This limits you to 30K total for everything on your page. Strive to achieve that size by keeping your images small.

☐ For larger images, consider using thumbnails on your main page and then linking to the larger image, rather than putting the larger image inline.

☐ Interlace your larger GIF files.

☐ Try the tests to see whether JPEG or GIF creates a smaller file for the type of image you are using.

☐ In GIF files, the fewer colors you use in the image, the smaller the image will be; you should try to use as few colors as possible to avoid problems with system-specific color allocation.

☐ You can reduce the physical size of your images by cropping them (using a smaller portion of the overall image), or by scaling (shrinking) the original image. Note that when you scale the image, you might lose some of the detail from the original image.

☐ You can use the Netscape WIDTH and HEIGHT attributes to scale the image presented in Netscape to a larger size than the image actually is. Note that, of course, this works only in Netscape, and the scaled result might not be what you expect. Test it before trying it.

Watch Out for Display Assumptions

Many people create problems for their readers by making a couple of careless assumptions about other people's hardware. When developing Web pages, be kind and remember these two guidelines:

☐ Don't assume that everyone has screen or browser dimensions the same as yours.

Just because that huge GIF you created is wide enough to fit on your screen in your browser doesn't mean it'll fit someone else's. And coming across an image that is too wide is annoying because it requires the reader to resize their window all the time or scroll sideways.

To fit in the width of a majority of browsers' windows, try to keep the width of your images to less than 450 pixels (most browsers on the Macintosh have a screen width of about 465).

☐ Don't assume that everyone has full-color displays.

Test your images in resolutions other than full color (you can often do this in your image-editing program). Many of your readers may have display systems that have only 16 colors, grayscale, or even just black and white. You may be surprised at the results: colors drop out or dither strangely in grayscale or black and white, and the effect may not be what you had intended.

Make sure your images are visible at all resolutions, or provide alternatives for high- and low-resolution images on the page itself.

Be Careful with Backgrounds and Link Colors

Using HTML extensions, you can use background colors and patterns and change the color of the text on your pages. Using this feature can be very tempting, but be very careful if you decide to do so. The ability to change the page and font colors and to provide fancy backdrops can give you the ability to quickly and easily make your pages entirely unreadable. Here are some hints for avoiding this:

☐ Make sure you have enough contrast between the background and foreground (text) colors. Low contrast can be hard to read. Also, light-colored text on a dark background is harder to read than dark text on a light background.

☐ Avoid changing link colors at all. Because your readers have semantic meanings attached to the default colors (blue means unfollowed, purple or red means followed), changing the colors can be very confusing.

☐ Sometimes increasing the font size of all the text in your page using <BASEFONT> can make it more readable on a background. Both the background and the bigger text will be missing in other browsers that don't support the Netscape tags.

☐ If you're using background patterns, make sure the pattern does not interfere with the text. Some patterns may look interesting on their own but can make it difficult to read the text you put on top of them. Also, some backgrounds that look fine in lots of colors may interfere with the text when the page is viewed in a 16-color display system or in black and white. Keep in mind that backgrounds are supposed to be in the background. Subtle patterns are always better than wild patterns. Remember, your readers are still visiting your pages for the content on them, not to marvel at your ability to create faux marble in your favorite image editor.

When in doubt, try asking a friend to look at your pages. Because you are familiar with the content and the text, you may not realize how hard your pages are to read. Someone who hasn't read them before will not have your biases and will be able to tell you that your colors are too close or that the pattern is interfering with the text. Of course, you'll have to find a friend who will be honest with you.

Other Good Habits and Hints

In this section, I've gathered several other miscellaneous hints and advice about good habits to get into when working with groups of Web pages. These include notes on how big to make each page in your presentation and how to sign your pages.

Link Back to Home

Consider including a link back to the top level or home page on every page of your presentation. Providing this link allows readers a quick escape from the depths of your content. Using a home link is much easier than trying to navigate backwards through a hierarchy, or trying to use the "back" facility of a browser.

Don't Split Topics Across Pages

Each Web page works best if it covers a single topic in its entirety. Don't split topics across pages; even if you link between them, the transition can be confusing. It will be even more confusing if someone jumps in on the second or third page and wonders what is going on.

If you think that one topic is becoming too large for a single page, consider reorganizing the content so you can break that topic up into subtopics. This works especially well in hierarchical organizations. It allows you to determine exactly to what level of detail each "level" of the hierarchy should go, and exactly how big and complete each page should be.

Don't Create Too Many or Too Few Pages

There are no rules for how many pages you must have in your Web presentation, nor for how large each page should be. You can have one page or several thousand, depending on the amount of content you have and how you have organized it.

With this in mind, you may decide to go to one extreme or to another, each of which has advantages and disadvantages. For example, say you put all your content in one big page, and create links to sections within that page (as illustrated in Figure 11.20).

Advantages:

- [ ] One file is easier to maintain, and links within that file won't ever break if you move things around or rename files.

- [ ] Mirrors real-world document structure. If you are distributing documents both in hard copy and online, having a single document for both makes producing both easier.

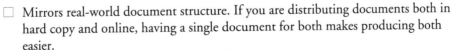

Figure 11.20.
One big page.

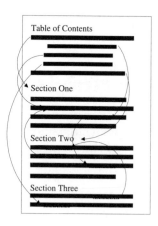

Disadvantages:

☐ A large file takes a very long time to download, particularly over slow network connections and especially if the page includes lots of graphics.

☐ Readers must scroll a lot to find what they want. Accessing particular bits of information can become tedious. Navigating at points other than at the top or bottom becomes close to impossible.

☐ The structure is overly rigid. A single page is inherently linear. Although you can skip around within sections in the page, the structure still mirrors that of the printed page and doesn't take advantage of the flexibility of smaller pages linked in a nonlinear fashion.

Or, on the other extreme, you could create a whole bunch of little pages with links between them (illustrated in Figure 11.21).

Figure 11.21.
Lots of little pages.

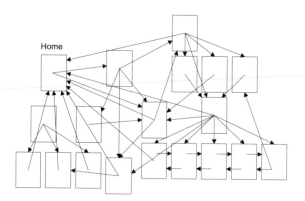

11

Advantages:

- [ ] Smaller pages load very quickly.
- [ ] You can often fit the entire page on one screen, and so the information in that page can be scanned very easily.

Disadvantages:

- [ ] Maintaining all those links will be a nightmare. Just adding some sort of navigational structure to that many pages may create thousands of links.
- [ ] If you have too many jumps between pages, the jumps may seem jarring. Continuity is difficult when your reader spends more time jumping than actually reading.

So what is the solution? Often the content you're describing will determine the size and number of pages you need, especially if you follow the one-topic-per-page suggestion. Testing your Web pages on a variety of platforms and network speeds will let you know if a single page is too large. If you spend a lot of time scrolling around in it or if it takes more time to load than you expected, it may be too large.

Sign Your Pages

Each page should contain some sort of information at the bottom of the page that acts as the "signature." I mention this briefly in Chapter 5, "More Text Formatting with HTML 3.2," as part of the description of the <ADDRESS> tag; that particular tag was intended for just this purpose.

Here is a list of some useful information to consider putting in the ADDRESS tag on each page:

- [ ] Contact information for the person who created this Web page or the person responsible for it, colloquially known as the "Webmaster." This should include at least his or her name and preferably an e-mail address.
- [ ] The status of the page. Is it complete? Is it a work-in-progress? Is it intentionally left blank?
- [ ] When this page was last revised. This is particularly important for pages that change a lot. Include a date on each page so that people know how old it is.
- [ ] Copyright or trademark information, if it applies.
- [ ] The URL of this page. Including a printed URL of a page that is found at that same URL may seem a bit like overkill, but what happens if someone prints out the page and loses any other reference to it in the stack of papers on their desk? Where did it come from? (I've done this many times and often wished for a URL to be typed on the document itself.)

Figure 11.22 shows a nice example of an address block.

Figure 11.22.
A sample address.

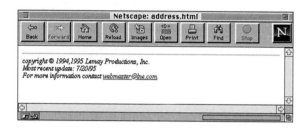

A nice touch to include on your Web page is to link a Mailto URL to the text containing the e-mail address of the Web master, like this:

```
<ADDRESS>
Laura Lemay <A HREF="mailto:lemay@lne.com">lemay@lne.com</A>
</ADDRESS>
```

This enables the readers of the page who have browsers that support the Mailto URL to simply select the link and send mail to the relevant person responsible for the page without having to retype the address into their mail programs.

> **NOTE**
> This will work only in browsers that support Mailto URLs. But even in browsers that don't accept it, the link text will appear as usual, so there's no harm in including the link regardless.

Finally, if you don't want to clutter each page with a lot of personal contact or boilerplate copyright information, a simple solution is to create a separate page for the extra information, and then link the signature to that page, like this:

```
<ADDRESS>
<A HREF="copyright.html">Copyright</A> and
<A HREF="webmaster.html">contact</A> information is available.
</ADDRESS>
```

Provide Non-Hypertext Versions of Hypertext Pages

Even though the Web provides a way to create pages in new and exciting ways, some readers still like to read many things offline, on the bus, or at the breakfast table. These kinds of readers have real problems with hypertext pages because once you start using hypertext to organize a document, it becomes difficult to be able to tell your browser to "print the whole thing"—the browser knows only the boundaries of individual pages.

If you are using the Web to publish anything that might be readable and usable outside the Web, consider also creating a single text or PostScript version. You can then make that available as an external document for downloading. That enables your readers both to browse the document online and, if they want to, print it out for reading offline. You can even link the location of the hardcopy document to the start of the hypertext version, like this:

```
A <A HREF="ftp://myhome.com/pub/mydir/myfile.ps">PostScript version</A> of
this document is available via ftp at myhome.com in the directory /pub/mydir/
myfile.ps.
```

And, of course, a handy cross-reference for the hardcopy version would be to provide the URL for the hypertext version:

```
This document is also available on hypertext form on
the World Wide Web at the URL:
http://myhome.com/pub/mydir/myfile/index.html.
```

Summary

The main dos and don'ts for Web page design from this chapter are as follows:

- ☐ Do understand the differences between HTML 2.0 and HTML extensions, and decide which design strategy to follow while using them.
- ☐ Do use HTML extensions with alternatives, if at all possible.
- ☐ Do test your pages in multiple browsers.
- ☐ Do write your pages clearly and concisely.
- ☐ Do organize the text of your page so that your readers can scan for important information.
- ☐ Don't write Web pages that are dependent on pages before or after them in the structure. Do write context-independent pages.
- ☐ Don't overuse emphasis (boldface, italic, all caps, link text, blink, marquees). Do use emphasis sparingly and only when absolutely necessary.
- ☐ Don't use terminology specific to any one browser (click here, use the back button, and so on).
- ☐ Do spell check and proofread your pages.
- ☐ Don't use heading tags to provide emphasis.
- ☐ Do group related information both semantically (through the organization of the content) and visually (through the use of headings or by separating sections with rule lines).
- ☐ Do use a consistent layout across all your pages.

11

☐ Do use link menus to organize your links for quick scanning.

☐ Do use descriptive links.

☐ Don't use "here" syndrome with your links.

☐ Do have good reasons for using links. Don't link to irrelevant material.

☐ Don't link repeatedly to the same site on the same page.

☐ Do keep your layout simple.

☐ Don't clutter the page with lots of pretty but unnecessary images.

☐ Do provide alternatives to images for text-only browsers.

☐ Do try and keep your images small so that they load faster over the network.

☐ Do be careful with backgrounds and colored text so that you do not make your pages flashy but unreadable.

☐ Do always provide a link back to your home page.

☐ Do match topics with pages.

☐ Don't split individual topics across pages.

☐ Do provide a signature block or link to contact information at the bottom of each page.

☐ Do provide single-page, non-hypertext versions of linear documents.

Q&A

Q I've seen statistics on the Web that say between 60 percent and 90 percent of people on the Web are using Netscape. Why should I continue designing my pages for other browsers and testing my pages in other browsers when most of the world is using Netscape anyhow?

A You can design explicitly to Netscape if you want to; your pages are your pages, and the decision is yours. But, given how easy it is to make small modifications that allow your pages to be viewed and read in other browsers without losing much of the design, why lock out 10 to 40 percent of your audience for the sake of a few tags? Remember, with estimates of the size of the Web growing all the time, 10 percent of your readers could very well be a million people or more.

Q I'm converting existing documents into Web pages. These documents are very text-heavy and are intended to be read from start to finish instead of being quickly scanned. I can't restructure or redesign the content to better follow the guidelines you've suggested in this chapter—that's not my job. What can I do?

A Some content is going to be like this, particularly when you're converting a document written for paper to online. Ideally, you would be able to rewrite and restructure for online presentation, but realistically you often won't be able to do anything with the content other than throw it online.

All is not lost, however. You can still improve the overall presentation of these documents by providing reasonable indexes to the content (summaries, tables of contents pages, subject indexes, and so on), and by including standard navigation links back out of the text-heavy pages. In other words, you can create an easily navigable framework around the documents themselves, which can go a long way towards improving content that is otherwise difficult to read online.

Q **I have a standard signature block that contains my name and e-mail address, revision information for the page, and a couple lines of copyright information that my company's lawyers insisted on. It's a little imposing, particularly on small pages, where the signature is bigger than the page itself!**

A If your company's lawyers agree, consider putting all your contact and copyright information on a separate page, and then linking it on every page instead of duplicating it every time. This way your pages won't be overwhelmed by the legal stuff, and if the signature changes, you won't have to change it on every single page.

Chapter **12**

Examples of Good and Bad Web Design

In this chapter, we'll walk through some simple examples of pages and presentations that you might find out on the Web. (Actually, you won't find these particular pages out on the Web; I developed these examples specifically for this chapter.) Each of these Web presentations is either typical of the kind of information being provided on the Web today or shows some unique method for solving problems you might run into while developing your own presentations. In particular, you'll explore the following Web presentations:

☐ A company profile for the Foozle Sweater Company

☐ An encyclopedia of motorcycles, with images, sounds, and other media clips

☐ The catalog for a small nursery, in which you can both browse and order cacti and succulents

☐ A Web-based book about making bread

In each example, I note some of the more interesting features of the page as well as some of the issues that you might want to consider as you develop your own pages and presentations.

Example One: A Company Profile

Foozle Industries, Inc. makes a wide variety of sweaters for all occasions. (They were responsible for the demon sweater mentioned in Chapter 3, "The Basics of HTML 3.2.") Customers visiting the Foozle Industries Web server would first be presented with the Foozle Industries Home Page (Figure 12.1).

Figure 12.1.

Foozle Industries home page.

From this simple and unpretentious home page, the customer has several choices of pages to visit on Foozle's Web site, arranged in a link menu. I won't describe all of them in this section, just a few that provide interesting features.

What's New at Foozle?

The first link to check out from the Foozle home page is the What's New page. The link to this page has been time stamped, noting the last time it changed. Selecting the What's New link takes you, appropriately, to the What's New page (Figure 12.2).

Organized in reverse chronological order (from the most recent event backwards), the What's New page contains information about interesting things going on at Foozle Industries, both inside and outside the company. This page is useful for announcing new products to customers on the Web, or just for providing information about the site, the company, and other Foozle information. What's New pages, in general, are useful for sites that are visited repeatedly and frequently, as they allow your readers to find the new information on your site quickly and easily without having to search for it.

Figure 12.2.

The Foozle What's New page.

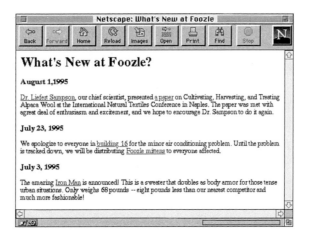

In this What's New page, the topmost item in the list of new things is a note about a paper presented by the Foozle chief scientist at a conference in Naples. That item has a link attached to it, implying that the paper itself is on the other side of that link, and, sure enough, it is (Figure 12.3).

Figure 12.3.

All about Foozle Alpaca wool.

12

Alpaca wool is fascinating, but where do you go from here? The links at the top of the page indicate that the reader has two navigation choices: back up to the Foozle home page, or go to an overview of technical papers.

We've visited the home page already, so let's go on to the technical papers.

Technical Papers

The Technical Papers section of the Foozle Web site (Figure 12.4) provides a list of the papers Foozle has published describing technical issues surrounding the making of sweaters. (Didn't know there were any, did you?)

Each link in the list takes you to the paper it describes. You can't see it in the figure, of course, but the link to the Alpaca wool paper is in a different color, indicating that it has already been visited.

From here, the reader can move down in the hierarchy and read any of the papers, or go back up the hierarchy to the overview page. From the overview page, the reader would then have the choice of exploring the other portions of the Web site: the company overview, the product descriptions, or the listing of open opportunities.

Figure 12.4.

The Technical Papers section.

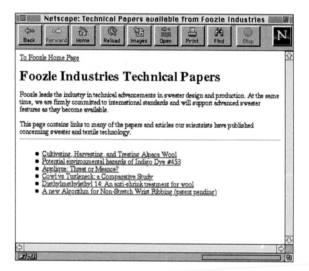

Features of This Web Site and Issues for Development

This Web presentation for a simple company profile is quite straightforward in terms of design; the structure is a simple hierarchy, with link menus for navigation to the appropriate pages. Extending it is a simple matter of adding additional "limbs" to the hierarchy by adding new links to the top-level page.

12

However, note the path we took through the few pages in this Web site. In a classic hierarchy the reader visits each "limb" in turn, exploring downward, and then creeping back up levels to visit new pages. However, remember the link between the What's New page and the paper on Alpaca wool? This link caused the reader to move sideways from one limb (the What's New page) to another (the Technical Papers section).

In this example, of course, given its simplicity, there is little confusion. But given a hierarchy much more complicated than this, with multiple levels and sub-trees, having links that cross hierarchical boundaries and allow the reader to break out of the structure can be confusing. After a few lateral links it is difficult to figure out where you are in the hierarchy. This is a common problem with most hypertext systems, and is often referred to as "getting lost in hyperspace."

Few really good solutions exist to the problem of getting lost. I prefer to avoid the problem by trying not to create lateral links across a hierarchy. If you stick with the rigid structure of the hierarchy and provide only navigational links, readers can usually figure out where they are, and if not, they usually have only two main choices: move back up in the hierarchy to a known point, or drill deeper into the hierarchy for more detailed information.

Example Two: A Multimedia Encyclopedia

The Multimedia Encyclopedia of Motorcycles is a set of Web pages that provides extensive information about motorcycles and their makers. In addition to text information about each motorcycle maker, the multimedia encyclopedia includes photographs, sounds (engine noises!), and video for many of the motorcycles listed.

The index is organized alphabetically, one page per letter (`A.html`, `B.html`, and so on). To help navigate into the body of the encyclopedia, the home page for this presentation is an overview page.

The Overview Page

The overview page is the main entry point into the body of the encyclopedia (Figure 12.5).

This page provides two main ways to get into the encyclopedia: by selecting the first letter of the marque or by selecting the name of one of the specific marques mentioned in the list itself.

NOTE

A *marque* is a fancy term used by motorcycle and sports car fanatics to refer to manufacturers of a vehicle.

Figure 12.5.

*The Motorcycle
Encyclopedia
overview page.*

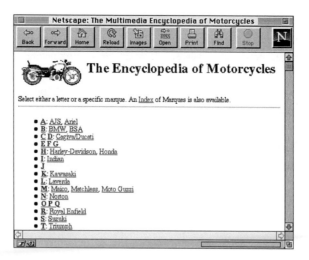

So, for example, if you wanted to find out information about the Norton motorcycle
company, you could select N for Norton and then scroll down to the appropriate entry in
the N page. But since Norton is one of the major manufacturers listed next to the N link, you
could select that link instead and go straight to the entry for Norton.

The Entry for Norton

Each individual page contains entries for all the marques starting with that letter. If the reader
has chosen a specific manufacturer, the link points directly to that specific entry (for example,
the entry for Norton, shown in Figure 12.6). Each entry contains information about the
marque and the various motorcycles it has produced over the years.

Figure 12.6.

Entry for Norton.

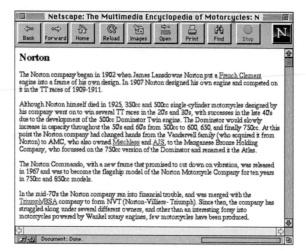

So where are the pictures? This was supposed to be a multimedia encyclopedia, wasn't it? In addition to the text describing Norton itself, the entry includes a list of external media files: images of various motorcycles, sound clips of what they sound like, and film of famous riders on their Nortons (Figure 12.7).

Figure 12.7.

The list of external media.

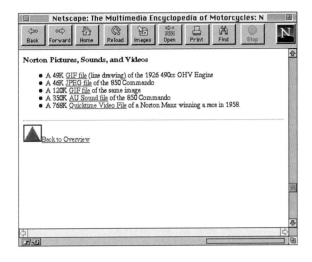

Each media file is described in text and contains links to those files so you can download them if you want to. For example, selecting the 850 Commando link accesses a JPEG image of the 850 Commando (Figure 12.8).

Figure 12.8.

The Norton 850 Commando.

Note also that in each point in the text where another manufacturer is mentioned, that manufacturer is linked to its own entry. For example, selecting the word BSA in the last paragraph takes you to the entry for BSA (Figure 12.9).

Figure 12.9.

Entry for BSA.

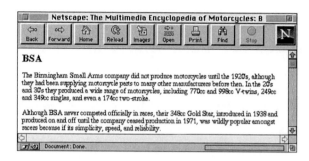

In this way, the reader can jump from link to link and manufacturer to manufacturer, exploring the information the encyclopedia contains based on what interests them. After they're done exploring, however, getting back to a known point is always important. For just this purpose, each entry in the encyclopedia contains a "Back to Overview" link. The duplication of this link in each entry means that the reader never has to scroll far to the top or bottom of the page in order to find the link back to the overview.

The Index of Marques

Back on the main overview page, there's one more feature I'd like to point out: The overview also contains a link to an Index of Marques, an alphabetical listing of all the manufacturers of motorcycles mentioned in the encyclopedia (Figure 12.10).

Each name in the index is, as you might expect, a link to the entry for that manufacturer in the encyclopedia itself, allowing you yet another way to quickly navigate into the alphabetic listings.

Figure 12.10.

The Index of Marques.

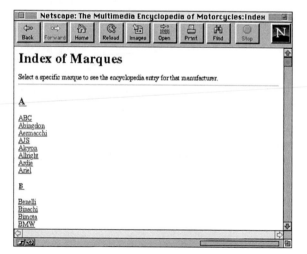

Features of This Web Site and Issues for Development

Probably the best feature of the design of this encyclopedia is the overview page. In many cases, an online encyclopedia of this sort would provide links to each letter in the alphabet, and leave it at that. If you wanted to check out Norton motorcycles, you would select the link for "N" and then scroll down to the entry for Norton. By providing links to some of the more popular motorcycle makers on the overview page itself, the author of this Web page provides a simple quick-reference that shortens the scrolling time and takes its readers directly to where they want to be.

The addition of the Index of Marques is also a nice touch, as it enables readers to jump directly to the entry of a particular manufacturer's name, reducing the amount of scrolling required to find the entry they want. Again, it's the same content in the encyclopedia. The overview page simply provides several different ways to find the information readers might be looking for.

The encyclopedia itself is structured in a loosely based Web pattern, making it possible for readers to jump in just about anywhere and then follow cross-references and graze through the available information, uncovering connections between motorcycles and marques and motorcycle history that might be difficult to uncover in a traditional paper encyclopedia. Also, by providing all the media files external to the pages themselves, the author of this Web presentation not only allows the encyclopedia to be used equally well by graphical and text-only browsers, but also keeps the size of the individual files for each letter small so they can be quickly loaded over the Net.

Finally, note that every listing in each letter has a link back to the overview page. If there were more than a single link, they would clutter the page and look ugly. The only explicit navigation choice is back to the overview, so including a single link enables readers to quickly and easily get back out of the encyclopedia, rather than having to scroll to the top or the bottom of a very long page to get to a set of navigation choices.

The biggest issue with developing a Web presentation of this kind is in setup and maintenance. Depending on the amount of material you have to put online, the task of arranging it all (Do you use exactly 26 files, one for each letter of the alphabet? Or more? Or less?) and creating the links for all the cross-references and all the external media can be daunting indeed. Fortunately, a presentation of this sort does not have to be updated very often, so after the initial work is done, the maintenance is not all that difficult.

12

Example Three: A Shopping Catalog

Susan's Cactus Gardens is a commercial nursery specializing in growing and shipping cacti and succulents. It offers over 120 species of cacti and succulents as well as books and other cactus-related items. Figure 12.11 shows the home page for Susan's Cactus Gardens.

Figure 12.11.

Susan's Cactus Gardens home page.

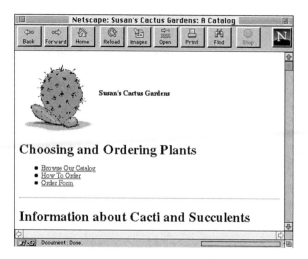

From here, customers have several choices: Read some background about the nursery itself, get information about specials and new plants, browse the catalog, get information about ordering, and actually order the cacti or succulents they have chosen.

Browsing the Catalog

Selecting the Browse Our Catalog link takes customers to another menu page, where they have several choices for how they want to browse the catalog (Figure 12.12).

By providing several different views of the catalog, the author is serving many different kinds of customers: those who know about cacti and succulents and just want to look up a specific variety, in which case the alphabetic index is most appropriate; those who know they would like, say, an Easter Cactus with pink flowers but are not sure which particular variety they want (the listing by category); as well as those who don't really know or care about the names but would like something that looks nice (the photo gallery).

The alphabetical links (A–F, G–R, S–Z) take customers to an alphabetical listing of the plants available for purchase. Figure 12.13 shows a sample listing from the alphabetical catalog.

12

Figure 12.12.

How to browse the catalog.

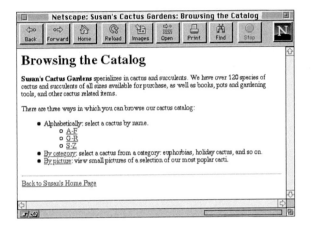

Figure 12.13.

The Cactus Catalog, arranged alphabetically.

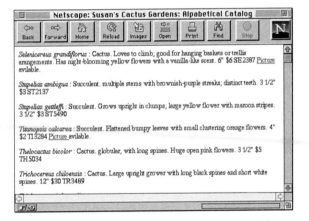

Each item indicates the Latin or scientific name of the cactus, a common name (if any), a simple description, size, order number, and price. If a photograph of this cactus is available in the photo gallery section of the catalog, a link is provided to that photograph so that readers can see what this cactus looks like before they buy it.

The catalog is also cross-referenced by each cactus's common name, if any. The link from the common name takes you back to the primary entry for the cactus. So if you really wanted a plant called Crown of Thorns, selecting that entry would take you to the true entry for that plant, Euphorbia Milii.

Each section of the alphabetical catalog also includes navigation buttons for returning back to the list of catalog views (Browsing the Catalog), or for returning to the home page.

The second view of the catalog (accessible from the Browsing the Catalog page) is the category view. Selecting this link takes the reader to yet another page of menus, listing the available categories (Figure 12.14).

Figure 12.14.

The category view.

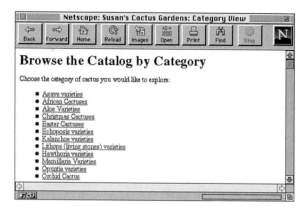

Selecting a particular category—for example, Orchid Cacti—takes customers to a list of the available plants in that category. Each element in the list should look familiar; they're the same elements as in the alphabetical list, sorted in a different order (Figure 12.15).

Figure 12.15.

The Cactus Catalog by category.

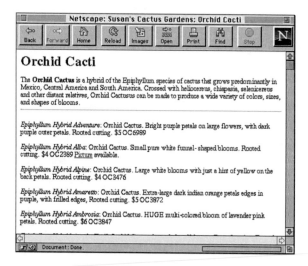

From the category index, customers can go back to the list of categories (one step up), or back to the list of catalog views (two steps up). On the Browsing the Catalog page, there's one more catalog view to examine: the photo gallery.

The photo gallery enables customers to browse many of the cacti available at the nursery by looking at pictures of them, rather than having to know their scientific names. This feature is obviously available only to graphical browsers but provides an excellent way to browse for interesting cacti.

The photo gallery page (shown in Figure 12.16) is organized as a series of icons, with each small picture of the cactus linked to a larger JPEG equivalent. The text description of each picture also takes you back to the appropriate entry in the main catalog.

Figure 12.16.

The Cactus Catalog photo gallery.

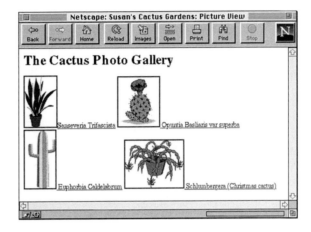

Ordering

After customers have finished browsing the catalog and they have an idea of the cacti they want to order, they can jump back up to the home page for Susan's Cactus Gardens and find out how to order. (It's the second bullet in the list shown previously in Figure 12.11.)

The page for ordering is just some simple text (Figure 12.17): information about where to call or send checks, tables for shipping costs, notes on when they will ship plants, and so on.

Figure 12.17.

Ordering plants.

12

In the section on ordering by mail, there is a link to an order form. The form itself is a PostScript file that customers will download, print out, and then fill out and send to the nursery. (It's an external file, specified in the HREF attribute to a link tag, just as you would specify any external media file.)

NOTE

> Why not order online? This page could easily have included an HTML form that allows readers to order their cacti online. I didn't include one here because you haven't learned about forms yet; we'll do that later in the book on Bonus Day.

And, lastly, note that the third bullet on the Susan's Cactus Gardens home page is a direct link to the order form file; it's provided here so that repeat customers won't have to take the added step of going back to the ordering, shipping, and payment page again.

Features of This Web Site and Issues for Development

In any online shopping service, the goals are to allow the reader to browse the items for sale and then to order those items. Within the browsing goal, there are several subgoals: What if the reader wants a particular item? Can it be found quickly and easily? What if someone just wants to look through the items for sale until he or she finds something interesting?

These two goals for browsing the online inventory may seem conflicting, but in this particular example they've been handled especially well through the use of multiple views of the content of the catalog. The multiple views do provide a level of indirection (an extra menu between the top-level page and the contents of the catalog itself), but that small step provides a branching in the hierarchy structure that helps each different type of customer accomplish his or her goals.

Probably the hardest part of building and maintaining a set of Web pages of this sort is maintaining the catalog itself, particularly if items need to be added or removed, or if prices change frequently. If the nursery had only one catalog view (the alphabetical one), this would not be so bad, as you could make changes directly to the catalog files. With additional views and the links between them, however, maintenance of the catalog becomes significantly more difficult.

Ideally, this sort of information could be stored in a database rather than as individual HTML files. Databases are designed to handle information like this and to be able to generate different views on request. But how do you hook up the database with the Web pages?

The Web has a mechanism for running programs on the server side. This could mean that given enough programming skill (and familiarity with your database) that you could create a program to do database queries from a Web page and return a neatly formatted list of items. Then, on the Web page, when someone requested the alphabetical listing, they would get an automatically generated list that was as up to date as the database was. But to do this, you'll need a database that can talk to your Web server, which, depending on the system your Web server runs on, may or may not be technically feasible. And you need the programming skill to make it work.

An alternate solution is to keep the data in the database and then dump it to text and format it in HTML every once in awhile. The primary difficulty with that solution, of course, is how much work it would take to do the conversion each time while still preserving the cross-references to the other pages. Could the process be automated, and how much setup and daily maintenance would that involve?

With this kind of application, these are the kinds of questions and technical challenges you might have to deal with if you create Web presentations. Sometimes the problem involves more than designing, writing, and formatting information on the screen.

Example Four: An Online Book

In this final example, we'll look at an online book called Bread & Circuses. This is a book that might very well have been published in hardcopy and has since been converted to HTML and formatted with few changes—the book-like structure has been retained in HTML, with each chapter a separate page. This is quite common on the Web, not necessarily with books, but with papers, articles, and otherwise linear forms of information. Does it work? Read on.

The home page for Bread & Circuses (shown in Figure 12.18) is, appropriately, a table of contents, just as it might be in a real book. Organized as lists within lists, this table of contents is essentially a large link menu with pointers to the various sections in the book.

Figure 12.18.

The Bread &
Circuses table of
contents.

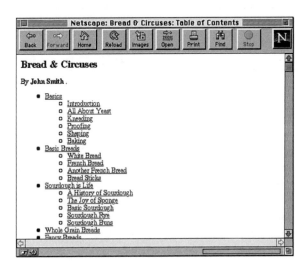

12

Readers who are interested in all the content the book has to offer could simply select the first link (Basics) and read all the way through from start to finish. Or, they could choose a topic and jump directly to that section in the book.

Proofing

Choosing the link for Proofing takes the reader to the file for Chapter One and then scrolls down to the appropriate section in that file (shown in Figure 12.19).

Figure 12.19.

The section on proofing.

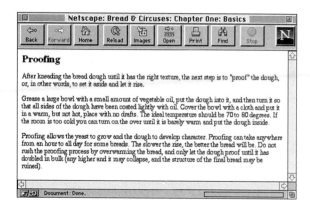

Here, the reader can read all about proofing. At the end of the section is the next section, "Shaping." And following it is the remainder of the chapter. Finally, at the end of the chapter, there are navigation links back to the table of contents, or on to the next chapter (Figure 12.20).

Figure 12.20.

Navigation links.

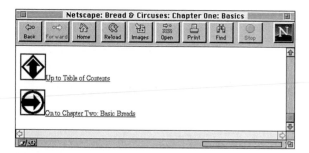

The two navigation links allow you either to progress linearly through the book by selecting the next chapter link, or to go back to the table of contents and choose another section or chapter to read. Note in this example the placement of the navigation links only at the end of each chapter file. The table of contents makes it easy to jump into the middle of the chapter, but to jump back out again you have to scroll all the way to the bottom (or go back using your browser).

The Index

On the table-of-contents page at the bottom of the list, there's a link to an index (the same place it would be in a hardcopy book—at the end). The index is similar to the table of contents in that it provides an overview of the content and links into specific places within the book itself. Like a paper index, the online version contains an alphabetical list of major topics and words, each one linked to the spot in the text where it is mentioned (Figure 12.21).

Figure 12.21.

The index.

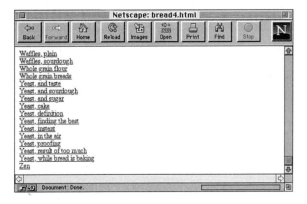

Yeast is mentioned multiple times in the book. Because online books do not (usually) have page numbers, linking index entries to multiple locations becomes more of a chore, as you'll have to construct your index so that each entry includes some kind of location reference (not to mention having to add all those anchors inside the chapters themselves).

So is this index useful? Like the table of contents, it does help readers jump to a specific place within the content. But also like the table of contents, it's harder for readers to get back out again once they're in the book—even more so for the index because the author does not provide a navigation link at the end of the chapter directly back to the index. This makes the index useful only in limited circumstances.

Features of This Web Site and Issues for Development

The biggest problem with putting books or other linear material online is that the material is often more difficult to navigate online than it is on paper. Online, readers can't flip through the pages as quickly and easily as they can on paper, and they can't use hints such as page numbers and chapter headings—both ways in which hardcopy books make finding where you are easy. For this reason, when you convert information intended for hardcopy to HTML, it is crucial to include overview pages, such as the table of contents in this example, to enable readers to jump in and out of the content and to find what they want.

12

More importantly, however, you have to provide methods of jumping back out again. In this example, the table of contents made it possible to jump into the middle of the content, but jumping back out again was less easy because there were few navigation links except at the end of the chapter. And jumping back to the index involved two links: back to the table of contents and then on to the index. In hardcopy, this isn't an issue. Online, it becomes one.

This example provided both a table of contents and an index. Multiple views of the same contents are usually a good thing, as I pointed out in the previous two examples, because they let your readers choose which way they want to find what they are looking for. Watch out for views that are intended for hardcopy, however, as they might not apply overly well. For example, a typical index, with a word or citations and a list of page numbers, doesn't work overly well in a Web presentation because you don't have page numbers. Consider some other method of linking to information in your document.

When converting a linear document to the Web, there may also be the temptation to add extra non-navigational links as well, for example, to refer to footnotes or citations or just related material. However, keep in mind with linear structures as with hierarchies that the structure can often keep your reader from getting lost or confused in your material. Links to other sections in the book can be confusing and muddle the structure you've tried so hard to preserve by converting the document to HTML.

Limited forms of non-navigational links can work well, however—for example, an explicit reference to another section of the book in the text such as, "For more information about yeast, see 'yeast' in Chapter One." In this case, it is clear where the link is leading, and readers understand where they are and where they are going so they can reorient their position in the presentation.

Summary

I've presented only a couple ideas for using and structuring Web pages here; the variations on these themes are unlimited for the Web pages you will design.

Probably the best way to find examples of the sort of Web pages you might want to design and how to organize them is to go out on the Web and browse what's out there. While you're browsing, in addition to examining the layout and design of individual pages and the content they describe, keep an eye out for the structures people have used to organize their pages, and try to guess why they might have chosen that organization. ("They didn't think about it" is a common reason for many poorly organized Web pages, unfortunately.) Critique other people's Web pages with an eye for their structure and design: Is it easy to navigate them? Did you get lost? Can you easily get back to a known page from any other location in their presentation? If you had a goal in mind for this presentation, did you achieve that goal, and if not, how would you have reorganized it?

Learning from other people's mistakes and seeing how other people have solved difficult problems can help you make your own Web pages better.

Q&A

Q These Web presentations are really cool. What are their URLs?

A As I noted at the beginning of this chapter, the Web presentations I've described here are mock-ups of potential Web presentations that could exist. Although many of the designs and organizations that I have created here were inspired by existing Web pages, these pages do not actually exist on the Web.

Q Three out of the four examples here used some sort of hierarchical organization. Are hierarchies that common, and do I have to use them? Can't I do something different?

A Hierarchies are extremely common on the Web, but that doesn't mean that they're bad. Hierarchies are an excellent way of organizing your content, especially when the information you're presenting lends itself to a hierarchical organization.

You can certainly do something different to organize your presentation. But the simplicity of hierarchies allows them to be easily structured, easily navigated, and easily maintained. Why make more trouble for yourself and for your reader by trying to force a complicated structure on otherwise simple information?

12

Advanced HTML Features: Tables and Frames

Chapter 13

Tables

Tables are an advanced HTML construct that allows you to arrange text, images, and other HTML content into rows and columns with or without borders. Tables were the first part of HTML 3.2 to hit the Web, and they've had an enormous influence on how pages are designed and constructed. In this chapter, you'll learn all about tables, including:

- ☐ The state of table development on the Web
- ☐ Defining tables in HTML
- ☐ Creating captions, rows, and heading and data cells
- ☐ Modifying cell alignment
- ☐ Creating cells that span multiple rows or columns
- ☐ Adding color to tables
- ☐ How to use (or not use) tables in your Web documents

A Note About the Table Definition

Tables were one of the first extensions to HTML that were proposed as part of HTML 3.2. In early 1995, Netscape and Mosaic almost simultaneously implemented a simple version of HTML 3.2 tables in their browsers (with Netscape adding a few extra features). Tables almost immediately revolutionized Web page design because tables can be used not just for presenting data in a tabular form, but also for page layout and control over placement of various HTML elements on a page. Tables have become so popular that most major browsers have now added table support.

At the time tables were originally implemented in Netscape and Mosaic, the actual definition for tables in HTML was still under considerable discussion, as was most of the HTML 3.2 specification. Although the definition of the basic table, as I'll describe in this chapter, is pretty much settled, and most browsers that support tables do support this definition, tables are still being discussed and refined by the WWW Consortium and by other interested parties. The new table specification contains lots of new features that have yet to be implemented in any browsers. You can read the current table specification at `http://www.w3.org/pub/WWW/TR/WD-tables` if you're interested.

Keep the fact that tables are still changing in mind as you design your own tables; although it's unlikely that anything you design now will break in the future, there probably will be changes still to come.

Creating Basic Tables

With that one small warning in mind, let's jump right in. To create tables in HTML, you define the parts of your table and which bits of HTML go where, and then you add HTML table code around those parts. Then you refine the table's appearance with alignments, borders, and colored cells. In this section, you'll learn how to create a basic table with headings, data, and a caption.

One more note, however. Creating tables by hand in HTML is no fun. The code for tables was designed to be easy to generate by programs, not to be written by hand, and as such it's rather confusing. You'll do a lot of experimenting, testing, and going back and forth between your browser and your code to get a table to work out right. HTML editors can help a great deal with this, as can working initially in a word processor's table editor or a spreadsheet to get an idea of what goes where. But I suggest doing at least your first bunch of tables the hard way so you can get an idea how HTML tables work.

Table Parts

Before we get into the actual HTML code to create a table, let me define some terms so we both know what we're talking about:

☐ The caption indicates what the table is about: for example, "Voting Statistics, 1950–1994," or "Toy Distribution Per Room at 1564 Elm St." Captions are optional.

☐ The table headings label the rows or columns, or both. Table headings are usually in a larger or emphasized font that is different from the rest of the table.

☐ Table data are the values in the table itself. The combination of the table headings and table data make up the sum of the table.

☐ Table cells are the individual squares in the table. A cell can contain normal table data or a table heading.

Figure 13.1 shows a typical table and its parts.

Figure 13.1.

The parts of a table.

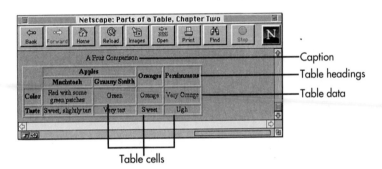

The <TABLE> Tag

To create a table in HTML, you use the <TABLE>...</TABLE> tags, which contain the code for a caption and then the contents of the table itself:

```
<TABLE>
...table contents...
</TABLE>
```

The most common attribute to the <TABLE> tag is the BORDER attribute. BORDER causes the table to be drawn with a border around it, which can be a fancy border in a graphical browser or just a series of dashes and pipes (¦) in a text-based browser.

Borderless tables are useful when you want to use the table structure for layout purposes, but you don't necessarily want the outline of an actual table on the page.

Rows and Cells

Inside the `<TABLE>`...`</TABLE>` tags, you define the actual contents of the table. Tables are specified in HTML row by row, and each row definition contains definitions for each of the cells in that row. So, to define a table, you start by defining a top row and each cell in turn, and then you define a second row and its cells, and so on. The columns are automatically calculated based on how many cells there are in each row.

Each table row is indicated by the `<TR>` tag and ends with the appropriate closing `</TR>`. Each table row, in turn, has a number of table cells, which are indicated using the `<TH>`...`</TH>` (for heading cells) and `<TD>`...`</TD>` tags (for data cells). You can have as many rows as you want to and as many cells in each row as you need for your columns, but you should make sure each row has the same number of cells so that the columns line up.

NOTE

> In early definitions of tables, the closing tags `</TR>`, `</TH>`, and `</TD>` were required for each row and cell. Since then, the table definition has been refined such that each of these closing tags is optional. However, many browsers that support tables still expect the closing tags to be there, and the tables may even break if you don't include the closing tags. Until tables become more consistently implemented across browsers, it's probably a good idea to continue using the closing tags even though they are optional.

Here's a simple example: a table with only one row, four cells, and one heading on the left side:

```
<TABLE BORDER>
<TR>
    <TH>Heading</TH>
    <TD>Data</TD>
    <TD>Data</TD>
    <TD>Data</TD>
</TR>
</TABLE>
```

The `<TH>` tag indicates a cell that is also a table heading, and the `<TD>` tag is a regular cell within the table (TD stands for Table Data). Headings are generally displayed in a different way than table cells, such as in a boldface font. Both `<TH>` and `<TD>` should be closed with their respective closing tags `</TH>` and `</TD>`.

If it's a heading along the top edge of the table, the `<TH>` tags for that heading go inside the first row. The HTML for a table with a row of headings along the top and one row of data looks like this:

```
<P>A Table with Headings Across the Top</P>
<TABLE BORDER>
<TR>
    <TH>Drive Plate</TH>
    <TH>Front Cover</TH>
</TR>
<TR>
    <TD>39-49</TD>
    <TD>19-23</TD>
</TR>
</TABLE>
```

If the headings are along the left edge of the table, put each <TH> in the first cell in each row, like this:

```
<P>A Table with Headings Along the Side</P>
<TABLE BORDER>
<TR>
    <TH>Drive Plate</TH>
    <TD>39-49</TD>
</TR>
<TR>
    <TH>Front Cover</TH>
    <TD>19-23</TD>
</TR>
</TABLE>
```

Figure 13.2 shows the results of both these tables.

Figure 13.2.

Small tables and headings.

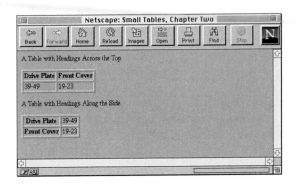

Both table headings and data can contain any text or HTML code or both, including links, lists, forms, and other tables.

The following input and output example shows a simple table. Figure 13.3 shows its result in Netscape.

```
INPUT        <HTML>
             <HEAD>
             <TITLE>Rows and Cells</TITLE>
             </HEAD>
             <BODY>
```

```
<TABLE BORDER>
<CAPTION>Soup of the Day</CAPTION>
<TR>
    <TH>Monday</TH>
    <TH>Tuesday</TH>
    <TH>Wednesday</TH>
    <TH>Thursday</TH>
    <TH>Friday</TH>
</TR>
<TR>
    <TD>Split Pea</TD>
    <TD>New England<BR>Clam Chowder</TD>
    <TD>Minestrone</TD>
    <TD>Cream of<BR>Broccoli</TD>
    <TD>Chowder</TD>
</TR>
</TABLE>
</BODY>
</HTML>
```

Figure 13.3.
Rows and cells.

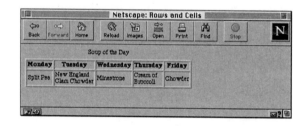

Empty Cells

What if you want a cell with nothing in it? That's easy. Just define a cell with a <TH> or <TD> tag with nothing inside it:

```
<TR>
    <TD></TD>
    <TD>10</TD>
    <TD>20</TD>
</TR>
```

Sometimes, an empty cell of this sort is displayed as if the cell doesn't exist (as shown in Figure 13.4).

Figure 13.4.
Empty cells.

An empty cell ——

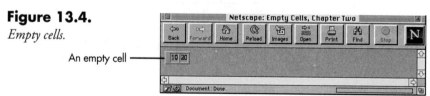

13

If you want to force a truly empty cell, you can add a line break in that cell by itself with no other text (see Figure 13.5).

```
<TR>
    <TD><BR></TD>
    <TD>10</TD>
    <TD>20</TD>
</TR>
```

Figure 13.5.
Really empty cells.

The empty cell, really empty ——

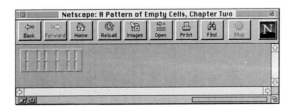

The following input and output example creates a pattern of empty cells (see Figure 13.6).

 INPUT

```
<HTML>
<HEAD>
<TITLE>A Pattern of Empty Cells, Chapter Two</TITLE>
</HEAD>
<BODY>
<TABLE BORDER>
<TR>
    <TH></TH><TH><BR></TH><TH></TH><TH></TH>
    <TH><BR></TH><TH></TH><TH><BR></TH><TH></TH>
    <TH></TH><TH><BR></TH><TH></TH><TH></TH>
    <TH><BR></TH><TH></TH><TH><BR></TH><TH></TH>
</TR>
<TR>
    <TH></TH><TH><BR></TH><TH></TH><TH></TH>
    <TH><BR></TH><TH></TH><TH><BR></TH><TH></TH>
    <TH></TH><TH><BR></TH><TH></TH><TH></TH>
    <TH><BR></TH><TH></TH><TH><BR></TH><TH></TH>
</TR>
</TABLE>
</BODY>
</HTML>
```

OUTPUT

Figure 13.6.
A pattern of empty cells.

13

Captions

Table captions tell your reader what the table is for. Although you could just use a regular paragraph or a heading as a label for your table, there is a <CAPTION> tag for just this purpose. Because the <CAPTION> tag labels captions as captions, tools to process HTML files could extract them into a separate file, or automatically number them, or treat them in special ways simply because they are captions.

But what if you don't want a caption? You don't have to include one. Captions are optional. If you just want a table and don't care about a label, leave the caption off.

The <CAPTION> tag goes inside the <TABLE> tag just before the table rows, and it contains the title of the table. It closes with the </CAPTION> tag.

```
<TABLE>
<CAPTION>Decapitated Tulips in Virginia, 1960-1980</CAPTION>
<TR>
```

The optional ALIGN attribute to the caption determines the alignment of the caption. However, depending on which browser you're using, you have different choices for what ALIGN means.

In most browsers, ALIGN can have one of two values: TOP and BOTTOM. By default, the caption is placed at the top of the table (ALIGN=TOP). You can use the ALIGN=BOTTOM attribute to the caption if you want to put the caption at the bottom of the table, like this:

```
<TABLE>
<CAPTION ALIGN=BOTTOM>Torque Limits for Various Fruits</CAPTION>
```

In Internet Explorer, however, captions are different. Using Internet Explorer, you use the VALIGN attribute to put the caption at the top or the bottom, and ALIGN has three different values: LEFT, RIGHT, and CENTER, which aligns the caption horizontally.

In general, unless you have a very short table, you should leave the caption in its default position—centered, at the top of the table—so that your readers will see the caption first and know what they are about to read, instead of seeing it after they're already done reading the table (at which point they've usually figured out what it's about anyway).

Exercise 13.1: Create a simple table.

Now that you know the basics of how to create a table, let's try a simple example. For this example, we'll create a table that indicates the colors you get when you mix the three primary colors together.

Figure 13.7 shows the table we're going to re-create in this example.

EXERCISE

13

Figure 13.7.

The simple color table.

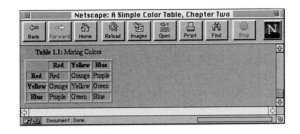

Here's a quick hint for laying out tables: because HTML defines tables on a row-by-row basis, it can sometimes be difficult to keep track of the columns, particularly with very complex tables. Before you start actually writing HTML code, it's useful to make a sketch of your table so you know what the heads are and the values of each cell. You might find that it's easiest to use a word processor with a table editor (such as Microsoft Word) or a spreadsheet to lay out your tables. Then when you have the layout and the cell values, you can write the HTML code for that table. Of course, eventually there will be filters so that you can simply save the file and automatically get HTML code out of the other end, but for now this is a good way of keeping track of everything.

Let's start with a simple HTML framework for the page that contains a table. Like all HTML files, you can create this file in any text editor:

```
<HTML><HEAD>
<TITLE>A Simple Color Table, Chapter Two</TITLE>
</HEAD>
<BODY>
<TABLE BORDER>
...add table rows and cells here...
</TABLE>
</BODY></HTML>
```

Note that the <TABLE> tag has the BORDER attribute. This draws the highlighted borders around the table.

Now start adding table rows inside the opening and closing <TABLE> tags (where the line "add table rows and cells here" was in the framework). The first row is the three headings along the top of the table. The table row is indicated by </TR>, and each cell by a <TH> tag:

```
<TR>
    <TH>Red</TH>
    <TH>Yellow</TH>
    <TH>Blue</TH>
</TR>
```

13

NOTE

You can format the HTML code any way you want to; like with all HTML, the browser ignores most extra spaces and returns. I like to format it like this, with the contents of the individual rows indented and the cell tags on separate lines, so I can pick out the rows and columns more easily.

Now add the second row. The first cell in the second row is the Red heading on the left side of the table, so it will be the first cell in this row, followed by the cells for the table data:

```
<TR>
    <TH>Red</TH>
    <TD>Red</TD>
    <TD>Orange</TD>
    <TD>Purple</TD>
</TR>
```

Continue by adding the remaining two rows in the table, with the Yellow and Blue headings. Here's what you have so far for the entire table:

```
<TABLE BORDER>
<TR>
    <TH>Red</TH>
    <TH>Yellow</TH>
    <TH>Blue</TH>
</TR>
<TR>
    <TH>Red</TH>
    <TD>Red</TD>
    <TD>Orange</TD>
    <TD>Purple</TD>
</TR>
<TR>
    <TH>Yellow</TH>
    <TD>Orange</TD>
    <TD>Yellow</TD>
    <TD>Green</TD>
</TR>
<TR>
    <TH>Blue</TH>
    <TD>Purple</TD>
    <TD>Green</TD>
    <TD>Blue</TD>
</TR>
</TABLE>
```

Finally, let's add a simple caption. The <CAPTION> tag goes just after the <TABLE BORDER> tag and just before the first <TR> tag:

```
<TABLE BORDER>
<CAPTION><B>Table 1.1:</B> Mixing Colors</CAPTION>
<TR>
```

13

Now, with a first draft of the code in place, test the HTML file in your favorite browser that supports tables. Figure 13.8 shows how it looks in Netscape.

Figure 13.8.
The color table.

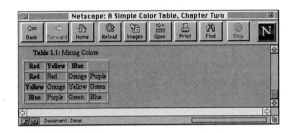

Oops! What happened with that top row? The headings are all messed up. The answer, of course, is that you need an empty cell at the beginning of that first row to space the headings out over the proper columns. HTML isn't smart enough to match it all up for you (this is exactly the sort of error you're going to find the first time you test your tables).

Let's add an empty table heading cell to that first row (here, the line <TH>
</TH>):

```
<TR>
    <TH><BR></TH>
    <TH>Red</TH>
    <TH>Yellow</TH>
    <TH>Blue</TH>
</TR>
```

NOTE

I used <TH> here, but it could just as easily be <TD>. Because there's nothing in the cell, its formatting doesn't matter.

If you try it again, you should get the right result with all the headings over the right columns.

Table and Cell Alignment

13

Once you've got your basic table layout with rows, headings, and data, you can start refining how that table looks. The first way to do this is to align the table on the page and to align the contents of the cells inside that table.

Table Alignment

By default, tables are displayed on a line by themselves along the left side of the page, with any text above or below the table.

Using the ALIGN attribute, however, you can align tables along the left or right margins and wrap text alongside them the same way you can with images. ALIGN=LEFT aligns the table along the left margin, and all text following that table is wrapped in the space between that table and the right side of the page. ALIGN=RIGHT does the same thing, with the table aligned to the right side of the page. Figure 13.9 shows an example of a table with text wrapped alongside of it.

Figure 13.9.

A table with text alongside it.

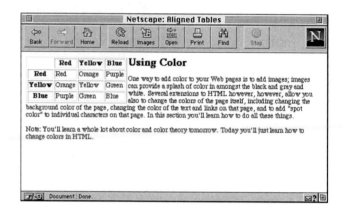

As with images, to stop wrapping text alongside an image, you can use the line break tag with the CLEAR attribute.

Centering tables is slightly more difficult. Currently, no browsers support ALIGN=CENTER on tables. However, you can use the <CENTER> or <DIV ALIGN=CENTER> tags (both of which you learned about in Chapter 5, "More Text Formatting with HTML 3.2") to center tables on the page.

Cell Alignment

When you have your rows and cells in place inside your table and the table properly aligned on the page, you can align the data within each cell for the best effect based on what your table contains. HTML tables give you several options for aligning the data within your cells both horizontally and vertically. Figure 13.10 shows a table (a real HTML one!) of the various alignment options.

Figure 13.10.

Cell alignment.

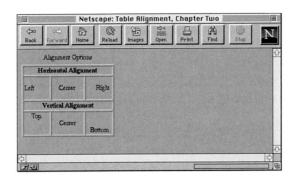

Horizontal alignment (the ALIGN attribute) defines whether the data within a cell is aligned with the left cell margin (LEFT), the right cell margin (RIGHT), or centered within the two (CENTER).

Vertical alignment (the VALIGN attribute) defines the vertical alignment of the data within the cell, meaning whether the data is flush with the top of the cell (TOP), flush with the bottom of the cell (BOTTOM), or vertically centered within the cell (MIDDLE). Netscape also implements VALIGN=BASELINE, which is similar to VALIGN=TOP, except that it aligns the baseline of the first line of text in each cell (depending on the contents of the cell, this might or might not produce a different result than ALIGN=TOP).

By default, heading cells are centered both horizontally and vertically, and data cells are centered vertically but aligned flush left.

You can override the defaults for an entire row by adding the ALIGN or VALIGN attributes to the <TR> tag, as in this example:

```
<TR ALIGN=CENTER VALIGN=TOP>
```

You can override the row alignment for individual cells by adding ALIGN to the <TD> or <TH> tags:

```
<TR ALIGN=CENTER VALIGN=TOP>
    <TD>14</TD>
    <TD>16</TD>
    <TD ALIGN=LEFT>No Data</TD>
    <TD>15</TD>
</TR>
```

The following input and output example shows the various cell alignments and how they look in Netscape (Figure 13.11).

```
<HTML>
<HEAD>
```

```
<TITLE>Aligned Buttons, Chapter Two</TITLE>
</HEAD>
<BODY>
<TABLE BORDER>
<TR>
    <TH></TH>
    <TH>Left</TH>
    <TH>Centered</TH>
    <TH>Right</TH>
</TR>
<TR>
    <TH>Top</TH>
    <TD ALIGN=LEFT VALIGN=TOP><IMG SRC="button.gif"></TD>
    <TD ALIGN=CENTER VALIGN=TOP><IMG SRC="button.gif"></TD>
    <TD ALIGN=RIGHT VALIGN=TOP><IMG SRC="button.gif"></TD>
</TR>
<TR>
    <TH>Centered</TH>
    <TD ALIGN=LEFT VALIGN=MIDDLE><IMG SRC="button.gif"></TD>
    <TD ALIGN=CENTER VALIGN=MIDDLE><IMG SRC="button.gif"></TD>
    <TD ALIGN=RIGHT VALIGN=MIDDLE><IMG SRC="button.gif"></TD>
</TR>
<TR>
    <TH>Bottom</TH>
    <TD ALIGN=LEFT VALIGN=BOTTOM><IMG SRC="button.gif"></TD>
    <TD ALIGN=CENTER VALIGN=BOTTOM><IMG SRC="button.gif"></TD>
    <TD ALIGN=RIGHT VALIGN=BOTTOM><IMG SRC="button.gif"></TD>
</TR>
</TABLE>
</BODY>
</HTML>
```

Figure 13.11.
Alignment options.

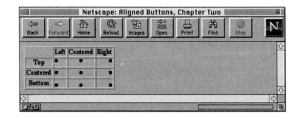

Exercise 13.2: A vegetable planting guide.

Tables are great when you have a lot of information—particularly technical or numeric information—that you want to present in a way that enables your readers to find what they need quickly and easily. Perhaps they're only interested in one bit of that information or a range of it. Presented in a paragraph or in a list, it might be more difficult for your readers to glean what they need.

For example, say you want to summarize information about planting vegetables, which includes the time in the year each vegetable should be planted, how long it takes before you can harvest that vegetable, whether you can transplant an already growing plant, and some common varieties that are known to grow especially well. You can present this information as a list, one paragraph per vegetable; but, because the data falls into neat categories, the data will look better and be more accessible as a table.

Figure 13.12 shows the vegetable-planting chart, the table you'll be building in this exercise. Like the last example, it's a rather simple table, but it does use links, images, and lists inside the table cells. In addition, it takes advantage of some of the alignment options that I described in the previous section. In this example, we'll start with a basic HTML framework, lay out the rows and the cells, and then adjust and fine-tune the alignment of the data within those cells. You'll find, as you work with more tables, that this plan is the easiest way to develop a table. If you worry about the alignment at the same time that you're constructing the table, it's easy to get confused.

Figure 13.12.

The vegetable planting schedule.

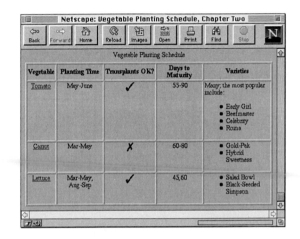

Here's the basic framework for the table, including the caption:

```
<HTML>
<HEAD>
<TITLE>Vegetable Planting Schedule</TITLE>
</HEAD>
<BODY>
<TABLE BORDER>
<CAPTION>Vegetable Planting Schedule</CAPTION>

</TABLE>
</BODY>
</HTML>
```

The first row we'll add is the heading for the top table. It's a row with five heading cells, and we'll add it to the table just beneath the <CAPTION> tag:

```
<TR>
    <TH>Vegetable</TH>
    <TH>Planting Time</TH>
```

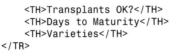

```
        <TH>Transplants OK?</TH>
        <TH>Days to Maturity</TH>
        <TH>Varieties</TH>
</TR>
```

The remaining rows are for the data for the table. Note that within a table cell (a <TH> or <TD> tag), you can put any HTML markup, including links, images, forms, or other tables. In this example, we've used links for each vegetable name (pointing to further information), a checkmark or X image for whether you can plant transplants of that vegetable, and an unordered list for the varieties. Here's the code so far for the headings and the three rows of the table:

```
<TABLE BORDER>
<CAPTION>Vegetable Planting Schedule</CAPTION>
<TR>
        <TH>Vegetable</TH>
        <TH>Planting Time</TH>
        <TH>Transplants OK?</TH>
        <TH>Days to Maturity</TH>
        <TH>Varieties</TH>
</TR>
<TR>
        <TD ><A HREF="tomato.html">Tomato</A></TD>
        <TD>May-June</TD>
        <TD><IMG SRC="check.gif"></TD>
        <TD>55-90</TD>
        <TD>Many; the most popular include:
            <UL>
            <LI>Early Girl
            <LI>Beefmaster
            <LI>Celebrity
            <LI>Roma
            </UL>
        </TD>
</TR>
<TR>
        <TD><A HREF="carrot.html">Carrot</A></TD>
        <TD>Mar-May</TD>
        <TD><IMG SRC="ex.gif"></TD>
        <TD>60-80</TD>
        <TD>
            <UL>
            <LI>Gold-Pak
            <LI>Hybrid Sweetness
            </UL>
        </TD>
</TR>
<TR>
        <TD><A HREF="lettuce.html">Lettuce</A></TD>
        <TD>Mar-May, Aug-Sep</TD>
        <TD><IMG SRC="check.gif"></TD>
        <TD>45,60</TD>
        <TD>
            <UL>
            <LI>Salad Bowl
```

```
        <LI>Black-Seeded Simpson
        </UL>
    </TD>
</TR>
</TABLE>
```

In Netscape, there's one exception to the rule that whitespace in your original HTML code doesn't matter in the final output. For images in cells, say you've formatted your code with the `<IMG>` tag on a separate line, like this:

```
<TD>
    <IMG SRC="check.gif">
</TD>
```

With this code, the return between the `<TD>` and the `<IMG>` tag is significant; your image will not be properly placed within the cell (this particularly shows up in centered cells). To correct the problem, just put the `<TD>` and the `<IMG>` on the same line:

```
<TD><IMG SRC="check.gif"></TD>
```

Figure 13.13 shows what the table looks like so far.

NOTE

Depending on how big your screen and your browser window are, your table may not look exactly like this one. Browsers reformat tables to the width of the window as they do with other HTML elements. You'll learn more about controlling the width of tables in "Defining Table and Column Widths," later in this chapter.

Figure 13.13.

The Vegetable Table, try one.

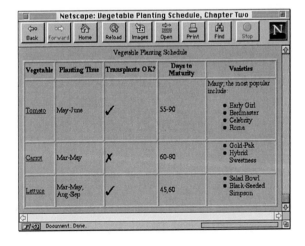

So far, so good, but the columns would look better centered. We can do this globally for each row by adding the ALIGN=CENTER attribute to each <TR> tag. (Note that you need to do it only for the data rows; the headings are already centered.)

```
<TR ALIGN=CENTER>
    <TD ><A HREF="tomato.html">Tomato</A></TD>
    <TD>May-June</TD>
    ...
```

Figure 13.14 shows the new table with the contents of the cells now centered:

Figure 13.14.

The Vegetable Table, try two.

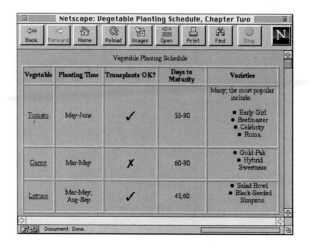

Now the table looks much better, except for the bullets in the Varieties column. They got centered, too, so now they're all out of whack. But that doesn't matter; we can fix that by adding the ALIGN=LEFT attribute to the <TD> tag for that cell in every row with the following code. The result is shown in Figure 13.15.

```
<TD ALIGN=LEFT>Many; the most popular include:
    <UL>
    <LI>Early Girl
    ...
```

NOTE

You could have just kept the default alignment for each row and then added an ALIGN=CENTER attribute to every cell that needed to be centered. But that would have been a lot more work. It's usually easier to change the default row alignment to the alignment of the majority of the cells and then change the cell alignment for the individual cells that are left.

Figure 13.15.

The Vegetable
Table, try three.

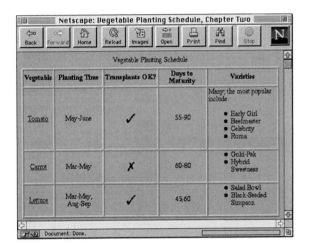

We're getting close, but let's try one more thing. Right now, all the cells are vertically centered. Let's add a VALIGN=TOP to each data row (next to the ALIGN=CENTER) so that they'll hug the top of the cells.

```
<TR ALIGN=CENTER VALIGN=TOP>
    <TD ><A HREF="tomato.html">Tomato</A></TD>
    <TD>May-June</TD>
```

You're done! Here's the final HTML text for the example:

```
<HTML>
<HEAD>
<TITLE>Vegetable Planting Schedule</TITLE>
</HEAD>
<BODY>
<TABLE BORDER>
<CAPTION>Vegetable Planting Schedule</CAPTION>
<TR>
    <TH>Vegetable</TH>
    <TH>Planting Time</TH>
    <TH>Transplants OK?</TH>
    <TH>Days to Maturity</TH>
    <TH>Varieties</TH>
</TR>
<TR ALIGN=CENTER VALIGN=TOP>
    <TD ><A HREF="tomato.html">Tomato</A></TD>
    <TD>May-June</TD>
    <TD><IMG SRC="check.gif"></TD>
    <TD>55-90</TD>
    <TD ALIGN=LEFT>Many; the most popular include:
        <UL>
        <LI>Early Girl
        <LI>Beefmaster
        <LI>Celebrity
        <LI>Roma
        </UL>
```

13

```
        </TD>
    </TR>
    <TR ALIGN=CENTER VALIGN=TOP>
        <TD><A HREF="carrot.html">Carrot</A></TD>
        <TD>Mar-May</TD>
        <TD><IMG SRC="ex.gif"></TD>
        <TD>60-80</TD>
        <TD ALIGN=LEFT>
            <UL>
            <LI>Gold-Pak
            <LI>Hybrid Sweetness
            </UL>
        </TD>
    </TR>
    <TR ALIGN=CENTER VALIGN=TOP>
        <TD><A HREF="lettuce.html">Lettuce</A></TD>
        <TD>Mar-May, Aug-Sep</TD>
        <TD><IMG SRC="check.gif"></TD>
        <TD>45,60</TD>
        <TD ALIGN=LEFT>
            <UL>
            <LI>Salad Bowl
            <LI>Black-Seeded Simpson
            </UL>
        </TD>
    </TR>
    </TABLE>
    </BODY>
    </HTML>
```

Cells That Span Multiple Rows or Columns

The tables we've created up to this point all had one value per cell or had the occasional empty cell. You can also create cells that span multiple rows or columns within the table. Those spanned cells can then hold headings that have subheadings in the next row or column, or you can create other special effects within the table layout. Figure 13.16 shows a table with spanned columns and rows.

Figure 13.16.

Tables with spans.

This cell spans two rows and two columns.

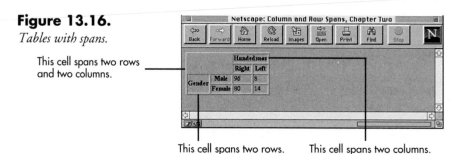

This cell spans two rows.   This cell spans two columns.

To create a cell that spans multiple rows or columns, you add the ROWSPAN or COLSPAN attribute to the <TH> or <TD> tags, along with the number of rows or columns you want the cell to span. The data within that cell then fills the entire width or length of the combined cells, as in the following example:

```
<TR>
    <TH COLSPAN=2>Gender
</TR>
<TR>
    <TH>Male</TH>
    <TH>Female</TH>
</TR>
<TR>
    <TD>15</TD>
    <TD>23</TD>
</TR>
```

Figure 13.17 shows how this table might appear when displayed.

Figure 13.17.

Column spans.

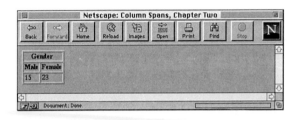

Note that if a cell spans multiple rows, you don't have to redefine that cell as empty in the next row or rows. Just ignore it and move to the next cell in the row; the span will fill in the spot for you.

Cells always span downward and to the right. So to create a cell that spans several columns, you add the COLSPAN attribute to the leftmost cell in the span, and for cells that span rows, you add ROWSPAN to the topmost cell.

The following input and output example shows a cell that spans multiple rows (the cell with the word "Piston" in it). Figure 13.18 shows the result in Netscape.

```
INPUT    <HTML>
         <HEAD>
         <TITLE>Ring Clearance</TITLE>
         </HEAD>
         <BODY>
         <TABLE BORDER>
         <TR>
             <TH COLSPAN=2></TH>
             <TH>Ring<BR>Clearance</TH>
         </TR>
         <TR ALIGN=CENTER>
             <TH ROWSPAN=2>Piston</TH>
             <TH>Upper</TH>
```

```
      <TD>3mm</TD>
  </TR>
  <TR ALIGN=CENTER>
      <TH>Lower</TH>
      <TD>3.2mm</TD>
  </TR>
  </TABLE>
  </BODY>
  </HTML>
```

Figure 13.18.

*Cells that span
multiple rows and
columns.*

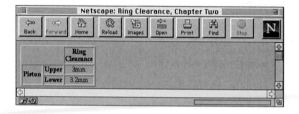

Exercise 13.3: A table of service specifications.

Had enough of tables yet? Let's do one more example that takes advantage of everything you've learned here: tables with headings and normal cells, alignments, and column and row spans. This is a very complex table, so we'll go step by step, row by row to build it.

Figure 13.19 shows the table, which indicates service and adjustment specifications from the service manual for a car.

Figure 13.19.

*The really complex
service specification
table.*

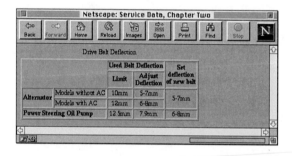

There are actually five rows and columns in this table. Do you see them? Some of them span columns and rows. Figure 13.20 shows the same table with a grid drawn over it so you can see where the rows and columns are.

With tables such as this one that use many spans, it's helpful to draw this sort of grid to figure out where the spans are and in which row they belong. Remember, spans start at the topmost row and the leftmost column.

Figure 13.20.

Five columns, five rows.

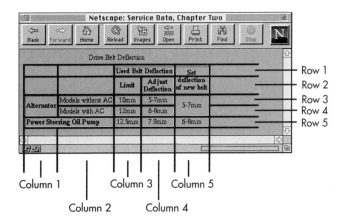

Ready? Start with the framework, just as you have for the other tables in this chapter:

```
<HTML>
<HEAD>
<TITLE>Service Data</TITLE>
</HEAD>
<BODY>
<TABLE BORDER>
<CAPTION>Drive Belt Deflection</CAPTION>

</TABLE>
</BODY>
</HTML>
```

Now create the first row. With the grid on your picture, you can see that the first cell is empty and spans two rows and two columns (see Figure 13.21). Therefore, the HTML for that cell would be as follows:

```
<TR>
<TH ROWSPAN=2 COLSPAN=2></TH>
```

Figure 13.21.

The first cell.

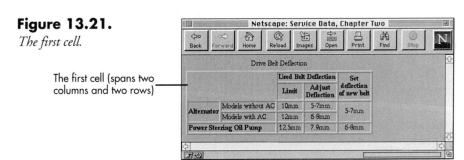

The second cell in the row is the Used Belt Deflection heading cell, which spans two columns (for the two cells beneath it). So the code for that cell is

 `<TH COLSPAN=2>Used Belt Deflection</TH>`

Now that you have two cells that span two columns each, there's only the one left in this row. But this one, like the first one, spans the row beneath it:

```
<TH ROWSPAN=2>Set deflection of new belt</TH>
</TR>
```

Now go on to the second row. This isn't the one that starts with the Alternator heading. Remember that the first cell in the previous row has a ROWSPAN and a COLSPAN of two, meaning that it bleeds down to this row and takes up two cells. You don't need to redefine it for this row; you just move on to the next cell in the grid. The first cell in this row is the Limit heading cell, and the second cell is the "Adjust Deflection" heading cell:

```
<TR>
    <TH>Limit</TH>
    <TH>Adjust Deflection</TH>
</TR>
```

What about the last cell? Just like the first cell, the cell in the row above this one had a ROWSPAN of two, which takes up the space in this row. So the only values you need for this row are the ones you already defined.

Are you with me so far? Now is a great time to try this out in your browser to make sure that everything is lining up. It will look kind of funny because we haven't really put anything on the left side of the table yet, but it's worth a try. Figure 13.22 shows what we've got so far.

Figure 13.22.

The table so far.

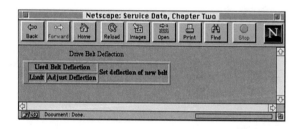

Next row! Check your grid if you need to. Here, the first cell is the heading for Alternator, and it spans this row and the one below it. Are you getting the hang of this yet?

```
<TR>
    <TH ROWSPAN=2>Alternator</TD>
```

The next three cells are pretty easy because they don't span anything. Here are their definitions:

```
<TD>Models without AC</TD>
<TD>10mm</TD>
<TD>5-7mm</TD>
```

The last cell in this row is just like the first one:

```
<TD ROWSPAN=2>5-7mm</TD>
</TR>
```

13

We're up to row number four. In this one, because of the ROWSPANs from the previous row, there are only three cells to define: the cell for Models with AC, and the two cells for the numbers:

```
<TR>
    <TD>Models with AC</TD>
    <TD>12mm</TD>
    <TD>6-8mm</TD>
</TR>
```

NOTE

In this table, I've made the Alternator cell a heading cell and the AC cells plain data. This is mostly an aesthetic decision on my part; I could just as easily have made all three into headings.

Now for the final row—this one should be easy. The first cell (Power Steering Oil Pump) spans two columns (the one with Alternator in it, and the With/Without AC column). The remaining three are just one cell each:

```
<TR>
    <TH COLSPAN=2>Power Steering Oil Pump</TD>
    <TD>12.5mm</TD>
    <TD>7.9mm</TD>
    <TD>6-8mm</TD>
</TR>
```

That's it. You're done laying out the rows and columns. That was the hard part; the rest is just fine-tuning. Let's try looking at it again to make sure there are no strange errors (see Figure 13.23).

Figure 13.23.

The table: the next step.

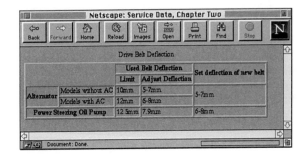

Now that you have all the rows and cells laid out, adjust the alignments within the cells. The numbers, at least, should be centered. Because they make up the majority of the table, let's center the default alignment for each row:

```
<TR ALIGN=CENTER>
```

But the labels along the left side of the table (Alternator, Models With/Without AC, and Power Steering Oil Pump) look funny if they're centered, so let's align them left:

```
<TH ROWSPAN=2 ALIGN=LEFT>Alternator</TD>
<TD ALIGN=LEFT>Models without AC</TD>

<TD ALIGN=LEFT>Models with AC</TD>

<TH COLSPAN=2 ALIGN=LEFT>Power Steering Oil Pump</TD>
```

Finally, the last bit of fine-tuning I've done is to put some line breaks in the longer headings so that the columns are a little narrower. Because the text in the data is pretty short to start with, I don't have to worry too much about the table looking funny if it gets too narrow. Here are the lines I modified:

```
<TH ROWSPAN=2>Set<BR>deflection<BR>of new belt</TH>
<TH>Adjust<BR>Deflection</TH>
```

Voilà—the final table, with everything properly laid out and aligned! Figure 13.24 shows the final result.

Figure 13.24.

The final Drive Belt Deflection table.

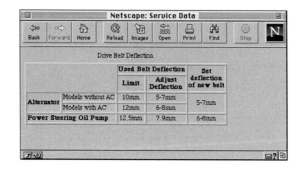

NOTE

If you got lost at any time, the best thing you can do is pull out your handy text editor and try it yourself, following along tag by tag. After you've done it a couple of times, it becomes easier.

Here's the full text for the table example:

```
<HTML>
<HEAD>
<TITLE>Service Data</TITLE>
</HEAD>
<BODY>
<TABLE BORDER>
<CAPTION>Drive Belt Deflection</CAPTION>
<TR>
```

13

```
    <TH ROWSPAN=2 COLSPAN=2></TH>
    <TH COLSPAN=2>Used Belt Deflection</TH>
    <TH ROWSPAN=2>Set<BR>deflection<BR>of new belt</TH>
</TR>
<TR>
    <TH>Limit</TH>
    <TH>Adjust<BR>Deflection</TH>
</TR>
<TR ALIGN=CENTER>
    <TH ROWSPAN=2 ALIGN=LEFT>Alternator</TD>
    <TD ALIGN=LEFT>Models without AC</TD>
    <TD>10mm</TD>
    <TD>5-7mm</TD>
    <TD ROWSPAN=2>5-7mm</TD>
</TR>
<TR ALIGN=CENTER>
    <TD ALIGN=LEFT>Models with AC</TD>
    <TD>12mm</TD>
    <TD>6-8mm</TD>
</TR>
<TR ALIGN=CENTER>
    <TH COLSPAN=2 ALIGN=LEFT>Power Steering Oil Pump</TD>
    <TD>12.5mm</TD>
    <TD>7.9mm</TD>
    <TD>6-8mm</TD>
</TR>
</TABLE>
</BODY>
</HTML>
```

Defining Table and Column Widths

All the tables we've created up to this point relied on the browser itself to decide how wide the table and column widths were going to be. In many cases, this is the best way to make sure your tables are viewable on different browsers with different screen sizes and widths; simply let the browser decide. In other cases, however, you may want to have more control over how wide your tables and columns are, particularly if the defaults the browser comes up with are really strange. In this section you'll learn a couple ways to do just this.

Setting Breaks in Text

Often the easiest way to make small changes to how a table is laid out is by using line breaks (
 tags), using the NOWRAP attribute, or using both <BR> and NOWRAP together.

Line breaks are particularly useful if you have a table in which most of the cells are small and only one or two cells have longer data. As long as the screen width can handle it, the browser generally just creates really long rows, which looks rather funny in some tables.

13

By putting in line breaks, you can wrap that row in a shorter column so that it looks more like the table shown in Figure 13.25.

Figure 13.25.

The long row fixed with <BR>.

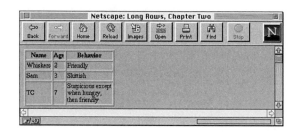

On the other hand, you might have a table in which a cell is being wrapped for which you want all the data on one line. (This can be particularly important for things such as form elements within table cells where you want the label and the input field to stay together.) In this instance, you can add the NOWRAP attribute to the <TH> or <TD> tags, and the browser keeps all the data in that cell on the one line. Note that you can always add <BR> tags by hand to that same cell and get line breaks exactly where you want them.

Be careful when you hard-code table cells with line breaks and NOWRAP attributes. Remember, your table might be viewed in many different screen widths. Try resizing the window in which your table is being viewed and see whether your table can still hold up under different widths with all your careful formatting in place. For the most part, you should try to let the browser itself format your table and make minor adjustments only when necessary.

Table Widths

The WIDTH attribute to the <TABLE> tag defines how wide the table will be on the page. WIDTH can have a value that is either the exact width of the table (in pixels) or a percentage (such as 50 percent or 75 percent) of the current screen width, which can therefore change if the window is resized. If WIDTH is specified, the width of the columns within the table can be compressed or expanded to fit the required width. For example, Figure 13.26 shows a table that would have been quite narrow if it had been left alone. But this table has stretched to fit a 100-percent screen width using the WIDTH attribute, which causes Netscape to spread out all the columns to fit the screen.

13

Figure 13.26.

Table widths in Netscape.

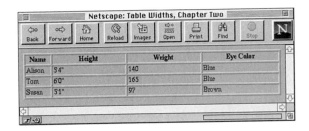

 NOTE

Trying to make the table too narrow for the data it contains might be impossible, in which case Netscape tries to get as close as it can to your desired width.

It's always a better idea to specify your table widths as percentages rather than as specific pixel widths. Because you don't know how wide the browser window will be, using percentages allows your table to be reformatted to whatever width it is. Using specific pixel widths may cause your table to run off the page.

Column Widths

The WIDTH attribute can also be used on individual cells (<TH> or <TD>) to indicate the width of individual columns. As with table width, the WIDTH tag in calls can be an exact pixel width or a percentage (which is taken as a percentage of the full table width). As with table widths, using percentages rather than specific pixel widths is a better idea because it allows your table to be displayed regardless of the window size.

Column widths are useful when you want to have multiple columns of identical widths, regardless of their contents (for example, for some forms of page layout). Figure 13.27 shows the same table from the previous example that spans the width of the screen, although this time the first column is 10 percent of the table width and the remaining three columns are 30 percent. Netscape adjusts the column widths to fit both the width of the screen and the given percentages.

Figure 13.27.

Column widths.

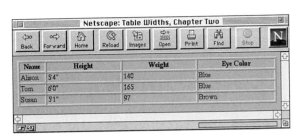

Other Features of Tables

Sick of tables yet? There are only a couple table features left: border widths, cell spacing, cell padding, and adding color.

Border Widths

You can also change the width of the border drawn around the table. If BORDER has a numeric value, the border around the outside of the table is drawn with that pixel width. The default is BORDER=1; BORDER=0 suppresses the border (just as if you had omitted the BORDER attribute altogether).

NOTE The border value applies only to the shaded border along the outside edge of the table, not to the borders around the cells. See the next section for that value.

Figure 13.28 shows an example of a table with a border of 10 pixels.

Figure 13.28.
Table border widths.

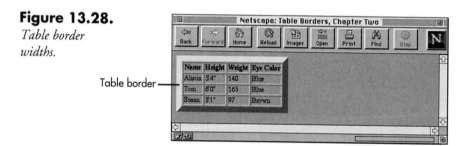

Cell Spacing

Cell spacing is similar to cell padding except that it affects the amount of space between cells—that is, the width of the shaded lines that separate the cells. The CELLSPACING attribute in the <TABLE> tag affects the spacing for the table. Cell spacing is 2 by default.

Cell spacing also includes the outline around the table, which is just inside the table's border (as set by the BORDER attribute). Experiment with it, and you can see the difference. For example, Figure 13.29 shows an example of a table with cell spacing of 8 and a border of 4.

13

Figure 13.29.

Cell spacing (and borders).

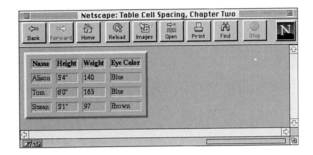

Cell Padding

Cell padding is the amount of space between the edges of the cells and the cell's contents. By default, Netscape draws its tables with a cell padding of 1 pixel. You can add more space by adding the CELLPADDING attribute to the <TABLE> tag, with a value in pixels for the amount of cell padding you want. Figure 13.30 shows an example of a table with cell padding of 10 pixels.

Figure 13.30.

Cell padding.

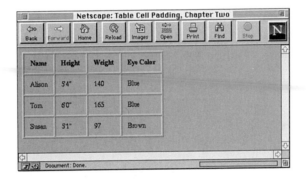

The CELLPADDING attribute with a value of 0 causes the edges of the cells to touch the edges of the cell's contents (which doesn't look very good).

Color in Tables

Just when tables were becoming consistent amongst browsers, someone had to come along and add a whole bunch of new features. That someone was Microsoft, with their Internet Explorer browser, which supports several attributes that allow you to change the color of various parts of the table. Netscape has since included support for background colors in the newest version of its browser, but for the most part these attributes are very new and not commonly supported by most browsers on the Web, and so keep this in mind if you choose to use these tags.

13

To change the background color of a table, a row, or a cell inside a row, use the BGCOLOR attribute to the <TABLE>, <TR>, <TH>, or <TD> tags. Just like in <BODY>, the value of BGCOLOR is a color specified as a hexadecimal triplet or, in Explorer only, one of the seven color names: Black, White, Green, Maroon, Olive, Navy, Purple, Gray, Red, Yellow, Blue, Teal, Lime, Aqua, Fuchsia, or Silver.

Each background color overrides the background color of its enclosing element. So, for example, a table background overrides the page background, a row background overrides the tables, and any cell colors override all other colors. If you nest tables inside cells, that nested table has the background color of the cell that encloses it.

Also, if you change the color of a cell, don't forget to change the color of the text inside it using <FONT COLOR...> so you can still read it.

Here's an example of changing the background and cell colors in a table. Here I've created a checkerboard using an HTML table. The table itself is white, with alternating cells in black. The checkers (here, red and black circles) are images. The result in Explorer is shown in Figure 13.31.

> **NOTE**
>
> In order for table cells to show up with background colors, they have to have some sort of contents. Simply putting a <BR> tag in empty cells works fine.

```
<HTML>
<HEAD>
<TITLE>Checkerboard</TITLE>
</HEAD>
<BODY>
<TABLE BGCOLOR="#FFFFFF" WIDTH=50%>
<TR ALIGN=CENTER>
   <TD BGCOLOR="#000000" WIDTH=33%><IMG SRC="redcircle.gif"></TD>
   <TD BGCOLOR="#000000" WIDTH=33%><IMG SRC="redcircle.gif"></TD>
   <TD BGCOLOR="#000000" WIDTH=33%><IMG SRC="redcircle.gif"></TD>
</TR>
<TR ALIGN=CENTER>
   <TD> <IMG SRC="blackcircle.gif"></TD>
   <TD BGCOLOR="#000000"><BR></TD>
   <TD><BR></TD>
</TR>
<TR ALIGN=CENTER>
   <TD BGCOLOR="#000000"><BR></TD>
   <TD><IMG SRC="blackcircle.gif"><BR></TD>
   <TD BGCOLOR="#000000"><IMG SRC="blackcircle.gif"> </TD>
</TR>
</TABLE>
</BODY>
</HTML>
```

Internet Explorer also allows you to change the colors of the elements of the table's border using the BORDERCOLOR, BORDERCOLORLIGHT, and BORDERCOLORDARK attributes. Each of these attributes takes either a color number or name and can be used in <TABLE>, <TD>, <TH>, or <TD>. Like background colors, the border colors each override the colors of the enclosing element. All three require the enclosing <TABLE> tag to have the BORDER attribute set.

These extensions are only (currently) supported in Internet Explorer.

☐ BORDERCOLOR sets the color of the border, overriding the 3D look of the default border.

☐ BORDERCOLORDARK sets the dark component of 3D-look borders.

☐ BORDERCOLORLIGHT sets the light component the 3D-look borders.

Figure 13.31.
Table cell colors.

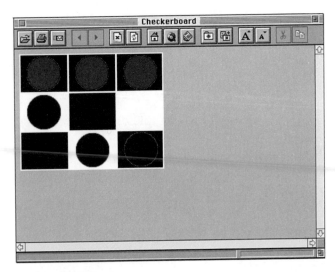

Alternatives to Tables

Tables are great for summarizing large amounts of information in a way that can be quickly and easily scanned. In terms of information design, tables are right up there with link menus (as described earlier in this book) for structuring data so that your reader can get in and out of your pages.

The difficulty with tables is that although most newer browsers do support them, they come out particularly messed up in browsers that don't. You won't lose all the data in the table, but you will lose the formatting, which can make your data just as unreadable as if it hadn't been included at all. For example, Figure 13.32 shows a table that looks pretty nice in Netscape.

13

Figure 13.32.

A table in Netscape 1.1.

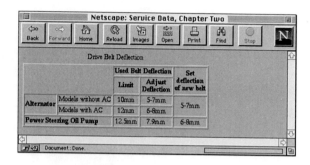

Figure 13.33 shows the same table as viewed by an earlier version of Netscape that didn't support tables.

Figure 13.33.

The same table in Netscape 1.0.

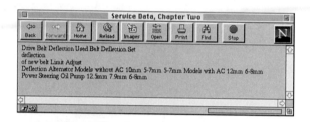

Pretty gross, huh? It's also really confusing for your readers if they're not using a browser that supports tables and you haven't warned them about it.

To work around tables for browsers that don't support them, you have several choices. Figure 13.34 shows a simple HTML table, and each of the following choices shows methods of working around that table:

Figure 13.34.

A simple table.

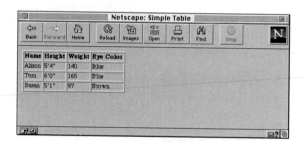

- ☐ Don't use a table at all. Some layouts can work just as well as a list or series of lists (Figure 13.35).

- ☐ Use an image of a table rather than an actual table. If the table is small enough and you use only black and white, this can be an excellent workaround to the lack of tables. And, with an image, you can also use preformatted text inside the ALT tag to mock the effect of the table in browsers that can't view images (Figure 13.36).

13

Figure 13.35.

The same table as a definition list.

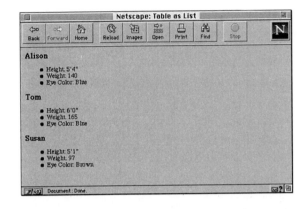

Figure 13.36.

The same table as an image.

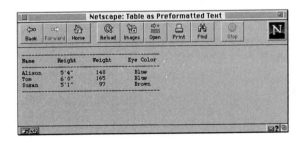

☐ Use preformatted text (the <PRE> tag) to line up your information in table-like columns—creating tables without the table tags. Keep in mind that preformatted text is usually displayed in a monospaced font such as Courier, so the appearance of the table will not be as nice as it was in table form (Figure 13.37).

Figure 13.37.

The same table as preformatted text.

☐ Link the table externally. Instead of putting the table directly on your page, consider putting the table on a separate page by itself and creating a link to it on the original page with a suitable description, for example:

```
<P><A HREF="heights.html">A table</A> of the various
heights, weights and eye colors of people in my group.
Your browser must support tables to be able to view this</P>
```

The most complicated way to create tables that work even in non-table-enabled browsers is to design your tables so that the layout works equally well in both. For example, if you use text elements such as headings and block quotes inside table cells, those elements will end up on their own lines if tables aren't supported. Using trial and error and testing your pages in both kinds of browsers, you can often come up with a layout that works equally well inside and outside tables.

One commonly used trick along those lines is to include <P> or <BR> tags at the end of selected cells. By including them at the end of the cell, they're ignored in browsers that support tables but provide line breaks at the appropriate spots in browsers that don't support tables. So, for example, with the color table you created in Exercise 13.1, let's add line breaks to the last cell in each row:

```
<TABLE BORDER>
<TR>
     <TH><BR></TH>
     <TH>Red</TH>
     <TH>Yellow</TH>
     <TH>Blue<BR></TH>
</TR>
<TR>
     <TH>Red</TH>
     <TD>Red</TD>
     <TD>Orange</TD>
     <TD>Purple<BR></TD>
</TR>
<TR>
     <TH>Yellow</TH>
     <TD>Orange</TD>
     <TD>Yellow</TD>
     <TD>Green<BR></TD>
</TR>
<TR>
     <TH>Blue</TH>
     <TD>Purple</TD>
     <TD>Green</TD>
     <TD>Blue<BR></TD>
</TR>
</TABLE>
```

The <BR> tags won't make any difference to the layout of the table in browsers that understand tables (because they're at the end of the cell), but they are significant to browsers that don't. The paragraph tags make actual paragraph breaks so that each row is on its own line. It's not a replacement for a table, but it does make it a little less confusing to read.

Summary

In this chapter, you've learned all about tables. Tables allow you to arrange your information in rows and columns so that your readers can scan the table quickly and get to the information they need.

While working with tables in this chapter, you've learned about headings and data, captions, defining rows and cells, aligning information within cells, and creating cells that span multiple rows or columns. With these features you can create tables for most purposes.

As you're constructing tables, it's helpful to keep the following steps in mind:

☐ Sketch your table and where the rows and columns fall. Mark which cells span multiple rows and columns.

☐ Start with a basic framework and lay out the rows, headings, and data row by row and cell by cell in HTML. Include row and column spans as necessary. Test frequently in a browser to make sure it's all working correctly.

☐ Modify the alignment in the rows to reflect the alignment of the majority of the cells.

☐ Modify the alignment for individual cells.

☐ Adjust line breaks, if necessary.

☐ Make other refinements such as cell spacing, padding, or color.

☐ Test your table in multiple browsers. Different browsers can have different ideas of how to lay out your table or be more accepting of errors in your HTML code.

Table 13.1 presents a quick summary of the HTML table-creating tags that you've learned about in this chapter.

Table 13.1. The table tags.

Tag	Attribute	Use
`<TABLE>...</TABLE>`		Indicates a table.
	BORDER	An attribute of the `<TABLE>` tag, indicating whether the table will be drawn with a border. The default is no border. If BORDER has a value, that value is the width of the shaded border around the table.
	CELLSPACING	Defines the amount of space between the cells in the table.
	CELLPADDING	Defines the amount of space between the edges of the cell and its contents.
`<CAPTION>...</CAPTION>`		Creates an optional caption for the table.
`<TR>...</TR>`		Defines a table row, which can contain heading and data cells.

13

continues

Table 13.1. continued

Tag	Attribute	Use
<TH>..</TH>		Defines a table cell containing a heading. Heading cells are usually indicated by boldface and centered both horizontally and vertically within the cell.
<TD>...</TD>		Defines a table cell containing data. Table cells are in a regular font, and are left-justified and vertically centered within the cell.
	ALIGN	When used with <TABLE>, possible values are LEFT and RIGHT. Determines the alignment of the table and indicates that text following the table will be wrapped alongside it.
		When used with <CAPTION>, the possible values for most browsers are TOP and BOTTOM. ALIGN indicates whether the caption will be placed at the top of the table (the default) or the bottom. In Internet Explorer, the possible values are LEFT, RIGHT, and CENTER, and indicate the horizontal alignment of the caption.
		When used with <TR>, the possible values are LEFT, CENTER, and RIGHT, which indicate the horizontal alignment of the cells within that row (overriding the default alignment of heading and table cells).
		When used with <TH> or <TD>, the possible values are also LEFT, CENTER, and RIGHT, which override both the row's alignment and any default cell alignment.
	VALIGN	When used with captions in Internet Explorer, possible values are TOP and BOTTOM and indicate the positioning of

Tag	Attribute	Use
		the caption relative to the table (same as ALIGN in most other browsers).
		When used with <TR>, possible values are TOP, MIDDLE, and BOTTOM. VALIGN indicates the vertical alignment of the cells within that row (overriding the defaults).
		When used with <TH> or <TD>, the same possible values are used, and VALIGN overrides both the row's vertical alignment and the default cell alignment.
		In Netscape, VALIGN can also have the value BASELINE.
	ROWSPAN	Used within a <TH> or <TD> tag, ROWSPAN indicates the number of cells below this one that this cell will span.
	COLSPAN	Used within a <TH> or <TD> tag, COLSPAN indicates the number of cells to the right of this one that this cell will span.
	BGCOLOR	(Internet Explorer and Netscape 3.0 extension) Can be used with any of the table tags to change the background color of that table element. Cell colors override row colors, which override table colors. The value can be a hexadecimal color number or a color name.
	BORDERCOLOR	(Internet Explorer extension) Can be used with any of the table tags to change the color of the border around that element. The value can be a hexadecimal color number or a color name.

continues

13

Table 13.1. continued

Tag	Attribute	Use
	BORDERCOLORLIGHT	(Internet Explorer extension) Same as BORDERCOLOR, except it affects only the light component of a 3D-look border.
	BORDERCOLORDARK	(Internet Explorer extension) Same as BORDERCOLOR, except it affects only the dark component of a 3D-look border.
	NOWRAP	Used within a `<TH>` or `<TD>` tag, NOWRAP prevents the browser from wrapping the contents of the cell.
	WIDTH	When used with `<TABLE>`, indicates the width of the table, in exact pixel values or as a percentage of page width (for example, 50 percent).
		When used with `<TH>` or `<TD>`, WIDTH indicates width of the cell, in exact pixel values or as a percentage of table width (for example, 50 percent).

Q&A

Q Tables are a real hassle to lay out, especially when you get into row and column spans. Exercise 13.3 was awful.

A You're right. Tables are a tremendous pain to lay out by hand like this. However, if you're writing filters and tools to generate HTML code, having the table defined like this makes more sense because you can programmatically just write out each row in turn. Sooner or later, we'll all be working in HTML filters anyhow (let's hope), so you won't have to do this by hand for long.

Q My tables work fine in Netscape, but they're all garbled in many other browsers. What did I do wrong?

A Did you remember to close all your `<TR>`, `<TH>`, and `<TD>` tags? Make sure you've put in the matching `</TR>`, `</TH>`, and `</TD>` tags, respectively. The closing tags may be legally optional, but often other browsers need those tags in order to understand table layout.

13

Q **Can you nest tables, putting a table inside a single table cell?**

A Sure! As I mentioned in this chapter, you can put any HTML code you want to inside a table cell, and that can include other tables.

Q **Why does most of the world use ALIGN for positioning a caption at the top or bottom of a page, but Internet Explorer does something totally different?**

A I don't know. And, worse, Internet Explorer claims they got that definition from HTML 3.2, but no version of HTML 3.2 or the newer tables specification has it defined in that way. Hopefully, future versions of Internet Explorer will conform to the definition most of the world is following so that there isn't this confusion.

13

Chapter 14

Frames and Linked Windows

This week we have one final subject to cover: that of frames. Frames are a very advanced new feature that provides an entirely different way of looking at Web pages. However, they are also currently supported only in Netscape 2.0, and even worse, pages created using frames are not easily backward-compatible with other browers.

In this chapter you'll learn all about the following topics:

- ☐ What frames are, what they give you in terms of layout, and who supports them
- ☐ Working with linked windows
- ☐ Working with frames
- ☐ Creating complex framesets

What Are Frames and Who Supports Them?

Most of the features and tags discussed in previous chapters will, as a rule, basically work on just about any Web browser. The appearance of the page might not be exactly what you had expected, but at the very least, people with older Web browsers can still view the text and links contained on the page.

In this chapter, however, you'll learn about a new set of tags—used to create frames—that currently work only with Netscape 2.0 (and throughout this chapter, whenever I refer to Netscape, I'll mean specifically Netscape 2.0 or higher). In addition, due to the nature of these tags, Web pages created using frames simply won't display using other browsers. You can, however, use special tags to create separate frame-based and non-frame-based versions of your pages, as you'll learn later in this chapter. The fact that frames can't be displayed on other Web browsers has made frames one of the most hotly debated topics of the "Netscape versus the rest" debate.

NOTE

> Netscape plans to submit the new frame tags for recognition as part of the HTML 3.2 standard, but it will probably be some time before you see the arrival of other browsers that include the feature discussed in this chapter.

This having been said, if you plan to develop presentations specifically for Netscape 2.0, the capabilities provided by the use of frames bring an entirely new level of layout control to Web publishing. Take, for example, the demonstration Web page created by Netscape Communications that is shown in Figure 14.1.

In this one screen, Netscape has integrated information that would previously have taken many separate screen loads. In addition, because the information displayed on the page is separated into individual areas or frames, the contents of a single frame can be updated without the contents of any other frame being affected. For example, if you click any of the hotlinks associated with the photos in the left frame, the contents of the large frame on the right are automatically updated to display the personal details of the selected staff member. When this occurs, the contents of the left frame and the bottom frame are not affected.

Apart from the demonstration pages provided by Netscape, other sites are currently adding frame support to their Web pages. Of these, one site you might find handy is the color index page developed by InfiNet located at `http://www.infi.net/wwwimages/colorindex.html` (see Figure 14.2). This page provides a handy reference for many of the colors you can use for backgrounds and text colors, with the colors in the frame on the left and the results in the frame on the right.

14

Figure 14.1.

A sample Web page with frames.

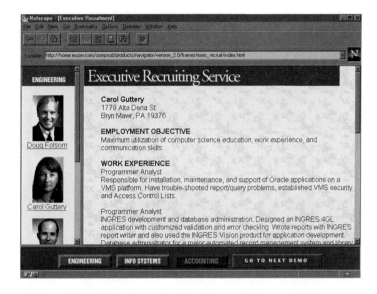

Figure 14.2.

The InfiNet color index.

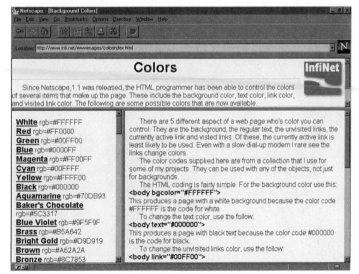

Working with Linked Windows

14

Before looking at how frames are added to a page, you first need to learn about a new attribute of the <A> tag called TARGET. This new attribute takes the following form:

TARGET="*window_name*"

Usually, when you click a hyperlink, the contents of the new page replace the current page in the browser window. In a windowed environment, however, there is technically no reason why the contents of the new page can't be displayed in a new window, leaving the contents of the calling page displayed onscreen in their own window.

The TARGET attribute enables you to do just that by telling the Web browser to display the information pointed to by a hyperlink in a window called *window_name*. You can basically call the new window anything you want, with the only proviso being that you not use names that start with an underscore (_). These names are reserved for a set of special TARGET values that you'll learn about later in the section "Magic TARGET Names."

When you use the TARGET attribute inside an <A> tag, Netscape first checks to see whether a window with the name *window_name* exists. If it does, the document pointed to by the hyperlink replaces the current contents of *window_name*. On the other hand, if no window called *window_name* currently exists, a new browser window is opened and given the name *window_name*. The document pointed to by the hyperlink is then loaded into the newly created window.

Exercise 14.1: Working with windows.

EXERCISE

In this exercise, you'll create four separate HTML documents that use hyperlinks, including the TARGET attribute. These hyperlinks will be used to open two new windows called first_window and second_window, as shown in Figure 14.3. The top window is the original Web browser window, first_window is on the bottom left, and second_window the bottom right.

Figure 14.3.

Hyperlinks can be made to open new windows for each of the pages they point to.

14

First, create the document to be displayed by the main Web browser window, shown in Figure 14.4, by opening your text editor of choice and entering the following lines of code:

 INPUT

```
<HTML>
<HEAD>
<TITLE>Target Parent Window</TITLE>
</HEAD>
<BODY>
<H1>Target Parent Window</H1>
<P>
<A HREF="target2.html" TARGET="first_window">Open</A>
 a new window called first_window.
<BR>
<A HREF="target3.html" TARGET="second_window">Open</A>
 a new window called second_window.
</P>
<P>
<A HREF="target4.html" TARGET="first_window">Load</A>
 some new text into first_window.
</P>
</BODY>
</HTML>
```

OUTPUT

Figure 14.4.
The Target Parent window.

Save this HTML source as target1.html.

Next, create a document called target2.html that looks like the page shown in Figure 14.5, by entering the following code:

INPUT

```
<HTML>
<HEAD>
<TITLE>Target First Window</TITLE>
</HEAD>
<BODY>
<H1>Target First Window</H1>
</BODY>
</HTML>
```

14

Figure 14.5.
`target2.html`
*displayed in the
Web browser
window named*
`first_window`.

After saving `target2.html`, create another document called `target3.html` that looks like the page shown Figure 14.6. Do this by entering the following code:

```
<HTML>
<HEAD>
<TITLE>Target Second Window</TITLE>
</HEAD>
<BODY>
<H1>Target Second Window</H1>
</BODY>
</HTML>
```

OUTPUT

Figure 14.6.
`target3.html`
*displayed in the
Web browser
window named*
`second_window`.

And finally, create a fourth document, called `target4.html`, that looks like this:

```
<HTML>
<HEAD>
<TITLE>Target First Window</TITLE>
</HEAD>
<BODY>
<H1>Target First Window</H1>
<P>But this time with new text...</P>
</BODY>
</HTML>
```

To complete the exercise, load `target1.html` into your Web browser, and click the top two hyperlinks. This action opens two new windows with the contents of the targets in each one.

Note that the new windows probably won't be laid out like the ones shown in Figure 14.3; instead they'll usually overlap each other.

Finally, click the third hyperlink to replace the contents of first_window with the Web page defined by target4.html, as shown in Figure 14.7.

Figure 14.7.
target4.html
displayed in the
Web browser
window named
first_window.

The <BASE> Tag

When using the TARGET attribute with links, you'll sometimes encounter a situation in which all or most of the hyperlinks on a Web page point to the same window—especially when using frames, as you'll discover in the following section.

In such cases, instead of including a TARGET attribute for each <A> tag, you can use another tag, <BASE>, to define a global target for all the links of a Web page. The <BASE> tag takes the following form:

```
<BASE TARGET="window_name">
```

If you include the <BASE> tag in the <HEAD>...</HEAD> block of a document, every <A> tag that does not have a corresponding TARGET attribute will display the document it points to in the window specified by <BASE TARGET="window_name">. For example, if the tag <BASE TARGET="first_window"> had been included in the HTML source for table1.html, the three hyperlinks could have been written this way:

```
<HTML>
<HEAD>
<TITLE>Target Parent Window</TITLE>
<BASE TARGET="first_window">        <!-- add BASE TARGET="value" here -->
</HEAD>
<BODY>
<H1>Target Parent Window</H1>
<P>
<A HREF="target2.html">Open</A>        <!-- no need to include a TARGET -->
 a new window called first_window.
<BR>
<A HREF="target3.html" TARGET="second_window">Open</A>
 a new window called second_window.
</P>
<P>
```

14

```
<A HREF="target4.html">Load</A>      <!-- no need to include a TARGET -->
 some new text into first_window.
</P>
</BODY>
</HTML>
```

In this case, `target2.html` and `target4.html` are loaded into the default window assigned by the `<BASE>` tag; `target3.html` overrides the default by defining its own target window.

You can also override the window assigned by the `<BASE>` tag by using one of two special window names. If you use `TARGET="_blank"` in a hyperlink, a new browser window is opened that does not have a name associated with it. Alternatively, if you use `TARGET="_self"`, the current window is used rather than the one defined by the `<BASE>` tag.

Working with Frames

The introduction of frames in Netscape 2.0 heralds a new era for Web publishers. With frames, you can create Web pages that look and feel entirely different from other Web pages—pages that have tables of tables, banners, footnotes, and sidebars, just to name a few common features that frames can give you.

At the same time, frames change what a "page" means to the browser and to the reader. Unlike all the previous examples, which use a single HTML page to display a screen of information, when you create Web sites using frames, a single screen actually consists of a number of separate HTML documents that interact with each other. Figure 14.8 shows how a minimum of four separate documents is needed to create the screen shown earlier in Figure 14.1.

Figure 14.8.

Separate HTML documents must be created for each frame.

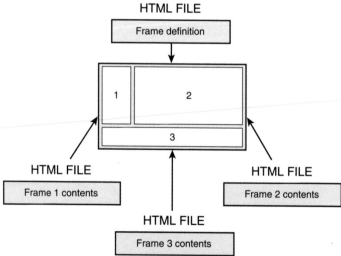

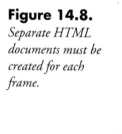

14

The first HTML document you need to create is called the frame definition document. In this document, you enter the HTML code that describes the layout of each frame and indicate the name of separate HTML document that contains the physical information to be displayed. The three remaining HTML documents contain normal HTML tags that define the physical contents of each separate frame area. These are the documents referenced by the frame definition document.

NEW TERM
> The *frame definition document* is the page that contains the layout of each frame and the names of the HTML documements that will fill that frame.

The <FRAMESET> Tag

To create a frame definition document, you use the <FRAMESET> tag. When used in an HTML document, the <FRAMESET> tag replaces the <BODY> tag, as shown here:

```
<HTML>
<HEAD>
<TITLE>Page Title</TITLE>
</HEAD>
<FRAMESET>
    your frame definition goes here.
</FRAMESET>
</HTML>
```

It's important to understand up front how a frame definition document differs from a normal HTML document. If you include a <FRAMESET> tag in an HTML document, you cannot also include a <BODY> tag. Basically, the two tags are mutually exclusive. In addition, no other formatting tags, hyperlinks, or document text should be included in a frame definition document, except in one special case (the <NOFRAME> tag) which you'll learn about in the section called, appropriately, "The <NOFRAME> Tag," later in this chapter. The <FRAMESET> tags contain only the definitions for the frames in this document: what's called the page's frameset.

NEW TERM
> A *frameset* is the set of frames defined by the <FRAMESET> tags in the frame definition document.

14

The COLS Attribute

When you define a <FRAMESET> tag, you must include one of two attributes as part of the tag definition. The first of these attributes is the COLS attribute, which takes the following form:

```
<FRAMESET COLS="column width, column width, ...">
```

The COLS attribute tells Netscape to split the screen into a number of vertical frames whose widths are defined by *column width* values separated by commas. You define the width of each frame in one of three ways: explicitly in pixels, as a percentage of the total width of the <FRAMESET>, or with an asterisk (*). When you use the *, Netscape uses as much space as possible for the specified frame.

When included in a complete frame definition, the following <FRAMESET> tag creates a screen with three vertical frames (see Figure 14.9). The first frame is 100 pixels wide, the second is 50 percent of the width of the screen, and the third uses all the remaining space.

INPUT   `<FRAMESET COLS="100,50%,*">`

OUTPUT

Figure 14.9.

The COLS attribute defines the number of vertical frames or columns in a frameset.

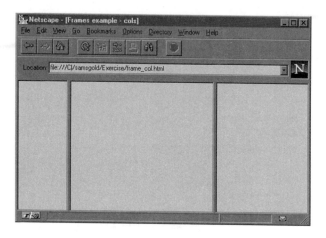

NOTE

Because you're designing Web pages that will be used on various screen sizes, you should use absolute frame sizes sparingly. And, whenever you do use an absolute size, ensure that one of the other frames is defined using an * to take up all the remaining screen space.

TIP

To define a frameset with three equal-width columns, use COLS="*, *, *". This way, you won't have to mess around with percentages, because Netscape automatically gives an equal amount of space to each frame assigned an * width.

14

The ROWS **Attribute**

The ROWS attribute works the same as the COLS attribute, except that it splits the screen into horizontal frames rather than vertical ones. For example, to split the screen into two equal-height frames, as shown in Figure 14.10, you could write either of the following:

INPUT
```
<FRAMESET ROWS="50%,50%">
```
```
<FRAMESET ROWS="*, *">
```

OUTPUT

Figure 14.10.
The ROWS attribute defines the number of horizontal frames or rows in a frameset.

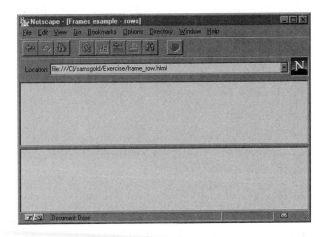

NOTE

If you try either of the preceding examples for yourself, you'll find that the <FRAMESET> tag does not appear to work. The reason for this is that currently no contents are defined for the rows or columns in the frameset. To define the contents, you need to used the <FRAME> tag, which is discussed in the next section.

The <FRAME> **Tag**

After you have your basic frameset laid out, you need to associate an HTML document with each frame. To do this, you use the <FRAME> tag, which takes the following form:

```
<FRAME SRC="document URL">
```

For each frame defined in the <FRAMESET> tag, you must include a corresponding <FRAME> tag, as shown here:

INPUT
```
<FRAMESET ROWS="*,*,*">
    <FRAME SRC="document1.html">
    <FRAME SRC="document2.html">
    <FRAME SRC="document3.html">
</FRAMESET>
```

14

In this example, a frameset with three equal-height horizontal frames has been defined (see Figure 14.11). The contents of document1.html are displayed in the first frame, document2.html in the second frame, and document3.html in the third frame.

Figure 14.11.

The <FRAME> tag is used to define the contents of each frame.

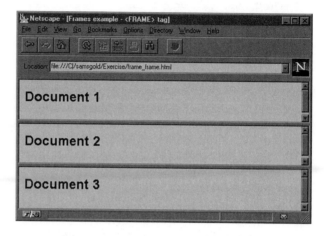

 TIP

When creating frame definition documents, you might find it helpful to indent the <FRAME> tags so they're separated from the <FRAMESET> tags in your HTML document. Doing so has no effect on the appearance of the resulting Web pages but does tend to make the HTML source easier to read.

Additional Attributes

A few extra attributes can be assigned to a <FRAME> tag to give you additional control over how the user interacts with your frames. Table 14.1 presents the details about them.

Table 14.1. Control attributes for the <FRAME> tag.

Attribute	Value	Description
SCROLLING	AUTO (default)	By default, if the contents of a frame take up more space than the area available to the frame, Netscape automatically adds scrollbars to either the side or the bottom of the frame so that the user can scroll through the document.
SCROLLING	NO	Setting the value of SCROLLING to NO disables the use of scrollbars for the current frame. (Note that if you set SCROLLING="NO" but there is more text in

Attribute	Value	Description
		the document than can fit inside the frame, the user will not be able to scroll the additional text into view.)
SCROLLING	YES	If you set SCROLLING to YES, the scrollbars are included in the frame regardless of whether they are required.
NORESIZE		By default, users can move the position of borders around each frame on the current screen by grabbing the border and moving it with their mouse. To lock the borders of a frame and prevent them from being moved, use the NORESIZE attribute.
MARGINHEIGHT	*pixels*	To adjust the margin that appears above and below a document within a frame, set the MARGINHEIGHT to the number indicated by *pixels*.
MARGINWIDTH	*pixels*	The MARGINWIDTH attribute enables you to adjust the margin on the left and right side of a frame to the number indicated by *pixels*.

The <NOFRAME> Tag

If you load a frame definition document into a Web browser that does not support frames, you get only a blank page. To get around this problem, Netscape 2.0 includes a special tag block called <NOFRAME> that enables you to include body text as part of the document. The <NOFRAME> tag takes the following form:

```
<HTML>
<HEAD>
<TITLE>Page Title</TITLE>
</HEAD>
<FRAMESET>
 your frame definition goes here.
<NOFRAME>
  Include any text, hyperlinks, and tags you want to here.
</NOFRAME>
</FRAMESET>
</HTML>
```

None of the text you include inside the <NOFRAME> block will be displayed by Netscape 2.0, but when the page is loaded into a Web browser that does not support frames, it will be displayed. Using both frames' content and tags inside <NOFRAME>, you can create pages that work nearly well with both kinds of browsers.

14

Creating Complex Framesets

The framesets you've learned about so far represent the most basic types of frames that can be displayed by Netscape . But in day-to-day use, you'll rarely use these basic frame designs. In all but the most simple sites, you'll most likely want to use more complex framesets.

Therefore, to help you understand the possible combinations of frames, links, images, and documents that can be used by a Web site, this final section of the chapter explores the topic of complex framesets.

Exercise 14.2: Combining ROWS and COLS.

EXERCISE

The frame layout presented by Figure 14.1, at the beginning of the chapter, provides a good basis for a simple example that explores how you can combine framesets to create complex designs. To remind you of the basic layout, Figure 14.12 shows a screen that uses a similar design but without any contents.

TIP

> When you're designing complex frame layouts, the use of storyboards is an invaluable tool. The storyboard helps you block out the structure of a frameset, and it can also be invaluable when you're adding hyperlinks, as you will see in the next exercise, "Using named frames and hyperlinks."

Figure 14.12.

The "Combining ROWS *and* COLS*" exercise.*

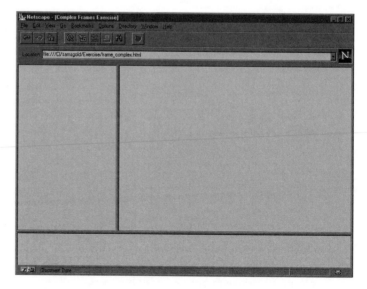

14

In Figure 14.12 the top section of the screen is split into two vertical frames, and the third frame, at the bottom of the page, spans the entire width of the screen. To create a frame definition document that describes this layout, open your text editor and enter the following basic HTML structural details:

```
<HTML>
<HEAD>
<TITLE>Complex Frames Exercise</TITLE>
</HEAD>
<FRAMESET>
</FRAMESET>
</HTML>
```

Next, you must decide whether you need to use a ROWS or COLS attribute in your base <FRAMESET>. To do this, take a look at your storyboard—in this case Figure 14.12—and work out whether any frame areas extend right across the screen or from the top to the bottom of the screen. If any frames extend from the top to the bottom, you need to start with a COLS frameset; otherwise, you need to start with a ROWS frameset. On the other hand, if no frames extend completely across the screen in either direction, you should start with a COLS frameset.

To put it more simply, here are three easily remembered rules:

- ☐ Left to right, use ROWS
- ☐ Top to bottom, use COLS
- ☐ Can't decide, use COLS

NOTE

The reasoning behind the use of the "left to right, use ROWS" rule relates to how Netscape creates frames. Each separate <FRAMESET> definition can split the screen (or a frame) either vertically or horizontally, but not both ways. For this reason, you need to define your framesets in a logical order to ensure that the desired layout is achieved.

In Figure 14.12, the bottom frame extends right across the screen from side to side. As a result, by using the rules mentioned previously, you need to start with a ROWS frameset. To define the base frameset, write this:

```
<FRAMESET ROWS="*, 80">
    <FRAME SRC="dummy.html">  <!-- this is the frame for row 1 -->
    <FRAME SRC="dummy.html">  <!-- this is the frame for row 2 -->
</FRAMESET>
```

Doing this splits the screen into two sections: a small frame at the bottom of the screen that is 80 pixels high, and a large frame at the top of the screen that uses the rest of the available space. Two <FRAME> tags have also been defined to represent the contents of each frame.

TIP
When laying out the basic structure of a frameset, you normally don't want to be bothered with such details as the actual contents of the frames. However, unless you define <FRAME> tags that include a valid document, your frameset will not be displayed properly when it is loaded into Netscape for testing. To get around this problem, create a small empty HTML document called `dummy.html`, and use it for all your frame testing.

Nesting <FRAMESET> Tags

The next step in the process is to split the top frame area into two vertical frames. You achieve this effect by placing a second <FRAMESET> block inside the base <FRAMESET> block. When one <FRAMESET> block is nested inside another, the nested block must replace one of the <FRAME> tags in the outside frameset.

Therefore, to split the top frame into two frame areas, you replace the <FRAME> tag for the first frame with an embedded <FRAMESET> block. Doing this embeds the new frameset inside the area defined for the <FRAME> tag it replaces. Inside the <FRAMESET> tag for this new block, you then need to define a COLS attribute as shown here:

```
<FRAMESET ROWS="*, 80">
    <FRAMESET COLS="30%, *">        <!-- the frame for row 1   -->
        <FRAME SRC="dummy.html">    <!-- has been replaced     -->
        <FRAME SRC="dummy.html">    <!--    by an embedded     -->
    </FRAMESET>                     <!--    frameset block      -->
    <FRAME SRC="dummy.html">  <!-- this is the frame for row 2 -->
</FRAMESET>
```

The embedded COLS frameset defines two columns, the first being 30 percent of the width of the embedded frame area and the second taking up all the remaining space in the embedded frame area. In addition, two <FRAME> tags are embedded inside the <FRAMESET> block to define the contents of each column.

NOTE
When used inside an embedded frameset, any percentage sizes are based on a percentage of the total area of the embedded frame and not as a percentage of the total screen.

Finally, save the finished HTML document to your hard drive, and test it by using Netscape 2.0 or higher. Also, if you happen to have a copy of a different Web browser, try loading the document into it. (You should not see anything when you use the alternative browsers.)

14

Exercise 14.3: Using named frames and hyperlinks.

EXERCISE

As mentioned earlier in this chapter, the frame definition document itself does not describe the contents of each frame. The documents indicated by the SRC attribute of the <FRAME> actually contain the text, images, and tags displayed by the frameset.

As a result, to turn the frame definition document created in the preceding exercise into a fully working, frame-based Web page, you need to add some valid HTML documents to the definition. The frames are so powerful because any HTML document you've created previously can become the SRC for an individual frame. Therefore, it's easy to take the HTML reference documents you've created and integrate them into a frameset. But first, so that you understand what you're about to create, Figure 14.13 shows the complete frameset you'll create in this exercise.

Figure 14.13.

The HTML reference document as a frameset.

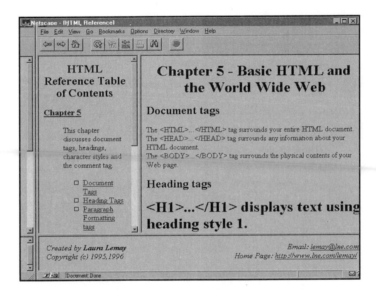

Adding Real Documents to Your Frameset

The first step in the process is a simple one. Take the frameset document you created in the exercise "Combining ROWS and COLS," and save a copy of it in the same directory as the HTML reference documents you created previously. Name the new file `html_frame.html`.

After you've created this new file, change the references to the `dummy.html` file to point to real HTML files (here the changes are highlighted in bold):

```
<FRAMESET ROWS="*, 80">
    <FRAMESET COLS="30%, *">
        <FRAME SRC="html_contents_frame.html">
        <FRAME SRC="05notes_frame.html">
```

14

```
    </FRAMESET>
    <FRAME SRC="html_footer.html">
</FRAMESET>
```

The first `<FRAME>` tag now points to a file called `html_contents_frame.html`. Simply copy the `html_contents.html` file to `html_contents_frame.html`.

TIP

If you're in DOS, you'll need to use an alternative naming scheme such as `cont_f.htm` and `05note_f.htm`.

Do the same for `05notes.html` by copying it to `05notes_frame.html`, and then work through each of the other chapter documents and any other pages they reference.

You next need to make some alterations to `05notes_frame.html`. With frames, you don't need to include `<ADDRESS>` blocks or navigation buttons because, in this exercise, they'll be handled in one way or another by other frames in the frameset. As a result, you should remove the signature and navigation buttons from the bottom of `05notes_frame.html`. In addition, remove any other hyperlinks that join the pages together.

Finally, you need to create a new HTML document called `html_footer.html`. In this document, you'll place the information previously shown in the `<ADDRESS>` block of your individual pages. What you place in this document is up to you; however, keep in mind that it will need to fit into the small 80-pixel-high frame at the bottom of the frameset.

To give you some idea about how you might create the contents of `html_footer.html`, here's the partial HTML source used for Figure 14.13:

```
<TABLE WIDTH="100%">
<TR>
    <TD WIDTH="50%">
        <ADDRESS>
        Created by <B>Laura Lemay</B><BR>
        Copyright (c) 1995,1996
        </ADDRESS>
    </TD>
    <TD WIDTH="50%" ALIGN="RIGHT">
        <ADDRESS>
        Email: <A HREF="mailto:lemay@lne.com">lemay@lne.com</A><BR>
        Home Page: <A HREF="http://www.lne.com/lemay/">
            http://www.lne.com/lemay/</A>
        </ADDRESS>
    </TD>
</TR>
</TABLE>
```

14

This example uses a table without borders to place my name on the left side of the screen and my e-mail addresses on the right.

Naming Individual Frames

If you were to load `html_frame.html` into Netscape at this stage, you would see a screen similar to the one shown in Figure 14.13. Some of the text sizes and spacing might be slightly different, but the general picture would be the same. If, however, you were to click any of the hyperlinks in the left frame, you would most likely get some very strange results. To be more specific, Netscape would attempt to load the contents of the file you select into the left frame, when what you really want it to do is load each document into the right frame.

To make this happen, you need to use a slight variation on the TARGET attribute discussed at the beginning of this chapter. But instead of the TARGET pointing to a new window, you want it to point to one of the frames in the current frameset.

You can achieve this by first giving each frame in your frameset a frame name, or window name. To do this, you include a NAME attribute inside the <FRAME> tag, which takes the following form:

```
<FRAME SRC="document URL" NAME="frame name">
```

Therefore, to assign a name to each of the frames in the `html_frame.html` document, you alter the <FRAME> tags to look like this:

```
<FRAMESET ROWS="*, 80">
    <FRAMESET COLS="30%, *">
        <FRAME SRC="html_contents_frame.html"  NAME="Contents">
        <FRAME SRC="05notes_frame.html"  NAME="Chapter">
    </FRAMESET>
    <FRAME SRC="html_footer.html"  NAME="Footer">
</FRAMESET>
```

This names the left frame "Contents", the right frame "Chapter", and the bottom frame "Footer". After this, resave the updated `html_frame.html` file, and you're just about finished with the exercise.

Linking Documents to Individual Frames

All you need to do now is make some minor alterations to `html_contents_frame.html` so that each chapter document is loaded into the right-hand frame of the frameset.

You may recall from the beginning of this chapter that the TARGET attribute was used with the <A> tag to force a document to load into a specific window. This is the same attribute that is used to control which frame a document is loaded into.

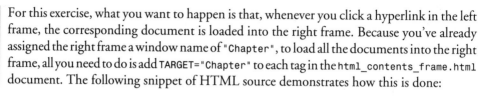

For this exercise, what you want to happen is that, whenever you click a hyperlink in the left frame, the corresponding document is loaded into the right frame. Because you've already assigned the right frame a window name of "Chapter", to load all the documents into the right frame, all you need to do is add TARGET="Chapter" to each tag in the html_contents_frame.html document. The following snippet of HTML source demonstrates how this is done:

```
<DT><A HREF="05notes_frame.html" TARGET="Chapter"><H3>Chapter 5</H3></A>
<DD>
<P>This chapter discusses document tags, headings,
character styles and the comment tag. </P>
<UL>
<LI><A HREF="05notes_frame.html#document_tags" TARGET="Chapter">
    Document tags</A>
<LI><A HREF="05notes_frame.html#heading_tags" TARGET="Chapter">
    Heading tags</A>
<LI><A HREF="05notes_frame.html#paragraph_tags" TARGET="Chapter">
    Paragraph Formatting tags</A>
</UL>
```

Alternatively, because every tag in the html_contents_frame.html document points to the same frame, you could also use the <BASE TARGET="*value*"> tag. In this case, you don't need to include TARGET="Chapter" inside each <A> tag. Instead, you place the following inside the <HEAD>...</HEAD> block of the document:

```
<BASE TARGET="Chapter">
```

The only other change you need to make to html_content_frame.html is purely cosmetic. In the original document, the main heading line uses <H1>; however, this is too large a heading size for the small left frame. Therefore, you should replace it with this:

```
<H2 ALIGN="CENTER">HTML Reference Table of Contents</H2>
```

With all the changes and new documents created, you should now be able to load html_frame.html into Netscape and view all of your HTML reference documents by selecting from the table of contents in the left frame.

TIP

> To get the layout exactly right, after you have gotten all your links working properly, you might need to go back and adjust the size of the rows and columns as defined in the <FRAMESET> tags. But remember, the final appearance of a frameset is still determined by the size of the screen and the operating system used by people viewing the documents.

14

Magic TARGET **Names**

You can assign four special values to a TARGET attribute, two of which (_blank and _self) you've already encountered. Netscape calls these values Magic TARGET names. Table 14.2 lists the Magic TARGET names and describes their use.

Table 14.2. Magic TARGET **names.**

TARGET Name	Description
TARGET="_blank"	Forces the document referenced by the <A> tag to be loaded into a new "unnamed" window.
TARGET="_self"	Causes the document referenced by the <A> tag to be loaded into the window or frame that held the <A> tag.
TARGET="_parent"	Forces the link to load into the <FRAMESET> parent of the current document. If, however, the current document has no parent, TARGET="_self" will be used.
TARGET="_top"	Forces the link to load into the full Web browser window, replacing the current <FRAMESET> entirely. If, however, the current document is already at the top, TARGET="_self" will be used.

Summary

If your head is hurting after reading this chapter, you're probably not alone. Although the basic concepts behind the use of frames are relatively straightforward, their implementation is somewhat harder to come to grips with. As a result, the best way to learn about frames is by experimenting with them.

In this chapter, you learned how to link a document to a new or an existing window. In addition, you learned how to create framesets and link them together by using the tags listed in Table 14.3.

Table 14.3. New tags discussed in this chapter.

Tag	Attribute	Description
<BASE TARGET="window">		Set the global link window for a document.
<FRAMESET>		Define the basic structure of a frameset.
	COLS	Defines the number of frame columns and their width in a frameset.

continues

14

Table 14.3. continued

Tag	Attribute	Description
	ROWS	Defines the number of frame rows and their height in a frameset.
<FRAME>		Define the contents of a frame within a frameset.
	SRC	The URL of the document to be displayed inside the frame.
	MARGINWIDTH	The size in pixels of the margin on each side of a frame.
	MARGINHEIGHT	The size in pixels of the margin above and below the contents of a frame.
	SCROLLING	Enable or disable the display of scroll bars for a frame. Values are YES, NO, and AUTO.
	NORESIZE	Don't allow the user to resize frames.
<NOFRAME>		Define text to be displayed by Web browsers that don't support the use of frames.

If you've made it this far through the book, you should give yourself a pat on the back. With the knowledge you've gained in the last week, you've done just about everything you can do while still working along on a single computer. You're now ready to place your Web pages onto the Internet itself and add more interactive features to those pages such as forms, image maps, and embedded animations. And tomorrow, with the first Bonus Day, you'll start doing just that.

Q&A

Q Is there any limit to how many levels of <FRAMESET> tags I can nest within a single screen?

A No, there isn't a limit. Practically speaking, however, when you get below about four levels, the size of the window space available starts to become unusable.

Q What would happen if I include a reference to a frame definition document within a <FRAME> tag?

A Netscape handles such a reference correctly, by treating the nested frame definition document as a nested <FRAMESET>. In fact, this technique is used regularly to reduce the complexity of nested frames.

14

There is, however, one limitation. You cannot include a reference to the current frame definition document in one of its own frames. This situation, called recursion, causes an infinite loop. Netscape Communications has included built-in protection to guard against this type of referencing.

14

Bonus Day 1

Chapter 15

Putting It All Online

For the past week you've been creating and testing your Web pages on your local machine, with your own browser. You might not have even had a network connection attached to your machine. And at this point you most likely have a Web presentation put together with a well-organized structure and a reasonable number of meaningful images (each with carefully chosen ALT text). You also will have written your text with wit and care, used only relative links, and tested it extensively on your own system.

Now, on this bonus day, it's finally time to publish it, to put it all online so that other people on the Web can see it and link their pages to yours. In this chapter, you'll learn everything you need to start publishing the work you've done. Today you'll learn about

- ☐ What a Web server does and why you need one
- ☐ Where you can find a Web server to put your presentation
- ☐ How to install your Web presentation

☐ How to find out your URL

☐ How to test your Web pages

☐ Methods for advertising your presentation

☐ Using log files and counters to find out who's viewing your pages

What Does a Web Server Do?

To publish Web pages, you'll need a Web server. A Web server is a program that sits on a machine on the Internet, waiting for a Web browser to connect to it and make a request for a file. Once a request comes over the wire, the server locates and sends the file back to the browser. It's as easy as that.

Web servers and Web browsers communicate using the HyperText Transfer Protocol (HTTP), a special "language" created specifically for the request and transfer of hypertext documents over the Web. Because of this, Web servers are often called HTTPD servers.

NOTE

> The "D" stands for "daemon." A daemon is a UNIX term for a program that sits in the background and waits for requests. When it receives a request, it wakes up, processes that request, and then goes back to sleep. You don't have to be on UNIX for a program to act like a daemon, so Web servers on any platform are still called HTTPDs. Most of the time I call them Web servers.

Other Things Web Servers Do

Although the Web server's primary purpose is to answer requests from browsers, there are several other things a Web server is responsible for. Some of these things you'll learn about today; others you'll learn about later this week.

File and Media Types

In Chapter 9, "External Files, Multimedia, and Animation," you learned a bit about content-types and how browsers and servers use file extensions to determine the type of the file. Servers are responsible for telling the browser the kind of content that a file contains. You can configure a Web server to send different kinds of media, or to handle new and different files and extensions. You'll learn more about this later in this chapter.

File Management

The Web server is also responsible for very rudimentary file management; mostly in determining where to find a file and keeping track of where it's gone. If a browser requests a file that doesn't exist, it's the Web server that sends back the page with the "404: File Not Found" message. Servers can also be configured to create aliases for files (the same file, but accessed with a different name), to redirect files to different locations (automatically pointing the browser to a new URL for files that have moved), and to return a default file or a directory listing if a browser requests a URL ending with a directory name.

Finally, servers keep log files for how many times each file on the site has been accessed, including the site that accessed it, the date, and, in some servers, the type of browser and the URL of the page it came from.

CGI Scripts, Programs, and Forms Processing

One of the more interesting (and more complex) things that a server can do is to run external programs on the server machine based on input that your readers provide from their browsers. These special programs are most often called CGI scripts, and are the basis for creating interactive forms and clickable image maps (images that contain several "hot spots" and do different operations based on the location within the image that has been selected). CGI scripts can also be used to connect a Web server with a database or other information system on the server side.

You'll learn more about CGI, forms, and image maps in Chapters 16, "Image Maps," 17, "Basic Forms," and 18, "Beginning CGI Scripting."

Server-Side File Processing

Some servers have the ability to process files before they send them along to the browser. On a simple level, these are called server-side includes, which can insert a date or a chunk of boilerplate text into each page, or run a program (many of the access counters you see on pages are run in this way). Server-side processing can also be used in much more sophisticated ways to modify files on-the-fly for different browsers or to execute small bits of scripting code.

Authentication and Security

Some Web sites require you to register for their service and make you log in using a name and password every time you visit their site. This is called authentication, and it's a feature most Web servers now include. Using authentication, you can set up users and passwords and restrict access to certain files and directories. You can also restrict access to files or to an entire site based on site names or IP addresses—for example, to prevent anyone outside your company from viewing files that are intended for internal use.

NEW TERM
> *Authentication* is the ability to protect files or directories on your Web server so that they require your readers to enter a name and password before the files can be viewed.

For security, some servers now provide a mechanism for secure connections and transactions using Netscape's SSL protocol. SSL provides authentication of the server (to prove that the server is who it says it is) and an encrypted connection between the browser and the server so that sensitive information between the two is kept secret.

Locating a Web Server

Before you can put your Web presentation on the Web, you'll need to find a Web server that you can use. Depending on how you get your access to the Internet, this might be really easy or not quite so easy.

Using a Web Server Provided by Your School or Work

If you get your Internet connection through school or work, that organization will most likely allow you to publish Web pages on its own Web server. Given that these organizations usually have fast connections to the Internet, and special people to administer the site for you, this is an ideal situation if you have it.

If you're in this situation, you'll have to ask your system administrator, computer consultant, Webmaster, or network provider if there is a Web server available, and, if so, what the procedures are for getting your pages installed. You'll learn more about what to ask later in this chapter.

Using a Commercial Internet or Web Service

If you pay for your access to the Internet through an Internet service provider (ISP) or a commercial online service, you might also be able to publish your Web pages using that service, although it might cost you extra to do so, and there might be restrictions on the kind of pages you can publish or whether or not you can run CGI scripts. Ask your provider's help line, online groups, or conferences related to Internet services to see how it has set up Web publishing.

Several organizations have popped up in the last year that provide nothing but Web publishing services. These services will usually provide you with some method for transferring your files to their site (usually FTP), and they provide the disk space and the network connection for access to your files. They also have professional site administrators on site to make sure the servers are running well all the time. Generally you are charged a flat monthly rate, with some additional cost if you use a large amount of disk space or if you have especially popular pages that take up a lot of network bandwidth. Some services even allow CGI scripts for forms and image maps and will provide consulting to help you set them up; a few will even set up their server with your own host name so that it looks as if you've got your own server running on the Web. These features can make commercial Web sites an especially attractive option. Appendix A, "Sources for Further Information," includes pointers to lists of these sites.

Note that, unlike your main Internet service provider, which you generally want to be in your city or somewhere close to minimize phone bills, services that publish Web pages can be located anywhere on the Internet, and you can shop for the cheapest prices and best service without having to worry about geographical location.

Using Anonymous FTP or Gopher

If all else fails and you cannot find a Web server, there is another option. If your work, school, or ISP doesn't provide a Web server but it does provide an anonymous FTP or Gopher server, you can use those to publish your Web pages. You'll have a different URL (an FTP or Gopher URL), and you won't have near the number of features of a real Web site (forms, scripts, image maps), but if it's all you've got, it'll work well enough for simple pages. And, often, it might be a cheaper option than a dedicated Web server.

Setting Up Your Own Server

For the ultimate in Web publishing, running your own Web site is the way to go. If you run your own site, you can publish as much as you want and include any kind of content you want. You can also use forms, CGI scripts, image maps, and many other special options that most other Web publishing services won't let you use. However, the cost, maintenance time, and technical background required to run your own server can be daunting, and running a server is definitely not for everyone. If you're interested in setting up your own server, consider Sams.net's *Web Site Construction Kit for Windows 95* or *Web Site Construction Kit for Windows NT*, both of which contain software and extensive information on setting up a Web site on those platforms. If you prefer to host your Web site on a UNIX or Macintosh system, books and software kits exist for those platforms as well.

Organizing and Installing Your HTML Files

Once you have access to a Web server, you can publish the Web presentation you've labored so hard to create. But before you actually move it into place on your server, it's best to have your files organized as well as a good idea of what goes where so you don't lose files or so your links don't break in the process.

Things To Ask Your Webmaster

The Webmaster is the person who runs your Web server. This person might also be your system administrator, help desk administrator, or network administrator. Before you can publish your files, there are several things you should learn from that Webmaster about how the server is set up. This list will also help you later on in this book when it's time to figure out what you can and cannot do with your server.

☐ Find out where to put your files on the server. In many cases, your Webmaster might create a special directory for you. Know where that directory is and how to gain access to it.

  In some other cases, particularly on UNIX machines, you might be able to just create a special directory in your home directory and store your files there. If that's the case, your Webmaster will tell you the name of that directory.

☐ Find out the URL of your top-level directory. That URL might be different than the actual pathname to your files.

☐ Find out the name of your system's default index file. This is the file that is loaded by default when a URL ends with a directory name. Usually it'll be `index.html`, but it might sometimes be `default.html`, `Homepage.html`, or something else.

☐ Find out if you can run CGI scripts. Depending on your server, the answer might be a flat-out "no," or you might be limited to certain programs and capabilities. For now you don't need extensive details about how to do CGI; you'll learn more about it later on.

☐ Find out if your site has limitations on what you can put up or how much. Some sites restrict pages to specific content (for example, only work-related pages) or allow you only a few pages on the system. They might prevent more than a certain number of people to access your pages at once or might have other restrictions on what sort of publishing you can do. Make sure you understand the limitations of the system and that you can work within those limitations.

15

Keep Your Files Organized Using Directories

Probably the easiest way to organize each of your presentations is to include all the files for that presentation in a single directory. If you have lots of extra files—for your images, for example—you can put those in a subdirectory to that main directory. Your goal is to contain all your files in a single place rather than scattering them around on your disk. Once you have your files contained, you can set all your links in your files to be relative to that one directory. If you follow these hints, you stand the best chance of being able to move that directory around to different servers without breaking the links.

Have a Default Index File and Correct Filenames

Web servers usually have a default index file that's loaded when a URL ends with a directory instead of a filename. As noted in the previous section, one of the things you should have asked your Webmaster is what the name of that file is. For most Web servers, this file is usually called index.html (index.htm for DOS). Your home page or top-level index for each presentation should be called by this name so that the server knows which page to send as the default page. Each subdirectory, in turn, if it contains any HTML files, should also have a default file. Using this default filename will also allow the URL to that page to be shorter because you don't have to include the actual filename. So, for example, your URL might be http://www.myserver.com/www/ rather than http://www.myserver.com/www/index.html.

Each file should also have an appropriate extension indicating what kind of file it is so that the server can map it to the appropriate file type. If you've been following along in the book so far, all your files should already have that special extension, so this should not be a problem. Table 15.1 shows a list of the common file extensions you should be using for your files and media, in case you've forgotten.

Table 15.1. Common file types and extensions.

Format	Extension
HTML	.html, .htm
ASCII Text	.txt
PostScript	.ps
GIF	.gif
JPEG	.jpg, .jpeg
AU Audio	.au

continues

Table 15.1. continued

Format	Extension
WAV Audio	`.wav`
MPEG Audio	`.mp2`
MPEG Video	`.mpeg, .mpg`
QuickTime Video	`.mov`
AVI Video	`.avi`

If you're using in your Web presentation special media that is not part of this list, you might have to have your server specially configured to handle that file type. You'll learn more about this later in this chapter.

Installing Your Files

Got everything organized? Then all that's left is to move everything into place on the server. Once the server can access your files, you're officially published on the Web. That's all there is to it.

But where is the appropriate spot on your server? You should have learned this from your Webmaster. You should also have found out how to get to that special spot on the server, whether it's simply copying files, using FTP to put them on the server, or using some other method.

Moving Files Between Systems

If you're using a Web server that has been set up by someone else, usually you'll have to move your Web files from your system to theirs using FTP, Zmodem transfer, or some other method. Although the HTML markup within your files is completely cross-platform, moving the actual files from one type of system to another sometimes has its gotchas. In particular, be careful to do the following:

☐ Transfer all files as binary.

Your FTP or file-upload program might give you an option to transfer files in binary or text mode (or might give you even different options altogether). Always transfer everything—all your HTML files, all your images, and all your media—in binary format (even the files that are indeed text; you can transfer a text file in binary mode without any problems).

15

If you're on a Macintosh, your transfer program will most likely give you lots of options with names such as MacBinary, AppleDouble, or other strange names. Avoid all of these. The option you want is flat binary or raw data. If you transfer files in any other format, they might not work when they get to the other side.

☐ Watch out for filename restrictions.

If you're moving your files to or from DOS systems, you'll have to watch out for the dreaded 8.3—the DOS rule that says filenames must be only eight characters long with three-character extensions. If your server is a PC and you've been writing your files on some other system, you might have to rename your files and the links to them to have the right file-naming conventions. (Moving files you've created on a PC to some other system is usually not a problem.)

Also, watch out if you're moving files from a Macintosh to other systems; make sure that your filenames do not have spaces or other funny characters in them. Keep your filenames as short as possible, use only letters and numbers, and you'll be fine.

☐ Be aware of carriage returns and line feeds.

Different systems use different methods for ending a line; the Macintosh uses carriage returns, UNIX uses line feeds, and DOS uses both. When you move files from one system to another, the vast majority of the time the end-of-line characters will be converted appropriately, but sometimes they aren't. This can result in your file coming out double-spaced or all on one single line on the system that it was moved to.

Most of the time it doesn't matter because browsers ignore spurious returns or line feeds in your HTML files. The existence or absence of either one is not terribly important. Where it might be an issue is in sections of text you've marked up with <PRE>; you might find that your well-formatted text that worked so well on one platform doesn't come out well-formatted after it's been moved.

If you do have end-of-line problems, you have a couple of options for how to proceed. Many text editors allow you to save ASCII files in a format for another platform. If you know what platform you're moving to, you can prepare your files for that platform before moving them. If you're moving to a UNIX system, small filters for converting line feeds called dos2unix and unix2dos might exist on the UNIX or DOS systems. And, finally, Macintosh files can be converted to UNIX-style files using the following command line on UNIX:

```
tr '\015' '\012' < oldfile.html > newfile.html
```

In this example, oldfile.html is the original file with end-of-line problems, and newfile.html is the name of the new file.

What's My URL?

At this point, you have a server, your Web pages are installed and ready to go, and all that's left is to tell people that your presentation exists. All you need now is a URL.

If you're using a commercial Web server, or a server that someone else administers, you might be able to easily find out what your URL is by asking the administrator (and, in fact, this is one of the things you were supposed to ask your Webmaster). Otherwise, you'll have to figure it out yourself. Luckily, this isn't that hard.

As I noted in Chapter 4, "All About Links," URLs are made of three parts: the protocol, the host name, and the path to the file. To determine each of these parts, use the following questions:

☐ What are you using to serve the files?

If you're using a real Web server, your protocol is http. If you're using FTP or Gopher, the protocol is ftp or gopher, respectively. (Isn't this easy?)

☐ What's the name of your server?

This is the network name of the machine your Web server is located on, typically beginning with www; for example, www.mysite.com. If it doesn't start with www, don't worry about it; that doesn't affect whether or not people can get to your files. Note that the name you'll use is the fully qualified host name—that is, the name that people elsewhere on the Web would use to get to your Web server, which might not be the same name you use to get to your Web server. That name will usually have several parts and end with .com, .edu, or the code for your country (for example, .uk, .fr, and so on).

With some SLIP or PPP connections, you might not even have a network name, just a number—something like 192.123.45.67. You can use that as the network name.

If the server has been installed on a port other than 80, you'll need to know that number, too. Your Webmaster will know this.

☐ What's the path to my home page?

The path to your home page most often begins at the root of the directory where Web pages are stored (part of your server configuration), which might or might not be the top level of your file system. For example, if you've put files into the directory /home/www/files/myfiles, your pathname in the URL might just be /myfiles. This is a server-configuration question, so if you can't figure it out, you might have to ask your server administrator.

If your Web server has been set up so that you can use your home directory to store Web pages, you can use the UNIX convention of the tilde (~) to refer to the Web

15

pages in your home directory. You don't have to include the name of the directory you created in the URL itself. So, for example, if I had the Web page `home.html` in a directory called `public_html` in my home directory (`lemay`), the path to that file in the URL would be

```
/~lemay/home.html
```

Once you know these three things, you can construct a URL. You'll probably remember from Chapter 4 that a URL looks like this:

```
protocol://machinename.com:port/path
```

You should be able to plug your values for each of those elements into the appropriate places in the URL structure. For example:

```
http://www.mymachine.com/www/tutorials/index.html
ftp://ftp.netcom.com/pub/le/lemay/index.html
http://www.commercialweb.com:8080/~lemay/index.html
```

Test, Test, and Test Again

Now that your Web pages are available on the Net, you can take the opportunity to test them on as many platforms using as many browsers as you possibly can. It is only when you've seen how your documents look on different platforms that you'll realize how important it is to design documents that can look good on as many platforms and browsers as possible.

Try it and see…you might be surprised at the results.

Troubleshooting

What happens if you upload all your files to the server, try to bring up your home page in your browser, and something goes wrong? Here's the first place to look.

Can't Access the Server

If your browser can't even get to your server, this is most likely not a problem you can fix. Make sure that you have the right server name and that it's a complete hostname (usually ending in .com, .edu, .net, or some other common ending name). Make sure you haven't mistyped your URL and that you're using the right protocol. If your Webmaster told you your URL included a port number, make sure you're including that port number in the URL after the hostname.

Also make sure your network connection is working. Can you get to other Web servers? Can you get to the top-level home page for the site itself?

If none of these ideas are solving the problem, perhaps your server is down or not responding. Call your Webmaster and see if he or she can help.

Can't Access Files

What if all your files are showing up as Not Found or Forbidden? First, check your URL. If you're using a URL with a directory name at the end, try using an actual filename at the end and see if that works. Double-check the path to your files; remember that the path in the URL might be different from the path on the actual disk. Also, keep in mind that uppercase and lowercase are significant. If your file is MyFile.html, make sure you're not trying myfile.html or Myfile.html.

If the URL appears to be correct, the next thing to check is file permissions. On UNIX systems, all your directories should be world-executable, and all your files should be world-readable. You can make sure all the permissions are correct using these commands:

```
chmod 755 filename
chmod 755 directoryname
```

Can't Access Images

You can get to your HTML files just fine, but all of your images are coming up as icons or broken icons. First of all, make sure your references to your images are correct. If you've used relative pathnames, this should not be a problem. If you've used full pathnames or file URLs, the references to your images might very well have broken when you moved the files to the server. (I warned you...)

In some browsers, notably Netscape, if you select an image with the right mouse button (hold down the button on a Mac mouse), you'll get a popup menu. The View This Image menu item will try to load the image directly, which will give you the URL of the image where the browser thinks it's supposed to be (which might not be where you think it's supposed to be). You can often track down strange relative pathname problems this way.

If the references all look fine, and the images worked just fine on your local system, the only other place a problem could have occurred is in transferring the files from one system to another. As I mentioned earlier in this chapter, make sure you transfer all your image files in binary format. If you're on the Mac, make sure you transfer as raw data or just data; don't try to use MacBinary or AppleDouble format, or you'll get problems on the other side.

Links Don't Work

If your HTML and image files are working just fine, but your links don't work, you most likely used pathnames for those links that applied only to your local system—for example, you used absolute pathnames or file URLs to refer to the files you're linking to. As I mentioned for images, if you used relative pathnames and avoided file URLs, this should not be a problem.

Files Are Displaying Wrong

Say you've got an HTML file or a file in some media format that displays or links just fine on your local system. But once you upload the file to the server and try to view it, the browser gives you gobbledygook—for example, it displays the HTML code itself, instead of the HTML file, or it tries to display an image or media file as text.

There are two cases where this could happen. The first is when you're not using the right file extensions for your files. Make sure that you're using one of the right file extensions with the right uppercase and lowercase letters.

The second case where this could happen is when your server is misconfigured to handle your files. For example, if you're working on a DOS system where all your HTML files have extensions of .htm, your server might not understand that .htm is an HTML file (most modern servers do, but some older ones don't). Or, you might be using a newer form of media that your server doesn't understand. In either case, your server might be using some default content-type for your files (usually text/plain), which your browser then tries to handle (and doesn't often succeed).

To fix this, you'll have to configure your server to handle the file extensions for the media you're working with. If you're working with someone else's server, you'll have to contact your Webmaster and have them set things up correctly. Your Webmaster will need two types of information to make this change: the file extensions you're using, and the content-type you want them to return. If you don't know the content-type you want, there's a listing of the most popular types in Appendix D, "MIME Types and File Extensions."

Registering and Advertising Your Web Pages

The "build it, and they will come" motto from the movie *Field of Dreams* notwithstanding, people won't simply start to visit your site of their own accord after you've put it online. In fact, with more than 10 million Web pages online already and that number set to double again in the next year, it's highly unlikely that anyone could ever just stumble across your site by accident.

As a result, to get people to visit your Web site, you need to advertise its existence in as many ways as possible. After all, the higher the visibility, the greater the prospect of your site receiving lots of *hits*.

NEW TERM

> *Hits* is Web-speak for the number of visits your Web site receives. It does not differentiate between people, but instead, is simply a record of the number of times a copy of your Web page has been downloaded.

In this section you'll learn about many of the avenues available for you to promote your site, including:

- ☐ Getting your site listed on major WWW directories
- ☐ Getting your site listed on the major WWW indexes
- ☐ Getting listed in "What's New" Sites
- ☐ Using bulk submission tools
- ☐ Using Usenet to announce your site
- ☐ Using Business cards, letterheads, and brochures

Listings in WWW Directories

When the Web was young, pages and sites were linked together in a hodge-podge cooperative fashion; if someone found your site cool, they linked to it, and you linked to the sites you thought were cool, and the people you linked to had their own links. While this made the Web a fun place to browse during a spare moment, it made it difficult to find pages on specific topics. You had to stumble across a page that had a subject that interested you.

Obviously something had to be done to organize the jumble of sites into something that could be more easily used. A number of mechanisms for organizing the Web quickly evolved including Web directories and indexes. I'll talk about the former in this section and the latter in the next.

Web directories are sites that organize a list of links to other sites on the Web library-style, breaking down those sites into categories such as Business, Entertainment, or Computers. Each category could have subcategories, and so on down until the actual site was listed. Directories allow you to find sites based on a particular topic that interests you instead of haphazardly jumping from link to link and hoping you stumble across something good.

NEW TERM

> A Web *directory* is a list of links organized into categories and subcategories that allow you to find the sites that interest you quickly and easily.

Because Web directories are so popular as starting points for Web exploration, having your site listed in a Web directory will help the people who are interested in your site find that site. While there are hundreds of directories on the Web these days, three in particular are extremely popular: Yahoo!, the WWW Virtual Library, and Excite.

Yahoo!

By far, the most well-known directory of Web sites is the Yahoo! site (see Figure 15.1), created by David File and Jerry Yang at http://www.yahoo.com/. This site started in April 1994 as a small private list of David and Jerry's favorite Web sites. But since then, it has grown to be a highly regarded catalog and index of Web sites and is now its own company.

Figure 15.1.

Yahoo!.

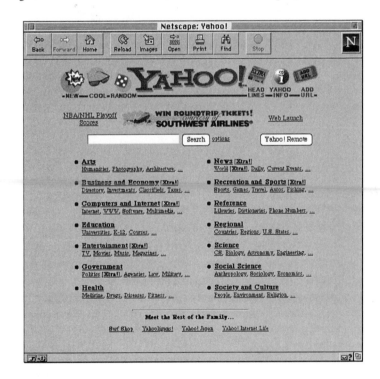

To add your site to the list maintained by Yahoo!, return to the Yahoo! home page at http://www.yahoo.com/, and select the category appropriate to your site. Work your way down the directory through any subcategories until you locate a list of sites similar to your own. On this page, click the Add URL button (it's in the banner along the top of the page). Yahoo! then displays a form like the one shown in Figure 15.2, where you can enter the URL and other details about your Web site.

Figure 15.2.

*The form to add your
URL to Yahoo!.*

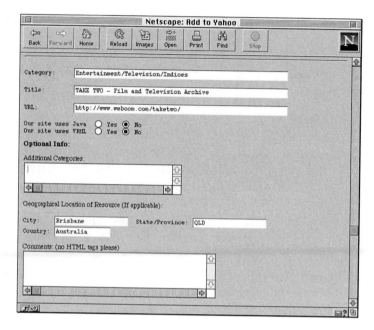

After you submit the form, a new link is automatically added to the category you selected previously. In addition, your site is also listed in the daily and weekly Yahoo! What's New list, which can be found at http://www.yahoo.com/New/.

The World Wide Web Virtual Library

The World Wide Web (W3) Virtual Library, located at http://www.w3.org/pub/DataSources/bySubject/Overview.html, was one of the very first Web directories. Unlike Yahoo!, which is operated by a single group of people, the W3 Virtual Library is a distributed effort. As such, the contents of each separate category are maintained by different people (all volunteers) and sometimes housed on different computers all over the world.

As a result, to submit your URL for inclusion in a category of the Virtual Library, you need to send an e-mail request to the person maintaining it. To obtain a list of the e-mail addresses for the maintainers, point your Web browser to http://www.w3.org/pub/DataSources/bySubject/Maintainers.html.

The top-level directory (see Figure 15.3) maintained by the W3 Consortium also contains a link to the Maintainers page, along with other links that describe the submission process in greater detail. In addition, you'll find information on this page that describes how people can add their own categories to the W3 Virtual Library and become maintainers themselves.

15

Figure 15.3.

The World Wide Web Virtual Library.

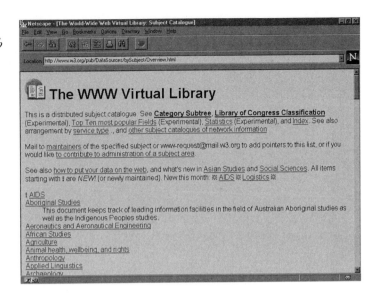

Excite

Excite, like Yahoo! and the Virtual Library, is a directory of Web sites. Excite, however, goes a step further by describing many of the sites listed in its database in concise 2–3 sentence reviews (the reviews are done by Excite's own editorial team, as opposed to relying on how the submitter describes the site).

Excite also offers news, information about various different U.S. cities, and searchable "yellow pages" services for e-mail addresses, maps, software, and other features. All of these features are available from the Excite home page at `http://www.excite.com/` (shown in Figure 15.4).

Figure 15.4.

Excite.

To add your site to Excite's database, first you might want to search for it to see if it's already there. If not, you can add it to the database using the page at http://www.excite.com/Search/ add_url.html (shown in Figure 15.5).

Figure 15.5.

Excite's Add URL page.

Other Directories

In addition to the broad mainstream directories such as Yahoo! and the Virtual Library, there are also hundreds of smaller more specialized directories that list sites based on special interests, for example, online commerce, education, business, or entertainment. Depending on the topic of your own site, you might want to seek out some of these directories and list your site with them as well.

The best way to find these other directories is to use the Web. A good place to start is Yahoo!'s Announcement Services page (shown in Figure 15.6), which contains several dozen directories and other places to list your site. You can find the Announcement Services page at http://www.yahoo.com/Computers_and_Internet/Internet/World_Wide_Web/ Announcement_Services/.

Listings in Web Indexes and Search Engines

A Web directory is one way to organize the multitude of sites on the World Wide Web. A different approach is to collect all the pages on the Web and then provide a way of searching those pages for keywords. This second type of approach is called a Web index or, sometimes, just a Web search engine.

15

Figure 15.6.

The Announcement Services category in Yahoo!.

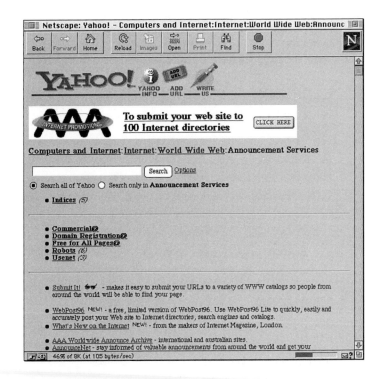

The index itself is a database of pages that exist on the Web. The database stores links to those pages, but also often the contents of the pages themselves, or perhaps a subset of important keywords. To collect those pages, the Web index uses what's called a robot, worm, or spider. Web robots wander the net on their own, jumping from link to link and collecting pages for the database. The best robots can get an updated collection of the entire World Wide Web in a little over a week (considering how large the Web is, and how fast its growing, that's an awesome task).

The second half of the Web index is the search engine. Search engines are simply tools that allow you to search something for keywords. Many Web directories and Web sites have their own search engines; they are not unique to Web indexes. But the search engine, in combination with the database of pages, gives you a mechanism for tracking down topics that interest you across the entire Web.

Because Web indexes rely on robots to find new pages, they have an advantage over Web directories in that they can locate pages that have not been specifically added to the directory. Some people, however, find directories easier to use, as searching for some keywords can return an incredibly large set of pages to choose from.

So how do you get listed on a Web index? Once you publish your site on the Web and other people link to your site, chances are a search engine will get around to finding and exploring your site fairly quickly. However, you can tell these indexes that your site exists ahead of time and get indexed that much faster.

Four search engines vie for the title of most popular on the Web: AltaVista, Lycos, WebCrawler, and Infoseek.

AltaVista

One of the most popular and fastest Web indexes is Digital Equipment's AltaVista index at `http://www.altavista.digital.com/`. AltaVista indexes a good portion of the Web but stands out by having an extremely fast search engine. So, looking up specific search terms on the Web is quick and thorough.

You can submit your page to AltaVista using the form at `http://www.altavista.digital.com/cgi-bin/query?pg=addurl` (shown in Figure 15.7:

Figure 15.7.

AltaVista's Add URL page.

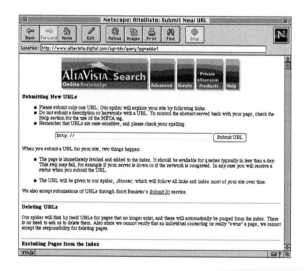

Lycos

Lycos was one of the earliest search engines and still claims to have the largest overall coverage of the Web. Lycos is located at `http://www.lycos.com/` (see Figure 15.8), and its registration form for asking your site to be visited is at `http://www.lycos.com/register.html`.

15

Figure 15.8.
Lycos's Registration page.

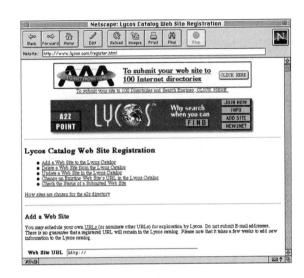

WebCrawler

Following its recent move onto the Internet, America Online has taken over the operation of the WebCrawler indexing system located at `http://webcrawler.com/GNN/WebQuery.html` (see Figure 15.9).

Figure 15.9.
WebCrawler is operated by America Online.

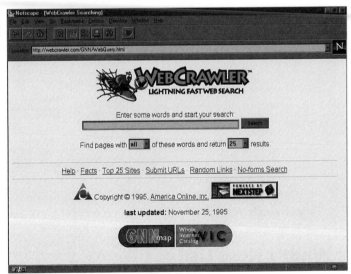

WebCrawler does not have as wide a coverage as Lycos or AltaVista, with less than an estimated 40 percent of the World Wide Web index, but it does have the advantage of being the Internet index system of choice for more than 3.5 million America Online and Global Network Navigator (GNN) users.

The Submit URL form for WebCrawler is located at `http://webcrawler.com/WebCrawler/SubmitURLS.html`.

Infoseek

PC Computing magazine recently voted Infoseek at `http://www.infoseek.com/` (shown in Figure 15.10) the Most Valuable Internet Tool for 1995. Like Lycos and WebCrawler, Infoseek is a Web indexing tool, but what makes it even more powerful is its capability to search through many kinds of additional services and databases in addition to the World Wide Web. Such functionality, however, does come at a cost—only the Web search engine can be used without charge.

Figure 15.10.
Infoseek.

The other main difference between Infoseek and other search tools is that you send your URL submission request via e-mail to `www-request@infoseek.com`.

What's New Listings

A special type of Web directory, called a What's New listing, was designed with one purpose in mind: to announce the arrival of new Web sites. Many of the directories and indexes I've already mentioned have their own What's New pages; by submitting your site to be included

on those sites, you'll automatically get included in their What's New listings. Other sites, however, are dedicated to nothing more than announcing new sites.

The granddaddy of all the What's New listings is the one operated by the NCSA, creators of NCSA Mosaic (see Figure 15.11).

Figure 15.11.

The NCSA What's New pages.

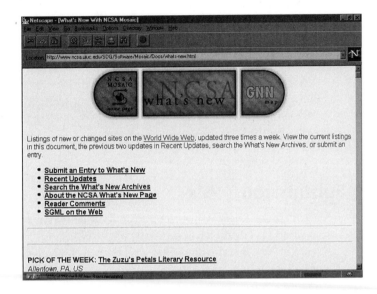

To submit your site for inclusion on the NCSA listing, follow the instructions outlined on the What's New home page at `http://www.ncsa.uiuc.edu/SDG/Software/Mosaic/Docs/whats-new.html`. Currently, you need to submit an e-mail request, but it's highly likely that this requirement will change in the future.

What's New Too! is an entire site dedicated to nothing but new Web pages (and usually there are an awful lot of them). You can visit What's New Too! at `http://newtoo.manifest.com/` or add your page using the form at `http://newtoo.manifest.com/WhatsNewToo/submit.html` (shown in Figure 15.12).

Figure 15.12.

Submitting a New Site to What's New Too!.

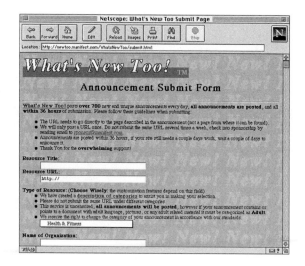

Submission Tools

Searching out relevant Web directories, indexes, and What's New pages, and then submitting your site to all of them, can be extremely time-consuming. To make the process easier, several services have been set up that will submit your site for inclusion into many of the major Web announcement services, including the sites listed above, as well as other sites that might be relevant. PostMaster and Submit It! are two of the most well known.

PostMaster

The PostMaster site, shown in Figure 15.13 and located at `http://www.netcreations.com/postmaster/index.html`, is an all-in-one submission page that asks you to fill out all the details required for more than 25 Web indexes and directories, including Yahoo!, Netscape's Escapes, JumpStation, Lycos, Infoseek, WebCrawler, World Wide Web, GNN Whole Internet Catalog, World Wide Yellow Pages, and NCSA's What's New. After completing the form, PostMaster submits your information to all these sites at once, so you don't have to do each one individually.

NOTE

PostMaster also offers a commercial version of its submission system that delivers announcements about your new site to almost 400 magazines, journals, and other periodicals, in addition to all the sites included in the free version. Using the commercial version, however, is an expensive exercise.

15

Figure 15.13.
PostMaster.

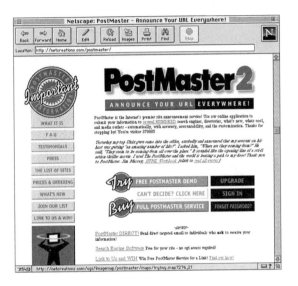

Submit It!

The Submit It! service is a lot like PostMaster in that it also helps you submit your URL to different directories and search indexes. It supports just about all the same services, but what sets it apart is the way that you submit your information. Figure 15.14 shows a list of all the search indexes and directories currently supported by Submit It!

Figure 15.14.
Submit It!

Submit It! doesn't ask you to complete one enormous page, something that many people find daunting. Instead, after you've filled out some general information, you select only the sites you want to submit an entry to and then perform each submission one site at a time.

To learn more about Submit It!, point your Web browser to `http://www.submit-it.com/`.

Usenet Announcements

The World Wide Web is not the only place on the Internet you can use to announce the launch of your new Web site. Many people make use of a small set of Usenet newsgroups that are designed especially for making announcements. To locate these newsgroups, look for newsgroup names that end with `.announce`. (Refer to the documentation that came with your Usenet newsreader for information about how this can be done.)

One newsgroup is even devoted just to World Wide Web–related announcements. The name of this newsgroup is `comp.infosystems.www.announce`. If your browser supports reading Usenet news, and you've configured it to point to your new server, you can view articles submitted to this newsgroup—and add your own announcements—by entering the following URL into the Document URL field:

`news:comp.infosystems.www.announce`

One post in particular to look for in `comp.infosystems.www.announce` is an excellent FAQ called "FAQ: How to Announce Your New Web Site." This FAQ contains an up-to-date list of all the best and most profitable means of promoting your Web site. If you can't locate the FAQ in this newsgroup, you can view an online version at `http://ep.com/faq/webannounce.html`.

NOTE

> `comp.infosystems.www.announce` is a moderated newsgroup. As such, any submissions you make to it are approved by a moderator before they appear in the newsgroup listing. To ensure that your announcement is approved, you should read the charter document that outlines the announcement process. You can read this document by pointing your Web browser to `http://boutell.com/%7Egrant/charter.html`.

Using Business Cards, Letterheads, and Brochures

Although the Internet is a wonderful place to promote your new Web site, there is another great advertising method that many people fail to even consider.

15

Most businesses spend a considerable amount of money each year producing letterheads, business cards, and other promotional material. Very few, however, consider printing their e-mail addresses and home page URLs on them. But why not? With more than 35 million people on the Internet, chances are that some of your customers are already on the Internet, or will be within a few years.

By printing your e-mail address and home page URL on all your correspondence and promotional material, you can reach an entirely new group of potential site visitors. And, who knows? Maybe you'll even pick up new clients by spending time explaining to people what all your new address information means.

The bottom line with the promotion of your Web site is lateral thinking. You need to use every tool at your disposal if you want to have a successful and active site.

Finding Out Who's Viewing Your Web Pages

Welcome to being happily published. At this point, you've got your pages up on the Web and ready to be viewed, you've advertised and publicized your site to the world, and people are (hopefully) flocking to your site in droves. Or are they? How can you tell? There are a number of ways to find out, including log files and access counters.

Log Files

The best way to figure out how often your pages are being seen, and by whom, is to see if you can get access to your server's log files. The server keeps track of all this information and, depending on how busy the server is, might keep this information around for weeks or even months. Many commercial Web publishing providers have a mechanism for you to view your own Web logs or to get statistics about how many people are accessing your pages and from where. Ask your Webmaster for help.

If you do get access to the raw log files, you'll most likely see a whole lot of lines that look something like this (I've broken this one up onto two lines so it fits on the page):

```
vide-gate.coventry.ac.uk - - [17/Apr/1996:12:36:51 -0700]
   "GET /index.html HTTP/1.0" 200 8916
```

What does this mean? This is the standard look and feel for most log files. The first part of the line is the site that accessed the file (in this case, it was a site from the United Kingdom). The two dashes are used for authentication (if you have login names and passwords set up, the user name of the person who logged in and the group he belonged to will appear here). The date and time the page was accessed is inside the brackets. The part after that is the actual filename that was accessed; here it's the `index.html` at the top level of the server. The `GET` part is the actual HTTP command the browser used; you usually see `GET` here. Finally, the last two numbers are the HTTP status code and the number of bytes transferred. The status code can be one of many things: 200 means the file was found and transferred correctly; 404 means the file was not found (yes, it's the same status code you get in error pages in your browser). Finally, the number of bytes transferred will usually be the same number of bytes in your actual file; if it's a smaller number, the reader interrupted the load in the middle.

Access Counters

If you don't have access to your server's log files for whatever reason, and you'd like to know at least how many people are looking at your Web pages, you can install an access counter on your page. You've probably seen these a number of times in your Web browsing; they look like odometers or little meters that say "Since July 15, 1900, this page has been accessed 5,456,234,432 times."

Lots of Web counters are available, but most of them require you to install something on your server or have what are called server-side includes set up. A few provide access counters that don't require server setup (but might cost you some money).

The Web counter at `http://www.digits.com/` is easy to set up and very popular. If you have a site without a lot of hits (less than 1,000 a day), the counter service is free. Otherwise you'll need to be part of the commercial plan, with the access counter costing $30 and up.

After you sign up for the `digits.com` counter service, you'll get an URL that you include on your pages as part of an `<IMG>` tag. Then, when your page is hit, the browser retrieves that URL at `digits.com`'s server, which generates a new odometer image for you.

For more information about access counters in general (as well as a huge archive of images for access counters), see the Digit Mania home page at `http://www.digitmania.holowww.com/`.

Summary

In this chapter, you've reached the final point in creating a Web presentation: publishing your work to the World Wide Web at large through the use of a Web server, either installed by you or available from a network provider. Here you learned what a Web server does and how to get one; how to organize your files and install them on the server; how to find out your URL and use it to test your pages; how to advertise your pages once they're available; and how to find out who's looking at those pages.

Q&A

Q **I have my pages published at an ISP I really like; my URL is something like `http://www.thebestisp.com/users/mypages/`. Instead of this URL, I'd like to have my own hostname—something like `http://www.mypages.com/`. How can I do this?**

A You have two choices. The easiest way is to ask your ISP if they allow you to have your own domain name. Many ISPs have a method for setting this up so you can still use their services and work with them—only your URL changes. Note that this might cost more money, but if you really must have that URL, then this might be the way to go.

The other option is to set up your own server with your own domain name. This option, as I noted earlier in this chapter, could be significantly more expensive than working with an ISP, and it requires at least some background in basic network administration.

Q **I created all my image files on a Mac, uploaded them to my UNIX server using the Fetch FTP program, tested it all, and it all works fine. But now I'm getting e-mail from people saying none of my images are working. What's going on here?**

A Usually when you upload files using Fetch, there'll be a pull-down menu you can choose from where the default format is MacBinary. Make sure you change it to Raw Data.

MacBinary files work fine when they're viewed on the Mac. And since I assume you're using a Mac to test your presentation, they'll work fine. But they won't work on any other system. To make sure your images work across platforms, upload them as Raw Data.

Q **I created my files on a DOS system, using the `.htm` extension, like you told me to earlier in the book. Now I've published my files on a UNIX system provided by my employer. The problem now is that when I try to get to my pages using my browser, I get the HTML code for those pages—not the formatted result! It all worked on my system at home...what went wrong?**

A Some older servers will have this problem. Your server has not been set up to believe that files with a `.htm` extension are actually HTML files, so they send them as the default content-type (text/plain) instead. Then, when your browser reads one of your files from a server, it reads that content-type and assumes you have a text file. So your server is messing everything up.

There are several ways you can fix this. By far the best way to fix this is to tell your Webmaster to change his or her server configuration so that .htm files are sent as HTML—usually a very simple step that will magically cause all your files to work properly from then on.

If you can't find your Webmaster, or for some strange reason he or she will not make this change, your only other option is to change all your filenames after you upload them to the UNIX system. Note that you'll have to change all the links within those files as well. (Finding a way to convince your Webmaster to fix this would be a *much* better solution.)

Chapter **16**

Image Maps

Image maps are a special kind of clickable image. Usually, when you embed an image inside a link, clicking anywhere on that image goes to a single location. Using image maps, you can go to different locations based on where inside the image you clicked. In this chapter you'll learn all about image maps and how to create them, including:

- ☐ What an image map is
- ☐ Creating server-side image maps
- ☐ Creating client-side image maps
- ☐ Supporting both types of image maps

What Is an Image Map?

In Chapter 7, "Using Images, Color, and Backgrounds," you learned how to create an image that doubles as a link, simply by including the `<IMG>` tag inside a link (`<A>`) tag. In this way, the entire image becomes a link. You could click the image, the background, or the border, and you'd get the same effect.

In image maps, different parts of the image activate different links. By using image maps, you can create a visual hyperlinked map that links you to pages describing the regions you click. Or you can create visual metaphors for the information you're presenting: a set of books on a shelf or a photograph in which each person in the picture is individually described.

Figure 16.1.

Image maps: different places, different links.

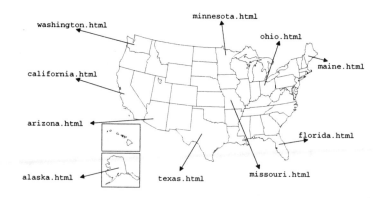

> **NEW TERM**
>
> *Image maps* are special images which have different areas that point to different link locations. Where you go on the site is determined by the place on the image where you click the mouse.

Server-Side Image Maps

Traditionally, image maps are created by using a special program that runs on the server. Such image maps are referred to as server-side image maps.

> **NEW TERM**
>
> *Server-side image maps* are implemented using an image displayed by the client and a program that runs on the server.

When a browser activates a link on an image map, it calls a special image map program stored on a Web server. In addition to calling the image map program, the browser also sends the program the x and y coordinates of the position on the image where the mouse was clicked. The image map program then looks up a special map file that matches regions in the image to URLs, does some calculations to figure out which page to load, and then loads that page.

Server-side image maps were one of the earliest Web features and are supported by most, if not all, graphical browsers.

Client-Side Image Maps

Although server-side image maps have been in common use for some time, the problems associated with them have led to the development of a new type of image map called a client-side image map. These are the main problems associated with server-side image maps:

☐ Normally, when you move your mouse over a hyperlink, the URL pointed to by the link is displayed in the Web browser's status bar. Because, however, the Web browser has no idea where the parts of a server-side image map point, all you see when you place your cursor over a server-side image map is either the URL of the image map program itself (not very helpful), or that URL and a set of x,y coordinates (still not very helpful).

☐ There is no way to use or to test server-side image maps with local files. Image maps require the use of a Web server to run the image map program and process the x and y coordinates.

☐ Because a special program must be run by the server each time a user clicks a page that contains image maps, image maps are much slower to respond to mouse clicks than normal links or images as links. This often results in image maps that seem to take forever to respond to requests for a new page.

Client-side image maps, on the other hand, remove all these difficulties by removing the need for a special image map program on the server. Instead, they manage all the image map processing locally on the Web browser itself.

NEW TERM

Client-side image maps work in the same ways as server-side image maps, except there is no program that runs on the server. All the processing of coordinates and pointers to different locations occurs in the browser.

NOTE

Client-side image maps are currently supported by only a few of the very latest Web browsers, including Netscape 2.0. The proposal for client-side image maps, however, is a standard in discussion by the W3 Consortium, so client-side image maps are likely to be more widely supported as time goes by.

Image Maps and Text-Only Browsers

Because of the inherently graphical nature of image maps, they can work only in graphical browsers. In fact, if you try to view a document with an image map in a text-only browser such as Lynx, you don't even get an indication that the image exists. (Unless, of course, the image contains an ALT attribute.) But even with the ALT attribute, you won't be able to navigate the presentation without a graphical browser.

If you decide to create a Web page with an image map on it, it's doubly important that you also create a text-only equivalent so that readers with text-only browsers can use your page. The use of image maps can effectively lock out readers using text-only browsers; have sympathy and allow them at least some method for viewing your content.

Creating Server-Side Image Maps

In addition to the various disadvantages of using server-side image maps, there's one more that puts a wrinkle into how I explain them: Almost every Web server has a different way of creating them. The methods even vary among servers on the same platform. For example, the W3C (CERN) httpd server and NCSA HTTPd server have incompatible methods of implementing image files. All servers, however, use the same basic ingredients for image maps:

☐ Special HTML code to indicate that an image is a map

☐ A map file on the server that indicates regions on the image and the Web pages they point to

☐ An image-mapping CGI script that links it all together

This section explains how to construct clickable images in general, but its examples focus on the NCSA HTTP-style servers such as NCSA itself and Apache. If you need more information for your server, see the documentation that comes with that server, or get help from your Web administrator.

Getting an Image

To create an image map, you'll need an image (of course). The image that serves as the map is most useful if it has several discrete visual areas that can be individually selected; for example, images with several symbolic elements, or images that can be easily broken down into polygons. Photographs make difficult image maps because their various "elements" tend to blend together or are of unusual shapes. Figures 16.2 and 16.3 show examples of good and poor images for image maps.

Figure 16.2.
A good image map.

Figure 16.3.
*A not-so-good
image map.*

16

Creating a Map File

The heart of the server-side image map is a map file. Creating a map file involves sketching out the regions in your image that are clickable, determining the coordinates that define those regions, and deciding on the HTML pages where they should point.

NOTE

> The format of the map file depends on the image-mapping program you're using on your server. In this section, I'll talk about image maps on the NCSA HTTP server and the map files it uses by default. If you're using a different server, you might have several image-mapping programs to choose from with several map formats. Check with your Web administrator or read your server documentation carefully if you're in this situation.

You can create a map file either by sketching regions and noting the coordinates by hand or by using an image map-making program. The latter method is easier because the program will automatically generate a map file based on the regions you draw with the mouse.

The Mapedit and MapThis programs for Windows and WebMap for the Macintosh can all help you create map files in NCSA format. In addition, MapThis also includes support for the creation of client-side image map definitions.

If you use a UNIX-based system, there is a version of Mapedit available via FTP. (See Appendix A, "Sources for Further Information," for a full list of related FTP sites.)

If you need your map file in a different format, you can always use these programs to create a basic map and then convert the coordinates you get into the map file format your server needs.

If you must create your map files by hand, here's how to do it. First, make a sketch of the regions you want to make active on your image (for example, as in Figure 16.4).

Figure 16.4.

Sketching map-able regions.

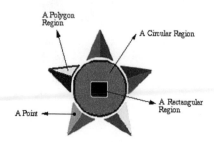

You next need to determine the coordinates for the endpoints of those regions (see Figure 16.5). Most image-editing programs have an option that displays the coordinates of the current mouse position. Use this feature to note the appropriate coordinates. (All the mapping programs mentioned previously will create a map file for you, but for now, following the steps manually will help you better understand the processes involved.)

Figure 16.5.

Getting the coordinates.

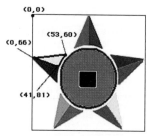

For circle regions, note the coordinates of the center point and the radius, in pixels. For rectangle regions, note the upper-left and lower-right corners. For polygon regions, note the coordinates of each corner. For points, note the coordinates of the point.

NOTE

The 0,0 origin is in the upper-left corner of the image, and positive y is down.

You're more than halfway there. The next step is to come up with a set of URLs to link for each region or point that is selected. You can have multiple regions pointing to the same URL, but each region must have only one link.

With all your regions, coordinates, and URLs noted, you can now write a map file for your server. NCSA HTTP map files look like this:

```
default URL
circle URL x,y radius
rect URL x,y x,y
poly URL x1,y1 x2,y2 ... xN,yN
point URL x,y
```

The map files for your particular image map program for your server might look different from this, but the essential parts are there. Substitute the values for the coordinates you noted previously in each of the *x* or *y* positions (or *x1*, *y1*, and so on). Note that the `radius` (in the `circle` line) is the radius for the circle region.

The URLs you specify for either format must be either full URLs (starting with `http`, `ftp`, or some other protocol) or the full pathnames to the files you are linking—that is, everything you could include after the hostname in a URL. You cannot specify relative pathnames in the image map file.

Here's a sample of an NCSA HTTPd map file:

```
circle /www/mapping.html 10,15 20
circle /www/mapping.html 346,23 59
poly /www/test/orange.html 192,3 192,170 115,217
rect /www/pencil.html 57,57 100,210
point /www/pencil.html 100,100
point /www/orange.html 200,200
```

Points enable you to specify that a given mouse click, if it doesn't land directly on a region, will activate the nearest point. Points are useful for photographs or other images with nondiscrete elements, or for a finer granularity than just "everything not in a region."

The order of regions in the map file is relevant; the further up a region is in the file, the higher precedence it has for mouse clicks. If part of the region that occurs on overlapping regions is selected, the first region listed in the map file is the one that is activated.

Finally, the map file includes a "default" region with no coordinates, just a URL. The default is used when a mouse click that is not inside a region is selected; it provides a catch-all for the parts of the image that do not point to a specific link. (Note that if you use an NCSA HTTPd map file and you include `default`, you shouldn't include any points. The existence of point elements precludes that of `default`.) Here's an example of using `default`:

```
default /www/none.html
```

16

Installing the Map File and the Image Map Program

Creating the map file is the hardest part of making an image map. Once you've got a map file written for your image, you'll have to install both the map file and the image map program on your server, and then hook everything up in your HTML files to use the image map.

Save your map file with a descriptive name (say, `myimage.map`). Where you install the map file on your server isn't important, but I like to put my map files in a central directory called `maps` at the top level of my Web files.

You'll also need your image map program installed on your server, usually in a special directory called `cgi-bin`, which has been specially set up to store programs and scripts for your server (you'll learn more about the `cgi-bin` directory in Chapter 18, "Beginning CGI Scripting"). Most servers have an image program set up by default, and if you're using someone else's server, that program will most likely be available to you as well. The program to look for is often called `htimage` or `imagemap`.

WARNING

Be careful with the NCSA server and the `imagemap` program. Older versions of `imagemap` were more difficult to work with and required an extra configuration file; the program that comes with the 1.5 version of the server works much better. If you aren't running the most recent version of the NCSA server, you can get the new `imagemap` program from `http://hoohoo.ncsa.uiuc.edu/docs/tutorials/imagemap.txt`.

Linking It All Together

So now you have an image, a map file, and an image map program. Now let's hook it all up. In your HTML page that contains the image map, you'll use the `<A>` and `<IMG>` tags together to create the effect of the clickable image. Here's an example using NCSA's image map program:

```
<A HREF="/cgi-bin/imagemap/maps/myimage.map">
<IMG SRC="image.gif" ISMAP></A>
```

Notice several things about this link. First, the link to the image map script (`imagemap`) is indicated the way you would expect, but then the path to the map file is appended to the end of it. The path to the map file should be a full pathname from the root of your Web directory (everything after the hostname in your URL), in this case `/maps/myimage.map`. (This weird-looking form of URL will be described in more detail when you learn more about CGI scripting in Chapter 18.)

The second part of the HTML code that creates a server-side map is the ISMAP attribute to the <IMG> tag. This is a simple attribute with no value that tells the browser to send individual mouse-click coordinates to the image map program on the server side for processing.

And now, with all three parts of the server-side image map in place (the map file, the image map program, and the special HTML code), the image map should work. You should be able to load your HTML file into your browser and use the image map to go to different pages on your server by selecting different parts of the map.

16

NOTE

If you're running the NCSA HTTPd server and you don't have the newest version of imagemap, you'll get the error Cannot Open Configuration file when you try to select portions of your image. If you get these errors, check with your Web administrator.

Exercise 16.1: A clickable bookshelf.

Image maps can get pretty hairy. The map files are prone to error if you don't have your areas clearly outlined and everything installed in the right place. In this exercise, you'll take a simple image and create a simple map file for it using the NCSA server map file format. This way you can get a feel for what the map files look like and how to create them.

The image you'll use here is a simple color rendering of some books (see Figure 16.6). You can't see the colors here, but from left to right, they are red, blue, yellow, and green.

Figure 16.6.
The bookshelf image.

First, you'll define the regions that will be clickable on this image. Because of the angular nature of the books, it's most appropriate to create polygon-shaped regions. Figure 16.7 shows an example of the sort of region it makes sense to create on the image. This one is for the leftmost (red) book. You can define similar regions for each book in the stack. (Draw on the figure here in this book, if you want to. I won't mind.)

Figure 16.7.

The bookshelf with an area defined.

Now that you have an idea of where the various regions are on your image, you'll need to find out the exact coordinates of the corners as they appear in your image. To find out those coordinates, you can use a mapping program such as Mapedit or WebMap (highly recommended), or you can do it by hand. If you do try it by hand, most image-editing programs should have a way of displaying the x and y coordinates of the image when you move the mouse over it. I used Adobe Photoshop's Info window to come up with the coordinates shown in Figure 16.8.

 TIP

Don't have an image-editing program? Here's a trick if you use Netscape as your browser: Create an HTML file with the image inside a link pointing to a fake file, and include the ISMAP attribute inside the <IMG> tag. You don't actually need a real link; anything will do. The HTML code might look something like this:

```
<A HREF="nothing"><IMG SRC="myimage.gif" ISMAP></A>
```

Now, if you load that HTML file into your browser, the image will be displayed as if it is an image map, and when you move your mouse over it, the x and y coordinates will be displayed in the status line of the browser. Using this trick, you can find out the coordinates of any point on that image for the map file.

Figure 16.8.

The bookshelf with coordinates.

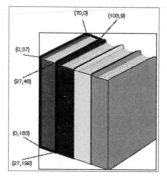

With regions and a list of coordinates, you just need the Web pages to jump to when the appropriate book is selected. These can be any documents, or they can be scripts; you can use anything you can call from a browser as a jump destination. For this example, I've created a document called redbook.html and stored it inside the www directory on my Web server. This is the page we'll define as the end-point of the jump when the red book is selected.

Now create the entry in the map file for this area, with the coordinates and the file to link to if that area is clicked on. In an NCSA map file, the information looks like this:

```
poly /www/redbook.html 70,0 0,37 0,183 27,192 27,48 103,9
```

Note that the URLs in the map file must be absolute pathnames from the top of the Web root (not from the top of the file system). They cannot be relative URLs from the map file; image maps don't work like that. In this case, my www directory is at the Web root, and the redbook.html file is in that directory, and so the URL for the purposes of the map file is /www/redbook.html.

You can now create similar entries for the other books in the image (blue, yellow, and green). Don't forget to include a default line in the map file to map mouse clicks that don't hit any books (here, a file called notabook.html):

```
default /www/notabook.html
```

You also can use points to refer to default pages; in this case, it was easier to use default.

Save your map file to your map directory on the server (or wherever you keep your maps). Finally, create a Web page that includes the books image, the ISMAP attribute in the <IMG> tag, and the link to the image mapping program. Here's an example that uses the imagemap program on my server:

```
<A HREF="http://www.lne.com/cgi-bin/imagemap/maps/books.map">
<IMG SRC="image.gif" ISMAP></A>
```

And that's it. With everything connected, clicking the image on each book should load the page for that part of the image.

Creating Client-Side Image Maps

When you creating a client-side image map, many of the steps for finding out the coordinates of each area on the map are exactly the same as they are for creating server-side image maps. Unlike a server-side image map, however, which uses a separate file to store the coordinates and references for each hyperlink, client-side image maps store all the mapping information as part of an HTML document.

The <MAP> and <AREA> Tags

To include a client-side image map inside an HTML document, you use the new <MAP> tag, which looks like this:

```
<MAP NAME="mapname"> coordinates and links  </MAP>
```

The value assigned to the NAME attribute is the name of this map definition. This is the name that will be used later to associate the clickable image with its corresponding coordinates and hyperlink references—so, if you have multiple image maps on the same page, you can have multiple <MAP> tags with different names.

Between the <MAP> and the </MAP> tags, you enter the coordinates for each area in the image map and the destinations of those regions using the same values and links that you determined in the section on server-side image maps. This time, however, the coordinates are defined inside yet another new tag—the one-sided <AREA> tag. For example, to define the polygon area from Excercise 16.1, you would write this:

```
<AREA SHAPE="POLY" COORDS="70,0, 0,37, 0,183, 27,192, 27,48, 103,9"
    HREF="/www/redbook.html">
```

The type of shape to be used for the region is declared by the SHAPE attribute, which can have the values RECT, POLY, and CIRCLE. The coordinates for each shape are noted using the COORDS attribute. So, for example, the COORDS attribute for the POLY shape is the following, where each x,y combination represents a point on the polygon:

```
<AREA SHAPE="POLY" COORDS="x1,y1,x2,y2,x3,y3,…,xN,yN" HREF="URL">
```

For RECT shapes, $x1,y1$ is the upper-left corner of the rectangle, and $x2,y2$ is the lower-right corner:

```
<AREA SHAPE="RECT" COORDS="x1,y1,x2,y2" HREF="URL">
```

And for CIRCLE shapes, x,y represents the center of a circular region of size $radius$:

```
<AREA SHAPE="CIRCLE" COORDS="x,y,radius" HREF="URL">
```

The last attribute you need to define for each <AREA> tag is the HREF attribute. HREF can be assigned any URL you would usually associate with an <A> link, including relative pathnames. In addition, you can assign HREF a value of "NOHREF" to define regions of the image that don't contain links to a new page.

NOTE

When using client-side image maps with frames, you can also include the TARGET attribute inside an <AREA> tag to open a new page in a specific window, as in this example:

```
<AREA SHAPE="RECT" COORDS="x1,y1,x2,y2" HREF="URL"
TARGET="window_name">
```

16

The USEMAP **Attribute**

After your client-side image map has been defined using the <MAP> tag, the last step is to put the image on your Web page. To do this, you use a special form of the <IMG> tag that includes a new attribute called USEMAP (this is different from the ISMAP for server-side image maps). USEMAP looks like this, where *mapname* is the name of a map defined by the <MAP NAME="#mapname"> tag:

```
<IMG SRC="image.gif" USEMAP="#mapname">
```

NOTE

Unlike with server-side image maps, you do not need to enclose the <IMG> tag inside an <A> tag. Instead, the USEMAP attribute tells the Web browser that the <IMG> contains a clickable image map.

TIP

The value assigned to USEMAP is a standard URL. This is why *mapname* has a pound (#) symbol in front of it. As with links to anchors inside a Web page, the pound symbol tells the browser to look for *mapname* in the current Web page. However, if you have a very complex image map, it can be stored in a separate HTML file and referenced using a standard URL.

Exercise 16.2: The clickable bookshelf exercise revisited.

EXERCISE

To conclude this discussion of image maps, take a look at how the image map example discussed in Exercise 16.1 would be written using client-side image maps. Because we already have the coordinates and the destination, all you really need is to convert the server-side map file into client-side HTML.

So, for the book image, the `<MAP>` tag and its associated `<AREA>` tag looks like this:

```
<MAP NAME="books">
<AREA SHAPE="POLY" COORDS="70,0, 0,37, 0,183, 27,192, 27,48, 103,9"
    HREF="/www/redbook.html">
</MAP>
```

The `<IMG>` tag to refer to the map coordinates is also different. It uses USEMAP instead of ISMAP, and doesn't have a link around it:

```
<IMG SRC="image.gif" USEMAP="#books">
```

Finally, put the whole lot together and test it. Here's a sample HTML file that contains both the `<MAP>` tag and the image that uses it. The result is shown in Figure 16.9.

INPUT

```
<HTML><HEAD>
<TITLE>The Virtual Bookshelf</TITLE>
</HEAD><BODY>
<H1>The Virtual Bookshelf</H1>
<P>Please select a book:</P>
<IMG SRC="books.gif" USEMAP="#books">
<MAP NAME="books">
<AREA SHAPE="POLY" COORDS="70,0, 0,37, 0,183, 27,192, 27,48, 103,9"
    HREF="/www/redbook.html" >
</MAP>
</BODY>
</HTML>
```

OUTPUT

Figure 16.9.

The finished image map.

Building Web Pages That Support Both Types of Image Maps

The main problem with using client-side image maps in your Web pages is that although client-side image maps are faster and easier to implement than server-side image maps, they're not supported by very many browsers at all. Because of this, if you do use client-side image maps, it's a good idea to also create a server-side equivalent, and then modify your HTML files so that they support both forms of image map. This way your pages will work equally well with both newer and older image map formats while taking advantage of the newer client-side capabilities in browsers that support them.

To create an image map that uses client-side support, if available, but falls back to server-side support when needed, take the following standard server-side definition:

```
<A HREF="/cgi-bin/imagemap/maps/myimage.map">
<IMG SRC="image.gif" ISMAP>
</A>
```

And add the client-side image map details as part of the <IMG SRC="image.gif" ISMAP> text, like this:

```
<A HREF="/cgi-bin/imagemap/maps/myimage.map">
<IMG SRC="image.gif" USEMAP="#books" ISMAP>
</A>
```

You will, of course, need to have installed the myimage.map file on your server and to have included the "books" <MAP> tag definition somewhere in your HTML document.

Summary

In this chapter you learned how to add image maps to your Web pages. You should now know the difference between server-side and client-side image maps and which ones are available in which browsers. You also learned how to find regions and the coordinates that defined them and to create map files for client-side image maps. You now should know how to connect clickable images, map files, and image map programs on the appropriate servers.

It's been a very full chapter, so to help refresh your memory, Table 16.1 presents a summary of the tags and attributes you learned about in this chapter.

Table 16.1. HTML tags presented in this chapter.

Tag	Attribute	Use
	ISMAP	An attribute of the <IMG> tag that indicates this image is a server-side image map.
	USEMAP	An attribute of the <IMG> tag used to associate an image with a client-side image map specified by <MAP NAME="#mapname">.
<MAP>		Defines a map for a client-side image map.
	NAME	An attribute of the <MAP> tag used to define the map's name.
<AREA>		The individual regions within a <MAP> element.
	SHAPE	An attribute of the <AREA> tag indicating the type of region. Possible values are RECT, POLY, and CIRCLE.
	COORDS	An attribute of the <AREA> tag indicating the point bounding the region.
	HREF	An attribute of the <AREA> tag indicating the URL of the region.

Q&A

Q Do I need a server to create image maps? I want to create and test all of this offline, the same way I did for my regular HTML files.

A If you're using client-side image maps, you can create and test them all on your local system (assuming, of course, that your map destinations all point to files in your local presentation as well). If you're using server-side image maps, however, because you need the image map program on the server, you'll have to be connected to the server for all of this to work.

Q My server-side image maps aren't working. What's wrong?

A Here are a couple things you can look for:

☐ Make sure that the URLs in your map file are absolute pathnames from the top of your root Web directory to the location of the file where you want to link. You cannot use relative pathnames in the map file. If absolute paths aren't working, try full URLs (starting with http).

☐ Make sure that when you append the path of the map file to the image map program, you also use an absolute pathname (as it appears in your URL).

16

☐ If you're using NCSA, make sure that you're using the newest version of imagemap. Requests to the new imagemap script should not look for configuration files.

Q My client-side image maps aren't working. What's wrong?

A Here are a couple suggestions:

☐ Make sure the pathnames or URLs in your <AREA> tags point to real files.

☐ Make sure the map name in the <MAP> file and the name of the map in the USEMAP attribute in the <IMG> tag match. Only the latter should have a pound sign in front of it.

16

Bonus Day 2

Chapter **17**

Basic Forms

Everything you've learned up to this point has involved your giving information to your readers. That information may just be text or images, it may be multimedia, or it may be a sophisticated, complex presentation using frames, image maps, and other bits of advanced Web publishing. But basically you're doing all the work, and your readers are simply sitting and reading and following links and digesting the information they've been presented.

Fill-in forms change all that. Forms make it possible for you to transform your Web pages from primarily text and graphics that your readers passively browse to interactive "toys," surveys, and presentations that can provide different options based on the readers' input.

Forms are the last of the major groups of HTML tags you'll learn about in this book. And unlike many of the other tags you've learned about, forms are part of HTML 2.0 and are widely supported by just about every browser on the market. In this chapter you'll learn about the HTML part of forms; tomorrow you'll learn about the server-side programs you use to process information you get back from forms. In particular, in this chapter you learn about:

- [ ] Each part of the form on both the browser and server side, and how it all works
- [ ] The basic form input elements: text fields, radio buttons, and checkboxes, as well as buttons for submitting and resetting the form
- [ ] Other form elements: text areas, menus of options, and hidden fields
- [ ] Some basic information about form-based file upload, a new feature that allows your readers to send whole files to you via a form

Anatomy of a Form

Creating a form usually involves two independent steps: creating the layout for the form itself and then writing a script program on the server side (called a CGI script or program) to process the information you get back from a form. Today you'll learn about the HTML side of the process, and tomorrow you'll learn all about CGI scripts.

To create a form, you use (guess!) the <FORM> tag. Inside the opening and closing FORM tags are each of the individual form elements plus any other HTML content to create a layout for that form (paragraphs, headings, tables, and so on). You can include as many different forms on a page as you want to, but you can't nest forms—that is, you can't include a <FORM> tag inside another FORM.

The opening tag of the FORM element usually includes two attributes: METHOD and ACTION. The METHOD attribute can be either GET or POST, which determines how your form data is sent to the script to process it. You'll learn more about GET and POST in Chapter 18, "Beginning CGI Scripting."

The ACTION attribute is a pointer to the script that processes the form on the server side. The ACTION can be indicated by a relative path or by a full URL to a script on your server or somewhere else. For example, the following <FORM> tag would call a script called form-name in a cgi-bin directory on the server www.myserver.com:

```
<FORM METHOD=POST ACTION="http://www.myserver.com/cgi-bin/form-name">
...
</FORM>
```

Again, you'll learn more about both of these attributes in Chapter 18 when we delve more into CGI scripts. For today, so we can test the output of our forms, we're going to be using a boilerplate form template that simply spits back what it gets. In each of the forms today, you'll be using POST as the METHOD, and the action will be the URL of a special script called post-query:

```
<FORM METHOD=POST ACTION="http://www.mcp.com/cgi-bin/post-query">
...
</FORM>
```

NOTE

> This particular example uses the post-query script on the server
> www.mcp.com (the server for the publisher of this book). The post-query
> script is part of the standard NCSA server distribution and may be
> available on your own server. Check with your Webmaster to see if it
> exists on your server; your forms will work that much faster if you work
> with a copy closer to you.

Exercise 17.1: Tell me your name.

EXERCISE

Let's try a simple example. In this example, you'll create the form shown in Figure 17.1. This
form does absolutely nothing but prompt you for your name. In this form, you would enter
your name and press the Submit button (or select the Submit link, in nongraphical browsers).
Submit is what sends all the form data back to the server for processing. Then, on the server,
a script would do something to that name (store it in a database, mail it to someone for further
processing, plaster it across Times square, and so on).

17

Figure 17.1.

*The Tell Me Your
Name form.*

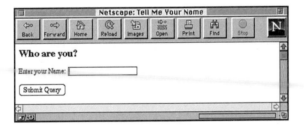

TIP

> Most browsers provide a shortcut: If there is only one text field on the
> page (besides Submit), you can just press Return to activate the form.

In this chapter we're just going to do the layout. Let's create this form so that you can get the
basic idea of how it works. As with all HTML documents, start with a basic framework, with
just a single level-two heading that says Who are you?:

```
<HTML><HEAD>
<TITLE>Tell Me Your Name</TITLE>
</HEAD><BODY>
<H2>Who are you?</H2>
</BODY>
</HTML>
```

Now, add the form. First, add that template for post-query I mentioned earlier:

```
<HTML><HEAD>
<TITLE>Tell Me Your Name</TITLE>
</HEAD><BODY>
```

```
<H2>Who are you?</H2>
<FORM METHOD=POST ACTION="http://www.mcp.com/cgi-bin/post-query">
</FORM>
</BODY>
</HTML>
```

With the form framework in place, we can add the elements of the form. Note that `<FORM>` doesn't specify the appearance and layout of the form; you'll have to use other HTML tags for that (and, in fact, if you looked at this page in a browser now, you wouldn't see anything on the page that looked like a form).

The first element inside the form is the text-entry area for the name. First, include the prompt, just as you would any other line of text in HTML:

```
<P>Enter your Name:
```

Then add the HTML code that indicates a text-input field:

```
<P>Enter your Name: <INPUT NAME="theName"></P>
```

The `<INPUT>` tag indicates a simple form element. (There are also several other form elements that use tags other than `<INPUT>`, but `<INPUT>` is the most common one.) `<INPUT>` usually takes at least two attributes: TYPE and NAME.

The TYPE attribute is the kind of form element this is. There are several choices, including "text" for text-entry fields, "radio" for radio buttons, and "check" for checkboxes. If you leave the TYPE attribute out, as we've done here, the element will be a text-entry field.

The NAME attribute indicates the name of this element. When your form is submitted to the server, the CGI script that processes it gets the form data as a series of name and value pairs. The value is the actual value your reader enters; the name is the value of this attribute. By including a sensible name for each element, you can easily match up which answer goes with which question.

You can put anything you want as the name of the element, but as with all good programming conventions, it's most useful if you use a descriptive name. Here we've picked the name theName. (Descriptive, yes?)

Now add the final form element: the submit button (or link). Most forms require the use of a submit button; however, if you have only one text field in the form, you can leave it off. The form will be submitted when the reader presses Return.

```
<P><INPUT TYPE="submit"></P>
```

You'll use the `<INPUT>` tag for this element as well. The TYPE attribute is set to the special type of "submit" which creates a submit button for the form. The submit button doesn't require a name if there's only one of them; you'll learn how to create forms with multiple submit buttons later on.

It's a good practice to always include a submit button on your form, even if there's only one text field. The submit button is so common that your readers may become confused if it's not there.

Note that each element includes tags for formatting, just as if this were text; form elements follow the same rules as text in terms of how your browser formats them. Without the `<P>` tags, you'd end up with all the elements in the form on the same line.

So, now you have a simple form with two elements. The final HTML code to create this form looks like this:

```
<HTML><HEAD>
<TITLE>Tell Me Your Name</TITLE>
</HEAD><BODY>
<H2>Who are you?</H2>
<FORM METHOD="POST" ACTION="http://www.mcp.com/cgi-bin/post-query">
<P>Enter your Name: <INPUT NAME="theName"></P>
<P><INPUT TYPE="submit"></P>
</FORM>
</BODY></HTML>
```

So what happens if you do submit the form? The form data is sent back to the server, and the post-query CGI script is called. The post-query script does nothing except return the names and values that you had in the original form. Figure 17.2 shows the output from a form submitted with my name in it.

Figure 17.2.

The output from post-query.

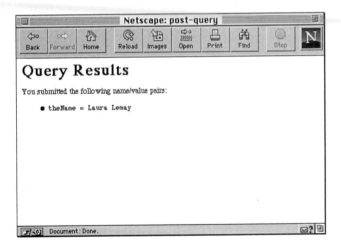

17

Simple Form Layout

So now that you've got the basics down, I'm sure you want to know exactly what kind of nifty interface elements you can put in a form.

In this section, you'll learn about the `<INPUT>` tag and the simple form elements you can create with it. There are a few other elements you can use for complex form input; you'll learn about those later in the chapter.

Each of the elements described in this section goes inside a `<FORM>...</FORM>` tag. In these examples, we'll continue to use the post-query script as the form's ACTION, which returns the name and value pairs it is given.

The Submit Button

Submit buttons (or submit links in nongraphical browsers; for the sake of simplicity, let's just call them buttons) tell the browser to send the form data to the server. You should include at least one submit button on every form even though forms with only one text field don't require them. To create a submit button, use "SUBMIT" as the TYPE attribute in an `<INPUT>` tag:

```
<INPUT TYPE="SUBMIT">
```

You can change the label text of the button by using the VALUE attribute:

```
<INPUT TYPE="SUBMIT" VALUE="Submit Query">
```

You can have multiple submit buttons in a form by including the NAME attribute inside the `<INPUT>` tag. Both the NAME and the VALUE of the submit button are then sent to the server for processing; you'll have to test for those name/value pairs when you write your CGI script to see which submit button was pressed. So, for example, you could use submit buttons inside a form for virtual directions, like this:

```
<INPUT TYPE="SUBMIT" NAME="left" VALUE="Left">
<INPUT TYPE="SUBMIT" NAME="right" VALUE="Right">
<INPUT TYPE="SUBMIT" NAME="up" VALUE="Up">
<INPUT TYPE="SUBMIT" NAME="down" VALUE="Down">
<INPUT TYPE="SUBMIT" NAME="forward" VALUE="Forward">
<INPUT TYPE="SUBMIT" NAME="back" VALUE="Back">
```

The following input and output example shows two simple forms with submit buttons: one with a default button and one with a custom label. Figure 17.3 shows the output in Netscape, and Figure 17.4 shows the output in Lynx.

NOTE

These figures show how the buttons appear in Netscape for the Macintosh. The buttons look slightly different in Netscape for other platforms, and may look entirely different in other browsers.

INPUT

```
<FORM METHOD=POST ACTION="http://www.mcp.com/cgi-bin/post-query">
<INPUT TYPE="SUBMIT">
</FORM>
<UL>
<FORM METHOD=POST ACTION="http://www.mcp.com/cgi-bin/post-query">
<INPUT TYPE="SUBMIT" VALUE="Press Here">
</FORM>
```

OUTPUT

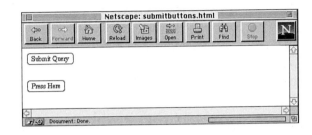

Figure 17.3.
*The output in
Netscape.*

OUTPUT

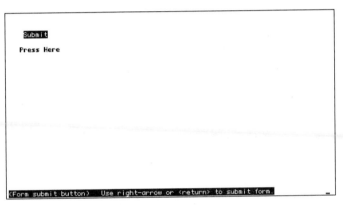

Figure 17.4.
*The output in
Lynx.*

Text Input Fields

Text fields enable your reader to type text into a single-line field. For multiple-line fields, use the <TEXTAREA> element, described later in this chapter.

To create a text-entry field, you can either use TYPE="text" in the <INPUT> tag or leave off the TYPE specification altogether. The default TYPE for the <INPUT> tag is "text". You must also include a NAME attribute. NAME indicates the name of this field as passed to the script processing the form.

```
<INPUT TYPE="text" NAME="myText">
```

You can also include the attributes SIZE and MAXLENGTH in the <INPUT> tag. SIZE indicates the length of the text-entry field, in characters; the field is 20 characters by default. Your readers can enter as many characters as they want. The field will scroll horizontally as your reader types. Try to keep the SIZE under 50 characters so that it will fit on most screens.

```
<INPUT TYPE="text" NAME="longText" SIZE="50">
```

MAXLENGTH enables you to limit the number of characters that your reader can type into a text field (refusing any further characters). If MAXLENGTH is less than SIZE, browsers will sometimes draw a text field as large as MAXLENGTH.

In addition to regular text fields, there are also password fields, indicated by TYPE=password. Password text fields are identical to ordinary text fields, except that all the characters typed are echoed back in the browser (masked) as asterisks or bullets (see Figure 17.5).

```
<INPUT TYPE="PASSWORD" NAME="passwd">
```

Figure 17.5.
Password fields.

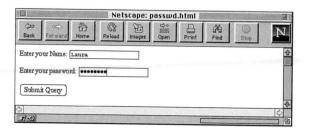

 NOTE

Despite the masking of characters in the browser, password fields are not secure. The password is sent to the server in clear text; that is, anyone could intercept the password and be able to read it. The masking is simply a convenience.

This input and output example shows several text fields and their results in Netscape (Figure 17.6) and Lynx (Figure 17.7).

INPUT

```
<P>Enter your Name: <INPUT TYPE="TEXT" NAME="theName"><BR>
Enter your Age:
<INPUT TYPE="TEXT" NAME="theAge" SIZE="3" MAXLENGTH="3"><BR>
Enter your Address:
<INPUT TYPE="TEXT" NAME="theAddress" SIZE="80"></P>
```

OUTPUT

Figure 17.6.
The output in Netscape.

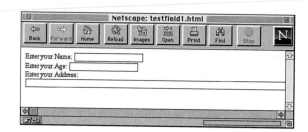

 17

Figure 17.7.
The output in Lynx.

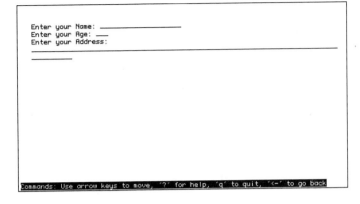

Radio Buttons

Radio buttons indicate a list of items, of which only one can be chosen. If one radio button in a list is selected, all the other radio buttons in the same list are deselected.

Radio buttons use "radio" for their TYPE attribute. You indicate groups of radio buttons using the same NAME for each button in the group. In addition, each radio button in the group must have a unique VALUE attribute, indicating the selection's value.

```
<OL>
<LI><INPUT TYPE="radio" NAME="theType" VALUE="animal">Animal<BR>
<LI><INPUT TYPE="radio" NAME="theType" VALUE="vegetable">Vegetable<BR>
<LI><INPUT TYPE="radio" NAME="theType" VALUE="mineral">Mineral<BR>
</OL>
```

You can use multiple, independent groups of radio buttons by using different names for each group:

```
<OL>
<LI><INPUT TYPE="radio" NAME="theType" VALUE="animal">Animal<BR>
<OL>
<LI><INPUT TYPE="radio" NAME="theAnimal" VALUE="cat">Cat
<LI><INPUT TYPE="radio" NAME="theAnimal" VALUE="dog">Dog
<LI><INPUT TYPE="radio" NAME="theAnimal" VALUE="fish">fish
</OL>
<LI><INPUT TYPE="radio" NAME="theType" VALUE="vegetable">Vegetable<BR>
<LI><INPUT TYPE="radio" NAME="theType" VALUE="mineral">Mineral<BR>
</OL>
```

By default, all radio buttons are off (unselected). With radio buttons, because you generally have at least one choice, it's a good idea to make one button selected by default. You can determine the default radio button in a group using the CHECKED attribute:

```
<OL>
<LI><INPUT TYPE="radio" NAME="theType" VALUE="animal" CHECKED>Animal<BR>
<LI><INPUT TYPE="radio" NAME="theType" VALUE="vegetable">Vegetable<BR>
<LI><INPUT TYPE="radio" NAME="theType" VALUE="mineral">Mineral<BR>
</OL>
```

When the form is submitted, a single name/value pair for the group of buttons is passed to the script. That pair includes the NAME attribute for each group of radio buttons and the VALUE attribute of the button that is currently selected.

Here's an input and output example that shows two groups of radio buttons and how they look in Netscape (Figure 17.8) and Lynx (Figure 17.9).

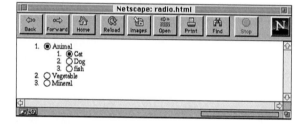

```
<OL>
<LI><INPUT TYPE="radio" NAME="theType" VALUE="animal"
CHECKED>Animal<BR>
<OL>
<LI><INPUT TYPE="radio" NAME="theAnimal" VALUE="cat" CHECKED>Cat
<LI><INPUT TYPE="radio" NAME="theAnimal" VALUE="dog">Dog
<LI><INPUT TYPE="radio" NAME="theAnimal" VALUE="fish">fish
</OL>
<LI><INPUT TYPE="radio" NAME="theType" VALUE="vegetable">Vegetable
<LI><INPUT TYPE="radio" NAME="theType" VALUE="mineral">Mineral
</OL>
```

OUTPUT

Figure 17.8.
*The output in
Netscape.*

OUTPUT

Figure 17.9.
*The output in
Lynx.*

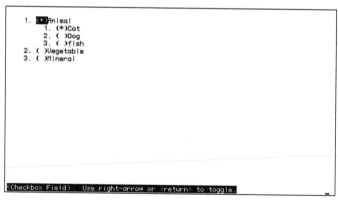

Checkboxes

Checkboxes make it possible to choose multiple items in a list. Each checkbox can be either checked or unchecked (the default is unchecked). Checkboxes use "checkbox" as their TYPE attribute:

```
<UL>
<LI><INPUT TYPE="checkbox" NAME="red">Red
<LI><INPUT TYPE="checkbox" NAME="green">Green
<LI><INPUT TYPE="checkbox" NAME="blue">Blue
</UL>
```

When the form is submitted, only the name/value pairs for each selected checkbox are submitted (unchecked checkboxes are ignored). By default, each name/value pair for a checked checkbox has a value of ON in the script that processes the form. You can also use the VALUE attribute to indicate a value you would prefer to see in your script. In this example, each checkbox that is selected will have the name given by the NAME attribute and the value chosen:

```
<UL>
<LI><INPUT TYPE="checkbox" NAME="red" VALUE="chosen">Red
<LI><INPUT TYPE="checkbox" NAME="green" VALUE="chosen">Green
<LI><INPUT TYPE="checkbox" NAME="blue" VALUE="chosen">Blue
</UL>
```

You can also implement checkbox lists such that elements have the same NAME attribute, similar to radio buttons. Notice, however, that this means your script will end up with several name/value pairs having the same name (each checkbox that is selected will be submitted to the script), and you'll have to take that into account when you process the input in your script.

As with radio buttons, you can use the CHECKED attribute to indicate that a checkbox is checked by default.

Here's another one of those input and output examples, with a series of checkboxes and how they look in Netscape (Figure 17.10) and Lynx (Figure 17.11).

```
<P>Profession (choose all that apply): </P>
<UL>
<LI><INPUT TYPE="checkbox" NAME="doctor" CHECKED>Doctor
<LI><INPUT TYPE="checkbox" NAME="lawyer">Lawyer
<LI><INPUT TYPE="checkbox" NAME="teacher" CHECKED>Teacher
<LI><INPUT TYPE="checkbox" NAME="nerd">Programmer
</UL>
```

OUTPUT

Figure 17.10.
The output in Netscape.

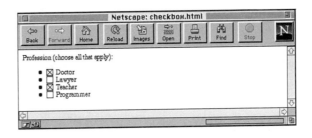

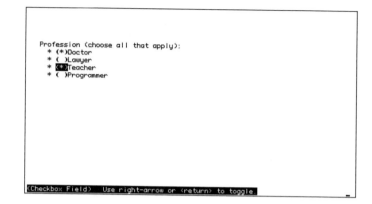

Figure 17.11.

The output in Lynx.

Images

Forms also give you an alternate way of implementing image maps using the TYPE=IMAGE attribute to the <INPUT> tag. Use TYPE=IMAGE with the SRC attribute which, just like SRC in <IMG>, indicates the pathname or URL to an IMAGE:

```
<INPUT TYPE="image" SRC="usamap.gif" NAME="map">
```

Images in forms behave just like image maps; when you click somewhere on the image, the form is submitted back to the server. The coordinates of the point where you clicked are submitted as part of that FORM data, with the value of the NAME attribute included twice with .x and .y appended for each coordinate. So, for example, if this image had the name map, the x-coordinate would be contained in the map.x value, and the y-coordinate would be contained in the map.y value.

In the CGI script to process the form, you'll have to handle those coordinates yourself. Since standard image maps do a much better job of this, TYPE=IMAGE is rarely used any more to create an image map. What is used much more commonly is as a replacement submit button. Because the image submits the form when it's selected, you can create an image for the submit button to replace the bland default button for submit.

Setting and Resetting Default Values

Each form element can have a default value that is entered or selected when the form is viewed:

☐ For text fields, use the VALUE attribute with a string for the default value. The VALUE is entered in the box automatically when the form is displayed.

☐ For checkboxes and radio buttons, the attribute CHECKED selects that element by default.

17

In addition to the default values for each element, you can include a reset button, similar to the submit button, on your form. The reset button clears all selections or entries your reader has made and resets them to their default values. Also like submit, a VALUE attribute indicates the label for the button:

```
<INPUT TYPE="RESET" VALUE="Reset Defaults">
```

Exercise 17.2: The Surrealist Census.

Now, let's create a more complicated form example. In this example, The Surrealist Society of America has created a small census via an interactive form on the World Wide Web. Figure 17.12 shows that census.

Figure 17.12.

The Surrealist Society's census form.

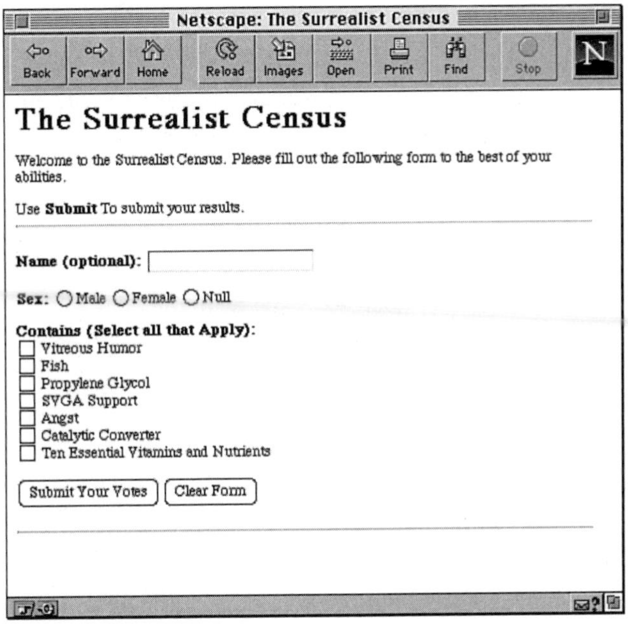

The form to create the census falls roughly into three parts: the name field, the radio buttons for choosing the sex, and a set of checkboxes for various other options.

Start with the basic structure, as with all HTML documents. We'll use that post-query script as we did in all the previous examples:

```
<HTML><HEAD>
<TITLE>The Surrealist Census</TITLE>
```

```
</HEAD><BODY>
<H1>The Surrealist Census</H1>
<P>Welcome to the Surrealist Census. Please fill out the following
form to the best of your abilities.</P>
<P>Use <STRONG>Submit Your Votes</STRONG> to submit your results.</P>
<HR>
<FORM METHOD=POST ACTION="http://www.mcp.com/cgi-bin/post-query">

</FORM>
<HR>
</BODY></HTML>
```

Note that in this example I've included rule lines before and after the form. Because the form is a discrete element on the page, it makes sense to visually separate it from the other parts of the page. This is especially important if you have multiple forms on the same page; separating them with rule lines or in some other way visually divides them from the other content on the page.

Now, let's add the first element for the reader's name. This is essentially the same element that we used in the previous example, with the name of the element theName:

```
<P><STRONG>Name: </STRONG><INPUT TYPE="TEXT" NAME="theName"></P>
```

The second part of the form is a series of radio buttons for Sex. There are three: Male, Female, and Null (remember, this is The Surrealist Census). Since radio buttons are mutually exclusive (only one can be selected at a time), we'll give all three buttons the same value for NAME (theSex):

```
<P><STRONG>Sex: </STRONG>
<INPUT TYPE="radio" NAME="theSex" VALUE="male">Male
<INPUT TYPE="radio" NAME="theSex" VALUE="female">Female
<INPUT TYPE="radio" NAME="theSex" VALUE="null">Null
</P>
```

Even though each <INPUT> tag is arranged on a separate line, the radio button elements are formatted on a single line. Always remember that form elements do not include formatting; you have to include other HTML tags to arrange them in the right spots.

Now, let's add the last part of the form: the list of Contains checkboxes:

```
<P><STRONG>Contains (select all that apply): </STRONG><BR>
<INPUT TYPE="checkbox" NAME="humor">Vitreous Humor<BR>
<INPUT TYPE="checkbox" NAME="fish">Fish<BR>
<INPUT TYPE="checkbox" NAME="glycol">Propylene Glycol<BR>
<INPUT TYPE="checkbox" NAME="svga">SVGA Support<BR>
<INPUT TYPE="checkbox" NAME="angst">Angst<BR>
```

```
<INPUT TYPE="checkbox" NAME="catcon">Catalytic Converter<BR>
<INPUT TYPE="checkbox" NAME="vitamin">Ten Essential Vitamins and Nutrients<BR>
</P>
```

Unlike radio buttons, any number of checkboxes can be selected, so each value of NAME is unique.

Finally, add the submit button so that the form can be submitted to the server. A nice touch is to also include a "Clear Form" button. Both buttons have special labels specific to this form:

```
<P><INPUT TYPE="SUBMIT" VALUE="Submit Your Votes">
<INPUT TYPE="RESET" VALUE="Clear Form"></P>
```

Whew! With all the elements in place, here's what the entire HTML file for the form looks like:

```
<HTML><HEAD>
<TITLE>The Surrealist Census</TITLE>
</HEAD><BODY>
<H1>The Surrealist Census</H1>
<P>Welcome to the Surrealist Census. Please fill out the following
form to the best of your abilities.</P>
<P>Use <STRONG>Submit</STRONG> to submit your results.</P>
<HR>
<FORM METHOD="POST" ACTION="http://www.mcp.com/cgi-bin/post-query">
<P><STRONG>Name: </STRONG><INPUT TYPE="TEXT" NAME="theName"></P>
<P><STRONG>Sex: </STRONG>
<INPUT TYPE="radio" NAME="theSex" VALUE="male">Male
<INPUT TYPE="radio" NAME="theSex" VALUE="female">Female
<INPUT TYPE="radio" NAME="theSex" VALUE="null">Null
</P>
<P><STRONG>Contains (Select all that Apply): </STRONG><BR>
<INPUT TYPE="checkbox" NAME="humor">Vitreous Humor<BR>
<INPUT TYPE="checkbox" NAME="fish">Fish<BR>
<INPUT TYPE="checkbox" NAME="glycol">Propylene Glycol<BR>
<INPUT TYPE="checkbox" NAME="svga">SVGA Support<BR>
<INPUT TYPE="checkbox" NAME="angst">Angst<BR>
<INPUT TYPE="checkbox" NAME="catcon">Catalytic Converter<BR>
<INPUT TYPE="checkbox" NAME="vitamin">Ten Essential Vitamins and Nutrients<BR>
</P>
<P><INPUT TYPE="SUBMIT" VALUE="Submit Your Votes">
<INPUT TYPE="RESET" VALUE="Clear Form"></P>
</FORM>
<HR>
</BODY></HTML>
```

Try selecting different parts of the form and seeing what you get back using post-query. Figure 17.13 shows one sample I used; Figure 17.14 shows the results I got back.

17

Figure 17.13.

A sample surrealist.

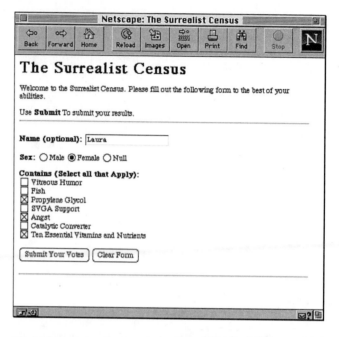

Figure 17.14.

The results back from the sample surrealist.

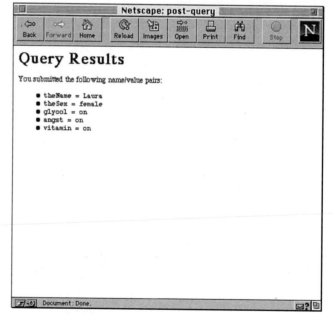

More Forms Layout

In addition to the <INPUT> tag with its many options, there are also two other tags that create form elements: SELECT, which has the ability to create pull-down menus and scrolling lists, and TEXTAREA, for allowing the reader to enter long blocks of text.

This section describes these other two tags. It also explains how to create "hidden" elements—form elements that don't actually show up on the page but exist in the form nonetheless.

Selections

Selections enable the reader to select one or more items from a menu or a scrolling list. They're similar in functionality to radio buttons or checkboxes, but they're displayed in a different way on-screen.

Selections are indicated by the <SELECT> tag, and individual options within the selection are indicated by the <OPTION> tag. The <SELECT> tag also contains a NAME attribute to hold its value when the form is submitted.

<SELECT> and <OPTION> work much like lists do, with the entire selection surrounded by the opening and closing <SELECT> tags. Each option begins with a single-sided <OPTION>, like this:

```
<P>Select a hair color:
<SELECT NAME="hcolor">
<OPTION>Black
<OPTION>Blonde
<OPTION>Brown
<OPTION>Red
<OPTION>Blue
</SELECT></P>
```

When the form is submitted, the value of the entire selection is the text that follows the selected <OPTION> tag—in this case, Brown, Red, Blue, and so on. You can also use the VALUE attribute with each <OPTION> tag to indicate a different value than the one that appears on the screen:

```
<OPTION VALUE="auburn">Red
```

Selections of this sort are generally formatted in graphical browsers as popup menus, as shown in Figure 17.15.

Figure 17.15.

Selections.

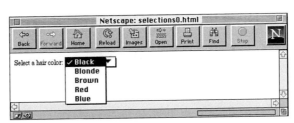

Usually, the first option in the list is the one that is selected and displayed as the initial value. You can set the default item to be initially selected by using the SELECTED attribute, part of the <OPTION> tag:

```
<P>Select a hair color:
<SELECT NAME="hcolor">
<OPTION>Black
<OPTION>Blonde
<OPTION SELECTED>Brown
<OPTION>Red
<OPTION>Blue
</SELECT></P>
```

By default, selections act like radio buttons; that is, only one item can be selected at a time. You can change the behavior of selections to allow multiple options to be selected by using the MULTIPLE attribute, part of the <SELECT> tag:

```
<P>Shopping List:
<SELECT NAME="shopping" MULTIPLE>
<OPTION>Butter
<OPTION>Milk
<OPTION>Flour
<OPTION>Eggs
<OPTION>Cheese
<OPTION>Beer
<OPTION>Pasta
<OPTION>Mushrooms
</SELECT></P>
```

Be careful when you use MULTIPLE in the script that will process this form. Remember that each selection list only has one possible NAME. This means that if you have multiple values in a selection list, all of those values will be submitted to your script, and the program you use to decode the input might store those in some special way.

NOTE

> Each browser determines how the reader makes multiple choices. Usually, the reader must hold down a key while making multiple selections, but that particular key may vary from browser to browser.

The optional <SIZE> attribute usually displays the selection as a scrolling list in graphical browsers, with the number of elements in the SIZE attribute visible on the form itself, as shown in the following code. (Figure 17.16 shows an example.)

```
<P>Shopping List:
<SELECT NAME="shopping" MULTIPLE SIZE="5">
<OPTION>Butter
<OPTION>Milk
<OPTION>Flour
<OPTION>Eggs
<OPTION>Cheese
<OPTION>Beer
```

17

```
<OPTION>Pasta
<OPTION>Mushrooms
</SELECT></P>
```

Figure 17.16.

Selections with
SIZE.

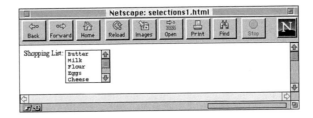

Here's an input and output example that shows a simple selection list and how it appears in Netscape for the Mac (Figure 17.17). Note that selection lists may have a different appearance if you're viewing them on different computer systems or in different browsers.

```
<FORM METHOD="POST" ACTION="http://www.mcp.com/cgi-bin/post-query">
<P>Select a hair color:
<SELECT NAME="hcolor">
<OPTION>Black
<OPTION>Blonde
<OPTION SELECTED>Brown
<OPTION>Red
<OPTION>Blue
</SELECT></P>
</FORM>
```

Figure 17.17.

*The output in
Netscape.*

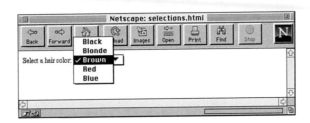

Text Areas

Text areas are input fields in which the reader can type. Unlike regular text-input fields (`<INPUT TYPE="text">`), text areas can contain many lines of text, making them extremely useful for forms that require extensive input. For example, if you wanted to create a form that enabled readers to compose electronic mail, you might use a text area for the body of the message.

To include a text area element in a form, use the `<TEXTAREA>` tag. `<TEXTAREA>` includes three attributes:

NAME	The name to be sent to the CGI script when the form is submitted
ROWS	The height of the text area element, in rows of text
COLS	The width of the text area element in columns (characters)

The <TEXTAREA> tag is a two-sided tag, and both sides must be used. If you have any default text you want to include in the text area, include it between the opening and closing tags. For example:

```
<TEXTAREA NAME="theBody" ROWS="14" COLS="50">Enter your message here.</TEXTAREA>
```

The text in a text area is generally formatted in a fixed-width font such as Courier, but it's up to the browser to decide how to format it beyond that. Some browsers will allow text wrapping in text areas; others will scroll to the right. Some will allow scrolling if the text area fills up, whereas some others will just stop accepting input.

Netscape provides an extension to HTML that allows you to control text wrapping in the browser. By default in Netscape, text in a text area does not wrap; it simply scrolls to the right. You have to press Enter to get to the next line. Using the WRAP attribute to TEXTAREA, you can change the wrapping behavior:

WRAP=OFF   The default; text will be all on one line, scrolling to the right, until the reader presses Enter.

WRAP=SOFT   Causes the text to wrap automatically in the browser window, but is sent to the server as all one line.

WRAP=HARD   Causes the text to wrap automatically in the browser window. That text is also sent to the server with new-line characters at each point where the text wrapped.

This input and output example shows a simple text area in Netscape (Figure 17.18) and Lynx (Figure 17.19).

INPUT
```
<FORM METHOD="POST" ACTION="http://www.mcp.com/cgi-bin/post-query">
<P>Enter any comments you have about this Web page here:
<TEXTAREA NAME="comment" ROWS="30" COLS="60">
</TEXTAREA>
</P>
</FORM>
```

Hidden Fields

One value for the TYPE attribute to the <INPUT> tag I haven't mentioned is "HIDDEN". Hidden fields do not appear on the actual form; they are invisible in the browser display. They will still appear in your HTML code if someone decides to look at the HTML source for your page.

Hidden input elements look like this:

```
<INPUT TYPE="HIDDEN" NAME="theName" VALUE="TheValue">
```

Why would you want to create a hidden form element? If it doesn't appear on the screen and the reader can't do anything with it, what's the point?

17

Figure 17.18.
*The output in
Netscape.*

Output

Figure 17.19.
*The output in
Lynx.*

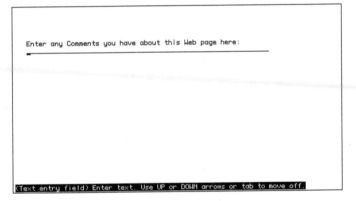

Let's take a hypothetical example. You create a simple form. In the script that processes the first form, you create a second form based on the input from the first form. The script to process the second form takes the information from both the first and second forms and creates a reply based on that information. Figure 17.20 shows how all this flows.

Figure 17.20.
*Form to form to
reply.*

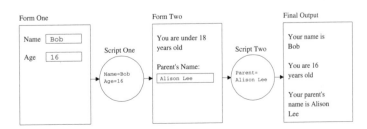

How would you pass the information from the first form to the script that processes the second form? You can do one of two things:

☐ Write the information from the first form to a temporary file, and then read that file back in again when the second form starts up.

☐ In the first script that constructs the second form, create hidden fields in the form with the appropriate information in NAME and VALUE fields. Then those names and values will be passed automatically to the second script when the reader submits the second form.

See? Hidden elements do make sense, particularly when you get involved in generating forms from forms.

Uploading Files Using Forms

A recent proposal for modifying the standard definition of forms includes allowing forms to be used for uploading whole files full of data to a server. With forms the way they are now, you can upload a text file by copying it into a text area, but there's no easy way to upload an image or other binary file.

NOTE   File upload is a proposed enhancement to HTML and has been extensively discussed by the various HTML standards organizations. At the moment, however, Netscape 2.0 is the only browser that supports form-based file upload, and even then, dealing with the input on the server side is significantly more difficult than dealing with simple form input. Keep all this in mind as you read this section; file upload is very new indeed.

If you do decide to play with form-based file upload, you'll need to make two simple changes to the HTML code for your form. The first is to include the ENCTYPE="multipart/form-data" attribute inside your <FORM> tag, like this:

```
<FORM METHOD=POST ENCTYPE="multipart/form-data"
ACTION="http://www.myserver.com/cgi-bin/uploadit">

...
</FORM>
```

NOTE   ENCTYPE (short for enclosure type) isn't new; it's actually part of standard HTML 2.0, and its default value is application/x-www-form-urlencoded. Because the vast majority of forms use that default

> enclosure type and few browsers or servers know how to deal with any
> other enclosure type, you don't really need to know anything about
> ENCTYPE unless you're working with file upload.

The second thing you'll need to add to your form is a new kind of <INPUT> tag. A new value
for the TYPE attribute, TYPE="file", inserts a file-upload element (a text field and a button
labeled "Browse" that lets you browse the local file system). Here's an example of a form with
nothing but a file-upload element in it. Figure 17.21 shows how this appears in Netscape.

```
<FORM ENCTYPE="multipart/form-data"
ACTION="http://www.myserver.com/cgi-bin/upload" METHOD=POST>
Send this file: <INPUT NAME="userfile" TYPE="file">
<INPUT TYPE="submit" VALUE="Send File">
</FORM>
```

Figure 17.21.
*Forms for file
upload.*

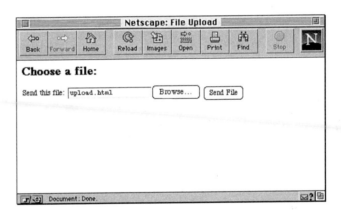

Note that because this is an entirely new kind of form, you won't be able to test this with the
post-query program we've been using up to this point. You'll need a special script on the
server side to deal with form-based file upload; I'll talk more about this in the next chapter
on CGI scripts.

Summary

Text fields, radio buttons, checkboxes, submit and reset buttons, selection lists, and text
areas—all of these are form elements you can include on your Web pages to get information

back from your reader. And in this chapter, you learned all about how to include each of these in your Web page, as well as how to construct the form itself so that when it's submitted it'll call the right programs on the server side to process the information.

Forms are an HTML 2.0 feature, and the tags for creating forms are widely supported in just about every available browser. Table 17.1 presents a summary of all the tags and attributes you learned about in this chapter.

Table 17.1. HTML tags from this chapter.

Tag	Use
<FORM>...</FORM>	A form. You can have multiple forms within a document, but forms cannot be nested.
ACTION	An attribute of the <FORM> tag indicating the CGI script to process the form input. Contains a relative path or URL to the script.
METHOD	An attribute of the <FORM> tag, indicating the method with which the form input is given to the script that processes the form. Possible values are GET and POST.
<INPUT>	A form element.
TYPE	An attribute of the <INPUT> tag indicating the type of form element. Possible values are CHECKBOX, HIDDEN, IMAGE, RADIO, RESET, SUBMIT, and TEXT.
	CHECKBOX	Creates a checkbox.
	HIDDEN	Creates a form element that is not presented but has a name and a value that can then be passed on to the script that processes the form input.
	IMAGE	Creates a clickable image, similar to an image map, that behaves like a submit button.
	RADIO	Creates a radio button.
	RESET	Creates a button which clears the user's selections and resets the default values of the form, if any.
	SUBMIT	Creates a button to submit the form to the script which processes the input.
	TEXT	Creates a single-line text input field.
VALUE	An attribute of the <INPUT> tag, indicating the default value for the form element, if any, or the value submitted with the NAME to the script. For SUBMIT and RESET buttons, VALUE indicates the label of the button.

17

Tag	Use
SIZE	An attribute of the <INPUT> tag used only when TYPE is TEXT. Indicates the size of the text field, in characters.
MAXLENGTH	An attribute of the <INPUT> tag used only when TYPE is TEXT. Indicates the maximum number of characters this text field will accept.
CHECKED	An attribute of the <INPUT> tag used only when TYPE is CHECKBOX or RADIO. Indicates that this element is selected by default.
SRC	An attribute of the <INPUT> tag used only when TYPE is IMAGE. Indicates the path or URL to the image file.
FILE	An attribute of the <INPUT> tag which inserts a file-uploading form element: a text field and a Browse button that allow you to browse the local file system.
<SELECT>	A menu or scrolling list of items. Individual items are indicated by the <OPTION> tag.
MULTIPLE	An attribute of the <SELECT> tag indicating that multiple items in the list can be selected.
SIZE	An attribute of the <SELECT> tag which causes the list of items to be displayed as a scrolling list with the number of items indicated by SIZE visible.
<OPTION>	Individual items within a <SELECT> element.
SELECTED	An attribute of the <OPTION> tag indicating that this item is selected by default.
VALUE	An attribute of the <OPTION> tag indicating the value this option should have when the form is submitted.
<TEXTAREA>	A text-entry field with multiple lines.
ROWS	An attribute of the <TEXTAREA> tag indicating the height of the text field, in rows.
COLS	An attribute of the <TEXTAREA> tag indicating the width of the text field, in characters.
WRAP	A (Netscape) attribute of the <TEXTAREA> tag indicating how the text inside that text area will behave. Possible values are OFF (the default), in which no wrapping occurs; SOFT, in which wrapping occurs on-screen but the text is sent to the server as a single line; or HARD in which wrapping occurs on-screen and newlines are included in the text as submitted to the server.

17

Q&A

Q I've got a form with a group of radio buttons, of which one has to be selected. When my form first comes up in a browser, none of them are selected, so if my reader doesn't choose one, I don't get any of the values. How can I make it so that one of them is selected?

A Use the CHECKED attribute to set a default radio button out of the group. If your reader doesn't change it, the value of that radio button will be the one that's submitted.

Q I'm having a hard time getting my form elements to lay out the way I want them. Nothing lines up right.

A Form elements, like all HTML elements, lay out based on the size of the screen and the browser's rules for where things go on the screen.

I've seen two ways of affecting how forms are laid out. The first is to use <PRE>; the monospaced text affects the labels for the forms, but not the form elements themselves.

The second solution is to use tables without borders. You can get all your form elements to line up nicely by aligning them inside table cells.

Q I have text areas in my forms. In Netscape, when I type into the text area, the line keeps going and going to the right; it never wraps onto the next line. Do I have to press Enter at the end of every line?

A When you set up your form, include the WRAP attribute to indicate in Netscape how text inside the form will behave. WRAP=SOFT would be a good choice.

Chapter 18

Beginning CGI Scripting

CGI stands for Common Gateway Interface, a method for running programs on the Web server based on input from a Web browser. CGI scripts enable your reader to interact with your Web pages—to search for an item in a database, to offer comments on what you've written, or to select several items from a form and get a customized reply in return. If you've ever come across a fill-in form or a search dialog on the Web, you've used a CGI script. You may not have realized it at the time because most of the work happens on the Web server, behind the scenes. You see only the result.

As a Web author, you create all the sides of the CGI script: the side the reader sees, the programming on the server side to deal with the reader's input, and the result given back to the reader. CGI scripts are an extremely powerful feature of Web browser and server interaction that can completely change how you think of a Web presentation.

In this chapter, you'll learn just about everything about CGI scripts, including

- ☐ What a CGI script is and how it works
- ☐ What the output of a CGI script looks like

☐ How to create CGI scripts with and without parameters or arguments

☐ How to create scripts that return special responses

☐ How to create scripts to process input from forms

☐ Troubleshooting problems with your CGI scripts

☐ CGI variables you can use in your scripts

☐ Scripts with non-parsed headers

☐ Searches using <ISINDEX>

NOTE

> This chapter and the next focus primarily on Web servers running on UNIX systems, and most of the examples and instructions will apply only to UNIX. If you run your Web server on a system other than UNIX, the procedures you'll learn in this section for creating CGI scripts may not apply. But this chapter will at least give you an idea of how CGI works, and then you can combine that with the documentation of CGI on your specific server.

What Is a CGI Script?

A CGI script, most simply, is a program that is run on a Web server, triggered by input from a browser. The script is usually a link between the server and some other program running on the system; for example, a database.

CGI scripts do not have to be actual scripts—depending on what your Web server supports, they can be compiled programs or batch files or any other executable entity. For the sake of a simple term for this chapter, however, I'll call them scripts.

NEW TERM

> A *CGI script* is any program that runs on the Web server. CGI stands for Common Gateway Interface and is a basic set of variables and mechanisms for passing information from the browser to the server.

CGI scripts are usually used in one of two ways: as the ACTION to a form or as a direct link on a page. Scripts to process forms are used slightly differently than regular CGI scripts, but both have very similar appearances and behavior. For the first part of this chapter you'll learn about generic CGI scripts and then move on to creating scripts that process forms.

How Do CGI Scripts Work?

CGI scripts are called by the server, based on information from the browser. Figure 18.1 shows the path of how things work between the browser, the server, and the script.

Figure 18.1.

Browser to server to script to program and back again.

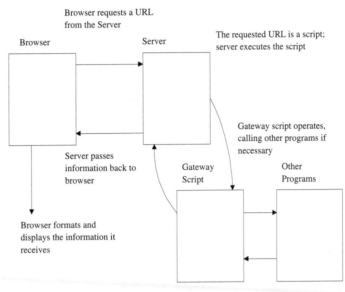

Here's a short version of what's actually going on:

1. A URL points to a CGI script. A CGI script URL can appear anywhere that a regular URL can appear; for example, in a link or in an image. Most often, a URL appears as the ACTION to a form. The browser contacts the server with that URL.

2. The server receives the request, notes that the URL points to a script (based on the location of the file or based on its extension, depending on the server), and executes that script.

3. The script performs some action based on the input, if any, from the browser. The action may include querying a database, calculating a value, or simply calling some other program on the system.

4. The script generates some kind of output that the Web server can understand.

5. The Web server receives the output from the script and passes it back to the browser, which formats and displays it for the reader.

Got it? No? Don't be worried; it can be a confusing process. Read on, it'll become clearer with a couple of examples.

A Simple Example

Here's a simple example, with a step-by-step explanation of what's happening on all sides of the process. In your browser, you encounter a page that looks like the page shown in Figure 18.2.

Figure 18.2.

A page with a script link.

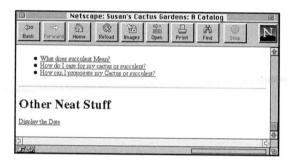

The link to `Display the Date` is a link to a CGI script. It is embedded in the HTML code for the page just like any other link. If you were to look at the HTML code for that page, that link might look like this:

```
<A HREF="http://www.somesite.com/cgi-bin/getdate">Display the Date</A>
```

The fact that there's a `cgi-bin` in the pathname is a strong hint that this is a CGI script. On many servers `cgi-bin` is the only place that CGI scripts can be kept.

When you select the link, your browser requests that URL from the server at the site `www.somesite.com`. The server receives the request and figures out from its configuration that the URL it's been given is a script called `getdate`. It executes that script.

The `getdate` script, in this case a shell script to be executed on a UNIX system, looks something like this:

```
#!/bin/sh

echo Content-type: text/plain
echo

/bin/date
```

The first line is a special command that tells UNIX this is a shell script; the real fun begins on the line after that. This script does two things. First, it outputs the line `Content-type: text/plain`, followed by a blank line. Second, it calls the standard UNIX date program, which prints out the date and time. So the complete output of the script looks something like this:

```
Content-type: text/plain

Sun Jul 16 17:50:23 PDT 1995
```

What's that `Content-type` thing? That's a special code the Web server passes on to the browser to tell it what kind of document this is. The browser then uses that code to figure out if it can display the document or not, or if it needs to load an external viewer. You'll learn specifics about this line later in this chapter.

So, after the script is finished executing, the server gets the result and passes it back to the browser over the Net. The browser has been waiting patiently all this time for some kind of response. When the browser gets the input from the server, it simply displays it (Figure 18.3).

Figure 18.3.
The result of the date script.

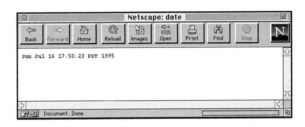

That's the basic idea. Although things can get much more complicated, it's this interaction between browser, server, and script that is at the heart of how CGI scripts work.

Can I Use CGI Scripts?

Before you can use CGI scripts in your Web presentations, there are several basic conditions that must be met by both you and your server. CGI scripting is an advanced Web feature and requires knowledge on your part as well as the cooperation of your Web server provider.

Make sure you can answer all the questions in this section before going on.

Is Your Server Configured To Allow CGI Scripts?

In order to write and run CGI scripts, you will need a Web server. Unlike with regular HTML files, you cannot write and test CGI scripts on your local system; you have to go through a Web server to do so.

But even if you have a Web server, that server has to be specially configured to run CGI scripts. That usually means that all your scripts will be kept in a special directory called `cgi-bin`.

Before trying out CGI scripts, ask your server administrator if you are allowed to install and run CGI scripts and, if so, where to put them when you're done writing them. Also, you must have a real Web server to run CGI scripts—if you publish your Web pages on an FTP or Gopher server, you cannot use CGI.

If you run your own server, you'll have to specially create a `cgi-bin` directory and configure your server to recognize that directory as a script directory (part of your server configuration, which of course varies from server to server). Also keep in mind the following issues that CGI scripts bring up:

☐ Each script is a program, and it runs on your system when the browser requests it, using CPU time and memory during its execution. What happens to the system if dozens or hundreds or thousands of these scripts are running at the same time? Your system may not be able to handle the load, making it crash or be unusable for normal work.

☐ Unless you are very careful with the CGI scripts you write, you can potentially open yourself up to someone breaking into or damaging your system by passing arguments to your CGI script that are different from those it expects.

Can You Program?

Beginner beware! In order to do CGI, process forms, or do any sort of interactivity on the World Wide Web, you must have a basic grasp of programming concepts and methods, and you should have some familiarity with the system on which you are working. If you don't have this background, I strongly suggest that you consult with someone who does, pick up a book in programming basics, or take a class in programming at your local college. This book is far too short for me to explain both introductory programming and CGI programming at the same time; in this chapter in particular, I am going to assume that you can read and understand the code in these examples.

What Programming Language Should You Use?

You can use just about any programming language you're familiar with to write CGI scripts, as long as your script follows the rules in the next section, and as long as that language can run on the system your Web server runs on. Some servers, however, may only support programs written in a particular language. For example, MacHTTP and WebStar use AppleScript for their CGI scripts; WinHTTPD and WebSite use Visual Basic. To write CGI scripts for your server, you must program in the language that server accepts.

In this chapter and throughout this book, I'm going to be writing these CGI scripts in two languages: the UNIX Bourne shell and the Perl language. The Bourne shell is available on nearly any UNIX system and is reasonably easy to learn, but doing anything complicated with it can be difficult. Perl, on the other hand, is freely available, but you'll have to download and compile it on your system. The language itself is extremely flexible and powerful (nearly as powerful as a programming language such as C), but it is also very difficult to learn.

Is Your Server Set Up Right?

To run any CGI scripts, whether they are simple scripts or scripts to process forms, your server needs to be set up explicitly to run them. This might mean your scripts must be kept in a special directory or they must have a special file extension, depending on which server you're using and how it's set up.

If you are renting space on a Web server, or if someone else is in charge of administering your Web server, you have to ask the person in charge whether CGI scripts are allowed and, if so, where to put them.

If you run your own server, check with the documentation for that server to see how it handles CGI scripts.

What If You're Not on UNIX?

If you're not on UNIX, stick around. There's still lots of general information about CGI that might apply to your server. But just for general background, here's some information about CGI on other common Web servers.

WinHTTPD for Windows 3.x, and WebSite for Windows 95 and NT, both include CGI capabilities with which you can manage form and CGI input. Both servers include a DOS and Windows CGI mode, the latter of which allows you to manage CGI through Visual Basic. The DOS mode can be configured to handle CGI scripts using Perl or Tcl (or any other language). WebSite also has a CGI mode for running Perl and Windows shell script CGI programs.

MacHTTP has CGI capabilities in the form of AppleScript scripts. (The new version of MacHTTP is called WebStar and is available from StarNine.) Jon Wiederspan has written an excellent tutorial on using AppleScript CGI, which is included as part of the MacHTTP documentation.

Anatomy of a CGI Script

If you've made it this far, past all the warnings and configuration, congratulations! You can write CGI scripts and create forms for your presentations. In this section you'll learn about how your scripts should behave so your server can talk to them and get the correct response back.

The Output Header

Your CGI scripts will generally get some sort of input from the browser by way of the server. You can do anything you want with that information in the body of your script, but the output of that script has to follow a special form.

18

NOTE

By "script output," I'm referring to the data your script sends back to the server. On UNIX, the output is sent to the standard output, and the server picks it up from there. On other systems and other servers, your script output may go somewhere else, for example, you may write to a file on the disk or send the output explicitly to another program. Again, this is a case where you should carefully examine the documentation for your server to see how CGI scripts have been implemented in that server.

The first thing your script should output is a special header that gives the server, and eventually the browser, information about the rest of the data your script is going to create. The header isn't actually part of the document; it's never displayed anywhere. Web servers and browsers actually send information like this back and forth all the time; you just never see it.

There are three types of headers that you can output from scripts: Content-type, Location, and Status. Content-type is the most popular, so I'll explain it here; you'll learn about Location and Status later in this chapter.

You learned about the Content-type header earlier in this book; Content-types are used by the browser to figure out what kind of data it's receiving. Because script output doesn't have a file extension, you have to explicitly tell the browser what kind of data you're sending back. To do this, you use the Content-type header. A Content-type header has the words `Content-type`, a special code for describing the kind of file you're sending, and a blank line, like this:

```
Content-type: text/html
```

In this example, the contents of the data to follow are of the type `text/html`; in other words, it's an HTML file. Each file format you work with when you're creating Web presentations has a corresponding Content-type, so you should match the format of the output of your script to the appropriate one. Table 18.1 shows some common formats and their equivalent Content-types.

Table 18.1. Common formats and Content-types.

Format	Content-Type
HTML	`text/html`
Text	`text/plain`
GIF	`image/gif`
JPEG	`image/jpeg`
PostScript	`application/postscript`
MPEG	`video/mpeg`

Note that the Content-type line *must* be followed by a blank line. The server will not be able to figure out where the header ends if you don't include the blank line.

The Output Data

The remainder of your script is the actual data that you want to send back to the browser. The content you output in this part should match the Content-type you told the server you were giving it; that is, if you use a Content-type of text/html, the rest of the output should be in HTML. If you use a Content-type of image/gif, the remainder of the output should be a binary GIF file, and so on for all the Content-types.

Exercise 18.1: Try it.

This exercise is similar to the simple example from earlier in this chapter, the one that printed out the date. This CGI script checks to see if I'm logged into my Web server and reports back what it found (as shown in Figure 18.4).

Figure 18.4.

The pinglaura *script results.*

This is the most simple form of a CGI script, which can be called from a Web page by just linking to it like this:

```
<A HREF="http://www.lne.com/web/cgi-bin/pinglaura">Is Laura Logged in?</A>
```

When you link to a CGI script like this, selecting that link runs the script. There is no input to the script; it just runs and returns data.

First, determine the Content-type you'll be outputting. Since this will be an HTML document, the Content-type is text/html. So the first part of your script simply prints out a line containing the Content-type, and a blank line after that (don't forget that blank line!):

```
#!/bin/sh

echo Content-type: text/html
echo
```

Now, add the remainder of the script: the body of the HTML document, which you had to construct yourself from inside the script. Basically what you're going to do here is

- ☐ Print out the tags that make up the first part of the HTML document.
- ☐ Test to see if I'm logged in, and output an appropriate message.

☐ Print out the last bit of HTML tags to finish up the document.

Start with the first bit of the HTML. The following commands will do this in the UNIX shell:

```
echo "<HTML><HEAD>"
echo "<TITLE>Is Laura There?</TITLE>"
echo "</HEAD><BODY>"
```

Now test to see whether I'm logged into the system using the who command (my login ID is lemay), and store the result in the variable ison. If I'm logged in, the ison variable will have something in it; otherwise, ison will be empty.

```
ison=`who | grep lemay`
```

Test the result and return the appropriate message as part of the script output:

```
if [ ! -z "$ison" ]; then
        echo "<P>Laura is logged in."</P>
else
        echo "<P>Laura isn't logged in."</P>
fi
```

Finally, close up the remainder of the HTML tags:

```
echo "</BODY></HTML>"
```

And that's it. If you ran the program by itself from a command line to test its output, you would get a result that says I'm not logged into your system, something like this (unless, of course, I am logged into your system):

```
Content-type: text/html

<HTML><HEAD>
<TITLE>Are You There?</TITLE>
</HEAD><BODY>
<P>Laura isn't logged in.
</BODY></HTML>
```

Looks like your basic HTML document, doesn't it? That's precisely the point. The output from your script is what is sent back to the server and then out to the browser, so it should be in a format the server and browser can understand—here, an HTML file.

Now, install this script in the proper place for your server. This step will vary depending on the platform you're on and the server you're using. Most of the time, on UNIX servers, there will be a special cgi-bin directory for scripts. Copy the script there and make it executable.

NOTE

If you don't have access to the cgi-bin directory, you must ask your Web server administrator for access. You cannot just create a cgi-bin directory and copy the script there; that won't work. See your Webmaster.

Now that you've got a script ready to go, you can call it from a Web page by linking to it, as I mentioned earlier. Just for reference, here's what the final script looks like:

```
#!/bin/sh

echo "Content-type: text/html"
echo
echo "<HTML><HEAD>"
echo "<TITLE>Is Laura There?</TITLE>"
echo "</HEAD><BODY>"

ison=`who | grep lemay`

if [ ! -z "$ison" ]; then
        echo "<P>Laura is logged in"
else
        echo "<P>Laura isn't logged in"
fi

echo "</BODY></HTML>"
```

Scripts with Arguments

CGI scripts are most useful if they're written to be as generic as possible. For example, if you want to check whether different people are logged into the system using the script in the previous example, you might have to write several different scripts (`pinglaura`, `pingeric`, `pingelsa`, and so on). It would make more sense to have a single generic script, and then send the name you want to check for as an argument to the script.

To pass arguments to a script, specify those arguments in the script's URL with a question mark (?) separating the name of the script from the arguments, and with plus signs (+) separating each individual argument, like this:

```
<A HREF="/cgi-bin/myscript?arg1+arg2+arg3">run my script</A>
```

When the server receives the script request, it passes `arg1`, `arg2`, and `arg3` to the script as arguments. You can then parse and use those arguments in the body of the script.

This method of passing arguments to a script is sometimes called a query, because it is how browsers communicated search keys in an earlier version of searches called ISINDEX searches (you'll learn more about these later on). These days, most searches are done using forms, but this form of encoding arguments is still used; you should be familiar with it if you use CGI scripts often.

18

Exercise 18.2: Check to see whether anyone is logged in.

Now that you know how to pass arguments to a script, let's modify the `pinglaura` script so that it is more generic. We'll call this script `pinggeneric`.

Start with the beginning of the script we used in the previous example, with a slightly different title:

```
#!/bin/sh
echo "Content-type: text/html"
echo
echo "<HTML><HEAD>"
echo "<TITLE>Are You There?</TITLE>"
echo "</HEAD><BODY>"
```

In the previous example, the next step was to test whether I was logged on. Here's where the script becomes generic. Instead of the name `lemay` hardcoded into the script, use `${1}` instead, with `${1}` as the first argument, `${2}` as the second, `${3}` as the third, and so on.

```
ison=`who | grep "${1}"`
```

> **NOTE**
>
> Why the extra quotes around the `${1}`? That's to keep nasty people from passing weird arguments to your script. It's a security issue.

All that's left is to modify the rest of the script to use the argument instead of the hardcoded name:

```
if [ ! -z "$ison" ]; then
        echo "<P>$1 is logged in"
else
        echo "<P>$1 isn't logged in"
fi
```

Now finish up with the closing `<HTML>` tag:

```
echo "</BODY></HTML>"
```

With the script complete, let's modify the HTML page that calls that script. The `pinglaura` script was called with an HTML link, like this:

```
<A HREF="http://www.lne.com/web/cgi-bin/pinglaura">Is Laura Logged in?</A>
```

The generic version is called in a similar way, with the argument at the end of the URL, like this (this one tests for someone named John):

```
<A HREF="http://www.lne.com/web/cgi-bin/pinggeneric?john">Is John Logged in?</A>
```

Try it on your own server, with your own login ID in the URL for the script to see what kind of result you get.

Passing Other Information to the Script

In addition to the arguments passed to a script through query arguments, there is a second way of passing information to a CGI script (that still isn't forms). The second way is called path information and is used for arguments that can't change between invocations of the script, such as the name of a temporary file or the name of the file that called the script itself. As you'll see in the section on forms, the arguments after the question mark can indeed change based on input from the user. Path info is used for other information to be passed for the script (and indeed, you can use it for anything you want).

NEW TERM

Path information is a way of passing extra information to a CGI script that are not as frequently changed as regular script arguments. Path information often refers to files on the Web server such as configuration files, temporary files, or the file that actually called the script in question.

18

To use path information, append the information you want to include to the end of the URL for the script, after the script name but before the ? and the rest of the arguments, as in the following example:

```
http://myhost/cgi-bin/myscript/remaining_path_info?arg1+arg2
```

When the script is run, the information in the path is placed in the environment variable `PATH_INFO`. You can then use that information any way you want to in the body of your script.

For example, let's say you had multiple links on multiple pages to the same script. You could use the path information to indicate the name of the HTML file that had the link. Then, after you've finished processing your script, when you send back an HTML file, you could include a link in that file back to the page that your reader came from.

Creating Special Script Output

In the couple of examples you've created so far in this chapter, you've written scripts that output data, usually HTML data, and that data is sent to the browser for interpretation and display. But what if you don't want to send a stream of data as a result of a script's actions? What if you want to load an existing page instead? What if you just want the script to do something and not give any response back to the browser?

Fear not, you can do those things in CGI scripts. This section explains how.

Responding by Loading Another Document

CGI output doesn't have to be a stream of data. Sometimes it's easier just to tell the browser to go to another page you have stored on your server (or on any server, for that matter). To send this message, you use a line similar to the following:

```
Location: ../docs/final.html
```

The Location line is used in place of the normal output; that is, if you use Location, you do not need to use Content-type or include any other data in the output (and, in fact, you can't include any other data in the output). As with Content-type, however, you must also include a blank line after the Location line.

The pathname to the file can be either a full URL or a relative pathname. All relative pathnames will be relative to the location of the script itself. This one looks for the document final.html in a directory called docs one level up from the current directory:

```
echo Location: ../docs/final.html
echo
```

NOTE

> You cannot combine Content-type and Location output. For example, if you want to output a standard page and then add custom content to the bottom of that same page, you'll have to use Content-type and construct both parts yourself. Note that you could use script commands to open up a local file and print it directly to the output; for example, cat filename would send the contents of the file filename as data.

No Response

Sometimes it may be appropriate for a CGI script to have no output at all. Sometimes you just want to take the information you get from the reader. You may not want to load a new document, either by outputting the result or by opening an existing file. The document that was on the browser's screen before should just stay there.

Fortunately, doing this is quite easy. Instead of outputting a Content-type or Location header, use the following commands instead (with a blank line after it, as always):

```
echo Status: 204 No Response
echo
```

The Status header provides status codes to the server (and to the browser). The particular status of 204 is passed on to the browser, and the browser, if it can figure out what to do with it, should do nothing.

You'll need no other output from your script since you don't want the browser to do anything with it—just the one Status line with the blank line. Of course, your script should do something; otherwise, why bother calling the script at all?

NOTE

> Although No Response is part of the official HTTP specification, it may not be supported in all browsers or may produce strange results. Before using a No Response header, you might want to experiment with several different browsers to see what the result will be.

Scripts To Process Forms

Most uses of CGI scripts these days are for processing form input. Calling a CGI script directly from a link can execute only that script with the hardcoded arguments. Forms allow any amount of information to be entered by the reader of the form, sent back to the server, and processed by a CGI script. They're the same scripts, and they behave in the same ways. You still use Content-type and Location headers to send a response back to the browser. However, there are a few differences, including how the CGI script is called and how the data is sent from the browser to the server.

Remember, most forms have two parts: the HTML layout for the form and the CGI script to process that form's data. The CGI script is called using attributes to the <FORM> tag.

Form Layout and Form Scripts

As you learned in Chapter 17, "Basic Forms," most forms you see on the Web have two parts: the HTML code for the form, which is displayed in the browser, and the script to process the contents of that form, which runs on the server. They are linked together in the HTML code.

The ACTION attribute inside the <FORM> tag contains the name of the script to process the form:

```
<FORM ACTION="http://www.myserver.com/cgi-bin/processorscript">
```

In addition to this reference to the script, each input field in the form (a text field, a radio button, and so on) has a NAME attribute, which names that form element. When the form data is submitted to the CGI script you named in ACTION, the names of the tags and the contents of that field are passed to the script as name/value pairs. In your script you can then get to the contents of each field (the value) by referring to that field's name.

18

GET and POST

One part of forms I didn't mention yesterday (except in passing) was the METHOD attribute. METHOD indicates the way the form data will be sent from the browser to the server to the script. METHOD has one of two values, GET and POST.

GET is just like the CGI scripts you learned about in the previous section. The form data is packaged and appended to the end of the URL you specified in the ACTION attribute as the argument. So, if your action attribute looks like this:

```
ACTION="/cgi/myscript"
```

and you have the same two input tags as in the previous section, the final URL sent by the browser to the server when the form is submitted might look like this:

```
http://myhost/cgi-bin/myscript?username=Agamemnon&phone=555-6666
```

Note that this formatting is slightly different than the arguments you passed to the CGI script by hand; this format is called URL encoding and is explained in more detail later in this chapter.

When the server executes your CGI script to process the form, it sets the environment variable QUERY_STRING to everything after the question mark in the URL.

POST does much the same thing as GET, except that it sends the data separately from the actual call to the script. Your script then gets the form data through the standard input. (Some Web servers might store it in a temporary file instead of using standard input; UNIX servers do the latter.) The QUERY_STRING environment variable is not set if you use POST.

Which one should you use? POST is the safest method, particularly if you expect a lot of form data. When you use GET, the server assigns the QUERY_STRING variable to all the encoded form data, and there might be limits on the amount of data you can store in that variable. In other words, if you have lots of form data and you use GET, you might lose some of that data.

If you use POST, you can have as much data as you want, because the data is sent as a separate stream and is never assigned to a variable.

URL Encoding

URL encoding is the format that the browser uses to package the input to the form when it sends it to the server. The browser gets all the names and values from the form input, encodes them as name/value pairs, translates any characters that won't transfer over the wire, lines up all the data, and—depending on whether you're using GET or POST—sends them to the server either as part of the URL or separately through a direct link to the server. In either case, the form input ends up on the server side (and therefore in your script) as gobbledygook that looks something like this:

18

```
theName=Ichabod+Crane&gender=male&status=missing&headless=yes
```

URL encoding follows these rules:

☐ Each name/value pair itself is separated by an ampersand (&).

☐ The name/value pairs from the form are separated by an equal sign (=). In cases when the user of the form did not enter a value for a particular tag, the name still appears in the input, but with no value (as in "name=").

☐ Any special characters (characters that are not simple seven-bit ASCII) are encoded in hexadecimal preceded by a percent sign (%NN). Special characters include the =, &, and % characters if they appear in the input itself.

☐ Spaces in the input are indicated by plus signs (+).

Because form input is passed to your script in this URL-encoded form, you'll have to decode it before you can use it. However, because decoding this information is a common task, there are lots of tools for doing just that. There's no reason for you to write your own decoding program unless you want to do something very unusual. The decoding programs that are out there can do a fine job, and they might consider things that you haven't, such as how to avoid having your script break because someone gave your form funny input.

I've noted a few programs for decoding form input later on in this chapter, but the program I'm going to use for the examples in this book is called uncgi, which decodes the input from a form submission for you and creates a set of environment variables from the name/value pairs. Each environment variable has the same name as the name in the name/value pair, with the prefix WWW_ prepended to each one. Each value in the name/value pair is then assigned to its respective environment variable. So, for example, if you had a form with a name in it called username, the resulting environment variable uncgi created would be WWW_username, and its value would be whatever the reader typed in that form element. Once you've got the environment variables, you can test them just as you would any other variable.

You can get the source for uncgi from http://www.hyperion.com/~koreth/uncgi.html. Compile uncgi using the instructions that come with the source, install it in your cgi-bin directory, and you're ready to go.

Exercise 18.3: Tell me your name, Part 2.

Remember the form you created yesterday that prompts you for your name? Let's create the script to handle that form (the form is shown again in Figure 18.5, in case you've forgotten). Using this form, you would type in your name and submit the form using the Submit button.

The input is sent to the script, which sends back an HTML document that displays a hello message with your name in it (see Figure 18.6).

What if you didn't type anything at the Enter your Name prompt? The script would send you the response shown in Figure 18.7.

Figure 18.5.

The Tell Me Your Name form.

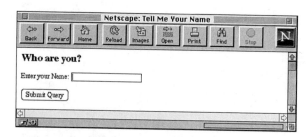

Figure 18.6.

The result of the name form.

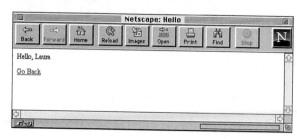

Figure 18.7.

Another result.

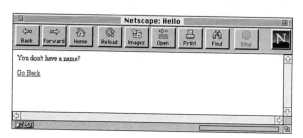

Modify the HTML for the Form

In the examples in Chapter 17, we used a testing program called post-query as the script to call in the ACTION attribute to the <FORM> tag. Now that we're working with real scripts, we'll modify the form so that it points to a real CGI script. The value of ACTION can be a full URL or a relative pathname to a script on your server. So, for example, the following <FORM> tag would call a script called form-name in a cgi-bin directory one level up from the current directory:

```
<FORM METHOD=POST ACTION="../cgi-bin/form-name">
</FORM>
```

If you're using uncgi to decode form input, as I am in these examples, things are slightly different. To make uncgi work properly, you call uncgi first, and then append the name of the actual script as if uncgi were a directory, like this:

```
<FORM METHOD=POST ACTION="../cgi-bin/uncgi/form-name">
</FORM>
```

18

Other than this one modification, you don't need to modify the HTML for the form at all; the original HTML code works just fine. Let's move on to the script to process the form.

The Script

The script to process the form input is a CGI script, just like the ones you've been creating up to this point in the chapter. All the same rules apply for Content-type headers and passing the data back to the browser.

The first step in a form script is usually to decode the information that was passed to your script through the POST method. In this example however, because we're using uncgi to decode form input, the form decoding has already been done for you. Remember how you put uncgi in the ACTION attribute to the form, followed by the name of your script? What happens there is that when the form input is submitted, the server passes that input to the uncgi program, which decodes the form input for you, and then calls your script with everything already decoded. Now, at the start of your script, all the name/value pairs are there for you to use.

Moving on, print out the usual CGI headers and HTML code to begin the page:

```
echo Content-type: text/html
echo
echo "<HTML><HEAD>"
echo "<TITLE>Hello</TITLE>"
echo "</HEAD><BODY>"
echo "<P>"
```

Now comes the meat of the script. You have two branches to deal with: one to accuse the reader of not entering a name, and one to say hello when they do.

The value of the theName element, as you named the text field in your form, is contained in the WWW_theName environment variable. Using a simple Bourne shell test (-z), you can see if this environment variable is empty and include the appropriate response in the output:

```
if [ ! -z "$WWW_theName" ]; then
    echo "Hello, "
    echo $WWW_theName
else
    echo "You don't have a name?"
fi
```

Finally, add the last bit of HTML code to include the "go back" link. This link points back to the URL of the original form (here, called name1.html) in a directory one level up from cgi-bin:

```
echo "</P><P><A HREF="../lemay/name1.html">Go Back</A></P>"
echo "</BODY></HTML>"
```

And that's it! That's all there is to it. Learning how to do CGI scripts is the hard part; linking them together with forms is easy.

18

Troubleshooting

Here are some of the most common problems with CGI scripts and how to fix them:

☐ The content of the script is being displayed, not executed.

Have you configured your server to accept CGI scripts? Are your scripts contained in the appropriate CGI directory (usually `cgi-bin`)? If your server requires CGI files with `.cgi` extensions, does your script have that extension?

☐ Error 500: Server doesn't support POST.

You'll get this error from forms that use the POST method. This error most often means that you either haven't set up CGI scripts in your server, or you're trying to access a script that isn't contained in a CGI directory (see the previous bullet).

It can also mean, however, that you've misspelled the path to the script itself. Check the pathname in your form, and if it's correct, make sure that your script is in the appropriate CGI directory (usually `cgi-bin`) and that it has a `.cgi` extension (if your server requires this).

☐ Document contains no data.

Make sure you included a blank line between your headers and the data in your script.

☐ Error 500: Bad Script Request.

Make sure your script is executable (on UNIX, make sure you've done `chmod +x yourscript.cgi` to the script). You and other users on your system should be able to run your scripts from a command line before you try to call them from a browser.

CGI Variables

CGI variables are a set of special variables that are set in the environment when a CGI script is called. All of these variables are available to you in your script to use as you see fit. Table 18.2 summarizes these variables.

Table 18.2. CGI environment variables.

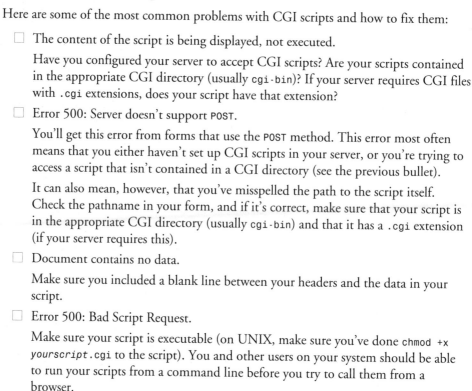

Environment Variable	What It Means
SERVER_NAME	The hostname or IP address on which the CGI script is running, as it appears in the URL.
SERVER_SOFTWARE	The type of server you are running: for example, CERN/3.0 or NCSA/1.3.
GATEWAY_INTERFACE	The version of CGI running on the server. For UNIX servers, this should be CGI/1.1.

Environment Variable	What It Means
SERVER_PROTOCOL	The HTTP protocol the server is running. This should be HTTP/1.0.
SERVER_PORT	The TCP port on which the server is running. Usually port 80 for Web servers.
REQUEST_METHOD	POST or GET, depending on how the form was submitted.
HTTP_ACCEPT	A list of Content-types the browser can accept directly, as defined by the HTTP Accept header.
HTTP_USER_AGENT	The browser that submitted the form information. Browser information usually contains the browser name, the version number, and extra information about the platform or extra capabilities.
HTTP_REFERER	The URL of the document that this form submission came from. Not all browsers send this value; do not rely on it.
PATH_INFO	Extra path information, as sent by the browser using the query method of GET in a form.
PATH_TRANSLATED	The actual system-specific pathname of the path contained in PATH_INFO.
SCRIPT_NAME	The pathname to this CGI script, as it appears in the URL (for example, /cgi-bin/thescript).
QUERY_STRING	The arguments to the script or the form input (if submitted using GET). QUERY_STRING contains everything after the question mark in the URL.
REMOTE_HOST	The name of the host that submitted the script. This value cannot be set.
REMOTE_ADDR	The IP address of the host that submitted the script.
REMOTE_USER	The name of the user that submitted the script. This value will be set only if server authentication is turned on.
REMOTE_IDENT	If the Web server is running ident (a protocol to verify the user connecting to you), and the system that submitted the form or script is also running ident, this variable contains the value returned by ident.
CONTENT_TYPE	In forms submitted with POST, the value will be application/x-www-form-urlencoded. In forms with file upload, Content-type will be multipart/form-data.
CONTENT_LENGTH	For forms submitted with POST, the number of bytes in the standard input.

18

Programs To Decode Form Input

The one major difference between a plain CGI script and a CGI script that processes a form is that, because you get data back from the form in URL-encoded format, you need a method of decoding that data. Fortunately, because everyone who writes a CGI script to process a form needs to do this, programs exist to do it for you and to decode the name/value pairs into something you can more easily work with. I like two programs: uncgi for general-purpose use, and cgi-lib.pl, a Perl library for use when you're writing CGI scripts in Perl. You can, however, write your own program if the ones I've mentioned here aren't good enough.

Programs also exist to decode data sent from form-based file uploads, although there are fewer of them. At the end of this section, I mention a few that I've found.

uncgi

Steven Grimm's uncgi is a program written in C that decodes form input for you. You can get information and the source to uncgi from http://www.hyperion.com/~koreth/uncgi.html.

To use uncgi, it's best to install it in your cgi-bin directory. Make sure you edit the makefile before you compile the file to point to the location of that directory on your system so that it can find your scripts.

To use uncgi in a form, you'll have to slightly modify the ACTION attribute in the FORM tag. Instead of calling your CGI script directly in ACTION, you call uncgi with the name of the script appended. So, for example, if you had a CGI script called sleep2.cgi, the usual way to call it would be this:

```
<FORM METHOD=POST ACTION="http://www.myserver.com/cgi-bin/sleep2.cgi">
```

If you were using uncgi, you would do this:

```
<FORM METHOD=POST ACTION=" http://www.myserver.com/cgi-bin/uncgi/sleep2.cgi">
```

NOTE
The uncgi program is an excellent example of how path information is used. The uncgi script uses the name of the actual script from the path information to know which script to call.

The uncgi program reads the form input from either the GET or POST input (it figures out which automatically), decodes it, and creates a set of environment variables with the same names as the values of each NAME attribute, with WWW_ prepended to them. So, for example, if your form contained a text field with the name theName, the uncgi variable containing the value for theName would be WWW_theName.

If there are multiple name/pairs in the input with the same name, uncgi creates only one environment variable with the individual values separated by hash signs (#). For example, if the input contains the name/value pairs shopping=butter, shopping=milk, and shopping=beer, the resulting WWW_shopping environment variable contains butter#milk#beer. It is up to you in your script to handle this information properly.

cgi-lib.pl

The cgi-lib.pl package, written by Steve Brenner, is a set of routines for the Perl language to help you manage form input. It can take form input from GET or POST and put it in a Perl list or associative array. Newer versions can also handle file upload from forms. You can get information about (and source for) cgi-lib.pl from http://www.bio.cam.ac.uk/cgi-lib. If you decide to use the Perl language to handle your form input, cgi-lib.pl is a great library to have.

To use cgi-lib.pl, retrieve the source from the URL listed in the previous paragraph and put it in your Perl libraries directory (often /usr/lib/perl). Then in your Perl script itself, use the following line to include the subroutines from the library in your script:

```
require 'cgi-lib.pl';
```

Although there are several subroutines in cgi-lib.pl for managing forms, the most important one is the ReadParse subroutine. ReadParse reads either GET or POST input and conveniently stores the name/value pairs as name/value pairs in a Perl associative array. It's usually called in your Perl script something like this:

```
&ReadParse(*in);
```

In this example, the name of the array is in, but you can call it anything you want to.

Then, after the form input is decoded, you can read and process the name/value pairs by accessing the name part in your Perl script like this:

```
print $in{'theName'};
```

This particular example just prints out the value of the pair whose name is theName.

If there are multiple name/pairs with the same name, cgi-lib.pl separates the multiple values in the associative array with null characters (\0). It's up to you in your script to handle this information properly.

Decoding File Upload Input

Because form-based file upload is a newer feature requiring a different kind of form input, there are few programs that will decode the input you get back from a form used to upload local files.

Recent versions of cgi-lib.pl handle file uploads very nicely, encoding them into associative arrays without the need to do anything extra to deal with them. See the home page for cgi-lib.pl at http://www.bio.cam.ac.uk/cgi-lib/ for more information.

Another library for handling CGI data in Perl 5, CGI.pm, also deals with file uploads. See http://valine.ncsa.uiuc.edu/cgi_docs.html for details.

Doing It Yourself

Decoding form input is the sort of task that most people will want to leave up to a program such as the ones I've mentioned in this section. But, in case you don't have access to any of these programs, if you're using a system that these programs don't run on, or you feel you can write a better program, here's some information that will help you write your own.

The first thing your decoder program should check for is whether the form input was sent via the POST or GET method. Fortunately, this is easy. The CGI environment variable REQUEST_METHOD, set by the server before your program is called, indicates the method and tells you how to proceed.

If the form input is sent to the server using the GET method, the form input will be contained in the QUERY_STRING environment variable.

If the form input is sent to the server using the POST method, the form input is sent to your script through the standard input. The CONTENT_LENGTH environment variable indicates the number of bytes that the browser submitted. In your decoder, you should make sure you only read the number of bytes contained in CONTENT_LENGTH and then stop. Some browsers might not conveniently terminate the standard input for you.

A typical decoder script performs the following steps:

1. Separate the individual name/value pairs (separated by &).
2. Separate the name from the value (separated by =).

   If there are multiple name keys with different values, you should have some method of preserving all those values.

3. Replace any plus signs with spaces.
4. Decode any hex characters (%NN) to their ASCII equivalents on your system.

Interested in decoding input from file uploads? The rules are entirely different. In particular, the input you'll get from file uploads conforms to MIME multipart messages, so you'll have to deal with lots of different kinds of data. If you're interested, you'll want to see the specifications for file upload, which will explain more. See those specifications at ftp://ds.internic.net/rfc/rfc1867.txt.

18

Nonparsed Headers Scripts

If you followed the basic rules outlined in this section for writing a CGI script, the output of your script (headers and data, if any) will be read by the server and sent back to the browser over the network. In most cases, this will be fine because the server can then do any checking it needs to do and add its own headers to yours.

In some cases, however, you might want to bypass the server and send your output straight to the browser: for example, to speed up the amount of time it takes for your script output to get back to the browser, or to send data back to the browser that the server might question. For most forms and CGI scripts, however, you won't need a script that does this.

CGI scripts to do this are called NPH (non-processed headers) scripts. If you do need an NPH script, you'll need to modify your script slightly:

☐ The script should have an `nph-` prefix: for example, `nph-pinglaura` or `nph-fixdata`.

☐ Your script must send extra HTTP headers instead of just the Content-type, Location, or Status headers.

The headers are the most obvious change you'll need to make to your script. In particular, the first header you output should be an HTTP/1.0 header with a status code, like this:

```
HTTP/1.0 200 OK
```

This header with the 200 status code means "everything's fine, the data is on its way." Another status code could be

```
HTTP/1.0 204 No Response
```

As you learned earlier in this section, this means that there is no data coming back from your script, and so the browser should not do anything (such as try to load a new page).

A second header you should probably include is the Server header. There is some confusion over whether this header is required, but it's probably a good idea to include it. After all, by using an NPH script you're trying to pretend you are a server, so including it can't hurt.

The Server header simply indicates the version of the server you're running, as in the following example:

```
Server: NCSA/1.3
Server: CERN/3.0pre6
```

After including these two headers, you must also include any of the other headers for your script, including Content-type or Location. The browser still needs this information in order to know how to deal with the data you're sending it.

Again, most of the time you won't need NPH scripts; the normal CGI scripts should be just fine.

`<ISINDEX>` Scripts

To finish off the discussion on CGI, let's talk about what are called `<ISINDEX>` searches. The use of the `<ISINDEX>` tag was the way browsers sent information (usually search keys) back to the server in the early days of the Web. `<ISINDEX>` searches are all but obsolete these days because of forms; forms are much more flexible both in layout and with different form elements, and also in the scripts you use to process them. But since I'm a completist, I'll include a short description of how ISINDEX searches work here as well.

`<ISINDEX>` searches are CGI scripts that take arguments, just like the scripts you wrote earlier in this chapter to find out if someone was logged in. The CGI script for an `<ISINDEX>` search operates in the following ways:

☐ If the script is called with no arguments, the HTML that is returned should prompt the reader for search keys. Use the `<ISINDEX>` tag to provide a way for the reader to enter them (remember, this was before there were forms).

☐ When the reader submits the search keys, the ISINDEX script is called again with the search keys as the arguments, which are appended to the URLs as they would be if you had included them in a link. Your ISINDEX script then operates on those arguments in some way, returning the appropriate HTML file. Just as you would pass arguments to CGI scripts through links, you can get to `<ISINDEX>` search keys using $1, $2, and so on in a UNIX shell script.

The core of the `<ISINDEX>` searches is the `<ISINDEX>` tag. It is a special HTML tag used for these kinds of searches. It doesn't enclose any text, nor does it have a closing tag.

So what does `<ISINDEX>` do? It "turns on" searching in the browser that is reading this document. Depending on the browser, this may involve enabling a search button in the browser itself (see Figure 18.8). For newer browsers, it may involve including an input field on the page (see Figure 18.9). The reader can then enter a string to search for, and then press Enter or click on the button to submit the query to the server.

Figure 18.8.

A search prompt in the browser window.

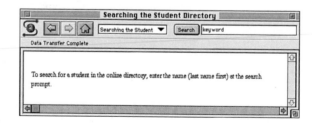

Figure 18.9.

A search prompt on the page itself.

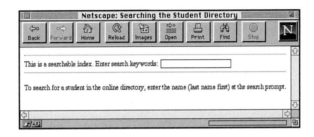

According to the HTML 2.0 specification, The <ISINDEX> tag should go inside the <HEAD> part of the HTML document (it's one of the few tags that goes into <HEAD>, <TITLE> being the other obvious example). In older browsers, where there was a single location for the search prompt, this made sense because neither the search prompt nor the <ISINDEX> tag was actually part of the data of the document. However, because more recent browsers display the input field on the HTML page itself, it is useful to be able to put <ISINDEX> in the body of the document so that you can control where on the page the input field appears (if it's in the <HEAD>, it'll always be the first thing on the page). Most browsers will now accept an <ISINDEX> tag anywhere in the body of an HTML document and will draw the input box wherever that tag appears.

Finally, there is an HTML extension to the <ISINDEX> tag that allows you to define the search prompt. Again, in older browsers, the search prompt was fixed (it was usually something confusing like "This is a searchable index. Enter keywords"). The new PROMPT attribute to <ISINDEX> allows you to define the string that will be used to indicate the input field, as in the following code for example. Figure 18.10 shows the result of this tag in Netscape.

```
<P> To search for a student in the online directory,
enter the name (last name first):
<ISINDEX PROMPT="Student's name:   ">
```

18

Figure 18.10.

A Netscape search prompt.

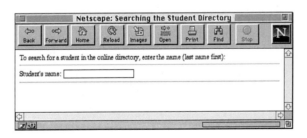

<ISINDEX> is useful only in the context of an ISINDEX search. Although you can put it into any HTML document, it won't do anything unless it was a CGI script that generated that HTML page to begin with.

Most of the time creating HTML forms is a far easier way of prompting the user for information.

Summary

CGI scripts, sometimes called server-side scripts or gateway scripts, make it possible for programs to be run on the server, and HTML or other files to be generated on the fly.

In this chapter, you reviewed all the basics of creating CGI scripts: both simple scripts and scripts to process forms, including the special headers you use in your scripts; the difference between GET and POST in form input; and how to decode the information you get from the form input. Plus you learned some extras about path information, URL encoding, <ISINDEX> searches, and the various CGI variables you can use in your CGI scripts. From here, you should be able to write CGI scripts to accomplish just about anything.

Q&A

Q What if I don't know how to program? Can I still use CGI scripts?

A If you have your access to a Web server through a commercial provider, you may be able to get help from the provider with your CGI scripts (for a fee, of course). Also, if you know even a little programming, but you're unsure of what you're doing, there are many examples available for the platform and server you're working with. Usually these examples are either part of the server distribution or at the same FTP location. See the documentation that came with your server; it often has pointers to further help. In fact, for the operation you want to accomplish, there may already be a script you can use with only slight modification. But be careful; if you don't know what you're doing, you can rapidly get in over your head, or end up creating scripts with security holes that you don't know about.

Q My Web server has a cgi-bin directory, but I don't have access to it. So I created by own cgi-bin directory and put my script there, but calling it from my Web pages didn't work. What did I do wrong?

A Web servers must be specially configured to run CGI scripts, and usually that means indicating specific directories or files that are meant to be scripts. You cannot just create a directory or a file with a special extension without knowing how your Webmaster has set up your server; most of the time you'll guess wrong and your scripts will not work. Ask your Webmaster for help with installing your scripts.

Q My Webmaster tells me I can just create a cgi-bin directory in my home directory, install my scripts there, and then call them using a special URL called cgiwrap. You haven't mentioned this way of having personal cgi-bin directories.

A cgiwrap is a neat program that provides a secure wrapper for CGI scripts and allows users of public UNIX systems to have their own personal CGI directories.

However, your Webmaster has to specifically set up and configure cgiwrap for your server before you can use it. If your Webmaster has allowed the use of cgiwrap, congratulations! CGI scripts will be easy for you to install and use. If you are a Webmaster and you're interested in finding out more information, check out `http://wwwcgi.umr.edu/~cgiwrap/` for more information.

Q My scripts aren't working!

A Did you look in the section on troubleshooting for the errors you're getting and the possible solutions? I covered most of the common problems you might be having in that section.

Q My Web provider won't give me access to `cgi-bin` at all. No way, no how. I really want to use forms. Is there any way at all I can do this?

A There is one way; it's called a Mailto form. Using Mailto forms, you use a Mailto URL with your e-mail address in the ACTION part of the form, like this:

```
<FORM METHOD=POST ACTION="mailto:lemay@lne.com"> ... </FORM>
```

Then, when the form is submitted by your reader, the contents of the form will be sent to you via e-mail (or at least they will if you include your e-mail address in the mailto instead of mine). No server scripts are required to do this.

There are a few major problems with this solution, however. The first is that the e-mail you get will have all the form input in encoded form. Sometimes you may be able to read it anyhow, but it's messy. To get around URL encoding, there are special programs created just for Mailto forms that will decode the input for you. Check out `http://homepage.interaccess.com/~arachnid/mtfinfo.html` for more information.

The second problem with Mailto forms is that they don't give any indication that the form input has been sent. There's no page to send back saying "Thank you, I got your form input." Your readers will just click Submit, and nothing will appear to happen. Because there's no feedback to your readers, they may very well submit the same information to you repeatedly. It might be useful to include a warning to your readers on the page itself to let them know that they won't get any feedback.

The third problem with Mailto forms is that they are not supported by all browsers, so your forms may not work for everyone who reads your page. Most of the major commercial browsers do support Mailto forms, however.

Q I'm writing a decoder program for form input. The last `name=value` pair in my list keeps getting all this garbage stuck to the end of it.

A Are you reading only the number of bytes indicated by the CONTENT_LENGTH environment variable? You should test for that value and stop reading when you reach the end, or you might end up reading too far. Not all browsers will terminate the standard input for you.

18

APPENDIX A

Sources for Further Information

by Laura Lemay

Haven't had enough yet? In this appendix you'll find the URLs for all kinds of information about the World Wide Web, HTML, developing Web presentations, and locations of tools to help you write HTML documents. With this list you should be able to find just about anything you need on the Web.

NOTE

Some of the URLs in this section refer to FTP sites. Some of these sites may be very busy during local business hours, and you may not be able to immediately access the files. Try again during non-prime hours.

Also, some of these sites, for mysterious reasons, may be accessible through an FTP program, but not through Web browsers. If you are consistently getting refused from these sites using a browser, and you have access to an FTP program, try that program instead.

The sites are divided into the following categories and listed in alphabetical order under each category:

Access Counters
Browsers
Collections of HTML and WWW Development Information
Forms and Image Maps
HTML Editors and Converters
HTML Validators, Link Checkers, and Simple Spiders
Java, JavaScript, and Embedded Objects
Log File Parsers
Other
Servers and Server Administration
Sound and Video
Specifications for HTML, HTTP, and URLs
The Common Gateway Interface (CGI) and CGI Scripting
The Future of HTML and the Web
Tools and Information for Images
Web Providers
WWW Indexes and Search Engines

Access Counters

Access Counters Without Server Programs
```
http://www.digits.com/
```

A Good Access Counters Tutorial

`http://members.aol.com/htmlguru/access_counts.html`

Lots of Access Counter Info

`http://www.digitmania.holowww.com/`

Yahoo's List of Access Counters

`http://www.yahoo.com/Computers/World_Wide_Web/Programming/Access_Counts/`

Browsers

Arena (X)

`http://www.w3.org/pwb/WWW/Arena/`

Emacs-W3 (for Emacs)

`http://www.cs.indiana.edu/elisp/w3/docs.html`

A general list

`http://www.w3.org/hypertext/WWW/Clients.html`

Internet Explorer

`http://www.microsoft.com/ie/`

Lynx (UNIX and DOS)

`http://www.cc.ukans.edu/about_lynx/`

NCSA Mosaic (X, Windows, Mac)

`http://www.ncsa.uiuc.edu/SDG/Software/Mosaic/NCSAMosaicHome.html`

Netscape (X, Windows, Mac)

`http://home.netscape.com/comprod/products/navigator/index.html`

WinWeb (Windows) and MacWeb (Macintosh)

`http://www.einet.net/EINet/WinWeb/WinWebHome.html`

Collections of HTML and WWW Web Sites Development Information

The Developer's JumpStation

`http://oneworld.wa.com/htmldev/devpage/dev-page.html`

The Home of the WWW Consortium

`http://www.w3.org/`

The HTML Writer's Guild
http://www.hwg.org/

Netscape's HTML Assistance Pages
http://home.netscape.com/assist/net_sites/index.html

The Repository
http://cbl.leeds.ac.uk/nikos/doc/repository.html

The Spider's Web Pages on the Web
http://miso.wwa.com/~boba/spider1.html

The Virtual Library
http://WWW.Stars.com/

The World Wide Web FAQ
http://www.boutell.com/faq/

Yahoo's WWW Section
http://www.yahoo.com/Computers/World_Wide_Web/

Forms and Image Maps

Carlos' Forms Tutorial
http://robot0.ge.uiuc.edu/~carlosp/cs317/cft.html

Client-Site Image Maps
http://ds.internic.net/internet-drafts/draft-seidman-clientsideimagemap-02.txt

File Upload in Forms
ftp://ds.internic.net/rfc/rfc1867.txt

HotSpots (a Windows Image Map Tool)
http://www.cris.com/~automata/hotspots.html

Image Maps in NCSA
http://hoohoo.ncsa.uiuc.edu/docs/tutorials/imagemapping.html

The Mailto Formatter
http://homepage.interaccess.com/~arachnid/mtfinfo.html

Mapedit: A Tool for Windows and X11 for Creating Imagemap Map Files
http://www.boutell.com/mapedit/

Mosaic Form Support Documenation
http://www.ncsa.uiuc.edu/SDG/Software/Mosaic/Docs/fill-out-forms/overview.html

The Original NCSA Forms Documentation
http://hoohoo.ncsa.uiuc.edu/cgi/forms.html

WebMap (Macintosh map creator)

```
http://www.shareware.com/code/engine/SearchOption?frame=none
```
(Search for the program and platform you're interested in.)

Yahoo Forms Index

```
http://www.yahoo.com/Computers_and_Internet/Internet/World_Wide_Web/
Programming/Forms/
```

HTML Editors and Converters

A List of Converters and Editors, Updated Regularly

```
http://www.w3.org/hypertext/WWW/Tools/
```

A Better List of Converters

```
http://www.yahoo.com/Computers/World_Wide_Web/HTML_Converters/
```

A Great List of Editors

```
http://www.yahoo.com/Computers/World_Wide_Web/HTML_Editors/
```

HTML Validators, Link Checkers, and Simple Spiders

The HTML Validator

```
http://www.webtechs.com/html-val-svc/
```

Htmlchek

```
http://uts.cc.utexas.edu/~churchh/htmlchek.html
```

Lvrfy (link checker)

```
http://www.cs.dartmouth.edu/~crow/lvrfy.html
```

MOMSpider

```
http://www.ics.uci.edu/WebSoft/MOMspider/
```

Weblint

```
http://www.unipress.com/cgi-bin/wwweblint
```

Yahoo's List of HTML Validation and HTML Checkers

```
http://www.yahoo.com/Computers/World_Wide_Web/HTML/Validation_Checkers/
```

Yahoo's List of Web Spiders and Robots

```
http://www.yahoo.com/computers_and_Internet/Internet/World_
Wide_Web/Searching_the_Web/Robots__Spiders__etc__Documentation
```

Java, JavaScript, and Embedded Objects

Gamelan, an Index of Java Applets
http://www.gamelan.com/

JavaScript Author's Guide
http://www.netscape.com/eng/mozilla/2.0/handbook/javascript/index.html

Netscape's Information about Java
http://home.netscape.com/comprod/products/navigator/version_2.0/java_applets/

Netscape's Information about JavaScript
http://www.netscape.com/comprod/products/navigator/version_2.0/script/

Sun's Java Home Page
http://www.javasoft.com/

Yahoo Java directory
http://www.yahoo.com/Computers_and_Internet/Languages/Java/

Log File Parsers

Getstats
http://www.eit.com/software/getstats/getstats.html

Wuasage
http://www.boutell.com/wusage

Yahoo's List
http://www.yahoo.com/Computers/World_Wide_Web/HTTP/Servers/Log_Analysis_Tools/

Other

Tim Berners-Lee's Style Guide
http://www.w3.org/hypertext/WWW/Provider/Style/Overview.html

The Yale HyperText Style Guide
http://info.med.yale.edu/caim/StyleManual_Top.HTML

Servers and Server Administration

Access Control in NCSA HTTPD

http://hoohoo.ncsa.uiuc.edu/docs/setup/access/Overview.html

http://hoohoo.ncsa.uiuc.edu/docs/tutorials/user.html

http://hoohoo.ncsa.uiuc.edu/docs/setup/admin/UserManagement.html

Apache (Unix)

http://www.apache.org/

Avoiding Robots

http://web.nexor.co.uk/mak/doc/robots/norobots.html

CERN HTTPD (UNIX)

http://www.w3.org/pub/WWW/Daemon/

Current List of Official MIME Types

ftp://ftp.isi.edu/in-notes/iana/assignments/media-types/media-types

MacHTTP and WebStar (Macintosh)

http://www.starnine.com/

Microsoft Internet Information Server (Windows NT)

http://www.microsoft.com/infoserv/index.html

NCSA HTTPD (UNIX)

http://hoohoo.ncsa.uiuc.edu/

NCSA Server Includes

http://hoohoo.ncsa.uiuc.edu/docs/tutorials/includes.html

NCSA winHTTPD (Windows 3.x)

http://www.city.net/win-httpd/

Netscape's Web Servers (UNIX, Windows NT)

http://home.netscape.com/comprod/server_central

O'Reilly WebSite (Windows 95/NT)

http://website.ora.com/

Sound and Video

Alison Zhang's Multimedia File Formats on the Internet: Movies
http://ac.dal.ca/~dong/movies.htm

Alison Zhang's Multimedia File Formats on the Internet: Sound and Music
http://ac.dal.ca/~dong/music.htm

Audio Applications (Commercial, Bundled, Shareware) for SGI Systems
http://reality.sgi.com/employees/cook/audio.apps/

Audio Formats FAQ
http://www.cis.ohio-state.edu/hypertext/faq/usenet/audio-fmts/top.html

SoundHack (Sound Editor for Macintosh)
SoundMachine (Sound Capture/Converter/Editor for Macintosh)
SoundAPP (Macintosh Sound Converter)
Sparkle (MPEG Player and Converter for Macintosh)
WHAM (Windows Sound Converter)
http://www.shareware.com/code/engine/SearchOption?frame=none
(Search for the program and platform you're interested in.)

CoolEdit, a Sound Editor for Windows
http://www.netzone.com/syntrillium/

FastPlayer (Macintosh QuickTime Player and "Flattener")
ftp://ftp.ncsa.uiuc.edu/Mosaic/Mac/Helpers/fast-player-110.hqx

Information about Indeo Video
http://www.intel.com/pc-supp/multimed/indeo/OVERVIEW.HTM

The Internet Underground Music Archive (IUMA)
http://www.iuma.com/

The MPEG FAQ
http://www.crs4.it/~luigi/MPEG/mpegfaq.html

QFlat (Windows QuickTime "Flattener")
ftp://venice.tcp.com/pub/anime-manga/software/viewers/qtflat.zip

QuickTime Information
http://quicktime.apple.com/

SOX (UNIX and DOS Sound Converter)
http://www.spies.com/Sox/

XingCD (AVI to MPEG Converter)
http://www.xingtech.com

Yahoo's Movies Information
http://www.yahoo.com/Computers/Multimedia/Movies/

Yahoo's Sound Information
http://www.yahoo.com/Computers/Multimedia/Sound/

Specifications for HTML, HTTP, and URLs

Frames
http://home.netscape.com/assist/net_sites/frames.html

The HTML 3.2 Specification
http://www.w3.org/hypertext/WWW/MarkUp/Wilbur/

The HTML Level 2 Specification
http://www.w3.org/hypertext/WWW/MarkUp/html-spec/index.html

HTML Tables (Working Draft)
http://www.w3.org/hypertext/WWW/TR/WD-tables

The HTTP Specification
http://www.w3.org/hypertext/WWW/Protocols/HTTP/HTTP2.html

Mosaic Tables
http://www.ncsa.uiuc.edu/SDG/Software/XMosaic/table-spec.html

Netscape Extensions to HTML 3.2
http://home.netscape.com/assist/net_sites/html_extensions_3.html

Netscape Extensions to HTML 2.0 (Includes Tables)
http://home.netscape.com/assist/net_sites/html_extensions.html

Pointers to URL, URN, and URI Information and Specifications
http://www.w3.org/hypertext/WWW/Addressing/Addressing.html

The Common Gateway Interface (CGI) and CGI Scripting

An Archive of CGI Programs at NCSA
ftp://ftp.ncsa.uiuc.edu/Web/httpd/Unix/ncsa_httpd/cgi

The CGI Specification
http://hoohoo.ncsa.uiuc.edu/cgi/interface.html

`cgi-lib.pl`, a Perl Library to Manage CGI and Forms
http://www.bio.cam.ac.uk/cgi-lib/

An Index to HTML-Related Programs Written in Perl
http://www.seas.upenn.edu/~mengwong/perlhtml.html

The Original NCSA CGI Documentation
http://hoohoo.ncsa.uiuc.edu/cgi/

Un-CGI, a Program to Decode Form Input
http://www.hyperion.com/~koreth/uncgi.html

Yahoo's CGI List
http://www.yahoo.com/Computers_and_Internet/Internet/World_Wide_Web/
CGI__Common_Gateway_Interface/

The Future of HTML and the Web

Adobe Acrobat
http://www.adobe.com/Acrobat/Acrobat0.html

Animate (Tools for Server Push)
http://www.homepages.com/tools/

General Information About PDF
http://www.ep.cs.nott.ac.uk/~pns/pdfcorner/pdf.html

Netscape's Dynamic Documents (Client Pull and Server Push)
http://home.netscape.com/assist/net_sites/dynamic_docs.html
http://home.netscape.com/assist/net_sites/pushpull.html

SHTTP Information
http://www.eit.com/projects/s-http/

SSL Information
http://www.netscape.com/info/security-doc.html

Style Sheets Overview
http://www.w3.org/hypertext/WWW/Style/

VRML FAQ
http://vag.vrml.org/VRML_FAQ.html

VRML Home Site
http://vrml.wired.com/

VRML Repository
http://www.sdsc.edu/SDSC/Partners/vrml/

Web Security Overview
http://www.w3.org/hypertext/WWW/Security/Overview.html

Yahoo's List on Security, Encryption, and Authentication
http://www.yahoo.com/Science/Mathematics/Security_and_Encryption/

Tools and Information for Images

Anthony's Icon Library
http://www.cit.gu.edu.au/~anthony/icons/index.html

Barry's Clip Art Server
http://www.barrysclipart.com

Frequently Asked Questions About JPEG
http://www.cis.ohio-state.edu/hypertext/faq/usenet/jpeg-faq/top.html

Frequently Asked Questions from `comp.graphics`
http://www.primenet.com/~grieggs/cg_faq.html

GIFConverter for Macintosh
GraphicConverter for Macintosh
LView Pro for Windows
Transparency for Macintosh
http://www.shareware.com/code/engine/SearchOption?frame=none
(Search for the program and platform you're interested in.)

GIFTool (UNIX)
http://www.homepages.com/tools/

Giftrans
ftp://ftp.rz.uni-karlsruhe.de/pub/net/www/tools/giftrans.c

PNG (Portable Network Graphics) Specification
http://boutell.com/boutell/png

Some Good Information About Transparent GIFs
http://members.aol.com/htmlguru/transparent_images.html

Yahoo's Clip Art List
http://www.yahoo.com/Computers/Multimedia/Pictures/Clip_Art/

Yahoo's GIF List
http://www.yahoo.com/Computers/Software/Data_Formats/GIF/

Yahoo's Icons List
http://www.yahoo.com/Computers/World_Wide_Web/Programming/Icons/

Web Providers

An Index from HyperNews

http://union.ncsa.uiuc.edu/HyperNews/get/www/leasing.html

WWW Indexes and Search Engines

AltaVista

http://www.altavista.digital.com/

Excite

http://www.excite.com

An Index of Indexes

http://www.biotech.washington.edu/WebCrawler/WebIndexes.html

Lycos

http://lycos.cs.cmu.edu/

WebCrawler

http://www.webcrawler.com/

Yahoo!

http://www.yahoo.com/

APPENDIX B

HTML 3.2 Language Reference

by Laura Lemay

This appendix is a reference to the HTML tags you can use in your documents, according to the HTML 3.2 proposed Specification. Tags in common use that are either HTML 3.2 or Netscape or Internet Explorer extensions are noted as such. Note that some browsers other than Netscape may support the Netscape extensions.

NOTE

> A few of the tags in this section have not been described in the body of the book. If a tag is mentioned here that you haven't seen before, don't worry about it; that means that the tag is not in active use or is for use by HTML-generating and -reading tools, and not for general use in HTML documents.

HTML Tags

These tags are used to create a basic HTML page with text, headings, and lists.

Comments

`<!--.....-->`
Creates a comment.

Structure Tags

`<HTML>...</HTML>`
Encloses the entire HTML document.

Can Include: `<HEAD> <BODY>`

`<HEAD>...</HEAD>`
Encloses the head of the HTML document.

Can Include: `<TITLE> <ISINDEX> <BASE> <LINK> <META> <SCRIPT> <STYLE>`

Allowed Inside: `<HTML>`

`<BODY>...</BODY>`
Encloses the body (text and tags) of the HTML document.

Attributes:

`BACKGROUND="..."` (HTML 3.2 only) The name or URL for an image to tile on the page background.

`BGCOLOR="..."` (Netscape 1.1) The color of the page background.

`TEXT="..."` (Netscape 1.1) The color of the page's text.

`LINK="..."` (Netscape 1.1) The color of unfollowed links.

`ALINK="..."` (Netscape 1.1) The color of activated links.

`VLINK="..."` (Netscape 1.1) The color of followed links.

Can Include: `<H1> <H2> <H3> <H4> <H5> <H6> <P> <OL> <UL> <DIR> <MENU> <DL> <PRE> <BLOCKQUOTE> <FORM> <ISINDEX> <HR> <ADDRESS>`

Allowed Inside: `<HTML>`

`<BASE>`
Indicates the full URL of the current document.

Attribute:

`HREF="..."` The full URL of this document.

Allowed Inside: `<HEAD>`

`<ISINDEX>`
Indicates that this document is a gateway script that allows searches.

Attribute:

`PROMPT="..."` (HTML 3.2) The prompt for the search field.

Allowed Inside: `<BLOCKQUOTE> <BODY> <DD> <FORM> <HEAD> <LI>`

`<LINK>`
Indicates a link between this document and some other document. Generally used only by HTML-generating tools. `<LINK>` represents document links to this one as a whole, as opposed to `<A>` which can create multiple links in the document. Not commonly used.

Attributes:

HREF="..." The URL of the document to be linked to this one.

NAME=... If the document is to be considered an anchor, the name of that anchor.

REL="..." The relationship between the linked-to document and the current document; for example, "TOC" or "Glossary."

REV="..." A reverse relationship between the current document and the linked-to document.

URN="..." A Uniform Resource Number (URN), a unique identifier different from the URL in HREF.

TITLE="..." The title of the linked-to document.

METHODS="..." The method with which the document is to be retrieved; for example, FTP, Gopher, and so on.

Allowed Inside: <HEAD>

<META>

Indicates metainformation about this document (information about the document itself); for example, keywords for search engines, special HTTP headers to be used for retrieving this document, expiration date, and so on. Metainformation is usually in a key/value pair form.

Attributes:

HTTP-EQUIV="..." Creates a new HTTP header field with the same name as the attributes value, for example HTTP-EQUIV=Expires. The value of that header is specified by CONTENT.

NAME=... If meta data is usually in the form of key/value pairs, NAME indicates the key; for example, Author or ID.

CONTENT=... The content of the key/vaue pair (or of the HTTP header indicated by HTTP-EQUIV).

Allowed Inside: <HEAD>

<NEXTID>

Indicates the "next" document to this one (as might be defined by a tool to manage HTML documents in series). <NEXTID> is considered obsolete.

Headings and Title

All heading tags have the following characteristics:

Attribute:

`ALIGN=CENTER`: (HTML 3.x only) Centers the heading.

Can Include: `<A>` `<IMG>` `<BR>` `<EM>` `<STRONG>` `<CODE>` `<SAMP>` `<KBD>` `<VAR>` `<CITE>` `<TT>` `<B>` `<I>`

Allowed Inside: `<BLOCKQUOTE>` `<BODY>` `<PRE>` `<ADDRESS>` `<FORM>` `<TH>` `<TD>`

`<H1>...</H1>`
A first-level heading.

`<H2>...</H2>`
A second-level heading.

`<H3>...</H3>`
A third-level heading.

`<H4>...</H4>`
A fourth-level heading.

`<H5>...</H5>`
A fifth-level heading.

`<H6>...</H6>`
A sixth-level heading.

`<TITLE>...</TITLE>`
Indicates the title of the document.

Allowed Inside: `<HEAD>`

Paragraphs

`<P>...</P>`

A plain paragraph. The closing tag (`</P>`) is optional.

Attribute:

`ALIGN=CENTER` (HTML 3.x only) Centers the paragraph.

Can Include: `<A>` `<IMG>` `<BR>` `<EM>` `<STRONG>` `<CODE>` `<SAMP>` `<KBD>` `<VAR>` `<CITE>` `<TT>` `<B>` `<I>`

Allowed Inside: `<BLOCKQUOTE>` `<BODY>` `<DD>` `<FORM>` `<LI>`

Links

`<A>...</A>`

With the `HREF` attribute, creates a link to another document or anchor; with the `NAME` attribute, creates an anchor which can be linked to.

Attributes:

`HREF="..."` The URL of the document to be linked to this one.

`NAME=...` The name of the anchor.

`REL="..."` The relationship between the linked-to document and the current document; for example, "TOC" or "Glossary." Not commonly used.

`REV="..."` A reverse relationship between the current document and the linked-to document. Not commonly used.

`TITLE="..."` The title of the linked-to document. Not commonly used.

Can Include: `<IMG>` `<BR>` `<EM>` `<STRONG>` `<CODE>` `<SAMP>` `<KBD>` `<VAR>` `<CITE>` `<TT>` `<B>` `<I>`

Allowed Inside: `<ADDRESS>` `<B>` `<CITE>` `<CODE>` `<DD>` `<DT>` `<EM>` `<H1>` `<H2>` `<H3>` `<H4>` `<H5>` `<H6>` `<I>` `<KBD>` `<LI>` `<P>` `<PRE>` `<SAMP>` `<STRONG>` `<TT>` `<VAR>` `<TH>` `TD>`

Lists

`<OL>...</OL>`

An ordered (numbered) list.

Attributes:

`compact`

`TYPE="..."` (Netscape and HTML 3.2 only) The type of numerals to label the list with. Possible values are A, a, I, i, and 1.

`START="..."` (Netscape) The value to start this list with.

Can Include: `<LI>`

Allowed Inside: `<BLOCKQUOTE>` `<BODY>` `<DD>` `<FORM>` `<LI>` `<TH>` `TD>`

`<UL>...</UL>`

An unordered (bulleted) list.

Attributes:

`compact`

`TYPE="..."` (Netscape and HTML 3.2) The bullet dingbat to use to mark list items. Possible values are DISC, CIRCLE, and SQUARE.

Can Include: `<LI>`

Allowed Inside: `<BLOCKQUOTE>` `<BODY>` `<DD>` `<FORM>` `<LI>` `<TH>` `TD>`

`<MENU>...</MENU>`

A menu list of items.

Attributes:

`compact`

Can Include: `<LI>`

Allowed Inside: `<BLOCKQUOTE>` `<BODY>` `<DD>` `<FORM>` `<LI>` `<TH>` `TD>`

`<DIR>...</DIR>`

A directory listing; items are generally smaller than 20 characters.

Attributes:

`compact`

Can Include: `<LI>`

Allowed Inside: `<BLOCKQUOTE>` `<BODY>` `<DD>` `<FORM>` `<LI>` `<TH>` `TD>`

`<LI>`

A list item for use with `<OL>`, `<UL>`, `<MENU>`, or `<DIR>`.

Attributes:

TYPE=" . . . " (Netscape and HTML 3.2) The type of bullet or number to label this item with. Possible values are DISC, CIRCLE, SQUARE, A, a, I, i, and 1.

VALUE=" . . . " (Netscape and HTML 3.2) The numeric value this list item should have (affects this item and all below it in `<OL>` lists).

Can Include: `<A>` `<IMG>` `<BR>` `<EM>` `<STRONG>` `<CODE>` `<SAMP>` `<KBD>` `<VAR>` `<CITE>` `<TT>` `<B>` `<I>` `<P>` `<OL>` `<UL>` `<DIR>` `<MENU>` `<DL>` `<PRE>` `<BLOCKQUOTE>`

Allowed Inside: `<DIR>` `<MENU>` `<OL>` `<UL>`

`<DL>...</DL>`

A definition or glossary list. The COMPACT attribute specifies a formatting that takes less whitespace to present.

Attribute: COMPACT

Can Include: `<DT>` `<DD>`

Allowed Inside: `<BLOCKQUOTE>` `<BODY>` `<DD>` `<FORM>` `<LI>` `<TH>` TD>

`<DT>`

A definition term, as part of a definition list.

Can Include: `<A>` `<IMG>` `<BR>` `<EM>` `<STRONG>` `<CODE>` `<SAMP>` `<KBD>` `<VAR>` `<CITE>` `<TT>` `<B>` `<I>`

Allowed Inside: `<DL>`

`<DD>`

The corresponding definition to a definition term, as part of a definition list.

Can Include: `<A>` `<IMG>` `<BR>` `<EM>` `<STRONG>` `<CODE>` `<SAMP>` `<KBD>` `<VAR>` `<CITE>` `<TT>` `<B>` `<I>` `<P>` `<OL>` `<UL>` `<DIR>` `<MENU>` `<DL>` `<PRE>` `<BLOCKQUOTE>` `<FORM>` `<ISINDEX>` `<TABLE>`

Allowed Inside: `<DL>`

Character Formatting

All the character formatting tags have these features:

Can Include: <A> <IMG>
 <EM> <STRONG> <CODE> <SAMP> <KBD> <VAR> <CITE> <TT> <B> <I>

Allowed Inside: <A> <ADDRESS> <B> <CITE> <CODE> <DD> <DT> <EM> <H1> <H2> <H3> <H4> <H5> <H6> <I> <KBD> <LI> <P> <PRE> <SAMP> <STRONG> <TT> <VAR> <TH> TD>

<EM>...</EM>
Emphasis (usually italic).

<STRONG>...</STRONG>
Stronger emphasis (usually bold).

<CODE>...</CODE>
Code sample (usually Courier).

<KBD>...</KBD>
Text to be typed (usually Courier).

<VAR>...</VAR>
A variable or placeholder for some other value.

<SAMP>...</SAMP>
Sample text.

<DFN>...</DFN>
(HTML 3.2 only) A definition of a term.

<CITE>...</CITE>
A citation.

<B>...</B>
Boldface text.

`<I>...</I>`

Italic text.

`<TT>...</TT>`

Typewriter font.

`<U>...</U>`

Underline text.

`<STRIKE>...</STRIKE>`

Strikethru font.

`<BIG>...</BIG>`

Changes the physical rendering of the text to be bigger, if practical.

`<SMALL>...</SMALL>`

Changes the physical rendering of the text to be smaller, if practical.

`<SUB>...</SUB>`

Subscript text.

`<SUP>...</SUP>`

Superscript text.

Other Elements

`<HR>`

A horizontal rule line.

Attributes:

`SIZE="..."` (Netscape) The thickness of the rule, in pixels.

`WIDTH="..."` (Netscape) The width of the rule, in pixels.

`ALIGN="..."` (Netscape) How the rule line will be aligned on the page. Possible values are `LEFT`, `RIGHT`, and `CENTER`.

NOSHADE="..." (Netscape) Causes the rule line to be drawn as a solid black.

Allowed Inside: <BLOCKQUOTE> <BODY> <FORM> <PRE>

A line break.

Attribute:

CLEAR="..." (HTML 3.0) Causes the text to stop flowing around any images. Possible values are RIGHT, LEFT, and ALL, or NONE.

Allowed Inside: <A> <ADDRESS> <B> <CITE> <CODE> <DD> <DT> <EM> <H1> <H2> <H3> <H4> <H5> <H6> <I> <KBD> <LI> <P> <PRE> <SAMP> <STRONG> <TT> <VAR>

<NOBR>...</NOBR> **(Netscape)**
Causes the enclosed text not to wrap at the edge of the page.

Allowed Inside: <A> <ADDRESS> <B> <CITE> <CODE> <DD> <DT> <EM> <H1> <H2> <H3> <H4> <H5> <H6> <I> <KBD> <LI> <P> <PRE> <SAMP> <STRONG> <TT> <VAR>

<WBR> **(Netscape)**
Wraps the text at this point only if necessary.

Allowed Inside: <A> <ADDRESS> <B> <CITE> <CODE> <DD> <DT> <EM> <H1> <H2> <H3> <H4> <H5> <H6> <I> <KBD> <LI> <P> <PRE> <SAMP> <STRONG> <TT> <VAR>

<BLOCKQUOTE>... </BLOCKQUOTE>
Used for long quotes or citations.

Can Include: <H1> <H2> <H3> <H4> <H5> <H6> <P> <OL> <UL> <DIR> <MENU> <DL> <PRE> <BLOCKQUOTE> <FORM> <ISINDEX> <HR> <ADDRESS> <TABLE>

Allowed Inside: <BLOCKQUOTE> <BODY> <DD> <FORM> <LI> <TH> TD>

<CENTER>...</CENTER>
All the content enclosed within these tags is centered.

Can Include: <A> <IMG>
 <EM> <STRONG> <CODE> <SAMP> <KBD> <VAR> <CITE> <TT> <B> <I>

Allowed Inside: <BLOCKQUOTE> <BODY> <DD> <FORM> <LI> <TH> TD>

<ADDRESS>...</ADDRESS>

Used for signatures or general information about a document's author.

Can Include: <A> <IMG>
 <EM> <STRONG> <CODE> <SAMP> <KBD> <VAR> <CITE> <TT> <B> <I>

Allowed Inside: <BLOCKQUOTE> <BODY> <FORM>

<BLINK>...</BLINK> (Netscape)

Causes the enclosed text to blink irritatingly.

Font Sizes

<FONT>...</FONT>

Changes the size of the font for the enclosed text.

Attribute:

SIZE="..." The size of the font, from 1 to 7. Default is 3. Can also be specified as a value relative to the current size; for example, +2.

Can Include: <A> <IMG>
 <EM> <STRONG> <CODE> <SAMP> <KBD> <VAR> <CITE> <TT> <B> <I>

Allowed Inside: <A> <ADDRESS> <B> <CITE> <CODE> <DD> <DT> <EM> <H1> <H2> <H3> <H4> <H5> <H6> <I> <KBD> <LI> <P> <PRE> <SAMP> <STRONG> <TT> <VAR>

<BASEFONT> (Netscape)

Sets the default size of the font for the current page.

Attribute:

SIZE="..." The default size of the font, from 1 to 7. Default is 3.

Allowed Inside: <A> <ADDRESS> <B> <CITE> <CODE> <DD> <DT> <EM> <H1> <H2> <H3> <H4> <H5> <H6> <I> <KBD> <LI> <P> <PRE> <SAMP> <STRONG> <TT> <VAR>

Images

<IMG>

Inserts an inline image into the document.

Attributes:

ISMAP This image is a clickable image map.

SRC="..." The URL of the image.

ALT="..." A text string that will be displayed in browsers that cannot support images.

ALIGN="..." Determines the alignment of the given image. If LEFT or RIGHT (HTML 3.2, Netscape), the image is aligned to the left or right column, and all following text flows beside that image. All other values such as TOP, MIDDLE, BOTTOM, or the Netscape only (TEXTTOP, ABSMIDDLE, BASELINE, ABSBOTTOM), determine the vertical alignment of this image with other items in the same line.

VSPACE="..." The space between the image and the text above or below it.

HSPACE="..." The space between the image and the text to its left or right.

WIDTH="..." (HTML 3.2) The width, in pixels, of the image. If WIDTH is not the actual width, the image is scaled to fit.

HEIGHT="..." (HTML 3.2) The height, in pixels, of the image. If HEIGHT is not the actual height, the image is scaled to fit.

BORDER="..." (Netscape only) Draws a border of the specified value in pixels to be drawn around the image. In the case of images that are also links, BORDER changes the size of the default link border.

LOWSRC="..." (Netscape only) The path or URL of an image that will be loaded first, before the image specified in SRC. The value of LOWSRC is usually a smaller or lower resolution version of the actual image.

Allowed Inside: <A> <ADDRESS> <B> <CITE> <CODE> <DD> <DT> <EM> <H1> <H2> <H3> <H4> <H5> <H6> <I> <KBD> <LI> <P> <SAMP> <STRONG> <TT> <VAR>

Forms

<FORM>...</FORM>

Indicates a form.

Attributes:

ACTION="..." The URL of the script to process this form input.

METHOD="..." How the form input will be sent to the gateway on the server side. Possible values are GET and POST.

ENCTYPE="..." Only one value right now: application/x-www-form-urlencoded.

Can Include: `<H1>` `<H2>` `<H3>` `<H4>` `<H5>` `<H6>` `<P>` `<OL>` `<UL>` `<DIR>` `<MENU>` `<DL>` `<PRE>` `<BLOCKQUOTE>` `<ISINDEX>` `<TABLE>` `<HR>` `<ADDRESS>` `<INPUT>` `<SELECT>` `<TEXTAREA>`

Allowed Inside: `<BLOCKQUOTE>` `<BODY>` `<DD>` `<LI>` `<TH>` `<TD>`

`<INPUT>`

An input widget for a form.

Attributes:

`TYPE="..."` The type for this input widget. Possible values are `CHECKBOX`, `HIDDEN`, `RADIO`, `RESET`, `SUBMIT`, `TEXT`, or `IMAGE`.

`NAME="..."` The name of this item, as passed to the gateway script as part of a name/value pair.

`VALUE="..."` For a text or hidden widget, the default value; for a checkbox or radio button, the value to be submitted with the form; for Reset or Submit buttons, the label for the button itself.

`SRC="..."` The source file for an image.

`CHECKED` For checkboxes and radio buttons, indicates that the widget is checked.

`SIZE="..."` The size, in characters, of a text widget.

`MAXLENGTH="..."` The maximum number of characters that can be entered into a text widget.

`ALIGN="..."` For images in forms, determines how the text and image will align (same as with the `<IMG>` tag).

Allowed Inside: `<FORM>`

`<TEXTAREA>...</TEXTAREA>`

Indicates a multiline text entry widget.

Attributes:

`NAME="..."` The name to be passed to the gateway script as part of the name/value pair.

`ROWS="..."` The number of rows this text area displays.

`COLS="..."` The number of columns (characters) this text area displays.

Allowed inside: `<FORM>`

`<SELECT>...</SELECT>`

Creates a menu or scrolling list of possible items.

Attributes:

NAME="..." The name that is passed to the gateway script as part of the name/value pair.

SIZE="..." The number of elements to display. If SIZE is indicated, the selection becomes a scrolling list. If no SIZE is given, the selection is a pop-up menu.

MULTIPLE Allows multiple selections from the list.

Can Include: <OPTION>

Allowed Inside: <FORM>

B

<OPTION>

Indicates a possible item within a <SELECT> widget.

Attributes:

SELECTED With this attribute included, the <OPTION> will be selected by default in the list.

VALUE="..." The value to submit if this <OPTION> is selected when the form is submitted.

Allowed Inside: <SELECT>

<FRAMESET>...</FRAMESET>
(Netscape 2.0 and up)

The main container for a frame document.

Attributes:

COLS="column_width_list" The size of the frame's columns in pixels, percentages, or relative scale.

ROWS="row_height_list" The size of the frame's rows in pixels, percentages, or relative scale.

<FRAME>...</FRAME>
(Netscape 2.0 and up)
Attributes:

MARGINHEIGHT="value" The height of the frame, in pixels.

MARGINWIDTH="value" The width of the frame, in pixels.

NAME="window_name" Naming the frame enables it for targeting by link in other documents. (Optional)

NORESIZE A flag to denote the frame cannot be resized.

SCROLLING="yes¦no¦auto" Indicates (*yes/no/auto*) whether a frame has scrollbars.

SRC The URL of the document displayed in the frame.

<NOFRAMES>...</NOFRAMES>
(Netscape 2.0 and up)

Creates frames that can be viewed by non-frame browsers only. A frames-capable browser ignores the data between the start and end <NOFRAMES> tags.

Tables (HTML 3.2)

<TABLE>...</TABLE>

Creates a table, which can contain a caption (<CAPTION>) and any number of rows (<TR>).

Attributes:

ALIGN="..." Indicates LEFT, CENTER, or RIGHT

BORDER="..." Indicates whether the table should be drawn with or without a border. In Netscape, BORDER can also have a value indicating the width of the border.

CELLSPACING="..." The amount of space between the cells in the table.

CELLPADDING="..." The amount of space between the edges of the cell and its contents.

WIDTH="..." The width of the table on the page, in either exact pixel values or as a percentage of page width.

Can Include: <CAPTION> <TR>

Allowed Inside: <BLOCKQUOTE> <BODY> <DD> <LI> <FORM>

<CAPTION>...</CAPTION>

The caption for the table.

Attribute:

ALIGN="..." The position of the caption. Possible values are TOP and BOTTOM.

<TR>...</TR>

Defines a table row, containing headings and data (<TR> and <TH> tags).

Attributes:

ALIGN="..." The horizontal alignment of the contents of the cells within this row. Possible values are LEFT, RIGHT, and CENTER.

VALIGN="..." The vertical alignment of the contents of the cells within this row. Possible values are TOP, MIDDLE, BOTTOM, and BASELINE.

Can Include: <TH> <TD>

Allowed Inside: <TABLE>

<TH>...</TH>

Defines a table heading cell.

Attributes:

ALIGN="..." The horizontal alignment of the contents of the cell. Possible values are LEFT, RIGHT, and CENTER.

VALIGN="..." The vertical alignment of the contents of the cell. Possible values are TOP, MIDDLE, BOTTOM, and BASELINE.

ROWSPAN="..." The number of rows this cell will span.

COLSPAN="..." The number of columns this cell will span.

NOWRAP Do not automatically wrap the contents of this cell.

HEIGHT="..." The height of the cell, in exact pixel values or a percentage of the table height.

WIDTH="..." The width of this column of cells, in exact pixel values or as a percentage of the table width.

Can Include: <H1> <H2> <H3> <H4> <H5> <H6> <P> <OL> <UL> <DIR> <MENU> <DL> <PRE> <BLOCKQUOTE> <FORM> <ISINDEX> <HR> <ADDRESS> <TABLE>

Allowed Inside: <TR>

<TD>...</TD>

Defines a table data cell.

Attributes:

ALIGN="..." The horizontal alignment of the contents of the cell. Possible values are LEFT, RIGHT, and CENTER.

VALIGN="..." The vertical alignment of the contents of the cell. Possible values are TOP, MIDDLE, BOTTOM, and BASELINE.

ROWSPAN="..." The number of rows this cell will span.

COLSPAN="..." The number of columns this cell will span.

NOWRAP Do not automatically wrap the contents of this cell.

HEIGHT="..." The height of the cell, in exact pixel values or a percentage of the table height.

WIDTH="..." The width of this column of cells, in exact pixel values or as a percentage of the table width.

Can Include: <H1> <H2> <H3> <H4> <H5> <H6> <P> <OL> <UL> <DIR> <MENU> <DL> <PRE> <BLOCKQUOTE> <FORM> <ISINDEX> <HR> <ADDRESS> <TABLE>

Allowed Inside: <TR>

Internet Explorer Tags

<BODY>

You can add BGPROPERTIES=FIXED to the <BODY> tag to get a nonscrolling background. <BODY BACKGROUND="*mybackground.gif*" BGPROPERTIES=FIXED>

<TABLE>

Internet Explorer fully supports tables as specified in the HTML 3.2 draft standard. Using the ALIGN=RIGHT or ALIGN=LEFT attributes, you can set the alignment of your tables. Using the BGCOLOR=#*nnnnnn* attribute, you can specify a different color for each cell in a table.

<IMG>

You can add video clips (.AVI files) to your pages with a string of new attributes to the <IMG> tag, most notably the dynamic source feature, DYNSRC=*URL*. You can integrate video clips in such a way as to not exclude viewers without video-enabled browsers. If your browser supports inline clips, you see the video; if not, you see a still image. <IMG SRC="earth.gif" DYNSRC="spinearht.avi">

You can use START=FILEOPEN or START=MOUSEOVER and a variety of LOOP commands to gauge when and for how long the clip is played.

<BGSOUND>

You can now use soundtracks for your Web pages. Samples or MIDI formats are accepted.

`<BGSOUND SRC="whistle.wav">`

You can use LOOP features to specify the repetition of the background sound.

<MARQUEE>

As you might guess, this new tag offers your pages a scrolling text marquee. Your text can appear using different attributes, such as ALIGN=RIGHT, and can have behaviors of SLIDE, SCROLL (the default), and ALTERNATE. `<MARQUEE ALIGN=MIDDLE>Buy Low, Sell High! </MARQUEE>`

Character Entities

Table B.1 contains the possible numeric and character entities for the ISO-Latin-1 (ISO8859-1) character set. Where possible, the character is shown.

NOTE

Not all browsers can display all characters, and some browsers may even display different characters from those that appear in the table. Newer browsers seem to have a better track record for handling character entities, but be sure and test your HTML files extensively with multiple browsers if you intend to use these entities.

Table B.1. ISO-Latin-1 character set.

Character	Numeric Entity	Character Entity (if any)	Description
	&#00;–&#08;		Unused
	&#09;		Horizontal tab
	&#10;		Line feed
	&#11;–&#31;		Unused
	&#32;		Space
!	&#33;		Exclamation mark
"	&#34;	&quot;	Quotation mark

continues

Table B.1. continued

Character	Numeric Entity	Character Entity (if any)	Description
#	&#35;		Number sign
$	&#36;		Dollar sign
%	&#37;		Percent sign
&	&#38;	&amp;	Ampersand
'	&#39;		Apostrophe
(	&#40;		Left parenthesis
)	&#41;		Right parenthesis
*	&#42;		Asterisk
+	&#43;		Plus sign
,	&#44;		Comma
–	&#45;		Hyphen
.	&#46;		Period (fullstop)
/	&#47;		Solidus (slash)
0–9	0–9		Digits 0–9
:	&#58;		Colon
;	&#59;		Semicolon
<	&#60;	&lt;	Less than
=	&#61;		Equals sign
>	&#62;	&gt;	Greater than
?	&#63;		Question mark
@	&#64;		Commercial at
A–Z	A–Z		Letters A–Z
[	&#91;		Left square bracket
\	&#92;		Reverse solidus (backslash)
]	&#93;		Right square bracket
^	&#94;		Caret
—	&#95;		Horizontal bar
`	&#96;		Grave accent
a–z	a–z		Letters a–z
{	&#123;		Left curly brace

Character	Numeric Entity	Character Entity (if any)	Description
|	&#124		Vertical bar
}	&#125;		Right curly brace
~	&#126;		Tilde
	&#127;–Ÿ		Unused
			non-breaking space
¡	&#161;	&iexcl;	Inverted exclamation
¢	&#162;	&cent;	Cent sign
£	&#163;	&pound;	Pound sterling
¤	&#164;	&curren;	General currency sign
¥	&#165;	&yen;	Yen sign
¦	&#166;	¦ or &brkbar;	Broken vertical bar
§	&#167;	&sect;	Section sign
¨	&#168;	¨ or¨	Umlaut (dieresis)
©	&#169;	&copy;	Copyright
ª	&#170;	&ordf;	Feminine ordinal
«	&#171;	&laqo;	Left angle quote, guillemet left
¬	&#172;	&not;	Not sign
	&#173;	&shy;	Soft hyphen
®	&#174;	&reg;	Registered trademark
¯	&#175;	¯ or &hibar;	Macron accent
°	&#176;	&deg;	Degree sign
±	&#177;	&plusmn;	Plus or minus
²	&#178;	&sup2;	Superscript two
³	&#179;	&sup3;	Superscript three
´	&#180;	&acute;	Acute accent
µ	&#181;	&micro;	Micro sign
¶	&#182;	&para;	Paragraph sign
·	&#183;	&middot;	Middle dot
¸	&#184;	&cedil;	Cedilla
¹	&#185;	&sup1;	Superscript one

continues

Table B.1. continued

Character	Numeric Entity	Character Entity (if any)	Description
º	&#186;	&ordm;	Masculine ordinal
›	&#187;	&raquo;	Right angle quote, guillemet right
1/4	&#188;	&fraq14;	Fraction one-fourth
1/2	&#189;	&fraq12;	Fraction one-half
3/4	&#190;	&fraq34;	Fraction three-fourths
¿	&#191;	&iquest;	Inverted question mark
À	&#192;	&Agrave;	Capital A, grave accent
Á	&#193;	&Aacute;	Capital A, acute accent
Â	&#194;	&Acirc;	Capital A, circumflex accent
Ã	&#195;	&Atilde;	Capital A, tilde
Ä	&#196;	&Auml;	Capital A, dieresis or umlaut mark
Å	&#197;	&Aring;	Capital A, ring
Æ	&#198;	&AElig;	Capital AE dipthong (ligature)
Ç	&#199;	&Ccedil;	Capital C, cedilla
È	&#200;	&Egrave;	Capital E, grave accent
É	&#201;	&Eacute;	Capital E, acute accent
Ê	&#202;	&Ecirc;	Capital E, circumflex accent
Ë	&#203;	&Euml;	Capital E, dieresis or umlaut mark
Ì	&#204;	&Igrave;	Capital I, grave accent
Í	&#205;	&Iacute;	Capital I, acute accent
Î	&#206;	&Icirc;	Capital I, circumflex accent

Character	Numeric Entity	Character Entity (if any)	Description
Ï	&#207;	&Iuml;	Capital I, dieresis or umlaut mark
Đ	&#208;	Ð orĐ	Capital Eth, Icelandic
Ñ	&#209;	&Ntilde;	Capital N, tilde
Ò	&#210;	&Ograve;	Capital O, grave accent
Ó	&#211;	&Oacute;	Capital O, acute accent
Ô	&#212;	&Ocirc;	Capital O, circumflex accent
Õ	&#213;	&Otilde;	Capital O, tilde
Ö	&#214;	&Ouml;	Capital O, dieresis or umlaut mark
×	&#215;	&times;	Multiply sign
Ø	&#216;	&Oslash;	Capital O, slash
Ù	&#217;	&Ugrave;	Capital U, grave accent
Ú	&#218;	&Uacute;	Capital U, acute accent
Û	&#219;	&Ucirc;	Capital U, circumflex accent
Ü	&#220;	&Uuml;	Capital U, dieresis or umlaut mark
Ý	&#221;	&Yacute;	Capital Y, acute accent
Þ	&#222;	&THORN;	Capital THORN, Icelandic
β	&#223;	&szlig;	Small sharp s, German (sz ligature)
à	&#224;	&agrave;	Small a, grave accent
á	&#225;	&aacute;	Small a, acute accent
â	&#226;	&acirc;	Small a, circumflex accent

continues

B

Table B.1. continued

Character	Numeric Entity	Character Entity (if any)	Description
ã	&#227;	&atilde;	Small a, tilde
ä	&#228;	&auml;	Small a, dieresis or umlaut mark
å	&#229;	&aring;	Small a, ring
æ	&#230;	&aelig;	Small ae dipthong (ligature)
ç	&#231;	&ccedil;	Small c, cedilla
è	&#232;	&egrave;	Small e, grave accent
é	&#233;	&eacute;	Small e, acute accent
ê	&#234;	&ecirc;	Small e, circumflex accent
ë	&#235;	&euml;	Small e, dieresis or umlaut mark
ì	&#236;	&igrave;	Small i, grave accent
í	&#237;	&iacute;	Small i, acute accent
î	&#238;	&icirc;	Small i, circumflex accent
ï	&#239;	&iuml;	Small i, dieresis or umlaut mark
ð	&#240;	&eth;	Small eth, Icelandic
ñ	&#241;	&ntilde;	Small n, tilde
ò	&#242;	&ograve;	Small o, grave accent
ó	&#243;	&oacute;	Small o, acute accent
ô	&#244;	&ocirc;	Small o, circumflex accent
õ	&#245;	&otilde;	Small o, tilde
ö	&#246;	&ouml;	Small o, dieresis or umlaut mark
÷	&#247;	&divide;	Division sign
ø	&#248;	&oslash;	Small o, slash

Character	Numeric Entity	Character Entity (if any)	Description
ù	&#249;	&ugrave;	Small u, grave accent
ú	&#250;	&uacute;	Small u, acute accent
û	&#251;	&ucirc;	Small u, circumflex accent
ü	&#252;	&uuml;	Small u, dieresis or umlaut mark
ý	&#253;	&yacute;	Small y, acute accent
þ	&#254;	&thorn;	Small thorn, Icelandic
ÿ	&#255;	&yuml;	Small y, dieresis or umlaut mark

APPENDIX C

Colors by Name and Hexadecimal Value

by Wes Tatters

Table C.1 contains a list of all the color names recognized by Navigator 2.0 and also includes their corresponding hexadecimal Triplet values. To see all these colors correctly, you must have a 256-color or better video card and the appropriate video drivers installed. Also, depending on the operating system and computer platform you are running, some colors may not appear exactly as you expect them to.

Table C.1. Color values and HEX triplet equivalents.

Color Name	HEX Triplet	Color Name	HEX Triplet
ALICEBLUE	#A0CE00	DARKGREEN	#006400
ANTIQUEWHITE	#FAEBD7	DARKKHAKI	#BDB76B
AQUA	#00FFFF	DARKMAGENTA	#8B008B
AQUAMARINE	#7FFFD4	DARKOLIVEGREEN	#556B2F
AZURE	#F0FFFF	DARKORANGE	#FF8C00
BEIGE	#F5F5DC	DARKORCHID	#9932CC
BISQUE	#FFE4C4	DARKRED	#8B0000
BLACK	#000000	DARKSALMON	#E9967A
BLANCHEDALMOND	#FFEBCD	DARKSEAGREEN	#8FBC8F
BLUE	#0000FF	DARKSLATEBLUE	#483D8B
BLUEVIOLET	#8A2BE2	DARKSLATEGRAY	#2F4F4F
BROWN	#A52A2A	DARKTURQUOISE	#00CED1
BURLYWOOD	#DEB887	DARKVIOLET	#9400D3
CADETBLUE	#5F9EA0	DEEPPINK	#FF1493
CHARTREUSE	#7FFF00	DEEPSKYBLUE	#00BFFF
CHOCOLATE	#D2691E	DIMGRAY	#696969
CORAL	#FF7F50	DODGERBLUE	#1E90FF
CORNFLOWERBLUE	#6495ED	FIREBRICK	#B22222
CORNSILK	#FFF8DC	FLORALWHITE	#FFFAF0
CRIMSON	#DC143C	FORESTGREEN	#228B22
CYAN	#00FFFF	FUCHSIA	#FF00FF
DARKBLUE	#00008B	GAINSBORO	#DCDCDC
DARKCYAN	#008B8B	GHOSTWHITE	#F8F8FF
DARKGOLDENROD	#B8860B	GOLD	#FFD700
DARKGRAY	#A9A9A9	GOLDENROD	#DAA520

Color Name	HEX Triplet	Color Name	HEX Triplet
GRAY	#808080	MEDIUMBLUE	#0000CD
GREEN	#008000	MEDIUMORCHID	#BA55D3
GREENYELLOW	#ADFF2F	MEDIUMPURPLE	#9370DB
HONEYDEW	#F0FFF0	MEDIUMSEAGREEN	#3CB371
HOTPINK	#FF69B4	MEDIUMSLATEBLUE	#7B68EE
INDIANRED	#CD5C5C	MEDIUMSPRINGGREEN	#00FA9A
INDIGO	#4B0082	MEDIUMTURQUOISE	#48D1CC
IVORY	#FFFFF0	MEDIUMVIOLETRED	#C71585
KHAKI	#F0E68C	MIDNIGHTBLUE	#191970
LAVENDER	#E6E6FA	MINTCREAM	#F5FFFA
LAVENDERBLUSH	#FFF0F5	MISTYROSE	#FFE4E1
LEMONCHIFFON	#FFFACD	NAVAJOWHITE	#FFDEAD
LIGHTBLUE	#ADD8E6	NAVY	#000080
LIGHTCORAL	#F08080	OLDLACE	#FDF5E6
LIGHTCYAN	#E0FFFF	OLIVE	#808000
LIGHTGOLDENRODYELLOW	#FAFAD2	OLIVEDRAB	#6B8E23
LIGHTGREEN	#90EE90	ORANGE	#FFA500
LIGHTGREY	#D3D3D3	ORANGERED	#FF4500
LIGHTPINK	#FFB6C1	ORCHID	#DA70D6
LIGHTSALMON	#FFA07A	PALEGOLDENROD	#EEE8AA
LIGHTSEAGREEN	#20B2AA	PALEGREEN	#98FB98
LIGHTSKYBLUE	#87CEFA	PALETURQUOISE	#AFEEEE
LIGHTSLATEGRAY	#778899	PALEVIOLETRED	#DB7093
LIGHTSTEELBLUE	#B0C4DE	PAPAYAWHIP	#FFEFD5
LIGHTYELLOW	#FFFFE0	PEACHPUFF	#FFDAB9
LIME	#00FF00	PERU	#CD853F
LIMEGREEN	#32CD32	PINK	#FFC0CB
LINEN	#FAF0E6	PLUM	#DDA0DD
MAGENTA	#FF00FF	POWDERBLUE	#B0E0E6
MAROON	#800000	PURPLE	#800080
MEDIUMAQUAMARINE	#66CDAA	RED	#FF0000

C

continues

Table C.1. continued

Color Name	HEX Triplet	Color Name	HEX Triplet
ROSYBROWN	#BC8F8F	SPRINGGREEN	#00FF7F
ROYALBLUE	#4169E1	STEELBLUE	#4682B4
SADDLEBROWN	#8B4513	TAN	#D2B48C
SALMON	#FA8072	TEAL	#008080
SANDYBROWN	#F4A460	THISTLE	#D8BFD8
SEAGREEN	#2E8B57	TOMATO	#FF6347
SEASHELL	#FFF5EE	TURQUOISE	#40E0D0
SIENNA	#A0522D	VIOLET	#EE82EE
SILVER	#C0C0C0	WHEAT	#F5DEB3
SKYBLUE	#87CEEB	WHITE	#FFFFFF
SLATEBLUE	#6A5ACD	WHITESMOKE	#F5F5F5
SLATEGRAY	#708090	YELLOW	#FFFF00
SNOW	#FFFAFA	YELLOWGREEN	#9ACD32

MIME Types and File Extensions

by Laura Lemay

Table D.1 lists the file extensions and MIME Content-types supported by many popular Web servers. If your server does not list an extension for a particular Content-type or if the type you want to use is not listed at all, you will have to add support for that type to your server configuration.

Table D.1. MIME types and HTTPD support.

MIME Type	What It Is (If Noted)	File Extensions
application/acad	AutoCAD Drawing files	dwg, DWG
application/arj		arj
application/clariscad	ClarisCAD files	CCAD
application/drafting	MATRA Prelude drafting	DRW
application/dxf	DXF (AutoCAD)	dxf, DXF
application/excel	Microsoft Excel	xl
application/i-deas	SDRC I-DEAS files	unv, UNV
application/iges	IGES graphics format	igs, iges, IGS, IGES
application/mac-binhex40	Macintosh BinHex format	hqx
application/msword	Microsoft Word	word, w6w, doc
application/mswrite	Microsoft Write	wri
application/octet-stream	Uninterpreted binary	bin
application/oda		oda
application/pdf	PDF (Adobe Acrobat)	pdf
application/postscript	PostScript	ai, PS, ps, eps
application/pro_eng	PTC Pro/ENGINEER	prt, PRT, part
application/rtf	Rich Text Format	rtf
application/set	SET (French CAD standard)	set, SET
application/sla	Stereolithography	stl, STL
application/solids	MATRA Prelude Solids	SOL
application/STEP	ISO-10303 STEP data files	stp, STP, step, STEP
application/vda	VDA-FS Surface data	vda, VDA
application/x-director	Macromedia Director	dir, dcr, dxr
application/x-mif	FrameMaker MIF Format	mif

MIME Type	What It Is (If Noted)	File Extensions
application/x-csh	C-shell script	csh
application/x-dvi	TeX DVI	dvi
application/x-gzip	GNU Zip	gz, gzip
application/x-hdf	NCSA HDF Data File	hdf
application/x-latex	LaTeX source	latex
application/x-netcdf	Unidata netCDF	nc, cdf
application/x-sh	Bourne shell script	sh
application/x-stuffit	Stiffut Archive	sit
application/x-tcl	TCL script	tcl
application/x-tex	TeX source	tex
application/x-texinfo	Texinfo (Emacs)	texinfo, texi
application/x-troff	Troff	t, tr, roff
application/x-troff-man	Troff with MAN macros	man
application/x-troff-me	Troff with ME macros	me
application/x-troff-ms	Troff with MS macros	ms
application/x-wais-source	WAIS source	src
application/x-bcpio	Old binary CPIO	bcpio
application/x-cpio	POSIX CPIO	cpio
application/x-gtar	GNU tar	gtar
application/x-shar	Shell archive	shar
application/x-sv4cpio	SVR4 CPIO	sv4cpio
application/x-sv4crc	SVR4 CPIO with CRC	sv4crc
application/x-tar	4.3BSD tar format	tar
application/x-ustar	POSIX tar format	ustar
application/x-winhelp	Windows Help	hlp
application/zip	ZIP archive	zip
audio/basic	Basic audio (usually μ-law)	au, snd
audio/x-aiff	AIFF audio	aif, aiff, aifc
audio/x-pn-realaudio	RealAudio	ra, ram
audio/x-pn-realaudio-plugin	RealAudio (plug-in)	rpm
audio/x-wav	Windows WAVE audio	wav

continues

Table D.1. continued

MIME Type	What It Is (If Noted)	File Extensions
image/gif	GIF image	gif
image/ief	Image Exchange Format	ief
image/jpeg	JPEG image	jpg, JPG, JPE, jpe, JPEG, jpeg
image/pict	Macintosh PICT	pict
image/tiff	TIFF image	tiff, tif
image/x-cmu-raster	CMU raster	ras
image/x-portable-anymap	PBM Anymap format	pnm
image/x-portable-bitmap	PBM Bitmap format	pbm
image/x-portable-graymap	PBM Graymap format	pgm
image/x-portable-pixmap	PBM Pixmap format	ppm
image/x-rgb	RGB Image	rgb
image/x-xbitmap	X Bitmap	xbm
image/x-xpixmap	X Pixmap	xpm
image/x-xwindowdump	X Window dump (xwd) format	xwd
multipart/x-gzip	GNU ZIP Archive	gzip
multipart/x-zip	PKZIP Archive	zip
text/html	HTML	html, htm
text/plain	Plain text	txt, g, h, C, cc, hh, m, f90, pl, text
text/richtext	MIME Richtext	rtx
text/tab-separated-values	Text with tab-separated values	tsv
text/x-setext	Struct enhanced text	etx
video/mpeg	MPEG video	mpeg, mpg, MPG, MPE, mpe, MPEG, mpeg
video/quicktime	QuickTime Video	qt, mov
video/msvideo	Microsoft Windows Video	avi
video/x-sgi-movie	SGI Movieplayer format	movie
x-world/x-vrml	VRML Worlds	wrl

INDEX

Web Site Administrator's Survival Guide

— *Jerry Ablan, et al.*

The *Web Site Administrator's Survival Guide* is a detailed, step-by-step book that guides the Web administrator through the process of selecting Web server software and hardware, installing and configuring a server, and administering the server on an ongoing basis. Includes a CD-ROM with servers and administrator tools. The book provides complete step-by-step guidelines for installing and configuring a Web server.

Price: $49.99 USA/$67.99 CDN   User Level: Intermediate-Advanced
ISBN: 1-57521-018-5   700 pages

Web Publishing Unleashed

— *Stanek, et al.*

Includes sections on how to organize and plan your information, design pages, and become familiar with hypertext and hypermedia. Choose from a range of applications and technologies, including Java, SGML, VRML, and the newest HTML and Netscape extensions. The CD-ROM contains software, templates, and examples to help you become a successful Web publisher.

Price: $49.99 USA/$67.99 CDN   User Level: Casual-Expert
ISBN: 1-57521-051-7   1,000 pages

Web Site Construction Kit for Windows 95

— *Christopher Brown and Scott Zimmerman*

The *Web Site Construction Kit for Windows 95* provides readers with everything you need to set up, develop, and maintain a Web site with Windows 95. It teaches the ins and outs of planning, installing, configuring, and administering a Windows 95-based Web site for an organization, and it includes detailed instructions on how to use the software on the CD-ROM to develop the Web site's content: HTML pages, CGI scripts, image maps, etc.

Price: $49.99 USA/$67.99 CDN   User Level: Casual-Accomplished
ISBN: 1-57521-072-X   500 pages

Creating Web Applets with Java

—*David Gulbransen and Kendrick Rawlings*

Creating Web Applets with Java is the easiest way to learn how to integrate existing Java applets into your Web pages. This book is designed for the non-programmer who wants to use or customize preprogrammed Java applets with a minimal amount of trouble. It teaches the easiest way to incorporate the power of Java in a Web page and covers the basics of Java applet programming. Includes a CD-ROM full of useful applets.

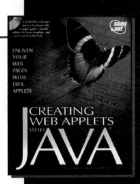

$39.99 USA/$53.99 CDN   User Level: Casual-Accomplished
ISBN: 1-57521-070-3   350 pages

Teach Yourself Netscape Web Publishing in a Week

— *Wes Tatters*

Teach Yourself Netscape Web Publishing in a Week is the easiest way to learn how to produce attention-getting, well-designed Web pages using the features provided by Netscape Navigator. Intended for both the novice and the expert, this book provides a solid grounding in HTML and Web publishing principles, while providing special focus on the possibilities presented by the Netscape environment. Learn to design and create attention-grabbing Web pages for the Netscape environment while exploring new Netscape development features such as frames, plug-ins, Java applets, and JavaScript!

Price: $39.99 USA/ $47.95 CDN   User Level: Beginner-Intermediate
ISBN: 1-57521-068-1   450 pages

Teach Yourself CGI Programming with Perl in a Week

— *Eric Herrmann*

This book is a step-by-step tutorial of how to create, use, and maintain Common Gateway Interfaces (CGI). It describes effective ways of using CGI as an integral part of Web development. Adds interactivity and flexibility to the information that can be provided through your Web site. Includes Perl 4.0 and 5.0, CGI libraries, and other applications to create databases, dynamic interactivity, and other enticing page effects.

Price: $39.99 USA/$53.99 CDN   User Level: Intermediate-Advanced
ISBN: 1-57521-009-6   500 pages

Teach Yourself Java in 21 Days

— *Laura Lemay and Charles Perkins*

The complete tutorial guide to the most exciting technology to hit the Internet in years—Java! A detailed guide to developing applications with the hot new Java language from Sun Microsystems, *Teach Yourself Java in 21 Days* shows readers how to program using Java and develop applications (applets) using the Java language. With coverage of Java implementation in Netscape Navigator and HotJava, along with the Java Developer's Kit, including the compiler and debugger for Java, *Teach Yourself Java* is a must-have!

Price: $39.99 USA/$53.99 CDN   User Level: Intermediate-Advanced
ISBN: 1-57521-030-4   600 pages

Presenting Java

— *John December*

Presenting Java gives you a first look at how Java is transforming static Web pages into living, interactive applications. Java opens up a world of possibilities previously unavailable on the Web. You'll find out how Java is being used to create animations, computer simulations, interactive games, teaching tools, spreadsheets, and a variety of other applications. Whether you're a new user, a project planner, or developer, *Presenting Java* provides an efficient, quick introduction to the basic concepts and technical details that make Java the hottest new Web technology of the year!

Price: $25.00 USA/$34.95 CDN   User Level: All Levels
ISBN: 1-57521-039-8   207 pages

Netscape 3 Unleashed

— Dick Oliver, et al.

This book provides a complete, detailed, and fully fleshed-out overview of the Netscape products. Through case studies and examples of how individuals, businesses, and institutions are using the Netscape products for Web development, *Netscape 3 Unleashed* gives a full description of the evolution of Netscape from its inception to today, and its cutting-edge developments with Netscape Gold, LiveWire, Netscape Navigator 2.0, Java and JavaScript, Macromedia, VRML, Plug-ins, Adobe Acrobat, HTML 3.0 and beyond, security, and Intranet systems.

Price: $49.99 USA/$61.95 CDN   User Level: All Levels
ISBN: 1-57521-164-5   Pages: 800 pages

The Internet 1996 Unleashed

— Barron, Ellsworth, Savetz, et al.

The Internet 1996 Unleashed is the complete reference to get new users up and running on the Internet while providing the consummate reference manual for the experienced user. *The Internet 1996 Unleashed* provides the reader with an encyclopedia of information on how to take advantage of all the Net has to offer for business, education, research, and government. The companion CD-ROM contains over 100 tools and applications. The only book that includes the experience of over 40 of the world's top Internet experts, this new edition is updated with expanded coverage of Web publishing, Internet business, Internet multimedia and virtual reality, Internet security, Java, and more!

Price: $49.99 USA/$67.99 CDN   User Level: All Levels
ISBN: 1-57521-041-X   1,456 pages

The World Wide Web 1996 Unleashed

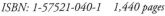

— December and Randall

The World Wide Web 1996 Unleashed is designed to be the only book a reader will need to experience the wonders and resources of the Web. The companion CD-ROM contains over 100 tools and applications to make the most of your time on the Internet. Shows readers how to explore the Web's amazing world of electronic art museums, online magazines, virtual malls, and video music libraries, while giving readers complete coverage of Web page design, creation, and maintenance, plus coverage of new Web technologies such as Java, VRML, CGI, and multimedia!

Price: $49.99 USA/$67.99 CDN   User Level: All Levels
ISBN: 1-57521-040-1   1,440 pages

Java Unleashed

—Michael Morrison, et al.

Java Unleashed is the ultimate guide to the year's hottest new Internet technologies, the Java language and the HotJava browser from Sun Microsystems. *Java Unleashed* is a complete programmer's reference and a guide to the hundreds of exciting ways Java is being used to add interactivity to the World Wide Web. It describes how to use Java to add interactivity to Web presentations, and it shows how Java and HotJava are being used across the Internet. Includes a helpful and informative CD-ROM.

$49.99 USA/$67.99 CDN   User Level: Casual-Expert
ISBN: 1-57521-049-5   1,000 pages

Teach Yourself JavaScript in a Week

—Arman Danesh

Teach Yourself JavaScript in a Week is the easiest way to learn how to create interactive Web pages with JavaScript, Netscape's Java-like scripting language. It is intended for non-programmers and will be equally of value to users on the Macintosh, Windows, and UNIX platforms. It teaches how to design and create attention-grabbing Web pages with JavaScript and shows how to add interactivity to Web pages.

$39.99 USA/$53.99 CDN   User Level: Intermediate-Advanced
ISBN: 1-57521-073-8   450 pages

Web Page Construction Kit (Software)

Create your own exciting World Wide Web pages with the software and expert guidance in this kit! Includes HTML Assistant Pro Lite, the acclaimed point-and-click Web page editor. Simply highlight text in HTML Assistant Pro Lite, and click the appropriate button to add headlines, graphics, special formatting, links, etc. No programming skills needed! Using your favorite Web browser, you can test your work quickly and easily without leaving the editor. A unique catalog feature allows you to keep track of interesting Web sites and easily add their HTML links to your pages. Assistant's user-defined toolkit also allows you to add new HTML formatting styles as they are defined. Includes the #1 best-selling Internet book, *Teach Yourself Web Publishing with HTML 3.0 in a Week, Second Edition,* and a library of professionally designed Web page templates, graphics, buttons, bullets, lines, and icons to rev up your new pages!

PC Computing magazine says, "If you're looking for the easiest route to Web publishing, HTML Assistant is your best choice."

Price: $39.95 USA/$53.99 CAN   User Level: Beginner-Intermediate
ISBN: 1-57521-000-2   518 pages

HTML 3.2 & CGI Unleashed, Professional Reference Edition

— John December and Marc Ginsburg

Targeted to professional developers who have a basic understanding of programming and need a detailed guide. Provides a complete, detailed reference to developing Web information systems. Covers the full range of languages—HTML, CGI, Perl C, editing and conversion programs, and more—and how to create commercial-grade Web applications. Perfect for the developer who will be designing, creating, and maintaining a Web presence for a company or large institution.

Price: $59.99 USA/$53.99 CDN   User Level: Intermediate-Advanced
ISBN: 1-57521-177-7   830 pages

Web Site Construction Kit for Windows NT

— Christopher Brown and Scott Zimmerman

The *Web Site Construction Kit for Windows NT* has everything you need to set up, develop, and maintain a Web site with Windows NT—including the server on the CD-ROM! It teaches the ins and outs of planning, installing, configuring, and administering a Windows NT–based Web site for an organization, and it includes detailed instructions on how to use the software on the CD-ROM to develop the Web site's content—HTML pages, CGI scripts, imagemaps, and so forth.

Price: $49.99 USA/$67.99 CDN   User Level: All Levels
ISBN: 1-57521-047-9   430 pages

Add to Your Sams.net Library Today
with the Best Books for Internet Technologies

ISBN	Quantity	Description of Item	Unit Cost	Total Cost
1-57521-039-8		Presenting Java	$25.00	
1-57521-030-4		Teach Yourself Java in 21 Days (Book/CD)	$39.99	
1-57521-049-5		Java Unleashed (Book/CD)	$49.99	
1-57521-164-5		Netscape 3 Unleashed (Book/CD)	$49.99	
1-57521-041-X		The Internet Unleashed, 1996 (Book/CD)	$49.99	
1-57521-040-1		The World Wide Web Unleashed, 1996 (Book/CD)	$49.99	
1-57521-177-7		HTML 3.2 and CGI Unleashed Professional Reference (Book/CD)	$59.99	
1-57521-051-7		Web Publishing Unleashed (Book/CD)	$49.99	
1-57521-009-6		Teach Yourself CGI Scripting with Perl in a Week (Book/CD)	$39.99	
0-672-30735-9		Teach Yourself the Internet in a Week	$25.00	
1-57521-004-5		Teach Yourself Netscape 2 Web Publishing in a Week (Book/CD)	$35.00	
0-672-30718-9		Navigating the Internet, Third Edition	$25.00	
		Shipping and Handling: See information below.		
		TOTAL		

Shipping and Handling: $4.00 for the first book, and $1.75 for each additional book. If you need to have it NOW, we can ship product to you in 24 hours for an additional charge of approximately $18.00, and you will receive your item overnight or in two days. Overseas shipping and handling adds $2.00. Prices subject to change. Call between 9:00 a.m. and 5:00 p.m. EST for availability and pricing information on latest editions.

201 W. 103rd Street, Indianapolis, Indiana 46290

1-800-428-5331 — Orders   1-800-835-3202 — FAX   1-800-858-7674 — Customer Service

Book ISBN 1-57521-192-0